Business Law

THIRD EDITION

S. B. Marsh

B.Com., LL.B., Ph.D., Barrister-at-Law
Formerly Head of the Department of Law, Manchester Polytechnic

and

J. Soulsby

LL.B., Solicitor
Principal Lecturer in Law, Manchester Polytechnic

McGRAW-HILL BOOK COMPANY

London · New York · St Louis · San Francisco · Auckland · Bogotá
Guatemala · Hamburg · Lisbon · Madrid · Mexico
Montreal · New Delhi · Panama · Paris · San Juan · São Paulo
Singapore · Sydney · Tokyo · Toronto

Published by
McGRAW-HILL Book Company (UK) Limited
MAIDENHEAD · BERKSHIRE · ENGLAND

British Library Cataloguing in Publication Data
Marsh, S. B.
  Business law.—3rd ed.
  1. Commercial law—England
  I. Title   II. Soulsby, J.
  344.206'7   KD1629

ISBN 0-07-084876-9

345 WC 887

Typeset by Eta Services (Typesetters) Ltd, Beccles, Suffolk
Printed and bound in Great Britain by William Clowes Limited, Beccles

Contents

Preface

This book was written initially to cover the examination syllabus in Business Law of the Institute of Cost and Management Accountants. It has proved of value to others who are required to study aspects of law which affect business relationships and transactions for the examinations of professional bodies and the Business and Technician Education Council (BTEC).

The early units provide an outline of the English legal system, its procedure and certain fundamental concepts, for those who are studying law for the first time. In this edition, we have followed this by a fuller introduction to the law of business organizations, particularly companies and partnerships. This in turn is followed by the principles of contract and tort, and to a lesser extent the criminal law, since these principles underlie most business activities. The final units deal with specific legal problems arising from the sale of goods, agency, credit, and employment.

The text is not divided into chapters according to subject, but into units, each containing approximately the same amount of material. It is hoped that this approach will help a student to plan a timetable of study, even though the time available will vary from one to another. Because of this approach, the book is ideally suited to those students on BTEC or Higher BTEC courses.

Examination questions are included at the end of each unit, so as to provide written practice which many candidates appear to lack. Our thanks are due to the Institute for permission to reproduce many of these questions.

We would like to thank Mr John Stone, Senior Lecturer at Manchester Polytechnic, who has looked at our units on employment law and given us his valuable comments. If any mistakes remain, we still of course accept responsibility.

There have been many changes in the law since the last edition in 1981. The present edition attempts to cover such changes up to March 1985.

S. B. Marsh
J. Soulsby

Table of Cases

Table of Statutes

Unit 1. The Nature and Development of English Law

A. The nature of law

The word 'law' suggests the idea of rules; rules affecting the lives and activities of people. Some of these rules, such as the laws of science, enable us to predict what will happen in a given situation, but we have no control over them. We must accept, for example, the law of gravity; we regulate our conduct by it, but we cannot alter it.

In any community or group of people, man-made rules will develop to control the relationships between members. These rules are essential if the community is to work and will be found in all forms of activity which depend upon some form of cooperation—in games, in schools, in clubs. The rules come into existence in varying ways, although in most cases there must have been agreement between at least some of the members of the community that the rule was desirable. When a person or persons having power in the community enforces the rule, then that rule will acquire the status of a 'law' in the generally accepted meaning of the word.

Even in primitive societies, traditions and customs will affect conduct. Such customary rules tend to be too vague and imprecise at this stage to merit the use of the term 'law' although they may provide the basis of later law. As the society develops and becomes more complex, rules of a more definite nature emerge and a body of law comes into existence. At the same time some machinery for its enforcement must be established.

B. Civil and criminal law

As legal systems develop, the different rules tend to fall into two main categories, criminal law and civil law, and the objectives of each, although closely connected, are different. Criminal law is concerned with conduct of which the state disapproves so strongly that it will punish the wrongdoer. It is felt that society cannot work if people are allowed to take the property of others at will; therefore theft is forbidden and thieves are punished to deter them, and others of a like mind, from repeating this conduct. It is not the objective of criminal law to compensate the victim, except perhaps incidentally.

Civil law has a complementary function. If a dispute arises between two individuals, each believing himself to be in the right, a quarrel may ensue and violence or other criminal conduct may result. To prevent this, rules of civil law were developed in order to determine which of the two parties was in the right. The party in the wrong was then obliged to make redress by compensating the other for any loss he may have caused. The object of the civil law therefore is to resolve disputes and give a remedy to the persons wronged, not to punish wrongdoers.

Most countries, including England, find it convenient to set up separate systems of criminal courts and civil courts. In England, a criminal prosecution is usually begun in the name of the Crown (i.e., the state) through the machinery of the police, and the decision as to whether or not to press the prosecution is not the concern of the victim. In a civil case, the law is set in motion by a private individual, or a firm, who has the right to determine how far the action shall continue.

Thus the parties and the terminology differ. In the criminal case of *R.* v. *Smith*, the Crown (*R.* signifying *Regina* or the Queen) prosecutes the accused, who may also be referred to as the prisoner or defendant. In the civil case of *Jones* v. *Smith*, the plaintiff sues the defendant.

Differences also exist in the rules of evidence and procedure, reflecting the fact that a criminal conviction is likely to be far more damaging to a person's character than failure in a civil action. The rules of evidence are much stricter in criminal cases; for example, a confession will be carefully examined to see if any pressure was brought to bear upon the accused, but an admission in a civil case will be freely accepted. The standard of proof required in criminal cases is greater, for the accused must be proved guilty beyond all reasonable doubt. A plaintiff in a civil action will succeed if he can convince the court that he has only a marginally stronger case than the defendant.

Finally, it is important to note that the same series of events may sometimes give rise both to criminal and civil proceedings. For instance, if an employer is alleged to have left dangerous factory machinery unguarded causing injury to a worker, two types of issue arise. Failure to guard such machinery is conduct which has been made a criminal offence and the employer may be prosecuted in a criminal court and, if found guilty of the offence, punished (Unit 24). The issue of whether the employer caused loss to the injured worker through negligence and failure to comply with his statutory duty will be determined in a separate civil action brought by the worker in a civil court, where the worker will claim compensation (damages) from his employer (Unit 25). There are many other situations, such as road accidents and the sale of mis-described goods, where the same incident can give rise to both criminal and civil actions.

C. The development of English law

Origins of English law

Most legal systems in Europe, including that of Scotland, and indirectly those in many other parts of the world are based upon Roman law. In England and Wales, on the other hand, Roman law has had very little influence except in a few specialized fields such as marriage and the succession to property upon death, matters in which the Church was particularly interested.

The body of law which at present applies in England and Wales developed very gradually over a long period. Like so many of our institutions, it was not systematically created. Drawing upon many different sources, the English common law system finally emerged and has become the basis of law not only in this country but also in the United States and many Commonwealth countries.

The period of local justice

Until and for some time after the Norman Conquest, it could scarcely be said that there was such a thing as English law. The population was small, settlements were often widely separated and travel was difficult. Justice and other aspects of administration tended to be local. Each local community would have its own court in which, for the most part, *local customs* would be applied. These customs, the beginnings of legal rules, varied considerably from one area to another.

The emergence of the common law

The Norman Conquest made little immediate impact upon English law. William I promised that the English should keep their rights and their law, which meant the customary law. At the same time, the Normans developed a strong central government and over the following 200 years greatly increased central control over the administration of the law. This was a gradual process bringing with it the decline of the local courts.

Central courts, sitting permanently at Westminster, developed when special committees of the King's Council were entrusted with jurisdiction over legal disputes. At the same time, the practice grew up of sending royal judges to visit most parts of the country so as to establish closer royal control over the administration of justice. The sittings of these judges were known as Assizes.

These new institutions, particularly the travelling judges, brought with them a most important change in the law itself, the unification of the varying local customs. As they went around the country on circuit the judges tended to select and apply certain customary rules in all cases rather than rely in every case upon enquiring into local customs. This process was assisted by the King who sometimes created new legal rules which were to apply nationally and by the permanent courts which had nation-wide

3

jurisdiction. The different local customs were therefore replaced gradually by a body of rules applying throughout the whole country and known eventually as the common law. This process was substantially completed by the end of the thirteenth century.

The formulation of the common law took place when there were few statutes or other forms of written law. The judges accordingly looked to previous decisions for guidance in order to maintain consistency. In other words the doctrine of precedent, to be discussed in Unit 2, began to emerge in the common law courts. If previous decisions were to be followed, it was essential that the judges' decisions be recorded and we see the beginning of law reporting, at first by anonymous lawyers in the Year Books. The main stream of English law, therefore, began with the unification of local customs to form the common law and has been developed down to the present day by the judges as precedent has been built upon precedent.

Equity

A legal rule aims at making provision for a large number of cases of a particular kind. It is impossible to provide for every eventuality, however, and some special situations will arise where the application of the rule will cause hardship. Since 'hard cases make bad law', most legal systems develop some machinery to deal with these special cases which would otherwise bring the law into disrepute.

As the common law courts became separated from the King's Council, they became increasingly reluctant or unable to grant remedies for new and unfamiliar types of wrong. As conditions changed and new forms of property and interests in property developed, there came to be many types of wrong for which the courts could grant no remedy.

Subjects unable to obtain a remedy, therefore, would sometimes petition the King asking for justice, and these petitions were usually passed to the Chancellor. The latter was empowered to order the parties to appear before him under penalty (*subpoena*) for refusal and, after hearing the petition, he could make such order as appeared to him to be fair, just or 'equitable'. These sittings of the Chancellor became more regular and by the end of the fourteenth century had developed into a new Court of Chancery, administering its own form of justice known as equity.

The early Chancellors were clergymen and at first, and for a long time, each petition was simply dealt with at the entire discretion of the individual Chancellor on the basis of what he himself felt to be just. It gradually came to be recognized, however, that there were some situations in which the Chancellor would almost always grant relief and a doctrine of precedent began to appear even in the Court of Chancery. This process quickened from the seventeenth century onwards when the office of Chancellor was held by lawyers trained in the common law. By the early nineteenth century, equity was as much tied by precedent as was common law and we had the unique system of two bodies of legal rules administered in two sets of courts, each with its own particular procedure and remedies. Many litigants were not only disappointed if they eventually found that they had chosen the wrong court but were utterly bewildered.

A number of reforms were introduced culminating in the Judicature Acts 1873–75. These statutes swept away the common law courts and the Court of Chancery and replaced them by one Supreme Court of Judicature in which each branch had the power to administer both common law and equity according to the same rules of procedure. The rule that equity should prevail in the event of a conflict was also restated.

The administration of the two systems was therefore combined, although it is still necessary to distinguish between them for some purposes. Thus the common law remedy of damages may be claimed as of right but the action will be barred after a fixed period, normally six years. On the other hand, the award of equitable remedies still remains partly at the discretion of the court and will be refused if it is felt that the plaintiff has delayed unnecessarily, even for a short time, in seeking them.

Equity was never a comprehensive system of law as was common law, but was for the most part a collection of individual rules or principles. If common law was the book, equity was a page of errata. Nevertheless, equity played an important part in developing certain aspects of law. It recognized and protected the trust by compelling the trustees, the legal owners, to deal with the property on behalf of the beneficiaries, the equitable owners. It treated the mortgage as the parties intended it to be treated, as a device for borrowing money, and would not allow the lender to exercise his legal rights over the property if repayment was not made on the exact contractual date. It granted relief where a contract was entered into as a result of misrepresentation or undue influence by allowing the innocent party to abandon the contract and be returned to his original position—the remedy of rescission. It also provided the remedies of specific performance and injunction which are court orders compelling the performance or non-performance respectively of certain acts under pain of fine or imprisonment for contempt if not obeyed.

It should be noted that the phrase 'common law' is sometimes used today to describe the whole body of judge-made rules of law whether the rules originated in equity in the Court of Chancery or were common law rules in the strict sense, emanating from the old common law courts. In this wider sense, common law is contrasted with statute law which is discussed later.

Law merchant

The early common law courts were concerned largely with problems of land tenure and gave little attention to the growing number of mercantile transactions and the disputes arising therefrom. Procedure in the common law courts was slow and in order to obtain the quick decisions they needed, the merchants set up their own tribunals. These were of two types. The Courts of Staple were found mainly in the ports and dealt with external trade. The Courts of Pie Powder, as they came to be called were found more widely and dealt with trade generally. The name of the latter is probably derived from *pieds poudrés* or the dusty feet of the traders who required speedy settlements before they moved on to the next fair.

The rules administered in these courts were based upon mercantile customs and became known as the law merchant. Some of these customs became internationally recognized, while others were applied only in a particular locality or trade.

The common law courts realized the growing importance of this work and gradually took it over. Various types of commercial documents and procedures were recognized in legal decisions, thereby forming precedents and becoming part of the common law itself. At the same time the modern law of contract was developed. The law merchant had been incorporated into the common law by about the end of the eighteenth century and the mercantile courts had disappeared. Even today, however, the ordinary courts will often take account of business practice in reaching a decision and this still plays a part in the evolution of English law.

Statute law

Statute law, or legislation, consists of rules which are formally enacted by a body which has constitutional power to do so. Parliament is now the only body with inherent power to legislate under English law and statutes today take the form of Acts of Parliament. Sometimes legislative powers are delegated to subordinate bodies.

From earliest days, legislation, often in the form of royal decrees, played some part in the growth of English law. The early statutes would supplement or amend the rules of common law, and later equity, but the main framework of law grew through the decisions of the courts.

Over the last 150 years, the Government has concerned itself to an unprecedented degree with such matters as public health, education, transport, the use and conservation of natural resources, the management of the economy and the concept of the welfare state.

Industrialization, the population explosion and the growth of large conurbations created social, economic and human problems to which the common law and equity could not adapt. New institutions and new legal rules and concepts had to be created quickly and this was done through Parliament. A vast number of statutes has been enacted creating new areas of law and, as will become apparent in later units, legislation has become a major source of new legal rules.

The courts have recognized the legislative sovereignty of Parliament and will always obey and apply an Act of Parliament even where it conflicts with or abolishes the rules of common law or equity. Legislation as a source of law today will be examined in the next unit.

D. Entry into Europe

Accession of the United Kingdom

One of the most potentially important legal developments in the history of this country took place in January 1972 when the United Kingdom signed the Treaty of Accession in Brussels. By this Treaty, the United Kingdom and two other states joined the original six member states in the enlarged European Communities as from the 1 January 1973. Greece has since joined as the tenth member state.

The Treaty was made by the Government under the Crown's prerogative power to enter into agreements with other states. The United Kingdom thereby accepted an international obligation but, since the internal law of this country was not affected, the approval of Parliament was not strictly required. Membership of the Communities, however, requires that Community law shall become part of the internal law of the member states and shall be accepted and applied by the national courts. It was therefore necessary to change our internal law by Act of Parliament and this was subsequently done by the European Communities Act 1972.

The Act provides that the Treaties, and all secondary legislation such as regulations which are intended to take direct effect within the member states, shall become part of the law of the United Kingdom. This includes legislation already made and that which may be made in the future. No further enactment by Parliament is necessary. Thus while Parliament may in future devise a procedure whereby draft regulations are considered and representations made to the Commission or Council, there is no direct Parliamentary control over whether or not such regulations become law.

Some legislation enacted by the Communities before the Treaty of Accession has already been given effect in English law, by the Act itself. For instance, section 9 of the European Communities Act was intended to implement the requirements of the First Directive on Company Law, enacted by the Council of the EEC in 1968.

Further provisions of the Act include the obligation to take account of the principles laid down by the European Court where these are relevant to legal proceedings before our courts. It is also provided that future Acts of Parliament are to be interpreted, and have effect, subject to the European Communities Act, that is, on the assumption that Community law is part of our internal law.

As a condition of the United Kingdom becoming a member state, Parliament has therefore been obliged to give up its sovereignty so far as Community matters are concerned. In theory, there is no reason why the 1972 Act should not be repealed by a later Act but this would mean the renunciation of membership.

The European Communities

Although it is convenient to speak of the European Community, there are in fact three distinct communities, each with its own constitution in the form of the treaty which established it. These are:

1. *European Coal and Steel Community* (*ESSC*). This was established by the Treaty of Paris 1951 for the purpose of managing a common market in coal and steel.
2. *European Atomic Energy Community* (*Euratom*). This was set up by the second Treaty of Rome 1957 for the purpose of developing a common market in nuclear energy and distributing the power produced.
3. *European Economic Community* (*EEC*). This was set up by the first Treaty of Rome 1957. Unlike the other two specialist communities, the EEC has wider and more general objectives. Its immediate aim is the integration of the economies of the participating states; the long-term aim is political integration.

There are four main institutions responsible for discharging the functions of the Communities.

1. *The Commission* is the executive body and consists of 14 Commissioners appointed by mutual agreement of the member Governments. While the Commission acts collectively, individual Commissioners specialize in certain aspects of Community affairs which are allotted to them. The Commission is responsible for the formulation of Community policy, it initiates and drafts most Community legislation and it also has executive functions to ensure that Community obligations are carried out.
2. *The Council of Ministers* represents the sovereignty of the member states and is composed of one representative from each state, normally the Foreign Minister. It is the legislative body for the Communities, but in most cases it may act only on proposals put forward by the Commission.
3. *The Assembly* represents the peoples of the member states, seats being allocated according to population. Although referred to as the European Parliament, it is not a parliament as understood in Britain. It has no legislative powers and is largely an advisory or consultative body in which Community problems may be discussed.
4. *The Court of Justice* holds the judicial power of the Communities with the function of ensuring that Community law is observed in the interpretation and implementation of the Treaties (Unit 4).

Effect of Community law

The immediate impact of Community law on English law is not likely to be very great. The Communities are concerned primarily with economic and commercial matters and the effect is being felt initially in those branches of law which govern relationships in these fields.

As already mentioned, some changes in the law relating to companies were made by the European Communities Act itself and further changes have been made in a gradual movement towards a uniform set of legal rules applicable to business organizations throughout the Communities. Commercial law, the law relating to taxation, and employment law have also been affected. For example, some rights of women regarding equal pay came directly from the Community Treaties (Unit 23). Article 100 of the EEC Treaty provides for the issue of directives for the harmonization or approximation of the laws of the member states where these directly affect the establishment or functioning of the Common Market.

For the time being there will be little effect upon our system of courts and our rules of procedure. Contract, tort, criminal law, property, and family law will remain essentially the same as before. On the other hand, the movement towards greater integration between the member states in general, and the greater contact between the legal professions and the work of the European Court in particular, must inevitably lead, albeit slowly, to more uniformity in the laws of the member states. This process will be quickened if the Communities should develop a policy of greater political integration. Nevertheless, complete integration of the laws and legal systems is many many years in the future.

Examination questions

1. Explain the difference between the prosecution of an employee for theft and an action for compensation against a supplier who has failed to honour a contract.
2. Distinguish between common law and statute law. Why is statute law a major source of new legal rules today?
3. What was the 'law merchant'? Do the specialized and complex business disputes of today justify special courts and procedures to deal with them?
4. What is meant by the European Community? Discuss the likely effect of Community law on English law.

Unit 2. Sources of Law

The expression 'sources of law' can mean several different things. It can refer to the historical origins from which the law has come, such as common law and equity which were discussed in the last unit. Secondly, it can refer to the body of rules which a judge will draw upon in deciding a case, and where these rules are to be found. In this second sense there are two main sources of English law today: legislation and precedent.

A. Legislation

The nature and effect of legislation

Legislation is the body of rules which have been formally enacted or made. Many bodies in England have power to lay down rules for *limited* purposes, for example social clubs, but fundamentally the only way in which rules can be enacted so as to apply *generally* is by Act of Parliament. For various reasons, some of Parliament's legislative functions are delegated to subordinate bodies which, within a limited field, are allowed to enact rules. Local authorities, for instance, are allowed to enact by-laws. But local authorities can only do this because an Act of Parliament has given them the power to do so.

In constitutional theory Parliament is said to have legislative sovereignty and, provided that the proper procedure is followed, the statute passed must be obeyed and applied by the courts. The judges have no power to hold an Act invalid or to ignore it, however unreasonable or 'unconstitutional' they may consider it to be.

In this respect England differs from many countries which have written constitutions. In the United States, for instance, the Supreme Court has power to declare legislation passed by Congress to be invalid if it is, in the opinion of the Court, inconsistent with the written constitution. The attitude of the courts in this country, on the other hand, is perhaps best expressed in words attributed to Holt, C. J., in a report of *City of London* v. *Wood* in 1702: 'An Act of Parliament can do no wrong, though it may do several things that look pretty odd.'

On the other hand, although they cannot question the validity of an Act, the courts do have the task of applying it to specific problems. The Government, by Act of Parliament, states what the law is to be but, having done so, it must then abide by the words which it has used. What those words *mean* is a matter for the courts to decide. If the Government disapproves of the interpretation it must pass another Act in an attempt to state its intentions more clearly. The courts have, in fact, evolved rules of interpretation which they will use to discover the 'true' meaning of the words of a statute. Parliament helped the courts to some extent by passing the Interpretation Act 1889, which is now repealed and replaced by the Interpretation Act 1978 (see page 17).

The legislative process

This is normally a long process. In most cases, the first and most important step is for the Government to decide that it wishes the bill to be passed. Once this decision has been taken, the legislation will normally pass through Parliament and become law, because of the Government's effective command of a majority in the House of Commons.

A formal requirement is that the bill must be approved by both Houses of Parliament, with ample opportunity for debate both in the Commons and in the Lords. In spite of Government control of the Commons, Parliament is not a mere rubber stamp, because it gives opportunities for members to criticize, publicize, explain and amend the detailed provisions of the bill, and few bills emerge without at least some amendment.

Finally, a bill must receive the Royal Assent, which today is never refused. It thereupon becomes an Act of Parliament and, unless otherwise provided, takes effect from the day of Assent. Many Acts now contain a section delaying commencement and providing for the Act to be brought into effect, if necessary part by part, by delegated legislation. Those affected by the Act are thereby given time to adapt to the change in the law.

Amendment and repeal

A statute, once enacted, remains in force permanently unless and until it is *repealed*, and it can only be repealed by another statute. The Distress Act of 1276 still appears in the current edition of Halsbury's *Statutes of England* for instance. Similarly, a statute can only be *amended* by another Act of Parliament unless, as rarely happens, an Act delegates to a Minister or some other body the power to make minor changes. Most Acts today, in fact, do have to repeal or amend some earlier statutory provisions, and they will usually contain a schedule specifying what earlier provisions have been affected.

Conversely, Parliament can never take away its own power to amend or repeal earlier legislation. Nor can it otherwise restrict its own freedom to legislate in future as it thinks fit. The European Communities Act 1972 could, for instance, be construed as purporting to restrict the power of Parliament to legislate in a manner inconsistent with the European Treaties. Nevertheless, this Act could always be repealed by a future Parliament, although this would mean the withdrawal of the United Kingdom from the European Communities.

Consolidating and codifying Acts

Governments have always tended to introduce legislation as and when some specific need arises, and several closely connected Acts on a particular topic may well exist side by side. In such circumstances the Government will often do some tidying up. A *consolidating* Act will be passed which will repeal all of the piecemeal provisions, and re-enact them in one logically arranged Act. This is periodically done, for instance, with tax legislation. Other examples include Acts dealing with road traffic, social security, safety at work, and companies.

Sometimes a Government may decide not only to consolidate all of the legislation, but also to replace some of the *case law* on the subject by a new Act. Such an Act is called a *codifying* one. It reduces most of the law on the subject into a single code. There are good examples in commercial law, particularly the Bills of Exchange Act 1882 and the Sale of Goods Act 1893. (The Sale of Goods Act 1893 was subsequently amended by several other Acts, and this legislation is now consolidated in the Sale of Goods Act 1979.)

B. Delegated legislation

Forms of delegated legislation

The vast extension of the functions of Government during the last 150 years was mentioned in Unit 1. The task of making the detailed rules needed to translate this new development into practice was beyond the capacity of any one legislative body. What the Government has often done, therefore, is to pass an 'enabling' Act setting up the main framework of the reform on which it has decided, and then empowering some subordinate body—often a Minister—to enact the detailed rules necessary to complete the scheme. Thus the Factories Act 1961 provides for sufficient and suitable lighting in factories but leaves to the responsible Minister the work of laying down specific standards of lighting that shall be deemed sufficient and suitable for different types of work. Rules enacted under such powers are called 'delegated legislation'. The following are the principal forms that this may take:

1. *Orders in Council* are enacted under powers delegated to the Privy Council. Most

senior members of the Government are also Privy Councillors, and effectively determine what shall be enacted.

2. *Ministerial regulations* are made by individual Ministers within some limited sphere relating to their departmental responsibilities, for example, traffic regulations. Most orders and rules of each of these kinds are published through HM Stationery Office under the description of *statutory instruments*.

3. *Local authorities* are given powers by many Acts of Parliament to make *by-laws* which will have the force of law within the geographical area of the authority.

4. *Other statutory authorities* such as nationalized industry boards, harbour commissions and bodies such as the Peak Park Planning Board are often given power to make *by-laws* within the scope of their functions.

5. *Certain professional bodies* are given power by Parliament to make rules governing the conduct of their members. The Law Society, for example, has this power under the Solicitors' Acts.

Advantages of delegation of powers

1. Parliamentary time is saved on relatively trivial matters.
2. Greater flexibility is assured by the ability to enact and change the rules quickly without lengthy Parliamentary procedure.
3. In national emergencies it may sometimes be necessary for the Government to act at short notice.
4. Many regulations cover technical subjects which few Members of Parliament are competent to discuss adequately.
5. Local and specialist knowledge may be drawn upon when local authority by-laws are passed.

Criticisms of the growth of delegated legislation

In the first half of this century there were widespread criticisms of the growth of delegated legislative powers. It was felt to be an erosion of the constitutional role of Parliament to allow such wide powers to be given to other bodies, particularly to individual Ministries. Moreover, it was pointed out, delegated legislation need not ever be debated or even mentioned in Parliament, and might therefore become law without people really being aware of the fact. There are usually over 2000 different statutory instruments alone coming into force each year, and some of these can make substantial changes in the law.

It is generally felt today that these criticisms were exaggerated, and to some extent simply an expression of resentment at the sheer volume of legislation needed in a modern industrialized country. Certainly some safeguards do exist against abuse of delegated powers; how adequate these safeguards are is a matter which is still sometimes discussed.

Control of delegated legislation

1. *Parliamentary control*
   (a) Parliament, having given the power to legislate, can obviously take the power away at a future date.
   (b) Ministers are usually answerable to Parliament for the content of regulations made by their departments.
   (c) The enabling Act will sometimes require that an instrument be laid before Parliament thereby permitting limited Parliamentary debate.
   (d) Committees of Members of Parliament examine and report on statutory instruments, EEC regulations and other delegated legislation.

2. *Judicial control*
   (a) *Ultra vires.* There is a vitally important distinction between the attitude of the courts to an Act of Parliament and their attitude to delegated legislation. The courts can never challenge the validity or reasonableness of a statute. They can, and do, sometimes challenge the validity of delegated legislation. The delegate body has power to legislate only in so far as Parliament has given it this power, and the courts keep it firmly within this limit. If it exceeds its powers in any way, the rules are *ultra vires* (outside of its powers) and therefore *void*.
   (b) *Unreasonableness.* The courts will sometimes take the view that Parliament has given the power only on the understanding that it be exercised *reasonably*. Some local authority by-laws have been held void, because the court felt that they were unreasonable.

C. Judicial precedent

The nature of precedent

The idea of binding judicial precedent is a special feature of common law jurisdictions, that is to say, systems of law based on that of England. The doctrine is based on the general principle that once a court has stated the legal position in a given situation, then the same decision will be reached in any future case where the material facts are the same.

Whether a court is bound to follow a previous decision depends to a very large extent on which court gave the previous decision. Generally, if the decision was of a superior court then the lower court must follow it, but a superior court is not bound by the previous decisions of an inferior one. The following table outlines the main rules:

1. Decisions of the House of Lords bind all other courts for the future, and until 1966 were even binding on the House of Lords itself in subsequent cases. In that year, however, the Lord Chancellor issued a statement on behalf of the House that it would no longer regard itself as rigidly bound if this would cause injustice by reason of changing social circumstances.

2. The Court of Appeal is bound by previous decisions of the Lords and, in most circumstances, by its own previous decisions. Its decisions are binding on all lower courts but not upon the House of Lords.
3. A High Court judge is bound by decisions of the House of Lords and the Court of Appeal but not by other High Court decisions.
4. A County Court judge is bound by decisions of all higher courts. The decisions of the County Courts themselves are not binding in any future case, and they are not normally reported at all.

This does not mean that decisions of lower courts will be disregarded by higher courts. These decisions may not be *binding* precedents, but they will have *persuasive* value. They may be long standing, recognized by people as the law, and acted upon accordingly. Similarly, decisions of the House of Lords in appeals from Scotland or Northern Ireland, and decisions of the Judicial Committee of the Privy Council in appeals from some Commonwealth countries, while not binding on English courts, have strong persuasive influence. Note, for instance, the *Wagon Mound* case in 1961 (Unit 10). An English court may even turn for guidance to a decision in the United States or the Commonwealth, where the legal systems have the same basis as our own.

When seen in operation, the doctrine of precedent works in quite a complex manner. When he gives his decision in a case the judge does, in effect, three things.

1. He gives his actual decision between the parties: 'I find for the plaintiff', or 'the appeal must fail'. This is obviously the part which is of most interest to the parties themselves.
2. He will also give his reasons for reaching that decision: what facts he regards as 'material', the legal principles which he is applying to those facts and why. This is called the *ratio decidendi* (the reasoning vital to the decision), and it is this part of the judgment which may bind future courts.
3. He may also, at the same time, discuss the law relating to this type of case generally, or perhaps discuss one or two hypothetical situations. These will be *obiter dicta* (other comments) and while they may have persuasive force in future cases, they are not binding.

Having become a precedent, a decision need not continue to be one indefinitely. It can cease to be binding in various ways. A decision can be *reversed* when the party who lost the case appeals to a higher court, which allows the appeal. Where similar facts come before the courts in a later case, then a higher court can *overrule* the previous decision of a lower one. This does not affect the parties of the earlier case; so far as they are concerned their decision still stands, but the earlier case is no longer binding in future. If a later court is not in a position to overrule a previous decision, for instance, because the legal principles involved are not the same, it may nevertheless *disapprove* it, usually by way of an *obiter dictum*. Disapproval by a higher court obviously casts doubt on the correctness of an earlier decision. Similarly, a later court which is not bound can simply *not follow* a previous decision, which will itself cast doubt on the earlier case. Finally, a previous decision can often be *distinguished* where the material facts of the earlier case differ from the present ones. There will always be some difference between the facts of two separate cases and if the later judge feels that the difference is sufficient to justify a different decision, he will distinguish the earlier case. In this way even a lower court can avoid holding itself bound by a previous higher decision.

Precedent or code?

Many other countries, particularly in Continental Europe, have no doctrine of binding precedent. Instead the main source of law in these countries will be a code. Almost all of the rules of civil and of criminal law have been written out fairly simply, and then formally enacted by the legislature.

It is largely for historical reasons that the English legal system is based mainly on precedent rather than on a code, and each alternative has its advantages.

1. In favour of the English system of judge-made or case law, it is argued that it gives more flexibility. The law steadily grows as new cases come before the courts, and new rules develop to meet new situations. A code, once enacted, can be changed only by a complex legislative process, and can sometimes work injustice as the rules become out-dated.
2. Systems based on precedent are claimed to be more realistic and practical in character, being based on actual problems that have come before the courts. On the other hand, it is sometimes necessary to wait until an actual dispute arises before the law can be known. This can lead to uncertainty, and bringing a case to find out the law can be a costly business. A code can, within limits, legislate in advance, so that the parties know what their legal position is without having to go to court to find out.
3. Finally, although case law provides us with many detailed rules, this can itself be a drawback. In English law there are at least 1000 volumes of law reports in which precedents are to be found. The ease with which cases may now be discovered by computerized retrieval methods has already led to the courts expressing concern at the number of precedents being cited.

Law reporting

The development of a doctrine of precedent has been very closely tied to the growth of good law reporting in this country. Without a clear and reliable record of earlier decisions, a doctrine of precedent simply could not work.

Law reporting in England began in the thirteenth century with the Year Books, which were very brief notes written by anonymous lawyers, often in a curious mixture of English and Norman French. From about 1530 the Year Books were replaced by private reports published under the names of those compiling them. These continued until the nineteenth century, but they vary considerably in value according to the accuracy of the reporter. In 1865 the Council of Law Reporting was established by the legal profession to provide for systematic publication of professionally prepared and officially revised volumes of reports.

Today the main reports are still produced by what is now the Incorporated Council of Law Reporting. It now publishes only one volume each year of reports of decisions in the Queen's Bench Division of the High Court, one of Chancery Division cases, and one of Family Division decisions. Court of Appeal cases are included in the volumes for the High Court Division from which the appeal came, but House of Lords decisions are found in a separate volume of Appeal Cases. Since 1953 the Council has also issued the Weekly Law Reports, to enable reports of certain cases to be available more quickly.

Some private reports did survive after the nineteenth century, but the only general ones now issued are the All England Law Reports, published in about three volumes each year, and also periodically, about weekly. Some very specialized private reports also continue in fields such as commercial law, taxation and industrial law.

The report of a civil case is referred to by the names of the parties as, for example, *Bolton* v. *Stone*, but in speech the 'v.' is said as 'and' (*not* 'versus'). The plaintiff's name is placed first and the defendant's second. If the case goes to appeal the parties are known as the appellant and the respondent, but the order is not changed unless it is a House of Lords case, when the appellant's name is placed first. After the name of the case will be found details for easy reference: the year, the series of reports with the volume number if necessary, and the page. Thus in the Law Reports, the House of Lords decision in *Bolton* v. *Stone* [1951] AC 850 is to be found on page 850 of the Appeal Cases reports for 1951. The Court of Appeal decision in the same case was reported under the name *Stone* v. *Bolton* [1950] 1 KB 201 (Miss Stone being the original plaintiff), and is found on page 201 of the first volume of King's Bench Division Reports for 1950. In the All England Law Reports, the Court of Appeal decision in this case is reported under the reference *Stone* v. *Bolton* [1949] 2 All ER 851, and the House of Lords decision as *Bolton* v. *Stone* [1951] 1 All ER 1078.

D. The judges and statutes

Construction and interpretation of statutes

The other major way in which the judges contribute to the development of English law is in interpreting and construing the words used in statutes and other legislation. Once a higher court has decided that the words of an Act apply in a particular way to a set of facts, this decision will form a precedent to be followed should a similar problem arise in a future case. Sometimes a complex body of case law may arise out of the interpretation of a single statute, as happened with parts of the Sale of Goods Act 1893.

The Interpretation Act 1978 gives certain statutory rules of interpretation, for example, that the masculine gender shall include the feminine, and the singular shall include the plural, and vice versa, unless a contrary intention is obvious. Moreover, almost all Acts contain a series of definitions of technical and other terms which the enactment contains.

Subject to this, it is for the judges to say what the words of an Act mean should any doubt arise. Words will be given their literal or everyday meaning unless this would lead to absurdity. If particular words are followed by general words, the general words are restricted to things similar to those specified particularly. Thus 'wheat, barley and other crops' would include oats but not potatoes. On the other hand, if there is particular mention only, nothing else is included. Thus 'wheat and barley' would not include oats.

If the words used are ambiguous, or if their application is uncertain, then more difficult questions of construction can arise. The courts will look at the Act as a whole; often the way in which a word is used in other parts of the Act will make it plain what it is intended to mean here. If the meaning is still not clear, the courts will try to discover from the wording of the Act what 'mischief' the Act was designed to deal with, and will try to interpret the words so as to give effect to what the Act was intended to achieve. The courts will *not*, however, ask the Government what the Act was intended to achieve, partly because the Government might be tempted to give a meaning which best suited its own immediate purposes; nor will account be taken of Parliamentary debates or statements published by Ministers when the bill was first proposed. It is the words of the Act alone which constitute the law.

Finally there are certain presumptions which a court will make. Thus it is presumed that a statute is not intended to bind the Crown unless the statute expressly so provides. Since 'the Crown' includes all crown servants (e.g., civil service departments) this presumption can be very important. Similarly, it is presumed that an Act is not intended to create a strict criminal offence; the courts will assume that the defendant is guilty only if he intended to commit the offence, or acted carelessly. This presumption will, of course, be rebutted if the words of the Act make it plain that the legislature wishes to impose strict liability.

Codes of practice

Section 45 of the Road Traffic Act 1930 (now section 60, Transport Act 1982) provided that 'The Minister shall . . . prepare a code (in this section referred to as the "Highway Code") comprising such directions as appear to him to be proper for the guidance of persons using roads . . .'. This code is *not* a piece of legislation; it does not have binding force, it is not a criminal offence to break it, nor will breach of it give rise to civil liability. It can always, however, be cited in evidence, and a person who breaks it is much more likely to be held negligent, or guilty of careless driving, than a person who observes the provisions. The code must be treated as a source of law to the extent that a court must accept its provisions in evidence.

The use of this type of code seems likely to increase in future. Under the Industrial Relations Act 1971, a Code of Industrial Relations practice was produced, having the same practical effect as the Highway Code. Subsequent legislation preserved this code of practice, which is still governed by the Employment Protection Act 1975, and further codes have since been added. Codes with similar effect are now being produced under several Acts, including the Health and Safety at Work, etc., Act 1974, the Control of Pollution Act 1974, and the Race Relations Act 1976.

In addition, there are many non-statutory codes of practice, produced by professional bodies, making recommendations as to safety in such matters as handling chemicals or other materials. Unlike statutory codes of practice, these are not sources of law, in that the courts have no *duty* to accept them in evidence. Nevertheless, they may in practice influence a court in deciding whether or not particular conduct is reasonable.

E. Other sources of law

Law of the European Communities

By section 2 of the European Communities Act 1972, Community law is incorporated in English law. The sources from which Community law is derived are as follows:

1. *The Treaties.* The primary sources are the three foundation Treaties (of Paris and Rome) with their supplementary schedules and appendices. To these must be added further treaties which have been made or will be made in the future between the member states, and treaties such as trade agreements concluded between the Communities and states in the outside world. These treaties are 'self-executing' in that the provisions automatically become part of the law of the member states without the states having the right to decide whether or not to implement them by their own legislation. Thus the courts in the United Kingdom must accept and apply Article 85 of the EEC Treaty which prohibits specified restrictive practice agreements between commercial undertakings.

2. *Secondary legislation.* The Council and Commission have been given law-making powers to enable the broad objects of the Treaties to be achieved. These administrative acts from which rules of law emanate may take various forms. *Regulations* are of general application, binding in their entirety and directly applicable in all member states without the need for further legislation. *Directives* also have a general scope but are simply addressed to member states requiring them to make changes in their own law to bring it into line with Community requirements. Each state will decide how this is to be done; for example, in the United Kingdom, it will be done by Order in Council or Ministerial regulation. *Decisions*, like regulations, take effect immediately without further implementation but they are only binding upon those to whom they are addressed and they do not have general legislative effect.

3. *Decisions of the Court of Justice.* The Court has no law-making powers and there is no doctrine of binding precedent. Nevertheless, through interpretation of 'statutory' provisions, a body of rules is emerging in the Court's judgments which has a strongly persuasive influence.

Custom

Historically, custom formed the basis of common law. General customs, almost without exception, have now fallen into disuse or been recognized by the courts and incorporated into precedent. Occasionally, a local custom may be put forward as still being law but the court will accept this only on very stringent conditions. More frequently, the courts will take into consideration what amount to special customs, such as commercial and business practice, in cases where they have to decide how existing legal rules should be applied in business situations.

Books by legal authors

These are not cited very frequently in the English courts, contrary to the practice in many continental countries. At one time this practice was seldom allowed here, and was restricted to a few notable authorities. More recently the rule has been relaxed and the number of acceptable authors increased.

Examination questions

1. Outline the sources from which a judge may draw the legal rules to apply in deciding a case.
2. Explain the meaning and purpose of delegated legislation using examples of a business nature.
3. A local authority by-law is preventing the expansion of your company. On what grounds, if at all, may the validity of the by-law be challenged?
4. Your company is considering whether or not to sue a supplier of faulty goods. There is a precedent when, on similar facts, the supplier was held to be liable. Explain the extent to which reliance may be placed upon this precedent.
5. What is meant by:
   (a) European Community law;
   (b) a code of practice?
   Explain in both cases the extent to which these are sources of English law.

Unit 3. The English Court System

A. County Courts

After the medieval local courts had largely disappeared, there was little provision for the hearing of minor civil claims until the County Courts were created in 1846. They were originally designed for the settlement of small claims and the collection of debts where the amount at stake did not exceed £20, but their jurisdiction has subsequently been extended by many statutes. Consolidating Acts have been passed from time to time, and they are now governed by the County Courts Act 1984.

There are some 400 of these courts in England and Wales. They have no connection either with the earlier courts which carried the same name or with the geographical counties. County Courts are grouped in circuits varying from as many as 15 courts in country areas to one court in almost continuous session in parts of London. They are presided over by Circuit judges, of whom there are just over 350, and, while it is usual for there to be one judge to each circuit, the busier courts may have more than one judge.

The majority of civil cases in this country are disposed of in the County Courts by the judge sitting without a jury. Procedure tends to be quicker and less formal than in the High Court and, particularly since the cases are heard locally, less costly. Solicitors, wearing gowns but not wigs, have a right of audience as well as barristers.

There are limits to the jurisdiction of the County Courts, normally based upon the amount of the claim. Actions in contract and tort, such as the collection of contractual debts and accident claims, can be brought where the amount claimed does not exceed £5000; this sum, and those in the following paragraph, may be raised further by Order in Council when it is deemed necessary. Since even a small claim can raise difficult issues of law, the amount at stake does not necessarily measure the

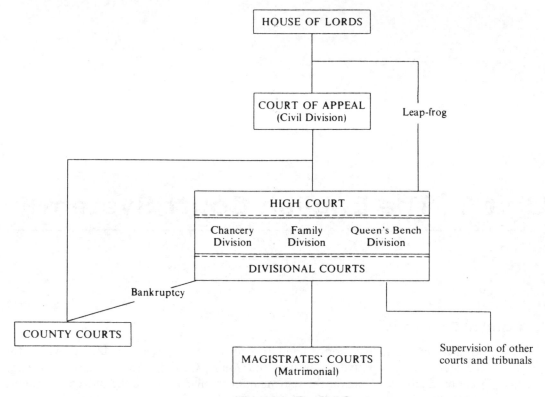

Figure 3.1 The Civil Courts

difficulty or complexity of the case. Actions for defamation, which invariably require trial by jury, must always be brought in the High Court.

In equity matters and related proceedings, which include actions on trusts and mortgages, the administration of estates and the dissolution of partnerships, the amount at issue must not exceed £30 000. In actions concerning land, such as the recovery of possession and the determination of title, the annual rateable value must not exceed £1000. Certain County Courts can deal with bankruptcies and the winding up of companies whose paid-up share capital does not exceed £120 000.

The County Courts also have jurisdiction in certain family matters such as undefended divorces, adoption, guardianship and legitimacy. Some courts near the coast can hear Admiralty cases, particularly small salvage claims. Many statutes confer jurisdiction in other matters, important examples being hire-purchase, rent restriction and complaints of racial discrimination. Actions begun in the High Court may be remitted to the County Court if the amount at issue is small and other actions may be so transferred with the consent of the parties.

In addition to the restrictions regarding the nature and amount of the claim as outlined above, there are also territorial limitations. In general, actions must be brought in the court for the district where either the defendant resides or carries on business or where the reason for the action arose. If possession of land is sought, the venue of the trial depends upon where the land is situated.

The administration of County Courts is carried out by *Registrars*, who must be solicitors of at least seven years' standing. Registrars also perform limited judicial functions and now have the power to act as judge if the action is not defended, if the amount at stake does not exceed £500, and in other cases if the judge and the parties agree.

In relation to very small claims, it is sometimes felt that the County Courts are no longer fulfilling the purpose for which they were originally created. Although procedure is much quicker and cheaper than that in the High Court, it is still expensive. A defended County Court action could now cost hundreds of pounds in fees and disbursements and many solicitors would advise against suing if only a small sum were at stake. The County Court arbitration scheme (Unit 4) has reduced costs considerably but, in consequence, costs of legal representation in court are not awarded to a successful party where the amount involved does not exceed the arbitration limit of £500.

B. The High Court

The Judicature Acts 1873–75 reorganized the system of civil courts by sweeping away the many separate courts which then existed and replacing them by the Supreme Court of Judicature (divided into the Court of Appeal and the High Court of Justice). The system then established has remained in operation with only minor alterations to the present day. It is now governed by the Supreme Court Act 1981.

Any civil action may be begun in the High Court, apart from a few matters such as rent restriction and hire-purchase where the County Courts are given exclusive jurisdiction by statute. There is, therefore, an overlap in the jurisdiction of the County Court and the High Court where small claims are concerned. In these cases litigants are encouraged to use the County Courts by the power of the High Court Registrars and Masters to transfer High Court actions to the County Courts, in some instances without the consent of the parties. If there is an insistence upon the use of the High Court, the successful party may be penalized by a smaller award of costs on the County Court and not the High Court scale.

The High Court is divided into three divisions, the Queen's Bench Division, the Chancery Division and the Family Division with some 80 judges in total. Any division is legally competent to deal with any matter arising, but in practice cases must be assigned to the division specializing in that particular type of action.

Before 1972, High Court cases outside London were tried at Civil Assizes. The cases were heard by High Court judges, mainly from the Queen's Bench Division, drawing their power from a special commission. The Courts Act 1971 abolished Civil Assizes and provided that the High Court might sit throughout the country wherever convenient. In practice this will be 24 'first-tier' centres where almost any type of High Court case may be heard. The exception concerns Chancery matters which will be confined to certain centres in the North of England; in effect, this is a continuation of the former jurisdiction of the old Palatine Courts of Lancaster and Durham which were abolished by the 1971 Act.

Queen's Bench Division

This division, presided over by the Lord Chief Justice, has succeeded to the jurisdiction formerly exercised by the old common law courts of Queen's (or King's) Bench, Common Pleas, and Exchequer. It deals with the greatest number of cases, notably those arising out of breaches of contract, the commission of torts and claims for the recovery of land. Typical cases would include an action for non-performance of a contract, an allegation that the defendant has published a defamatory statement, and a claim for damages arising out of a road accident or an injury suffered at work. Any action not specifically assigned to one of the other two divisions will be heard in the Queen's Bench Division.

In this division are to be found the few remaining civil juries. While most actions are now tried by a judge sitting alone, a jury will normally be empanelled whenever a person's character is likely to be in issue, as in actions based upon fraud and defamation. Majority verdicts can be reached.

Two specialized courts sit within the Queen's Bench Division, the Admiralty Court and the Commercial Court. Judges may be assigned to these courts and thereby specialize in these types of case.

Chancery Division

This division inherited the jurisdiction formerly exercised by the old Court of Chancery and other matters have since been allocated to it by statute. It is concerned with the administration of the estates of deceased persons, trusts, mortgages, partnerships, companies, bankruptcies and revenue and planning matters. The nominal president is the Lord Chancellor but his many other duties prevent him from taking any direct part in the work of the division; the organization of the day-to-day business is carried out by a senior judge, the Vice-Chancellor. The Patents Court and Companies Court are specialized courts within this division.

Family Division

This division was created in 1970 to deal with matters arising out of marriage, divorce, matrimonial property and children. The senior judge in the division is known as the President.

This was formerly the Probate, Divorce and Admiralty Division, a collection of apparently unrelated matters which were re-allocated in 1970. Admiralty cases, such as salvage claims and prize jurisdiction, were transferred to a special court within the

Queen's Bench Division. Probate cases were transferred to the Chancery Division, except for non-contentious matters which remained within the Family Division for administrative reasons. Jurisdiction over minors, for example, wardship, was transferred from the Chancery Division to the Family Division.

C. Appeals in civil cases

Divisional Courts

In addition to its original jurisdiction whereby cases are first tried by one judge, the High Court also exercises certain appellate jurisdiction. For this purpose two or three judges sit together and constitute a Divisional Court.

Divisional Courts of the Queen's Bench Division may exercise criminal and civil jurisdiction. Criminal appeals are heard by way of 'case stated' from Magistrates' Courts and the Crown Court. Civil appeals are heard from the decisions of certain tribunals. Divisional Courts in the Chancery Division hear appeals from the County Courts on bankruptcy questions.

The Divisional Court in the Queen's Bench also hears applications for various prerogative orders, through which various special courts and tribunals are kept under review (Unit 4). Thus if an administrative tribunal exceeds its jurisdiction or otherwise acts wrongfully, its decision can be quashed by the Divisional Court. This is not strictly an appellate jurisdiction, but in many cases it is so similar as to be almost indistinguishable.

Court of Appeal (Civil Division)

Appeals from the County Court (except on bankruptcy matters), the High Court and certain tribunals, for example the Lands Tribunal, are normally heard by three judges of this court. The court, for all practical purposes, is constituted by the Master of the Rolls and 18 Lord Justices of Appeal, though judges from the High Court may also be asked to sit if necessary. An appeal may generally be made as of right but leave is required in some cases. In County Court cases the permission of the trial judge or of the Court of Appeal is necessary except where the appeal concerns a claim in excess of one-half of the County Court limit or where an injunction is sought or the custody of or access to a child is involved, when an appeal then lies as of right.

The appeal takes the form of a rehearing of the case through the media of the judge's notes and the transcript of the official shorthand writer's notes, and by listening to argument from counsel. Witnesses are not heard again nor is fresh evidence usually admitted. The court has all the powers of the court below and may uphold or reverse the decision in whole or in part, it may alter the sum of damages awarded, and it may make a different order as to costs. In certain prescribed circumstances, for example the discovery of fresh evidence, a new trial may be ordered.

25

House of Lords

A further right of appeal exists from the Court of Appeal to the House of Lords; leave is required from the Court of Appeal or from the Appeals Committee of the House itself.

The House of Lords, when it sits as a judicial tribunal, differs in constitution from the legislative body which forms one of the Houses of Parliament. All the lay peers are now excluded, by convention if not by law, and the judges are drawn from the Lord Chancellor, peers who have held or are holding high judicial office such as ex-Lord Chancellors, and the 10 life peers who are known as Lords of Appeal in Ordinary or Law Lords. Some of the Law Lords are appointed from Scotland and Northern Ireland since the House is also the highest civil court of appeal for these countries and the highest criminal court of appeal for Northern Ireland.

Appeals heard by the House of Lords require a minimum of three judges but in practice five will normally sit. Since the court is technically part of the House, the judgments are given in the form of 'speeches', not usually read aloud today. If their lordships disagree, the view of the majority will prevail, and an appellant or respondent may succeed by only three votes to two. This was so in the case of *Donoghue* v. *Stevenson* (Unit 9).

It had long been felt in some quarters that two appeals from the High Court to the Court of Appeal and then to the House of Lords were unnecessary. Accordingly, the

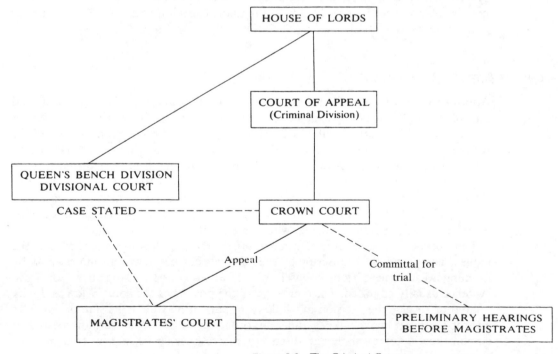

Figure 3.2 The Criminal Courts

Administration of Justice Act 1969 introduced a 'leap-frog' procedure whereby the Court of Appeal could be avoided and the appeal could go direct from the trial judge to the House of Lords.

The trial judge must grant a certificate that the case is suitable for an appeal direct to the House of Lords, on the grounds that it involves a point of law of general importance, which either relates to a matter of statutory interpretation or is a case in which the judge was bound by a previous decision of the Court of Appeal or the House of Lords. The parties must also consent to the 'leap-frog'. Finally, the House of Lords must grant leave for the direct appeal. It is worth noting that since this change was introduced there have been very few instances where it has been used.

D. Criminal Courts

Magistrates' Courts

These courts, sometimes known as petty sessions, are held in most centres of population; the number of courts and the frequency of their sitting depend upon the amount of work to be done. They deal with over 98 per cent of all crimes.

The court must be composed of at least two justices of the peace or magistrates, but three will usually sit so that a majority decision can be given in the event of a disagreement. Justices are appointed by the Lord Chancellor on the recommendation of local advisory committees and no legal qualifications or knowledge of law are required. The justices decide upon guilt or innocence, without the assistance of a jury, and upon the appropriate sentence to be imposed. Advice on questions of law is given by the Clerk to the Justices who will normally have had some legal training. In a few towns the place of the unpaid lay justices is taken by one full-time stipendiary magistrate who must be a barrister or solicitor.

The jurisdiction of Magistrates' Courts is regulated closely by statute. In general, there is the power to try all minor offences which will include, for example breaches of the Factories Act, false trade descriptions and the sale of adulterated food. The power of punishment depends upon the offence but a fine of more than £2000 may not normally be imposed nor a sentence of imprisonment exceeding six months. An offender may be committed to the Crown Court for sentence if the justices feel that their powers of punishment are inadequate.

Justices have another function to perform in the case of more serious crimes, which they cannot try, when they hear the evidence against the accused and decide whether there is a prima facie or reasonable case to go forward for trial. Their so-called committal proceedings avoid wasting the time of higher courts on frivolous charges. These proceedings may now take the form of merely handing in written statements of witnesses.

The Crown Court

The Courts Act 1971 reorganized a criminal structure dating back to the Middle Ages. Courts of Assize and Quarter Sessions were abolished and replaced by a system of Crown Courts sitting at convenient centres and trying cases committed for trial by Magistrates' Courts.

Criminal offences have been classified into four groups for the purpose of trial. The first class which comprises the most serious offences must be tried by a High Court judge. Less serious offences will be tried by (lesser) Circuit judges or by Recorders, barristers sitting as part-time judges. In some cases lay justices may form part of the bench.

The judge conducts the trial and decides any points of law that may arise. The guilt or innocence of the accused is determined by a jury of 12 laymen and, if the verdict is guilty, the judge will pass sentence.

E. Appeals in criminal cases

An appeal may be made from a Magistrates' Court against either the conviction or the severity of the sentence. The appeal takes the form of a complete re-hearing of the case in the Crown Court.

An appeal may be made on a point of law by either the prosecution or the defence to the Divisional Court of the Queen's Bench Division. This is known as 'case stated' since the magistrates are required to state their findings on the facts before them. The Divisional Court will decide the law applicable to those facts and, if necessary, remit the case to the justices, instructing them to decide the case again on the basis of this ruling on the law.

An appeal against a conviction or sentence in the Crown Court may be made by the defendant to the Criminal Division of the Court of Appeal where it will be heard by a bench of three judges. A further appeal by either the prosecution or the defence is possible to the House of Lords but this occurs infrequently. A point of law of general public importance must be involved and permission to appeal must be given by either the Court of Appeal or the House itself.

Examination questions

1. Explain the jurisdiction of the County Courts in matters likely to affect a business. What are the advantages and disadvantages of bringing an action in the County Court instead of the High Court?
2. Outline the system of appeals in civil cases.
3. Distinguish between the criminal jurisdiction of Magistrates' Courts and that of the Crown Courts.
4. Explain, with reasons, which court would hear the following cases:
    (a) a claim for damages for negligence which has caused an alleged loss of £10 000;
    (b) a petition to wind up a company with a capital of £100 000;
    (c) a prosecution for applying a false trade description;
    (d) a claim for £20 000 for breach of trust.
    State in each instance the court to which an appeal might lie.

Unit 4. Other Courts and Tribunals

A. Modern special courts and tribunals

The existence of special courts outside the ordinary system has always been a feature of the English legal system throughout its history. The mercantile courts and the Court of Chancery itself in its early days are examples which were mentioned in Unit 1. Most of these older special courts have been incorporated into the ordinary system, although there are still a few which, for various reasons, did not perish in the nineteenth-century reforms or in the Courts Act 1971.

More recently, in the last 100 years, governments have created a large number of new special courts and tribunals. This has been another result of the great expansion of government into social and economic fields. The special nature of some of the disputes arising from these new activities makes the composition and procedure of the ordinary courts inappropriate for this purpose.

Reasons for their creation

1. The ordinary courts are courts of *law*, and are not equipped to deal with the economic, social, business, industrial relations and other considerations that lie behind certain types of dispute.
2. The procedure of the ordinary courts is slow, for reasons which will be discussed later. Administrative decisions often have to be acted upon fairly quickly, otherwise the job will never be done. Special tribunals may therefore be set up to hear and decide on appeals very quickly. In other circumstances, delay can cause great financial hardship to the claimant. A person claiming to have been wrongly refused social security benefits can hardly be expected to starve while an appeal

awaits hearing in the ordinary courts. Such appeals, therefore, now go to special social security appeal tribunals which operate relatively quickly.

3. Procedure in the ordinary courts is also very expensive, again for reasons which will be discussed later. The quicker and less formal procedure of special tribunals can be much cheaper, and this can outweigh the fact that evidence may sometimes be presented and examined less thoroughly.

4. The formal atmosphere of the ordinary civil courts can be very forbidding, and can often deter claimants from pursuing certain types of claim. Most special tribunals operate in a much more relaxed and informal manner.

5. Finally, the rules of common law and equity concentrate on protecting and enforcing *individual* rights, and on giving the individual the right to help himself. The social legislation, which has played such an important part in the development of English law in the last century, has a rather different basic objective, and concentrates more on those who are not very good at helping themselves. This difference in approach has sometimes influenced governments in deciding that disputes over social legislation should normally go to special tribunals.

A description of some of the special courts and tribunals which have been created may help to illustrate some of these points.

Special courts with High Court status

In some instances it has been possible to create a new court very similar to a Division of the High Court, but in fact quite separate and specifically adapted to some special type of dispute. The principal example at the present time is the *Restrictive Practices Court*.

The Restrictive Trade Practices Act 1976, which consolidated earlier statutes, is aimed at suppressing restrictive trade agreements on matters such as price fixing and restraining the production or supply of goods. Such agreements will normally be valid only if the agreement can be shown to be in the public interest, to be determined by reference to certain criteria set out in the Act. Decisions on such issues demand business and economic knowledge not normally available in the ordinary courts, and a special court, the Restrictive Practices Court, is, therefore, constituted under the Act.

The Act provides that the court will have 15 members, 5 of whom are lawyers, the other 10 normally not. The 5 lawyers will be 3 judges of the High Court, and 1 judge each from Scotland and Northern Ireland. The 10 other members will be appointed on the recommendation of the Lord Chancellor, each being 'a person appearing to the Lord Chancellor to be qualified by virtue of his knowledge of or experience in industry, commerce or public affairs'. Cases are heard normally by one judge and two lay members sitting together. Points of law are decided by the judge, but the more important issues are usually questions of fact, which must be decided by a simple majority. Members with necessary business experience to judge properly whether a restrictive agreement is really justifiable are, therefore, involved in the decision, and can if they so wish outvote the judge on questions of fact.

The court does not operate particularly speedily, but this is not an area where delay is likely to cause great hardship. An appeal is possible on a point of law, and in England and Wales will be heard by the Court of Appeal.

Another example is the *Employment Appeal Tribunal* set up under the Employment Protection Acts to hear appeals from industrial tribunals (see later). Its work is concerned with redundancy payments and compensation for unfair dismissal, complaints of discrimination in employment on grounds of race or sex, and complaints of inadequate notice to terminate employment. An appeal on a point of law will also go to the Court of Appeal.

B. Administrative tribunals

Types of tribunals

In most cases where special courts were established, it was not felt necessary to set up a powerful body like the courts just described. The nature of the disputes likely to arise made smaller 'administrative' tribunals more appropriate, and very many of these have been created. The Franks Committee on Tribunals and Inquiries in 1957 estimated that there were then over 2000 different tribunals in existence. These differ from each other in many respects, but they do have some common features: the judges are usually not lawyers, although some do have legally qualified chairmen; they operate informally, cheaply and fairly quickly; most of them sit locally; there is usually no appeal to the courts on a point of fact, and only sometimes on a point of law. It is not possible here to describe all of these tribunals, but a few of the main categories will serve as an example.

1. *Tribunals dealing with social security and personal welfare.* The Social Security Acts 1975–80, provide that benefits shall be payable to people out of state funds, subject to certain conditions, in the event of sickness, death, unemployment, maternity or similar situations giving rise to financial problems. Under the industrial injuries provisions of the 1975–80 Acts, benefits may be paid to persons suffering injury or disease arising out of and in the course of employment. Disputes can often arise as to whether a claimant is entitled to benefit, and as to the amount due.

   If the local insurance officer rejects a claim, the claimant can appeal to a local tribunal, of which there are over 190 in England and Wales. The tribunal will have three members: a chairman who will usually be a local barrister or solicitor, and two lay members.

   A further right of appeal lies from the local tribunals to one of the Social Security Commissioners, who are barristers or solicitors of at least 10 years' standing, and are appointed full-time. Some decisions of the Commissioners are published in a series of reports and, while these decisions are normally followed by the tribunals, there is no system of binding precedent as in the ordinary courts.

Where an appeal under the industrial injuries provisions is on medical grounds, for example a dispute as to the extent of the injury, there is a slightly different procedure to allow the appeal to be heard by people who are medically qualified.

Other groups of tribunals in this broad category include supplementary benefit appeal tribunals (now fused with national insurance local tribunals under the name of social security appeal tribunals as from 1984), national health service tribunals, and mental health review tribunals.

2. *Tribunals concerned with the valuation and use of land.* Many permanent and *ad hoc* tribunals operate in connection with public control over land use and value. Appeals from rating valuations, for instance, go to local valuation courts composed of laymen. A further appeal from the local valuation court lies to the Lands Tribunal, which is a much more powerful body whose chairman and some other members will be legally qualified. The Lands Tribunal also hears appeals concerning compensation for compulsory purchase.

Other tribunals in this field are the rent assessment committees which have power to fix rents of residential tenancies, furnished or unfurnished, which fall within the terms of the Rent Act 1977.

Where a person wishes to appeal against a compulsory purchase order on his land, or against refusal of planning permission, there is no special tribunal to which he can go. He can, however, appeal to the Minister, who will send an 'inspector' to hold a public inquiry. This will be conducted almost like a court, with all interested parties having the right to give evidence, but unlike a court or tribunal this inquiry will not give a decision. It will merely make recommendations to the Minister, and the Minister need not follow these recommendations when he eventually makes the final decision.

3. *Transport.* A number of special tribunals exist in this field. One example is the Transport Tribunal which deals with appeals over road haulage licences, among other matters. The president must be an experienced lawyer and the four other members must include two who have experience in transport business, one with experience in commercial affairs and one with experience in financial matters or economics.

4. *Tribunals dealing with employment.* The industrial tribunals which have already been mentioned are some of the most important of all local tribunals. Their main work arises from disputed claims for redundancy payments and complaints of unfair dismissal, and they are extremely busy. They sit locally, and will have a legally qualified chairman with two other members, one from a panel representing employers, the other from a panel representing employees. They work informally and fairly quickly. An appeal lies to the Employment Appeal Tribunal.

Control over tribunals

Administrative tribunals have sometimes come in for criticism; it is suggested that the legal and lay members appointed by a Minister might be more likely to give a decision favourable to the Government and civil service than would the independent judges in the ordinary courts; and the looser procedure may sometimes make a wrong decision seem more likely. There is little evidence that these criticisms are justified, but in any event tribunals are subject to two main controls.

1. *Judicial control by the courts.* In the first place there is usually a provision for an appeal on a point of law to the ordinary courts. This can cause delay, however, and occasionally no right of appeal is allowed.

   Secondly, the courts exercise some other controls, often by an extended use of very old 'prerogative' orders. *Mandamus*, which means 'we command', is used to compel the performance of some duty, such as the duty of a tribunal to allow an appeal when it ought to do so. *Prohibition*, as the name suggests, is used to prevent a tribunal exceeding its jurisdiction or otherwise acting wrongfully. *Certiorari*, the most important of these orders, is used to compel a tribunal to inform the High Court of the facts of the case under discussion so that the High Court may certify whether the tribunal has acted wrongfully, in which event the decision will be quashed. It is no longer necessary to ask the High Court for a specific order; instead a request is made for a 'judicial review' of the decision in question and the High Court is able to make such order as it deems appropriate.

   These controls can be exercised if a tribunal has acted *ultra vires*, i.e., exceeded its powers. The tribunals only have the powers conferred on them by statute, and can only exercise them in the ways and for the purposes intended by Parliament. The courts can, therefore, intervene if these powers are, in the opinion of the court, exceeded or seriously abused. Thus the courts can insist that tribunals observe the principles of 'natural justice', for instance, that no man shall be judge in his own cause, that is, that no member of the tribunal shall have any personal interest in the subject-matter under discussion, and that both parties shall have a right to be heard.

   This supervisory jurisdiction of the courts is exercised largely by the Queen's Bench Division, usually by a Divisional Court.

2. *The Council on Tribunals.* Criticism of tribunals and inquiries led to the setting up of the Franks Committee, which reported in 1957. Following its recommendations, the Tribunals and Inquiries Act 1958 established a Council on Tribunals to keep under review the constitution and working of administrative tribunals. The members of the Council are appointed by the Lord Chancellor, and report to him on matters referred to it. The Council also has an important power to examine any rules of procedure that a tribunal may introduce. Thus, in most cases, tribunals must now give reasons for their decision upon request from one of the parties and give a right of appeal on a point of law to the ordinary court.

C. Domestic tribunals

When people form an association, they usually prescribe rules which members must obey, and provide a committee or other machinery for enforcement where necessary.

33

All persons joining the association agree to be bound and to submit to the judgment of the committee in the event of a dispute.

Thus, allegations of unprofessional conduct against solicitors, medical practitioners, dentists and architects are heard by disciplinary committees set up for this purpose. Trade associations often set up tribunals to enforce uniform trading practices on their members and trade unions ensure discipline in powers given to their committees.

Many such disciplinary bodies exercise wide powers, particularly where membership of the association may be a condition for carrying on the particular trade, profession or business, so that expulsion can take away a person's ability to earn a living in that field. The ordinary courts do exercise some controls where domestic tribunals exceed or abuse the power given them by the rules of the association, in much the same way as the courts can review the actions of administrative tribunals.

D. Arbitration

Arbitration is a means of settling disputes other than by court action and it arises when one or more persons are appointed to hear the arguments submitted by the parties and to give a decision on them. The type of arbitrator depends upon the nature of the case. In some instances a legal practitioner may be chosen, while in others of a highly technical nature it may be more appropriate to appoint a person with knowledge or experience of the subject-matter.

The most common way in which arbitration arises is by the voluntary agreement of the parties either before or after a dispute has arisen. Many commercial contracts, for example insurance policies, contain a clause providing for this method of settling disputes. It is often preferred to court action for it is usually cheaper, quicker, more informal, and does not involve publicity.

Provided that the submission is in writing, which is usually the case, arbitration procedure is governed by the Arbitration Acts 1950–79. Once arbitration has been agreed upon and is being carried out in a proper manner, the court will not interfere nor hear the dispute itself. An arbitration award properly arrived at will be enforced by the court. Points of law which arise may be submitted separately to the court for decision, by means of *case stated*. In these ways the court allows the parties to settle their own disputes, but at the same time maintains a supervisory role.

Various statutes provide for reference of certain types of issue to arbitration, and the courts themselves can refer a matter to arbitration where, for instance, the case requires prolonged examination of documents, scientific investigation or involved accounting.

Since 1973 there has also been an arbitration service within the County Court structure. When the claim does not exceed £500, the Registrar can refer the proceedings to arbitration, even against the wishes of the parties. If both parties agree to arbitration, it can be ordered even where the sum exceeds this amount. The Registrar himself usually hears the case. Legal representation is permitted but discouraged since the fees of a lawyer cannot be recovered as costs and must be paid by the litigants themselves even if they win the case. Arbitration awards are enforceable in the same ways as a County Court judgment. This procedure allows small claims to be settled privately and informally, without rigid adherence to the rules of evidence and procedure.

This development was influenced by earlier voluntary experiments such as the Manchester Arbitration Scheme for Small Claims. Now, sadly, most such local schemes have disappeared, largely because of lack of funds.

A specialized use of arbitration, which has sometimes been important in recent years, is for the purpose of settling industrial disputes. This is arbitration in a slightly different sense, in that the award here is not usually legally enforceable, although it can be none the less effective. This is outside the scope of the present work.

E. The Judicial Committee of the Privy Council

This body does not form part of the court structure of this country but, since it corresponds in structure with the House of Lords and its decisions have a strong persuasive influence, it is more conveniently dealt with here. The Judicial Committee is the final court of appeal from the Commonwealth in both civil and criminal matters, except where self-governing countries have exercised their right to abolish such appeals; most countries have now done this. The Committee also hears appeals from the Channel Islands, the Isle of Man, the Ecclesiastical Courts, the Prize Courts in wartime, and from certain other tribunals such as the Disciplinary Committee of the General Medical Council.

In practice, membership is restricted to those persons holding high legal qualifications and it is very similar in composition to the House of Lords when that body sits as a court of appeal, with the addition of certain judges from Commonwealth countries. Although its judgments are not binding upon English courts, they are treated with considerable respect in view of the Committee's composition. The judgment takes the form of advice to the Crown which is then formally implemented by Order in Council. Dissenting opinions can now be delivered.

F. The European Court of Justice

Constitution and procedure

The Court sits in Luxemburg and its decisions on Community matters, from which there is no appeal, must be accepted by national courts. Each member state appoints one judge who may be a professional judge, an academic lawyer or a public servant. The business of the Court is normally disposed of before all the judges.

Compared with English procedure, much greater emphasis is placed upon written submissions or pleadings than upon oral argument. The Bench plays a more active or inquisitorial part in the hearing and it will be assisted by an advocate-general whose function is to give an independent view of the case by way of a reasoned submission at the close of the proceedings. The Court will give a single judgment and dissenting opinions are not expressed. There is no machinery for enforcing judgments and, where this is necessary, it must be done by the member states through their national courts.

Jurisdiction

1. Actions may be brought against member states either by other member states or by the Commission on the grounds that Treaty obligations are not being fulfilled. The Court will give a declaratory judgment and it is a matter of good faith for the member state to comply with it; see *Commission of the European Communities* v. *United Kingdom* (1982) (Unit 23).
2. Actions may be brought against Community institutions by other institutions, by member states or by private individuals or corporate bodies who are directly concerned. In this way the legality of an act of, for example, the Commission may be challenged. The Court may declare the act to be void and, if appropriate, award compensation.
3. The Court may settle disputes between the Communities and their employees arising from the employees' contracts of employment. It may also deal with non-contractual liability of Community institutions for damage caused by their servants in the performance of their duties.
4. Any court or tribunal in a member state may ask the Court for a preliminary ruling on the interpretation of the Treaties or of any acts of Community institutions. A ruling must be sought by the final court of appeal in a member state if this is requested by one of the parties to an action.

Examination questions

1. (a) A change in the law may necessitate some new provision for the settlement of disputes. What are the advantages of making such provision a reference to some tribunal instead of leaving it to the courts?
   (b) Indicate which court or tribunal would settle the following matters and any provisions existing for an appeal:
      (i) a claim for a social security benefit which has been rejected by the local insurance officer;
      (ii) a dispute concerning an alleged restrictive trade agreement.
2. Write short notes on:
   (a) Restrictive Practices Court;
   (b) Industrial Tribunals;
   (c) Social Security Appeal Tribunals;
   (d) Council on Tribunals;
   (e) Judicial Committee of the Privy Council.
3. Outline the constitution, procedure and jurisdiction of the European Court of Justice.

4. (a) Your company is revising its standard form of contract which is used for its car-hire business and is considering the insertion of an arbitration clause.

   Draft a report explaining the effect of such a clause and the benefits that might arise from it in the event of a dispute.

   (b) Many contracts do not include an arbitration clause.

   Explain when a dispute concerning such a contract may be submitted to arbitration.

Unit 5. Court Proceedings

This unit will be concerned primarily with the course taken by typical civil proceedings, including matters likely to arise before trial, the trial itself, and the ways in which any judgment given by the court may be enforced. It will conclude with a brief outline of criminal proceedings.

Civil proceedings vary according to the type of action. It is not possible here to deal with petitions for divorce, for the bankruptcy of a private individual or for the winding up of a company. Cases in the Chancery Division and the Family Division are also governed by special rules. The emphasis here will be on common law actions in the Queen's Bench Division, such as are likely to arise following a breach of contract or an accident at work or on the road. It should be remembered that many such actions are brought in the County Courts, but the more important are heard in the High Court, and in any event the problems facing the litigant in the County Court are very similar.

A. Preliminary considerations

To sue or not to sue

Any person may begin and conduct proceedings himself without legal assistance, but because of the difficulties involved it is highly desirable to obtain legal advice by consulting a solicitor. The solicitor may advise that further legal action is not worth while at all. It has been said that only lawyers benefit from the law, and the litigant might be best advised simply to drop the matter. The following factors may be relevant:

1. Is the other party worth suing? There is always the possibility that, because of lack of means, he will not be able to pay any damages that may be awarded against him.

Even if he has the means it might be difficult to enforce the judgment against him; the methods of enforcing judgments will be discussed later in this unit. If there are two possible defendants, for example, a bus driver whose negligence caused the accident and his employers who are responsible for his actions, it is desirable to bring the action against the one most likely to be able to pay the damages, in this example the bus company.

2. Another consideration is the likely cost of the proceedings. The plaintiff's costs in a defended High Court action will run to hundreds, often thousands, of pounds. The costs of a defended County Court action may be hundreds of pounds. Moreover, unless there are good reasons for deciding otherwise, the unsuccessful party will be required to pay not only his own costs, but also those of his opponent, at the discretion of the court. The cost of losing an action can, therefore, be very substantial indeed.

   The winner does not, in fact, get all of his costs from the unsuccessful party. The actual legal costs incurred by the winner will be scrutinized by a court official known as a taxing-master, and anything not strictly essential to winning the case, such as a very high fee paid to counsel, will be struck out. Even winning the action, therefore, can still be expensive, and the action might not be worth while if the damages recovered are small. There may, of course, be good reasons for bringing an action at a loss, for example, a business firm does not wish to acquire a reputation among its debtors that it does not bother to collect small debts.

3. The length of time which proceedings will take must also be borne in mind, particularly in cases where an appeal is likely. The plaintiff might have to wait several years for his remedy, which would make it hardly worth the effort involved.

   In *Halsey* v. *Esso Petroleum Co. Ltd* (1961), Halsey sought damages for harm done to his property by chemical discharges from an Esso plant. He also sought an injunction ordering Esso to stop the discharges and reduce noise. The damage occurred in 1958, but he did not get compensation or an injunction until 1961. Many plaintiffs would not wish to engage in proceedings of this length, particularly since the damages ultimately awarded were only £235.

   Readers will be aware of the length of time taken to settle the action on behalf of the thalidomide children.

4. A final consideration may be the publicity which a court action will bring. Even a successful action by a business may have a bad effect upon its public reputation or on its industrial relations, for example, where the firm brings or defends an action against an employee.

Legal aid

If, in spite of the above considerations, a decision has been made to proceed with the action, the next step is to consider the finance of the proceedings. For the private client, there may be the possibility of obtaining legal aid if the client cannot himself afford the cost.

The statutory provisions for legal aid and advice are contained in the Legal Aid

Acts 1974 and 1979. Aid is available for most civil proceedings before the ordinary courts, but not in most instances for proceedings before administrative tribunals. The legal aid scheme is administered by the Law Society through a series of area and local committees which are made up of solicitors and barristers who practise locally.

The applicant must satisfy two requirements if he is to qualify for aid: (a) he must satisfy the local certifying committee that he has a good arguable case which, if he could pay his own costs, a solicitor would advise him to proceed with; and (b) he must show that he genuinely cannot afford to proceed.

The rules for determining what an applicant can afford are very detailed. The grant of legal aid and the amount of contribution, if any, which he must make, depend upon his income and capital remaining after certain allowances have been made.

B. Civil procedure before trial

Negotiating a settlement

As a first step it is customary for the solicitor to try to settle the dispute without litigation by writing to the opposing party or his solicitor. If no opportunity at all is given to the other party to settle, a successful plaintiff might be penalized by not getting some of his costs from the other side. In most cases this initial letter will be followed by other correspondence, and possibly meetings between representatives of the two sides with a view to reaching a settlement. In an accident claim the negotiations will usually be between the injured person's solicitor and the other party's insurance company.

Simultaneously with this, each side will be concerned with collecting evidence. In accident claims this will normally include medical reports, statements from witnesses, and possibly technical reports about, for example, the condition of the motor vehicle or the defective premises. Medical reports, in particular, can be extremely important, because the amount of any settlement will depend upon how bad, and how permanent, the injuries prove to be. Where the injuries take some time to heal, doctors cannot always answer these questions immediately, and this is often a major reason for delay in reaching a legal settlement. During this period, the solicitor will usually also obtain 'counsel's opinion' on any difficult points of law or of evidence which might arise.

The vast majority of claims in tort or for breach of contract are in fact settled without actual resort to the courts. As a rule, it is only where a settlement proves impossible that proceedings have to be started.

Commencing proceedings

The first formal steps in civil proceedings are designed to do two things: (a) to bring the parties together before the court, and (b) to ensure that everyone concerned clearly understands what issues are in dispute. The plaintiff, normally through his solicitor, takes the first step. In Queen's Bench Division cases, he prepares a draft *writ of summons*, notifying the defendant in general terms of the nature of the claim against him, and ordering him to submit to the jurisdiction of the court. The plaintiff (or more usually his solicitor) must attend at the court office to file the writ, which will be formally sealed by the court officers and returned to him. Either on the writ itself, or with it, there will normally appear a brief, clear *statement of claim*, indicating what facts the plaintiff alleges, and what remedy he seeks against the defendant. A copy will be retained by the court.

The next step is to notify the defendant that a claim has been made against him. The writ, together with the statement of claim, must therefore be 'served' on him, normally by being handed to him personally. If the statement of claim is not filed and served with the writ, it must be served within a limited time afterwards. In High Court proceedings it is the responsibility of the plaintiff or his solicitor to arrange for service, whereas service of the equivalent documents in County Court proceedings will be done by the court officers.

In High Court proceedings the defendant must then, within 14 days, *acknowledge service* of the writ. The acknowledgement must be filed in the court office, and state whether the defendant intends to contest the action. If he does not acknowledge, judgment can sometimes be entered against him in default. After acknowledgement, he has a further 14 days in which to submit a written *defence* if he so wishes. Indeed, if he so wishes, he can also make a *counterclaim*, alleging that it is he who is the injured party, and that it is the plaintiff who has broken the contract or committed a tort. The plaintiff has the right to deliver a *reply* to the defence within a specified period. All of this can sometimes be accompanied by further exchanges of documents; either party can ask for *further and better particulars* to clarify vague allegations made by the other side in any of these *pleadings*.

After the close of the pleadings, *discovery of documents* may take place. Each side will give the other the opportunity to inspect documents relevant to the case, and if either side refuses, disclosure can usually be compelled. If it is thought that the other party has further information which should be disclosed, it is possible to apply for permission to deliver *interrogatories*, written questions on issues of fact which must be answered on oath.

Meanwhile, the plaintiff may have to ask for some temporary court order so as to protect his position pending the hearing. For example, he might ask for a '*Mareva*' injunction (named after a case in 1975), restraining the defendant from removing his assets from the country before trial of the action.

Within a month of the close of pleadings, plaintiffs must usually take out a *summons for directions* to settle any outstanding matters preliminary to the trial itself. This summons will be heard before court officials known as Masters in London, or before Registrars in the local District Registries of the High Court. In the Queen's Bench Division these officials are barristers, and in the Chancery Division the Masters are solicitors. At the hearing of the summons for directions, the Master will fix a date and venue for the trial, for example, whether it is to be a case for the Commercial Court. He can also examine the evidence which the parties propose to call at the trial. Some allegations may be ones which the other side is willing to admit, and therefore formal proof is unnecessary; other matters can be proved by sworn written statements or *affidavits*, and attendance of witnesses in person is unnecessary. He can also restrict the number of expert witnesses, such as doctors, who can be called by either side. He will decide whether the case is one of the rare instances where there should be a jury. If the claim is a small one, he may order that it be transferred to a County Court.

These *interlocutory* steps can fulfil a useful function in saving the time of the judge and witnesses at the trial itself. On the other hand, they are sometimes felt to be unnecessarily complicated, with the result that a litigant finds it difficult to conduct the case himself and is obliged to seek expensive legal assistance. Procedure is governed in the High Court by the Rules of the Supreme Court, which are kept in continual review by a special Rules Committee which amends the rules as and when required. The rules are published regularly in the *Supreme Court Practice*, a weighty volume known as the *White Book* from the colour of its cover. A corresponding volume is the annual *County Court Practice*, with a green cover.

It must be added that procedure in the County Courts is usually a good deal simpler than the High Court procedure just described. In particular, interlocutory proceedings are generally less complex.

C. The civil trial

At the trial both parties are usually represented by counsel and, since the burden of proving the case generally rests upon the plaintiff, counsel for the plaintiff begins. He outlines the facts of the case and the evidence he proposes to call in support of these facts. This evidence is then produced, and any witnesses who are examined may be cross-examined by the defence. The defence will then put its case to the court in the same manner. After the defence case has been completed, each counsel will address the court in turn, first the counsel for the defendant and then the counsel for the plaintiff. During these closing speeches any points of law may be argued with the judge.

In the rare cases where a jury is present in civil proceedings, the judge will sum up the case, outlining the evidence, giving any directions on questions of law, and telling them what questions of fact are for their decision and the various conclusions open to them. If there is no jury, the judge will deliver his judgment, either immediately or, if the case is particularly complicated, at a later date. The latter is known as a *reserved judgment*.

A defended action in the County Court follows a similar pattern, except that in many areas the parties will usually be represented in court by solicitors rather than barristers. Reserved judgments, and indeed detailed arguments on points of law, are not very common.

If the plaintiff is successful in proving his case, there are several remedies which the judge may grant. The most common will be an order for the defendant to pay damages to the plaintiff, a fixed sum of money by way of compensation. If he has been asked to do so by the plaintiff, the judge has power to grant an injunction or to make various other orders, such as an order for the possession of land or goods.

Immediately after judgment has been given it is usual for counsel for the successful party to ask for costs and, as mentioned earlier, this is a matter for the judge's discretion. If an appeal is to be made against the judgment it must be made within a limited period of time.

D. Enforcement of civil judgments

It is one thing to obtain judgment, it can be another thing to force the defendant to comply with it. If the judgment orders the defendant to pay damages to the plaintiff, for instance, what happens if the defendant still refuses to pay? Equally important, what happens if the defendant fails to comply with an injunction, or an order to return the land or goods to the plaintiff?

Money judgments

In the High Court there are various ways by which money can be obtained from a judgment debtor who will not pay. For instance:

1. The plaintiff can obtain a writ of *fieri facias* (*fi. fa.*), ordering the sheriff to seize the defendant's goods and, if necessary, sell them to pay the plaintiff out of the proceeds.
2. The plaintiff can apply to the court for a *charging order* on the defendant's land or on shares held by him in a company. If the money is still not paid, the plaintiff can ultimately have the house or shares sold, and recover his damages from the proceeds.
3. The court may grant a *garnishee* order, under which money owed to the defendant by someone else must be paid directly to the plaintiff. In this way, the plaintiff can obtain payment directly from the defendant's bank account, if it is in credit.
4. The court has power to appoint a *receiver* who, if the defendant owns property, can intercept income such as rent, and apply it in payment of the plaintiff.
5. If the plaintiff applies by *writ of sequestration*, the court can, in effect, take control of all of the defendant's property, and deprive him of the right to manage it until the plaintiff has been paid. This can sometimes be useful where the defendant is a small company.
6. In addition to methods of enforcement such as these, High Court judgments can also be enforced through the County Courts. This can have several advantages, not least that the County Court can order payment by instalments, which is often the most practicable way of collecting the money from an individual.

The following are the main powers available in the County Courts:

1. The plaintiff can obtain a *warrant of execution* which, like the writ of *fi. fa.* in the High Court, directs a court officer—in this case the County Court bailiff—to seize the defendant's goods and, if necessary, sell them to pay the plaintiff.
2. Under the Attachment of Earnings Act 1971, the judgment creditor will be able to

obtain an *attachment of earnings* order through the County Court. Where the defendant is in employment, his employer can be ordered to deduct a specified sum each week or month from the defendant's wages or salary, and to pay this money into court to pay the plaintiff.

In addition to these methods of enforcement, the judgment creditor can also threaten to make the defendant bankrupt in certain circumstances.

Non-money judgments

If the defendant fails to obey an injunction, which is an order of the court to refrain from doing something, then he is in contempt of court, and the court can, on application by the plaintiff, punish him. The main methods of punishment are (a) by an *order for committal* under which, if he still refuses to comply, the defendant can ultimately be imprisoned; and/or (b) by a writ of sequestration.

An order to deliver land to the plaintiff can be enforced by a *writ of possession*, and an order to deliver goods by a *writ of delivery* or of *specific delivery*. In each of these instances, the sheriff is ordered to seize the property and deliver it to the plaintiff. Delivery may sometimes be obtained by the threat of committal or sequestration, as described above.

E. Criminal proceedings

Procedure before trial

In the case of less serious offences, a summons is served upon the accused directing him to appear before the court at a specified time, date and place. Proceedings against companies for such offences as false trade descriptions, unguarded factory machinery and incorrect weights and measures are invariably begun in this way. If the offence is more serious and the accused is unlikely to appear voluntarily, a warrant for his arrest will be signed by a magistrate and executed by the police. For some offences, usually the most serious ones, the offender may be arrested without a warrant.

As already mentioned, Magistrates' Courts deal with 98 per cent of all criminal prosecutions and therefore, once the attendance of the offender has been secured, the court may proceed to trial. If the offender has only recently been arrested, an adjournment may first be necessary to allow time for both parties to prepare their cases. The prosecution is normally conducted by a legal practitioner or police officer but various statutes give the power to prosecute to such officials as factory inspectors, inspectors of trading standards and public health inspectors, in respect of offences against statutes which it is their duty to enforce. If the offence is one that must be tried in the Crown Court, committal proceedings will be held to determine whether or not there is a sufficiently strong case against the accused to justify a trial.

The trial

In both the Magistrates' Court and the Crown Court the accused will be asked to plead guilty or not guilty. If the plea is guilty, the prosecution will summarize the evidence and give details of the background of the accused, the defence may plead for mitigation, and sentence is passed.

If the plea is not guilty, the prosecution will outline the case against the accused and call witnesses to give evidence on oath to support this; these witnesses may be cross-examined by the defence. The defence case will then be put in a like manner. After closing speeches by both sides, the verdict of the court will be given, either by the magistrates or by the jury following a summing-up by the judge. A verdict of guilty will place a duty upon the court of imposing the most appropriate form of sentence, for example a custodial sentence of imprisonment or the payment of a monetary sum by way of a fine.

Compensation

The punishment of the offender will not of itself compensate the victim of a crime. It is always possible for the latter to bring a civil action, normally in tort, but this may not be worth while (see above). To avoid hearing the same evidence twice in different courts it would seem desirable to settle small amounts of compensation in the same (criminal) proceedings.

A criminal court may, therefore, at its discretion, award compensation for personal injury, loss or damage, excluding loss arising from fatal and road traffic accidents. In Magistrates' Courts there is a restriction of £2000 for each offence for which there is a conviction. Any compensation ordered is deducted from any damages subsequently awarded in a civil action arising from the same facts.

This power is now contained in the Powers of Criminal Courts Act 1973. It has been used to compensate some victims of offences under the Trade Descriptions Acts 1968–72 (Unit 18) who might not have brought a separate civil action because of the time and cost involved.

Wide powers are also given to order the restitution of stolen goods or money which represents the proceeds of their sale. Another provision empowers the Crown Court to make a criminal bankruptcy order in the interests of the victims where the loss amounts to £15 000.

Examination questions

1. Your company has a number of debtors who appear to have no intention of paying for goods which have been supplied to them.
   (a) Explain the considerations affecting the decision whether or not to take proceedings to recover the sums owing.
   (b) To what extent, if at all, will the size of the debt affect (i) the decision whether to sue; and, if so, (ii) the subsequent court proceedings?

45

2. Why, in civil proceedings, is there normally a long period of time between the first consultation with a solicitor and the trial of the case?
3. Outline the course of proceedings in the trial of a civil case.
4. Your company has been successful in a claim for damages for breach of contract. What action may be taken if the judgment debtor refuses to pay?
5. You have suffered loss by reason of a faulty trade description. Compare the right to recover damages by a civil action with an award of compensation following a criminal prosecution.

Unit 6. Legal Personality and Capacity

A. Natural and legal persons

Legal personality

A legal person is anything recognized by law as having legal rights and duties. With one main exception, a legal person in this country is simply a person in the ordinary sense: a human being. In general, his or her rights begin at birth and end at death and, subject to rules such as those of capacity (below), the same rules apply to everyone.

In one important instance, English law also grants legal personality to an artificial person. This arises where a group of persons together form a *corporate* body of some sort. The corporate body can acquire a personality separate from that of its members, with some of the legal powers of a natural person. It can, for example, own property and make contracts, even with its own members, in its own name. The ways in which such *incorporation* can occur are described later.

Capacity

English law limits the legal capacity of certain categories of natural person. For example, special rules protect minors, i.e., those under 18 years of age. A minor is not generally liable on his contracts (Unit 13) and may escape liability in tort (Unit 8). He may own personal property, such as books or even a car, but he cannot own land except indirectly as beneficiary under a trust. He cannot make a will to dispose of his property on death unless he is on active military service. Other special rules apply at different ages: a person under 16 cannot marry, and there are special provisions for young criminal offenders. A young person is not allowed a full driving licence until 17.

The legal capacity of *mentally disordered* persons is similarly restricted. In general, they cannot enter into valid contracts, transfer property or make wills, or validly marry.

Many of the restrictions formerly placed on *aliens* have been removed, but generally they still do not have a right of free entry to the country. They remain liable to deportation in some circumstances, and they cannot vote or become MPs. There are now also restrictions on entry and powers to deport some Commonwealth citizens, but new rights of entry for citizens within the European Communities. *Foreign sovereigns* and some diplomatic staff are normally granted the privilege of immunity from legal actions.

The main limits on the capacity of *corporate bodies* arise from their very nature. First, there are things which they cannot physically do, such as marry. Second, they are the creation of law and, therefore, only have such powers as the law gives them; anything outside of those powers (*ultra vires*) is void.

B. Corporations

Corporations may come into being in one of three ways.

1. The earliest form of incorporation was by Royal Charter, issued under the Royal prerogative upon the advice of the Privy Council. This form of incorporation was used to create the Bank of England and the great trading companies such as the East India Company and the Hudson's Bay Company. The issue of a charter today is confined to non-commercial undertakings, for example, new universities.

2. A corporation may be created by Act of Parliament. This method was used for the early railway and gas companies and more recently for the nationalized industries such as the National Coal Board. Most undertakings of a public nature, for example, the Independent Broadcasting Authority, are statutory corporations. So far as local authorities are concerned, while some towns first received their status by Royal Charter, the authorities administering our system of local government from 1974 onwards owe their existence to the Local Government Act 1972. Some have also received new Royal Charters since then.

3. It was found in the nineteenth century that the cumbersome and expensive method of forming chartered and statutory corporations was not ideal for private business concerns. Hence the Companies Act 1844 provided a third and easier method of incorporation, by registration following a few relatively simple formalities. In 1855, limited liability was introduced, whereby shareholders who invested in companies could only be called upon for the amount they had agreed to contribute and were not liable to creditors to the extent of all their wealth. Formation by registration and limited liability together helped provide the capital which the increasing scale of business then needed. The law governing companies is now largely contained in the Companies Act 1985, which consolidates many earlier

Acts. Several other statutes allow incorporation by registration today. Building societies are created by registration under the Building Societies Acts, and many organizations such as working men's clubs and cooperative societies are incorporated under the Industrial and Provident Societies Acts.

As we have seen a corporation, once formed, acquires *separate legal personality*. It can sue its own members and be sued by them. It can employ its own members. Its property belongs to the corporation, not to the members. *Limited liability* developed naturally from this: the corporation's debts and liabilities are its own and, in general, members are not responsible for them.

> In *Salomon* v. *Salomon & Co. Ltd* (1897), Salomon, who manufactured boots, formed his business into a company. Six members of his family held one share each, and he held the remaining 20 000. He lent money to the company on the security of its assets and, when the company ran into financial difficulties, it was held that he took preference over the ordinary creditors. Although he *was*, in effect, the company, he was treated in law as an entirely separate person.

If a corporation exceeds its powers, the act in question will be *ultra vires* and void. While a natural person can do whatever the law does not prohibit, an artificial person can only do what the law and the documents creating it will permit. A statutory corporation only has the powers bestowed by legislation, and a company only has the powers given by the 'objects clause' in its memorandum of association.

> In *Ashbury Carriage Co.* v. *Riche* (1875), a company formed to make railway carriages contracted to finance the building of a railway in Belgium. Although the shareholders ratified the agreement, it was held *ultra vires* and the company was not bound.

> In *Introductions Ltd* v. *National Provincial Bank Ltd* (1969), a company formed in 1951 with the objects of promoting tourism was not bound by contracts made when it went into pig farming many years later.

> In *London Borough of Bromley* v. *Greater London Council* (1982), it was held *ultra vires* and unlawful for the GLC to subsidize public transport out of rates in the way in which it had done so.

The reason for the objects clause of a company was largely to protect shareholders who invested their money on the understanding that the company would only do the things specified therein. In practice, objects clauses are today drawn widely and may later be extended, so that little protection is actually given. The Companies Act 1985, section 35, makes further inroads. Outsiders dealing with a company in good faith may assume that a transaction entered into by the directors is within the company's capacity, so that the company is bound whether or not it is within its objects.

C. Unincorporated associations

People may combine to further a common interest without creating an independent legal personality. Such interests may be sporting, social, political or business. In the absence of incorporation, the law does not normally recognize the association as a separate entity but regards it instead as a number of individual persons. Any property belongs to the members jointly, not to the association.

49

In some instances, however, limited recognition is given to the association.

1. If its property is held by trustees on behalf of the members, the trustees are then the legal owners, and they may bring and defend actions and do other things necessary to safeguard it.
2. If the management of affairs is entrusted to a committee, all the members of that committee may be liable for an act done with their authority.
3. Under the rules of court it is possible for some members to sue or be sued on behalf of all the others in a representative action. In *Bolton and Others* v. *Stone* (Unit 9), Miss Stone sued Bolton, the secretary, and three other committee members of the cricket club, which was an unincorporated association.

Special rules exist for particular types of unincorporated association. For example, most *trade unions* are unincorporated. In the early nineteenth century, they were unlawful, and members could be prosecuted for the crime of conspiracy. Gradually their status was recognized by law and, since 1871, their status (if not always their activities) has been regarded as lawful. Today they can acquire some features similar to those of corporations, particularly if they register with the Certification Officer under the Trade Union and Labour Relations Act 1974.

Most unincorporated associations for *business* purposes are governed by the Partnership Act 1890 (below).

D. Partnerships

The Partnership Act 1890, section 1, defines a partnership as 'the relation which subsists between persons carrying on business in common with a view to profit'.

Formation

When a partnership is created, the parties often draw up a deed or 'articles' of partnership. This usually covers such matters as the provision of capital, management, and the sharing of profits. The Partnership Act provides for these matters, but only in the absence of agreement to the contrary by the partners. This contrasts sharply with the provisions of the Companies Acts, with which companies must comply.

In some instances, partnerships are not formal or long term. They may be created informally, or even inadvertently. If X and Y cooperate in a once-only business venture, being paid jointly to remove rubbish from Lord Z's back garden, then X and Y are partners under the Act, although the thought may never have occurred to them. It is similar with many very small or part-time businesses.

Difficulties do sometimes arise as to whether there is a partnership, and the Act contains rules to help determine this. First, the persons involved must be in *business*. Therefore, by section 2, the mere fact that two or more people are co-owners of property does not *of itself* render them partners, even if the property brings in income such as rent or dividends. Similarly, the sharing of *gross* returns (not profits) does not of itself create a partnership. Second, they must be carrying on the business 'in common'. If both carry on the business, then they are partners under section 1. If someone shares in the profits *without* taking part in the business, then section 2 applies. As a general rule anyone sharing profits is *presumed* a partner, but this can be rebutted. For example, repayment of a loan or debt out of profits, or at a rate varying with profits, does not necessarily make the creditor a partner; nor is the seller of a business who is being paid off out of the buyer's profits necessarily still a partner. The section also provides that paying an employee or agent at a rate varying with the profits does not necessarily make him a partner.

In forming a partnership, the ordinary rules of contract apply. It is voidable if induced by misrepresentation. It is void if formed for an illegal purpose; see *Foster* v. *Driscoll* (Unit 17). By the rules of capacity, a company, being a person, can be a partner. A minor can be a partner, but can repudiate before or within a reasonable time after majority. He is not liable for partnership debts, but cannot be credited with profits without also being debited with losses.

By the Companies Act 1985, section 716, a partnership cannot validly have more than 20 members, although exceptions exist for professions such as solicitors and accountants, who cannot practise as companies. A partnership is, therefore, at a disadvantage when raising large amounts of capital. It is a suitable form of business organization where close cooperation between members is required, and where they do not wish to have to publish their accounts (see later).

The partners are known collectively as a 'firm', and the name under which they carry on business is the 'firm name'. They can, within limits, choose whatever name they think fit, subject only to the Business Names Act 1985. This Act, like the Companies Act, consolidates earlier legislation, and provides that wherever a firm carries on business in a name which does not consist of the surnames of all partners, with or without 'permitted additions' such as first names, initials, phrases such as 'and Sons' or, where two or more partners have the same surname, the addition of an 's' at the end of that surname ('Smiths'), then it is subject to limits. It must not, for example, use a firm name which suggests Government or local authority connections, is offensive, or falsely suggests connection with another business. Other important checks are that a partnership must not use 'limited' or 'public limited company' as the last words of its name, although it can use 'company' or an abbreviation thereof. In any event, the true surnames of all partners must appear on letter headings (although there are exceptions for firms with more than 20 partners), and must be displayed in a prominent place to which customers have access at the firm's business premises. Non-compliance with any of the above provisions is a criminal offence.

Relations between the partners and outsiders

Four main issues arise under this head.

When can the acts of one partner render the whole firm liable?
By the Partnership Act, section 5, the rules are those of agency. The firm is bound by anything which an individual partner was *expressly* authorized to do. The firm may

also be bound if the partner does something for '*carrying on in the usual way business of the kind carried on by the firm*', so that there is nothing to make the outsider suspicious. The partner has *implied* authority, and the firm is bound even if he has exceeded his actual authority. It follows, however, that the firm will not be bound if the outsider either knows that the partner has no authority, or does not know or believe him to be a partner.

The key question as regards the unauthorized acts of a partner is what sort of thing *is* it 'usual' for an individual partner to do? This depends largely upon what sort of business it is, but the following can normally be assumed to be within a partner's powers, so long as his actions are not so unusual as to raise suspicions: selling the firm's goods; buying goods normally bought by the firm; giving receipts for debts; engaging and dismissing employees; signing ordinary cheques. In trading partnerships, as opposed to professional ones, it may also be usual for one partner to borrow money on the firm's behalf.

> In *Mercantile Credit Ltd* v. *Garrod* (1962), G and P were partners in a garage business concerned with *repairing* cars and letting lock-up garages. They had expressly agreed *not* to *sell* cars. Nevertheless P, without G's knowledge, sold a car to M Ltd for £700. It then transpired that P had had no title to the car, so M Ltd demanded back the £700. When P did not pay, G was held liable as his partner. There was nothing to make M Ltd suspect that P and G had restricted their authority to repairing contracts. Therefore the firm, all partners, were liable.

An outsider can doubly protect himself by contacting the other partners to see whether they do in fact agree with what the one partner proposes.

When is the firm liable for wrongs, such as torts, committed by one partner?
By section 10, where one partner commits an act which is wrong in itself, as opposed to merely being outside his authority, the firm will be civilly liable for any harm caused, and criminally for any penalty incurred if either:

(a) the act was done with the actual authority of his fellow partners; or
(b) the act was within his 'usual' authority, in the ordinary course of the firm's business.

> In *Hamlyn* v. *Houston & Co.* (1903), it was held to be quite 'usual' for a partner to obtain information about a rival business. His firm was therefore held liable when, without actual authority, he used bribery for this purpose.

Section 11 applies where a partner misapplies money or property received for, or in the custody of, the firm. The problem can arise in two ways. First, a *partner* may receive money or property *for* the firm, and misapply it before it reaches the firm. Here, the firm is liable if it was within the actual or 'usual' authority of that partner to receive the property. Second, the *firm* may already have custody of someone else's money or property, and a partner then takes it from the firm. In this case, so long as the money or property was in the firm's custody in the ordinary course of its business, the firm and all of its partners are liable.

When is an individual partner personally liable for the firm's debts and liabilities?
Partners do not have limited liability. By section 9, they are jointly liable on the firm's contracts. Each partner is liable for the full amount due, but can apply to the court to have the others joined as co-defendants. In practice, plaintiffs usually sue the firm in the firm's name, but can then enforce the full judgment against any partner. By section 12, partners are liable jointly and severally for torts committed by or on behalf of the firm. Again, each can be made liable for the full amount.

New partners are not liable for things done or debts incurred before they became partners. A *retiring partner* remains liable for debts incurred *before* his retirement, but can be discharged if a contract of 'novation' is made between himself, the other partners, and the creditor. He may also be liable for debts incurred *after* he leaves. Someone dealing with a firm after a change in its constitution is entitled to treat all apparent members of the old firm as still being members until he has notice of the change. The retiring partner should, therefore, protect himself by notifying all existing customers and suppliers of his retirement, so that he no longer appears to them to be a partner. He should also advertise his retirement in the *London Gazette*, which serves as notice to those who have not previously dealt with the firm. In any event, he is not liable to those who have not previously dealt with the firm, and who did not even know that he had been a partner.

> In *Tower Cabinet Co. Ltd* v. *Ingram* (1949), I and C traded as partners under the name 'Merry's' until 1947. I then left, but C carried on under the old name. In 1948, C ordered furniture from T Ltd, and failed to pay. T Ltd obtained judgment against 'Merry's', and tried to enforce this against I. It was held that I was not liable: T Ltd had never dealt with Merry's while I was a partner, and only knew of him because C had confirmed the order on some old headed notepaper which still showed I's name. Until then, T Ltd did not know that I had been a partner, and discovery at this late stage did not make I an 'apparent member'. (Nevertheless, he would have saved himself much trouble had he destroyed *all* of the old headed notepaper before leaving.)

The estate of a partner who dies or becomes bankrupt is not liable for partnership debts incurred after the death or bankruptcy.

When is a person who is not *a partner liable for the debts of the firm?*
We have seen that a retiring partner can sometimes be liable for debts incurred after he left. By section 14, others may also be liable. A non-partner can be liable for the debt if he has by his words, spoken or written, or by his conduct, represented himself to be a partner and, as a result, an outsider has given credit to the firm. Similarly, a non-partner can be liable if he has *allowed* himself to be 'held out' as being a partner, and the creditor has relied on this misapprehension. The 'apparent' partner can be liable whether or not he knows that the representations which he has made or allowed have been used to persuade a potential creditor in this way.

> In *Tower Cabinet* v. *Ingram*, I was not liable under section 14 because he had not *allowed* the use of the old headed paper.

Relations of partners to each other

This is basically a matter for agreement between the partners. Section 24, however, sets out rules which apply in the absence of express or implied agreement to the contrary.

1. All partners are entitled to share equally in capital and profits, and must contribute equally to losses.
2. The firm must indemnify partners in respect of expenses and personal liabilities incurred in the ordinary and proper conduct of the business, or in anything necessarily done to preserve the firm's business or property.
3. A partner is entitled to interest on payments or loans which he makes to the firm beyond his agreed capital.
4. He is not, however, entitled to interest on his capital before ascertainment of profits.
5. Every partner may take part in managing the firm's business.
6. No partner is entitled to remuneration (such as salary) for acting in the partnership business.
7. No new partner may be introduced without the consent of all the existing partners. (This is sometimes expressly varied in practice, so as to give a partner the right to introduce a son or daughter.)
8. Ordinary management decisions can be by a majority, but any change in the *nature* of the business must be unanimous.
9. The records and accounts must be kept at the main place of business, and be open to all partners, or their proper agents such as accountants, to inspect and copy.
10. By section 25, no majority can expel a partner unless a power to do so has been conferred by express agreement between the partners.

Partners also owe statutory duties of good faith to each other.

1. Section 28 imposes a statutory duty to account: 'Partners are bound to render true accounts and full information of all things affecting the partnership to any partner or his legal representative.'
2. Section 29 deals with secret or unauthorized profits: 'Every partner must account to the firm for any benefit derived by him without the consent of the other partners from any transaction concerning the partnership property, name or business connection.'

   In *Pathirana* v. *Pathirana* (1967), R and A were partners in a petrol service station. A gave R three months' notice that he intended to leave. Without waiting, R almost immediately took full control, and pocketed the entire profits. A was held entitled to his own share of profits for the rest of the notice period.

3. Section 30 imposes a duty not to compete with the firm: 'If a partner, without the consent of the other partners, carries on any business of the same nature as and competing with that of the firm, he must account for and pay over to the firm all profits made by him in that business.'

Dissolution of a partnership

Partnerships may be dissolved in various ways. For example, a partnership for a fixed term, or for a single venture or undertaking, *expires* automatically when the term or undertaking ends. If the partners continue working together after this, it is a new partnership.

If the partnership was for an indefinite period, as is more usual, it can be ended by any partner giving *notice* to *all* of the others. Notice can be oral unless the original partnership was created by deed, in which case notice must be written.

Death or *bankruptcy* of any partner automatically dissolves the entire partnership, unless otherwise provided. This can be inconvenient, so partnership agreements often exclude this rule and provide, for example, that the partnership shall continue, and that the others shall buy the deceased or bankrupt's share at a valuation.

If a court makes a *charging order* over any partner's share as a result of his private debts, the other partners may dissolve the firm.

A partnership is automatically dissolved by any event which makes it *illegal* to carry on the business, or for the members to carry it on in partnership.

> In *Stevenson Ltd* v. *Cartonnagen-Industrie* (1918), the outbreak of war in 1914 automatically ended the partnership between a British company and a German firm.

Any partner may apply for a *court order* to dissolve the partnership if any of the following conditions apply.

1. If any partner becomes a patient under the Mental Health Acts, or is shown to be permanently of unsound mind; application can be either on behalf of the mentally ill partner, or by the others.
2. If a partner other than the one applying becomes in any other way incapable of performing his partnership contract.
3. If a partner, other than the one suing, is guilty of such conduct as, in view of the nature of the business, is calculated to affect it prejudicially; an order might be made under this head if, for example, a solicitor, accountant or other professional partner was convicted of dishonesty, either within or outside of the business.
4. If a partner, other than the one suing, wilfully or persistently breaks the partnership agreement, or otherwise so conducts himself that it is not reasonably practicable for the others to carry on business with him; examples might include persistent absence or laziness, or simply unpleasantness.
5. If the partnership business can *only* be carried on at a loss; merely making a loss *at present* is not necessarily enough.
6. If circumstances have arisen which, in the court's opinion, render it just and equitable that the partnership be dissolved.

> In *Ebrahimi* v. *Westbourne Galleries Ltd* (1972), E and N had been equal members for many years in a successful partnership. They then formed a company to run the business, with themselves as the sole shareholders and directors. Later, as a favour, E allowed N to introduce N's son into the business, and E voluntarily transferred some of his shares to the son. N and his son then combined deliberately to force E out. The court granted E's

application to wind up (dissolve) the company, under provisions of the Companies Act 1948 very similar to those of the Partnership Act.

In *Re Yenidje Tobacco Co. Ltd* (1916), similarly, the court ordered winding up when a company's directors and sole shareholders quarrelled and could no longer work together, even though the company was profitable.

Finally, like any other contract, a partnership can be *rescinded* within a reasonable time of formation if it was induced by fraud or misrepresentation.

If a partnership is dissolved for any of the above reasons, the authority, rights, and duties of the partners continue, but only for the purpose of winding up. Any partner may publicize the dissolution, and the others must concur.

By section 39, partnership property must be applied in payment of the firm's debts and liabilities. Any surplus must then be paid to the individual partners as, in effect, repayment of capital. Any partner can insist on this and, if necessary, ask the court to supervise it.

In settling accounts between the partners, the rules in section 44 apply unless otherwise agreed. Losses, including deficiencies in capital, must be paid (a) out of profits, (b) then out of capital, and (c) lastly, if necessary, by the partners themselves in the proportions in which they were entitled to share profits. If there are no outstanding losses, assets are to be applied (a) in paying trade and other creditors, (b) then in repaying to partners any loans which they have made to the firm, (c) then in repaying to each partner what he has contributed in capital, and finally (d) anything left goes to the partners in the proportions to which they were entitled to profits.

When there ought to be a final settlement and it does not take place, for example, if a partner dies or retires and the remaining partners carry on without settling with him or his estate, then the outgoing partner may claim either such share of the profits after he left as are attributable to use of his share of the assets, or interest on the amount of his share; see *Pathirana* v. *Pathirana* again.

In practice, partnership agreements often expressly exclude this part of the Act. For example, the agreement may provide that the partnership shall not end on the death or retirement of one partner, but that the surviving partners shall buy the interest of outgoing partner at a valuation.

Limited partnerships

The Limited Partnerships Act 1907 allows the creation of firms where, unlike in ordinary partnerships, some members can have limited liability. Limited partners contribute a stated amount of capital, and then have no further liability for the firm's debts. At least one member, however, must have unlimited liability. A limited partner takes no part in management, his death, bankruptcy or mental illness do not dissolve the firm, and he cannot end the firm by notice. Unlike ordinary firms, limited partnerships must register details of the firm, the business, and the partners with the Companies' Registrar, who issues a certificate of registration. In practice, limited partnerships are rare.

E. The Crown

At common law, the Crown was above the law, and no action could be brought against the King in the King's courts. This was summarized in the maxim, 'The King (or Queen) can do no wrong'. This legal immunity applied also to public acts carried out in the King's name by Ministers and Government departments.

As the activities of state vastly increased, the extent of this immunity brought many cases of injustice. Thus, the Crown was not liable for the negligent driving of an army lorry or for a dangerous post office floor, as an ordinary employer would have been; nor were Government departments liable if they broke their contracts. At common law there was, in practice, some mitigation of this severe position, but the important changes were made by the Crown Proceedings Act 1947, which now largely governs the matter.

In tort, the Crown can now be liable for the wrongful acts of its servants, for injuries arising out of the ownership and control of premises and, where the statute expressly states that the Crown is to be bound, for breach of statutory duty. There are still some immunities, however: for example, no action lies for death or personal injury suffered during service in the armed forces if the Minister responsible certifies that this injury ranks for entitlement to pension. Although the Post Office changed in 1969 from a Government department to a public corporation, there is still no liability for loss or delay of unregistered letters, parcels, telegrams or for telephonic communications.

In contract, similarly, the Crown can be liable, particularly for commercial agreements. It is doubtful if it is bound by the service contracts of its employees (civil servants) but, in any event, they are now protected by the unfair dismissal provisions of the Employment Protection (Consolidation) Act 1978.

Civil actions may now be brought against the appropriate departments or against the Attorney-General, who is empowered to defend such actions on the Crown's behalf. There is still no legal way of enforcing judgments against the Crown, although this is normally not necessary. The Crown (i.e., the Government) can still stop disclosure of certain evidence for which Crown privilege is claimed. The Queen in her private capacity still enjoys complete immunity.

Examination questions

1. Discuss whether the following are partners within the Partnership Act 1890.
   (a) The committee of a tennis club.
   (b) Mr A and his son B who take turns in driving Mr A's van to deliver flowers and vegetables from a market garden to retail grocers' shops.
   (c) C and D who organize a jumble sale for charity.
   (d) E, who runs a business, and F who has loaned him money to help him expand it.
2. To what extent is a partnership firm liable in respect of contracts made in its name by one of the partners?

3. In what ways can a retiring partner protect himself against liability for the firm's debts?
4. 'The Queen can do no wrong.' Explain the legal meaning of this phrase, and discuss whether it is true today.
5. Explain briefly the meaning of the following
   (a) Separate legal personality
   (b) *Ultra vires*
   (c) A minor
   (d) An unincorporated association
   (e) The Crown

Unit 7. Companies

Since 1844, companies have been created by registration under various Acts. The position today is governed by the Companies Act 1985, which consolidates many earlier Acts. There are three main types of company. In an *unlimited* company, each member is fully liable for the company's debts in the same way as members of a partnership. In a company *limited by guarantee* a member, on joining, guarantees the company's debts, but only up to a stated figure. Again these are uncommon, but are sometimes used for non-business bodies such as cricket clubs. The vast majority of companies are *limited by shares*: each member holds one or more 'shares' issued by the company in return for payment. A shareholder's liability to the company's creditors is normally limited to that part of the nominal value of his shares which he has not yet paid to the company. Most shares today are fully paid up, and such shareholders, therefore, have no liability for the company's debts; see *Salomon* v. *Salomon & Co. Ltd* (page 49).

Most of this unit deals with companies limited by shares, of which there are two types. Some become *public limited companies*. To qualify for this status they must have issued at least £50 000 worth of shares, with at least one-quarter of the nominal capital (see later) paid up. The memorandum of association must specifically state that the company is public, and the name must end with the words 'public limited company' ('p.l.c.'). Any company not satisfying these requirements is a *private company* and therefore, by the Companies Act 1985, section 81, must not offer its shares for sale to the public. A private company can turn itself into a public one and vice versa. In practice, most companies are formed as, and remain, private.

There are other classifications for special purposes which have little to do with the Companies Acts. For example, if a public company wishes its shares (or debentures, see later) to be dealt with on a stock exchange, it must apply to the exchange, which will only grant permission if the requirements *of the exchange* (as to total value of the shares, and as to disclosure, etc.) are met. A stock exchange 'quotation' or 'listing' is often desirable in order to increase the saleability and value of a company's shares. By no means all public companies are 'listed'.

For tax purposes, it can be an advantage for a company to remain a 'close' company, that is, one 'controlled' by directors who are also shareholders or creditors, or 'controlled' by five or fewer shareholders or creditors.

One company can hold shares in another, and most large companies do control many subsidiary companies, for instance by holding most of the shares in the subsidiary. Although in law each of these companies is a separate person, in reality they are controlled by the 'parent' company. Often the arrangements are much more complex, and may involve companies or their equivalents in many different countries. Some such 'multinational' enterprises include hundreds of companies throughout the world.

A. Formation of companies

Those forming a company are called its 'promoters'. The term includes people doing any of the work necessary, those who acquire property or a business for the company, and those who set out to provide finance. The main tasks of the promoters are to prepare various documents, and to lodge these, with the necessary fees, with the Registrar of Companies (an official of the Department of Trade). Several documents must be lodged.

1. *The memorandum of association.* This, in effect, defines the company and what it can do. It must contain the following details.
   (a) It must state the *company's name.* The choice rests with the promoters but, under the Companies Act 1985, the Registrar must refuse a name which is misleading. For example, he will reject a name too like that of an existing company, or which falsely suggests Government or local authority connections. The last words must normally be 'public limited company' or simply 'limited', depending on the type of company. Members can later change the name by special resolution, but again the Registrar's consent is required.
   (b) If the company is to be a public one, the memorandum must expressly say so.
   (c) A clause must state whether the *registered office* is to be in England and Wales, or in Scotland. Every company must have a registered office, which is its *legal* home. It need not be anywhere near the main, or any, place of business. The actual address of the registered office must be given in the statement concerning directors, delivered with the memorandum.
   (d) The '*objects clause*' states the objects for which the company is formed, and the powers which it is to have. Anything which the company later does outside of these objects and powers is *ultra vires*, and may be void; see *Ashbury Carriage Co. Ltd* v. *Riche* and *Introductions Ltd* v. *National Provincial Bank* (Unit 6).
      A company can later extend its objects, within limits, by special resolution of shareholders under the 1985 Act, sections 4–6. In practice, objects clauses today are usually drafted very widely in the first place.

(e) A clause must state that the members have *limited liability*.

(f) There must be a statement of the *nominal capital*, and how it is to be divided into shares. This clause may be changed subsequently, for example, so as to increase the capital if the company expands.

The memorandum ends with a request by the 'subscribers', whose names and addresses appear at the end, to be formed into a company. There must be at least two subscribers. Each must take at least one share, and the memorandum must state how many he does take. Each must sign, and the signatures must be witnessed.

2. *Articles of association* are usually submitted too. These regulate the internal management, and the rights and duties of shareholders *vis-à-vis* the company and each other. They deal with matters such as transfer of shares, meetings, voting and other rights of shareholders, dividends, and the directors' powers of management.

   A company need not, in fact submit any articles. If it does not do so, it will be taken to have adopted Table A, a model set of articles in regulations made under the Companies Act. In any event, Table A always applies except in so far as it is expressly or impliedly overruled by actual articles.

   The articles of association may later be altered under the 1985 Act, section 9, but the alteration must not (a) clash with the memorandum; or (b) discriminate between members, or take away the rights of any class of shareholders; and (c) the alteration must be for the benefit of all shareholders.

3. There must be a separate *statement of the nominal capital*.

4. A statement containing *particulars of directors and company secretary* must be filed with the memorandum. It must be signed by the subscribers, and contain a signed consent by each director to act as such. It must also contain the address of the registered office.

5. A *statutory declaration* by a solicitor engaged in forming the company, or by a person named in the articles as a director or the company secretary, must also be filed. This must declare that the requirements of the Act have been complied with, and may be accepted by the Registrar as evidence of this.

If all the requirements in respect of registration and matters incidental to it have been satisfied, the Registrar issues a *certificate of incorporation*, which is the company's 'birth certificate'. A company registered as private can start business immediately. A public company, however, must not do business or borrow money until it has gone on to satisfy the Registrar that the necessary share capital has actually been raised. It must also show details of the expenses of formation, and of any payments to promoters. If he is satisfied, the Registrar issues a further certificate, whereupon the public company too can start to do business.

B. Capital

It takes money to set up and run a business. In companies with a share capital, the money is raised partly by issuing shares in the company. A shareholder must pay the company for each share allotted to him, and the money thus produced provides, in theory, the basic finance. In its memorandum, a company must state its *nominal capital*. This is the face value of the total number of shares which the company has, at present, *authorized* itself to issue. The nominal (or 'authorized') capital may, for example, be £60 000, divided into 60 000 shares of £1 each. This does not necessarily mean that all of these shares have been issued yet, only that the company *can* issue them.

The *issued capital* is so much of the £60 000 nominal capital as has actually been issued. The company need not even demand that the full nominal price be paid immediately by the new shareholders. It can issue £1 shares for 50p now, with the right to call for the other 50p later. The second 50p is known as 'uncalled' capital. This is rare today, because most shares are issued fully paid.

The real value of shares may be more than the nominal value. Thus if a company's assets are worth much more than its nominal capital, its shares may reflect this. If would-be shareholders pay £5 for each of the £1 shares issued, the shares are said to be issued at a premium of £4.

In theory, an amount equal to the money actually paid to a company in return for its shares has to be kept available in order, in the last resort, to pay off creditors and repay the shareholders if the company is wound up. The Companies Act, therefore, still contains detailed rules to prevent or control reduction of this capital, although the rules have been relaxed slightly since 1981.

When a company invites the public to buy its shares, it must issue a *prospectus*, which must contain detailed information about the company so that investors can make an informed choice. False statements in prospectuses can be a criminal offence, and can also render the share issue voidable.

When a company has allotted a share it must, within two months, issue a share certificate to the holder. This is evidence of ownership, and one certificate can cover a number of shares. The company must also keep a register of shareholders, normally at its registered office.

Once issued, shares can be transferred by the shareholder. For example, if the business prospers, the shares may increase in real value, and a shareholder may wish to sell his shares to someone else (at a profit to *himself*, not to the company). The company's capital is maintained; the shares are simply held by someone new. The procedure for transferring shares is set out in the Stock Transfer Act 1963, as amended; broadly, the share certificate and stock transfer form are sent to the company's secretary, who alters the register and issues a new certificate to the new holder.

Shareholders may periodically be rewarded by the company by the payment of a *dividend* out of profits. This must come either from current profits, or from money set aside from the profits of previous years. If it were paid otherwise than from profits, it could be regarded as a payment out of capital, which generally is not permitted.

Another way in which a company can raise finance is by borrowing it. A document issued by a company evidencing a loan to it is called a *debenture*. Debenture holders are not members of the company, although they can acquire rights to influence management. Money borrowed is not strictly 'capital', although in practice it is often called 'loan capital'. It will be discussed in Unit 21.

C. Membership and management

Shareholders

We have seen that there are three ways in which someone can become a shareholder: the subscribers of the memorandum must each take at least one share; new shares may later be issued by the company; or the shareholder may have acquired existing shares from another holder.

The general position of shareholders is set out in the 1985 Act, section 14: '. . . the memorandum and articles, when registered, bind the company and its members to the same extent as if they respectively had been signed and sealed by each member, and contained covenants on the part of each member to observe all the provisions of the memorandum and of the articles'. Shareholders, therefore, have rights, based on the memorandum and articles, as between themselves and the company, and as between themselves. Their rights also depend upon the terms of issue of the shares; some shares, for instance, carry voting rights while others do not. The following are some common types of share.

Ordinary shares usually carry rights to vote at company meetings, and therefore to take part in electing directors and in other management issues. Holders of ordinary shares are not, however, *entitled* to any dividend. The directors *may* (and usually will if they can) recommend at the annual general meeting that a stated dividend be paid that year. Shareholders then have a right to vote themselves a dividend up to, but not more than, that amount.

Holders of *preference shares*, on the other hand, *are* entitled to a fixed rate of dividend before anything becomes available for ordinary shareholders. Note, however, that even preference dividends can only be paid out of profits; no profits, no dividends. Moreover, the preference only extends to dividends. Unless the articles provide otherwise, preference shareholders receive no preferential repayment of capital on a winding up if, for example, the company is insolvent. Normally the articles give no voting rights to preference shareholders.

Different varieties of preference share exist. For example, preference shares are 'participating' if, in addition to the preferential dividend, the holders are also entitled to participate in the ordinary dividend, if one is declared. Unless otherwise provided, preference shares are presumed to be 'non-participating'. Preference shares are 'cumulative' if, should the preference dividend not be paid in one year, it is carried forward, so that in the next year all arrears of preference dividend must be paid before anyone else gets anything. Unless otherwise provided, preference shares *are* presumed cumulative.

If authorized by its articles, a company limited by shares can issue *redeemable* shares. Either the shareholder or the company can be empowered to insist that the shares be bought back by the company, and both preference and ordinary shares can be made redeemable. Normally, redemption must be made either out of profits, or out of the proceeds of a new share issue made for the purpose. Exceptionally, a private company may also redeem or buy its own shares out of capital.

Company meetings

Shareholders can exercise their voting rights by voting on resolutions at company meetings.

There are two types of meeting. An *annual general meeting* ('a.g.m.') must be held initially within 18 months of incorporation, and thereafter at least once in every calendar year, with not more than 15 months between any two meetings. At least 21 days' notice of the a.g.m. must be given to members. Any other general meeting is an *extraordinary general meeting* ('e.g.m.'). Under Table A, directors can call an e.g.m. whenever they think fit. Furthermore, they *must* call one if holders of at least one-tenth of paid-up shares so demand. Those requiring the meeting must say why they want it, and at least 14 days' notice must be given to members.

The notice calling a general meeting must, under Table A, include details of any *special business* to be discussed there. All business at an e.g.m. is 'special'. At an a.g.m., standard items such as declaring a dividend, considering the accounts, balance sheets, directors' and auditors' reports, and electing directors to replace those retiring, are *ordinary business* and need not be mentioned in the notice. Even at an a.g.m., however, anything else will be 'special' business.

Irrespective of the type of business, there are three different types of *resolution* at company meetings. *Ordinary resolutions* can be passed by a simple majority of those voting. It should be emphasized, however, that the normal rule is one vote *per share*, not one per person. Therefore, if one person holds most of the voting shares, he can determine what is passed and what is not. Sometimes the articles and terms of issue can give weighted voting rights, so that some shares carry several votes. Second, by the Companies Act and or the articles, some powers of shareholders can be exercised only by *extraordinary resolution*. This can be passed only by a three-quarters majority of votes cast. Notice of intention to move an extraordinary resolution must have been given when the meeting was called. Third, some things can be done only by *special resolution*—for example, altering the objects clause or the articles. Again a three-quarters majority is needed. Furthermore, in this case at least 21 days' notice of the resolution must be given to members, even if it is moved at an e.g.m. for which only 14 days' notice is required.

Finally, as we have seen, *notice* must be given of meetings and or resolutions, and the periods of notice required vary. In some situations, for instance on a resolution to dismiss a director, *special notice* of 28 days must be given to the company, which must then give notice of the resolution to members when it calls the necessary general meeting.

Directors and other officers

Every company must have directors, who are the persons responsible for managing the company. The actual numbers depend upon the articles, but a public company must have at least two, and a private company at least one. No qualifications are needed, except that a director of a public company must retire at 70 unless either the articles, or a resolution of which special notice has been given specifying his age, provide otherwise. The court can disqualify a person from being or acting as a director for up to five years if he has been convicted of an offence under the Act, and an undischarged bankrupt may not act as a director.

A director need not be a shareholder, although 'qualification' shares are often required by the articles in practice.

The first directors are those named in the statement filed with the memorandum. Subsequent elections normally take place at the a.g.m. Articles commonly provide that directors must retire or offer themselves for re-election every three years, with one-third doing so each year. Changes of directors must be notified to the Registrar of Companies.

Even if elected for a three-year term, directors can be removed at any time, under the 1985 Act, section 303, by an ordinary resolution of shareholders, with special notice. However, if a director holds voting shares, he can vote for himself.

> In *Bushell* v. *Faith* (1970), a director's shares validly gave him two votes per share on such a resolution, and this was enough to defeat the attempt to sack him.

Directors are not as such employees of the company, and they are not automatically entitled to payment. In practice, the articles often provide for directors to receive fees and expenses, and executive directors such as a 'managing director' often, in addition to being directors, have employment contracts under which they receive a salary.

Every company must also have a *company secretary*, who is the administrative officer responsible for meetings, notices, resolutions, records, registers, and accounts. A director, but not a sole director, may serve as secretary.

A company must keep a register of directors and secretaries at its registered office, and notify the Companies' Registrar of its contents. The register is open to public inspection. Detailed statutory provisions also require directors to disclose to the company and members matters such as their financial interests in this and connected companies.

Duties of directors

In addition to their duties to manage, the directors owe duties of good faith to the company. These duties are similar to those of partners (Unit 6) or agents (Unit 20). The following are some examples.

1. A director must not make a secret profit from his position.

> In *Boston Deep Sea Fishing and Ice Co.* v. *Ansell* (1888), a director received an undisclosed commission from the builders of a new boat for his company, and

65

undisclosed bonuses from a company supplying ice. After he had been dismissed as director, and his employment contract ended, he had to account to the company for the money.

2. A director must not allow an undisclosed conflict of interest to occur. For example, he must not take for himself contracts negotiated for the company.

> In *Cook* v. *Deeks* (1916), the directors of a construction company negotiated a contract in the usual way, as if they were making it for the company. Then, however, they made the contract in their own names, and took the profit. They ultimately had to account to the company for the profit.

> In *Regal (Hastings) Ltd* v. *Gulliver* (1942), the company bought and sold some cinemas at a profit. Some directors, who had also invested their own money in the project, shared in the profit without the knowledge or consent of the other shareholders. They had to account for their profits, which were only made because of knowledge and opportunities arising from their position as directors. (They could have protected themselves by making full disclosure and seeking the consent of the other shareholders in advance.)

Under the Companies Act, a director who is in any way, directly or indirectly, 'interested' in a contract which the company is making must disclose his 'interest' to the board of directors and, if it is a substantial property transaction, to a general meeting. Failure to do so is an offence. Subject to this and the above common law and equitable rules, however, there is no reason why a director should not contract with his own company. It is *undisclosed* conflicts of interest which are unlawful.

3. Directors must exercise their powers for the *company's* benefit, not for their own or for any other ulterior motive. This has often arisen when shares are issued:

> In *Piercy* v. *Mills Ltd* (1920), the directors issued extra voting shares to themselves and their supporters, not because the company needed the extra capital, but solely to prevent the election of rival directors. The share issue was held void.

> In *Howard Smith Ltd* v. *Ampol Petroleum Ltd* (1974), the directors of M Ltd issued 4.5 million new shares to Smith Ltd, so as to change the balance of power in M Ltd. After the issue, the previous majority shareholder, Ampol, would no longer have a majority. This issue was set aside, because destroying Ampol's majority was not a proper motive for issuing shares.

4. Directors must show reasonable care and skill.

> In *Re City Equitable Fire Insurance Co.* (1925), the managing director was able to defraud his own company partly because the ordinary directors were careless in not checking suspicious entries in the annual accounts. It was accepted that the negligence of the ordinary directors was a breach of their duties to the company.

Relations between members and management

Directors and officers owe their duties *to the company*, not to individual shareholders. Therefore, it is the company which must sue them if they break their duties, and if the company decides not to sue, then no further action can be taken. The company will not sue if the majority of votes in a general meeting resolve not to do so. Therefore, if the directors have the support of the majority of votes (or if they *have* the majority of votes), the wrong can be condoned.

> In *Foss* v. *Harbottle* (1843), two directors sold their own land to the company, allegedly for much more than its true value. Some shareholders tried to sue the directors, but the court would not hear the action. It was up to the company to decide whether or not to sue.

The rule in *Foss* v. *Harbottle* does not, however, allow the majority to get away with everything. In some situations, the court will hear an action by minority shareholders, even against the majority's wishes.

1. The majority cannot ratify something which is *ultra vires* the company; see *Ashbury Railway Carriage Co.* v. *Riche* (Unit 6). Even one shareholder can restrain an *ultra vires* act.
2. If the directors try to do something which requires a special or extraordinary resolution (with a three-quarters majority and appropriate notice) without first obtaining such a resolution, a *simple* majority cannot ratify it. To allow this would be to destroy the whole protection given to minorities by special or extraordinary resolutions, namely that a 26 per cent minority can defeat the resolutions.
3. Sometimes the directors may commit a wrong to the member personally, not to the company. If this occurs, the individual member can sue to protect his own rights.

> In *Pender* v. *Lushington* (1877), the chairman wrongfully refused to accept the votes of certain shareholders and, as a result, a resolution which they wished to oppose was passed. It was held that the chairman had infringed the shareholders' personal rights to vote, and the court granted them an injunction restraining the company from acting on the resolution.

4. The court will not permit a 'fraud on the minority'. 'Fraud' is used loosely here as meaning grossly inequitable conduct, not necessarily criminal.

> In *Cook* v. *Deeks* (page 66), the directors were made to account notwithstanding that, as majority shareholders, they had passed a resolution declaring that the company had no interest in the contract.

5. The court can also allow minority shareholders to sue to prevent directors from benefiting personally, at the company's expense, from their own negligence or misconduct.

> In *Daniels* v. *Daniels* (1978), it was alleged that the directors and majority shareholders had sold land belonging to the company to one member of the board for less than its value. It was sold by the company in 1970 for £4250, and re-sold by the director in 1974 for £120 000. It was held that, even though no fraud was alleged, a minority shareholder could sue the directors for breach of their duties.

Duties of majority shareholders

Unlike directors, shareholders as such owe no detailed duties of good faith to the company. Generally, they can exercise their powers for whatever motive they think fit. There are now, however, limits on this freedom. For example, as we have seen, the activities of directors cannot always be ratified by majority shareholders. Second, in altering the articles, it is established that shareholders must act in good faith for the benefit of the company. Third, oppression by the majority of the minority may be a ground for winding up the company. Fourth, a shareholder's powers are subject to equitable principles which may make it unjust to exercise them in a particular way.

> In *Clemens* v. *Clemens Bros Ltd* (1976), the defendant used her majority holding to pass resolutions issuing new shares, with the effect (and apparent motive) of increasing her own control, and reducing the plaintiff's holding to below 25 per cent. The court therefore set aside the resolutions.

D. The company and outsiders

Agency of directors and officers

Since a company is an artificial person and cannot do anything by itself, it must act through human beings. Most companies are larger than partnerships and, therefore, unlike partnerships, not every member is presumed to have authority to act on a company's behalf. A shareholder as such, even a majority shareholder, has no implied authority to make contracts for the company. Even an individual director has no implied authority to bind the company. Most of a company's activities are carried on by the directors, acting as a board.

A company will normally be bound by the activities of its board of directors. This can be the case even if the board is acting outside of its actual powers under the articles, or even *ultra vires* the company. By the Companies Act, section 35 (replacing the European Communities Act, section 9):

> '(1) In favour of a person dealing with a company in good faith, any transaction decided on by the directors is deemed to be one which it is within the capacity of the company to enter into, and the power of the directors to bind the company is deemed to be free of any limitation under the memorandum or articles.
> (2) A party to a transaction so decided on is not bound to enquire as to the capacity of the company to enter into it or as to any such limitation on the powers of the directors . . .'

The company only escapes liability for the acts of the *board*, therefore, if it proves that the outsider knew or suspected that the board was exceeding its or the company's powers, so that the outsider was not in good faith.

Almost invariably, boards of directors delegate some of their powers. Some directors will be given executive responsibilities, either specific (sales director), or more general (managing director). Similarly, powers are often delegated to officers such as the company secretary. Such *executive* directors or officers *are* agents of the company, and do have authority to bind it. If a delegate such as a managing director is acting within the actual authority given him by the board, then section 35 can protect outsiders. The main legal difficulties have arisen where a director or officer has exceeded the actual authority given him by the board, or has no such authority. Is the company still bound? Several other rules can protect outsiders.

1. By the 1985 Act, section 285, the acts of a director or manager shall be valid notwithstanding any defect which may later be discovered in his *appointment* or *qualification*. This is a limited provision, and does not cover either persons who purport to be executive directors without ever having been appointed at all, or who, having been properly appointed, exceed their actual authority.

2. If an outsider has no means of checking, he is entitled to assume that the internal procedures of the company have been properly carried out.

> In *Royal British Bank Ltd* v. *Turquand* (1856), two directors borrowed money on behalf of the company. They only had authority to borrow on such terms if they had first been authorized to do so by an ordinary resolution of members, and no such resolution had been passed. Nevertheless the company was bound to repay the loan, because the lender—who had no means of checking—was entitled to assume that the proper resolution had been passed.

3. In any event, an executive such as a managing director has, from his position, certain *implied* powers. An outsider is entitled to assume that such a director or officer, acting within his 'usual' authority, can in fact bind the company. The company will only escape liability if (a) the director or officer has no actual authority, and (b) there were suspicious circumstances which should have made the outsider enquire further.

> In *Panorama Developments Ltd* v. *Fidelis Furnishing Fabrics Ltd* (1971), the company secretary of Fidelis Ltd hired cars in the company's name, but used them for his own purposes. Although he had no authority from the board to do this, the company had to pay the bill. It was quite usual for a senior officer such as the secretary to hire cars for the firm, to meet important visitors, for example, and there was nothing to make the car company suspect that the secretary was acting outside his actual authority.

4. Furthermore, if a company has previously honoured contracts made by someone on its behalf, or has otherwise 'held him out' as having authority to bind the company, it may be estopped from denying his authority. The company may be bound by future unauthorized contracts which he makes.

> In *Freeman and Lockyer* v. *Buckhurst Park Properties Ltd* (1964), the board of B Ltd had allowed one of its number, K, to act as if he were managing director, although he had never been appointed to that position. The board had previously honoured contracts made by K, but now claimed not to be bound by a contract which he made with the plaintiffs. It was held that (a) B Ltd was estopped from denying that K was managing director, and (b) it was within the usual powers of a managing director to make such contracts. Therefore, B Ltd was bound.

Personal liability of members

We have seen in Unit 6 that fully paid-up shareholders in a company have no liability for the company's debts. There are only a few exceptions to this, two of which are the following.

1. Under the 1985 Act, section 24, if a company carries on business without at least two members for six months, then the remaining member is personally liable for

the company's debts incurred thereafter, if he knows that he is the only member. Creditors can sue the company and/or the member personally. (This section can affect a 'parent' company which owns *all* of the shares in a subsidiary.)

2. Under the 1985 Act, section 630, if, in the course of winding up a company, it appears that any business has been carried on with intent to defraud creditors, or for any fraudulent purpose, the court may declare that persons knowingly party to such 'fraudulent trading' shall be personally responsible for all or any of the company's debts or liabilities.

E. Public controls over companies

Companies have the privileges of separate legal personality and, usually, limited liability. In return, public controls are imposed, largely requiring disclosure and publication of material regarding membership, management, debts, and financial position generally. The purpose is mainly to protect members, creditors, and those dealing with the company. The following are some examples.

1. *Annual returns.* The Act requires a company to submit a detailed 'annual return' within 42 days after each a.g.m. (except in the year of incorporation). The returns must contain, for example, current particulars of members and officers, shares issued, and charges on the company's property. There must also be certified copies of balance sheets, profit and loss accounts, and auditors' and directors' reports.

2. *Registers* of various kinds must be kept at the company's registered office and/or at the Companies Registry. Examples are mentioned at several places in this unit. Most registers can be inspected by members and, in some instances, by outsiders. Accounts must also be kept, usually at the registered office, but these are normally only open to inspection by directors.

3. *Inspection and investigation.* The Department of Trade has wide powers under the Acts to inspect a company's books, and to conduct far-reaching investigations of its affairs if need be.

F. Winding up

Voluntary winding up

The shareholders can resolve at any time to end ('wind up') the company. The resolution must usually be a special one, needing a three-quarters majority. Alternatively an extraordinary resolution may be passed that the company is insolvent and should be wound up.

The job of winding up is carried out by a *liquidator* (unlike a partnership, which is dissolved by the members themselves). The liquidator's tasks are (a) to settle lists of contributories, (b) to collect the company's assets, (c) to pay off its creditors, and (d) to distribute any surplus to the contributories. The 'contributories' are present and past shareholders who, if the shares were not fully paid up, would have to contribute towards payments of debts. For practical purposes today, the relevant contributories are the current shareholders, and they will not in fact have to contribute if the shares are fully paid.

If the directors have made a statutory declaration that the company can within 12 months pay its debts in full, and filed this with the Registrar, matters will proceed as a *members' voluntary winding up*. The members appoint the liquidator, who is responsible to them. If the directors are unable to make a 'declaration of solvency', then it will be a *creditors' voluntary winding up*. The liquidator may be appointed by the creditors, and will largely be responsible to them.

Compulsory winding up

A petition may be presented to the court by the company itself, the Department of Trade or, most commonly, by a creditor, asking that the company be wound up by the court. There are various grounds on which such a petition may be granted, the most important being that the company cannot pay its debts, or that 'it is just and equitable that the company should be wound up'; see *Ebrahimi* v. *Westbourne Galleries*, and *Re Yenidje Tobacco* (Unit 6).

If a winding up order is made, a court officer, the Official Receiver, acts as liquidator unless and until the creditors or shareholders apply for the appointment of another. Having realized the assets, the receiver or liquidator pays debts in the following order:

1. Costs of winding up.
2. Preferential debts, such as rates and tax arrears for the last year, up to three months' arrears of employees' wages, to an £800 maximum, and arrears of national insurance contributions.
3. If all preferred creditors have been paid in full, the remaining money goes to pay off ordinary creditors.

If there is not enough to pay off any category, each gets a dividend of so much in the pound. If anything remains after ordinary creditors are fully paid, it goes in repayment of capital, and then division among shareholders.

Secured creditors are in a fortunate position in that they are entitled to payment in full from the proceeds of sale of the asset charged, before anyone else gets any part of that money.

The court can order that a winding up which started voluntarily shall be conducted thenceforth under the court's supervision. Such an order is rare today.

Examination questions

1. (a) If you and a friend were running a small company and needed extra money, discuss the factors which would influence you in deciding whether to issue further shares, or debentures.
   (b) Distinguish between nominal capital and issued capital.

2. What controls can shareholders exercise over the directors of a company limited by shares? In particular, discuss the position of the holders of
   (a) one share
   (b) 30 per cent of the shares
   (c) 51 per cent of the shares
3. To what extent do the following have power to make contracts on behalf of the company?
   (a) The holder of one share
   (b) The holder of 60 per cent of the shares
   (c) A single director
   (d) The board of directors
   In each instance, discuss whether the company would be bound by what was purportedly done on its behalf.
4. Distinguish between
   (a) a voluntary winding up and a compulsory winding up, and
   (b) a members' voluntary winding up and a creditors' voluntary winding up.
5. Explain briefly the meaning of
   (a) p.l.c.
   (b) Objects clause
   (c) Prospectus
   (d) Dividend
   (e) Preference share
   (f) Special resolution
   (g) Extraordinary general meeting
   (h) Annual return

Unit 8. Liability for Wrongful Acts

A. Crimes and torts

As has been noted in Unit 1, conflicts can arise in many ways in a complex society, and the law aims to regulate conduct in various different ways. First, certain conduct is deemed so undesirable that the law prohibits it, makes it a criminal offence, and provides that offenders may be punished. Secondly, some conduct harms other members of society, and the rules of civil law provide for the victim to receive compensation or some other civil remedy. Civil liability for breach of contract will be discussed in Units 11–17. The law of tort is concerned with some of the other matters which can give rise to civil liability.

There is a large overlap between crime and tort. If a criminal act harms the victim, it will usually be a tort as well, thus making the offender liable both to be prosecuted and to be sued for damages by the victim. The factory occupier who fails to fence dangerous machinery commits both a criminal offence and, if an employee is injured, a tort against that employee. He may also be liable to the employee for breach of contract, because he owes a duty, under the contract of employment, to provide a reasonably safe system of work (Unit 25).

A second preliminary point must be made. Not all undesirable conduct, however much we disapprove of it, is necessarily either a crime or a tort. If a builder erects a block of flats on the field behind your house, he may not only ruin your view, but also cause your house to fall in value. Nevertheless, the builder has probably committed neither a crime nor a tort. A similar situation arises where a new supermarket deliberately cuts prices with the sole intention of driving the old corner shop out of business, thereby depriving the shop-owner of his livelihood. No one is a criminal unless he has committed one or more of the crimes recognized by law; similarly, no one can be liable in tort unless he has committed one or more of the recognized torts.

Criminal offences and torts have either evolved through precedent, been created by statute, or arisen from a combination of both. Development has been influenced by external pressures, often of a political, social or economic nature. To a large extent, each crime has its own special features, as has each separate tort. On the other hand there are some common elements, and because many business situations give rise to both criminal and tortious liability, this unit is devoted to a comparison of the general features of each of these branches of law. The following two units deal with some aspects of tort in more detail.

B. Criminal liability

For convenience, criminal offences may be classified according to whether the crime is committed against the state and public order (treason, unlawful assembly), or against the person (murder, assault), or against property (theft, obtaining property by deception). There are, in addition, other offences, usually but not always of a minor nature, which do not fall neatly into any of these major categories and which may be of more direct concern to businessmen. Examples include unlawfully discharging polluting matters into a stream, applying a false trade description to goods in the course of business, or failing to fence dangerous machinery in a factory. Minor traffic offences are another example. These offences are frequently created by statute as part of a wider administrative scheme designed, for example, to control traffic or pollution, protect consumers or promote industrial safety.

The element of fault

In general, most offences require some measure of moral culpability or fault so that, in addition to committing the wrongful act, the accused must be shown to have a wrongful intention or guilty mind (*mens rea*). It follows that an accused may have a defence if, because of insanity or reasonable mistake of fact, he did not appreciate that his action was wrongful.

On the other hand, contrary to the general rule, in a growing number of statutory criminal offences there is no need for the prosecution to prove *mens rea*. The act alone constitutes the offence, and the very fact that the accused has done it, even without wrongful intent, is enough. These offences are sometimes called crimes of strict liability, and many of the statutory offences mentioned earlier fall into this category.

> In *Alphacell Ltd* v. *Woodward* (1972), a company accidentally polluted a river when poisonous liquid overflowed from some settling tanks because a valve was blocked by dead leaves. The company was found guilty even though it had acted neither intentionally nor carelessly.

Nevertheless, the difference between strict offences and other offences is not always so great as would appear at first sight. The statute creating the offence sometimes goes on to provide various defences if, for example, the accused can prove that he acted by mistake and was not careless in any way. In these instances, although the prosecution need not prove that the accused *did* have a guilty mind, it may be open for the defence to prove that he *did not*. Only the burden of proof is different.

> In *Tesco Supermarkets Ltd* v. *Nattrass* (1972), faulty supervision by a shop manager led to goods being sold with a false indication as to price, contrary to section 11 of the Trade Descriptions Act 1968. Liability for this offence is strict, but the Act provides a defence if the *accused* can prove that the offence was due to the default of another person and that the accused had exercised all due care and diligence. The company succeeded in proving that it had exercised all due diligence, and that the shop manager, although employed by the company, was 'another person'. The conviction, therefore, was quashed.

In addition, there is always a presumption that *mens rea* must be proved unless the statute clearly dispenses with the need for such proof. When a man is convicted of a criminal offence the consequences can be very severe, involving possible loss of liberty and probably social disgrace, and the courts are reluctant to contemplate such sanctions in the absence of moral guilt.

C. Liability in tort

Infringement of rights

> The law recognizes certain rights, both personal and in respect of property, which it will protect by compelling anyone who infringes the right to pay damages to the victim. In appropriate cases the court will issue an injunction restraining the wrongdoer from repeating his act.
>
> Infringement of one of these rights is known as a tort. Interference with the person of another, causing physical harm, could give rise to an action for the torts of battery or negligence. Damaging the reputation of another could lead to an action for defamation. Interests in land are protected by the torts of trespass and nuisance, and interests in goods by trespass to goods and conversion.

The element of fault

> As with crime, liability in tort normally requires an element of fault or blame on the part of the wrongdoer or 'tortfeasor'. On the other hand, the degree of moral fault required is normally smaller. Thus *careless* conduct which harms others will often constitute the tort of negligence without giving rise to criminal liability.
>
> There are some torts of strict liability which, like strict criminal offences, can be committed without fault. Examples occur in the case of dangerous things escaping from land (*Rylands* v. *Fletcher*) and breach of some statutory duties (Unit 10).

Loss suffered by the plaintiff

> An essential element of most torts is that the plaintiff must have suffered some physical or financial harm as a result of the defendant's conduct. Thus if someone

drives negligently, he does not necessarily commit the tort of negligence against anyone. It is only if the negligent driver harms or injures someone that the tort has been committed.

On the other hand, harm and tort do not always go together. First, there are still some torts where the defendant's wrongful act itself is sufficient to constitute the tort, without the plaintiff having to show loss. Notable examples are the torts of trespass and libel. These are said to be actionable *per se*, i.e., for themselves, without proof of loss. The man who stands on your lawn without permission commits the tort of trespass even if he does not damage the lawn (although in practice it might not be worth while to sue him for damages for, with no loss, damages might only be nominal).

Conversely, it must again be emphasized that merely causing harm to someone does not necessarily constitute a tort. There may be no infringement of a legal right. In many situations it is impossible to act without harming someone; for example, every sale by a shopkeeper means one less for his competitors.

> In *Bradford Corporation* v. *Pickles* (1895), the defendant, in order to induce the corporation to buy his land at a high price, dug wells and extracted water that would otherwise have found its way into the town's water supply. Although the corporation had suffered loss, there had been no infringement of a legal right, for Pickles had only done what he was fully entitled to do on his own land.

D. Parties

Subject to only a few exceptions, everyone may sue or be sued in tort or be liable to criminal prosecution. Reference has already been made in Unit 6 to some exceptional cases such as the Crown. In addition, foreign sovereigns may avoid liability for criminal prosecution or civil action, as may ambassadors and their staffs who claim 'diplomatic immunity'. To protect the administration of justice, actions for defamation cannot be brought in respect of statements made in the course of court proceedings, nor can actions be brought for false imprisonment against those executing court orders.

Minors are normally fully liable for their torts, but they may escape liability in some instances. First, the court will not allow an action in tort to be used as an indirect way of obtaining a remedy for a contract which would otherwise not be actionable (see Unit 13).

> In *Leslie Ltd* v. *Shiell* (1914), a minor fraudulently pretended to be of age in order to obtain a loan of money. The lender could not sue on the contract of loan, so he sued the minor for the tort of deceit. It was held that this was merely an indirect attempt to recover for breach of contract, and the action therefore failed.

On the other hand, if the infant does something quite outside the contract, then the general rule applies and he can be liable in tort.

> In *Ballet* v. *Mingay* (1943), a minor had an amplifier under a contract of loan. He could not have been sued for the tort of conversion for simply refusing to return the goods. He was held liable in tort, however, for parting with the goods to someone else, because this was quite outside the original contract of loan.

Secondly, a minor may escape liability if the tort requires a mental element, as with fraud and negligence, and the minor is too young for this to be present. A minor who is alleged to have been negligent will be judged by what might reasonably have been expected of a person of that age and not by what might have been expected of an adult. Thus a minor may escape liability where an adult would not.

In criminal law, a minor is given rather more protection as to the age at which he is deemed capable of *mens rea*, the courts in which cases will be heard and the sanctions which may be imposed; it is not appropriate to discuss this in detail here.

Trade unions and their members have, since 1906, enjoyed substantial immunity from actions in tort as regards things done in contemplation or furtherance of a trade dispute. This is now governed by the Trade Union and Labour Relations Act 1974, but the protection has been limited by the Employment Acts 1980 and 1982, and the Trade Union Act 1984.

In general, trade unions and their members are subject to the criminal law in the same way as everyone else, except that there is limited protection for peaceful picketing that might otherwise constitute an offence.

Joint wrongdoers

When a tort is committed by two or more persons acting together, for example, if *A* and *B* assault or defraud *C*, the position is governed by the Civil Liability (Contribution) Act 1978. Liability is 'joint and several', in that the plaintiff may sue both tortfeasors, or each separately, or only one of them. If *A* is sued and cannot pay, another action can be brought against *B*, provided that the total damages recovered do not exceed the amount awarded in the first action.

If *A* has to pay the whole of the damages, he can claim a *contribution* from *B*. The court will, if called upon to do so, apportion liability as between *A* and *B*, either in the course of *C*'s action, or in a separate action by *A* against *B*. In some circumstances, *B* might be ordered to *indemnify A* completely. None of this, however, affects *C*'s right to claim the whole amount from either of the defendants.

If several persons act together and commit a criminal offence, all or any of them may be prosecuted.

E. Liability for the acts of others in tort

Vicarious liability

In some situations, a person may be held liable for torts committed by others, even though the wrongful act was no fault of his. This is known as *vicarious liability*. Thus a principal may be liable for the torts of his agent, and a partner may be liable for the torts of another partner in connection with the partnership business. The owner of a car may be liable for another who is driving with the owner's permission and for the owner's benefit or purposes. The most important example is the liability of an employer for the torts of his servant committed by the latter in the course of employment. It depends upon two conditions:

1. *The employee must have been acting under a contract of service.* An employer will only be vicariously liable for the torts of employees, and not normally for those of independent contractors. The distinction between employees and independent contractors is sometimes straightforward: a chauffeur is an employee, a taxi driver is an independent contractor. It is not always so simple, however, and will be discussed in more detail in Unit 22.
2. *The tort must have been committed in the course of employment.* There has been considerable litigation upon what constitutes the course of employment. Broadly, it is enough if the wrongdoer was *doing what he was employed to do*, albeit carelessly, fraudulently, or even disobediently. More particularly, the following rules are suggested.

The employer will be liable:

(a) *Where the wrongful act is expressly or impliedly authorized by the employer.* Implied authority will arise, for example, where an employee acts in an emergency to protect his employer's property.

> In *Poland* v. *John Parr and Sons* (1927), a carter struck a boy whom he suspected to be stealing sugar from his employer's cart. The boy fell, and was injured when the wagon wheel ran over his foot. The employer was held vicariously liable because, although the carter had used excessive force, he did have implied authority to protect his employer's property.

(b) *Where the tort is a wrongful way of carrying out an authorized act.* The mere fact that the employee acts dishonestly or carelessly does not take him outside the course of his employment.

> In *Ricketts* v. *Thos. Tilling Ltd* (1915), a bus driver negligently allowed the conductor to drive and the plaintiff, a passenger, was injured. The employer was vicariously liable because the driver was doing, albeit negligently and disobediently, what he was employed to do, namely control the vehicle.

> On the other hand, in *Beard* v. *London General Omnibus Co.* (1900), the conductor turned a bus round in the *absence* of the driver, and injured the plaintiff. The employer escaped liability; the driver was not at fault, and the conductor was acting quite outside his duties.

The employer cannot escape liability merely by prohibiting the wrongful method of working. He is liable to third parties injured even if the employee was acting in breach of express instructions.

> In *Limpus* v. *London General Omnibus Co.* (1862), an accident was caused by the defendant's bus driver racing with a driver from another company. Although the defendant had expressly forbidden such racing, the driver's unauthorized and wrongful act was held to arise in the course of his employment.

On the other hand, if the prohibition limits the extent of the worker's duties, this may effectively protect the employer.

In *Twine* v. *Bean's Express Ltd* (1946), a van driver was forbidden to give lifts and there was a notice to this effect on the dashboard. He gave a lift and the passenger was killed through negligent driving. It was held that giving a lift was outside the course of the driver's employment.

(c) *Where the wrongful act was incidental to the course of employment.*

In *Century Insurance Co. Ltd* v. *Northern Ireland Road Transport Board* (1942), the respondents were held liable for the act of a driver who, while delivering petrol to a garage, lit a cigarette, threw away the lighted match and caused an explosion.

(d) *For wilful wrongdoing in respect of acts which the worker is employed to do.* Even if the employee is acting fraudulently, and solely for his own ends, his employer will still be vicariously liable if the wrongdoer obtained control over the property misappropriated in the course of his duties.

In *Lloyd* v. *Grace, Smith & Co.* (1912), a firm of solicitors were held liable when their managing clerk, while dealing with some property in the course of his duties, fraudulently induced a client to make over the property to him. The partners had employed the clerk to convey property, and were therefore liable to their client when the clerk did so dishonestly. (The client could have sued the clerk himself instead of the partners, but was obviously advised to sue the employers because they were more likely to have money to pay the damages.)

In *Morris* v. *C. W. Martin & Sons Ltd* (1965), the respondents were held liable in conversion for the loss of a mink stole which had been entrusted to them for cleaning, and which had been stolen by one of their workers. The thief had been entrusted with the stole in the course of the cleaning operations.

The employer will *not* be liable:

(a) *Where the worker departs from the course of his employment* and is said to be on a frolic of his own. An example would be the unauthorized use of the employer's property for the worker's own purposes, as where a lorry driver deviates from his authorized route to engage in some private business.

In *Hilton* v. *Thomas Burton Ltd* (1961), demolition workers were allowed to use the employer's van for reasonable purposes. At 3.30 p.m. one afternoon they drove seven miles to a café in order to pass the time until they finished work at 5.30 p.m. On the way back, the driver drove negligently and injured the plaintiff. The employer was not vicariously liable.

(b) *Where the worker is permitted to do something for his own purposes, but is not employed to do it for his employer.* An example would be permission to use the car for private business.

(c) *For an act which, although occurring while the wrongdoer is at work, is quite unconnected with the employment.* Thus there would be no vicarious liability if a coalman, while delivering coal, threw a piece of coal at a dog and broke a window.

In *Warren* v. *Henlys Ltd* (1948), a petrol pump attendant mistakenly thought that a driver was trying to avoid paying for petrol. An argument developed, the attendant lost his temper and struck the plaintiff. It was held that the employer was not vicariously liable, because the quarrel had become a personal matter, no longer sufficiently connected with the employment.

Loaned employees may give rise to problems as when an employer hires out a worker, with or without equipment, to another employer. Which employer will be vicariously liable for torts committed by the worker during the hiring? There is a strong presumption that liability will remain with the permanent or general employer unless there is clear evidence that control over the method of working has passed to the temporary or special employer. This will depend upon the facts of each particular case, and will be determined by such matters as the specialized skill of the worker and the intricacy of machinery hired out at the same time. Thus, responsibility is more likely to remain with the general employer if a complex piece of earthmoving equipment and a skilled operator are involved than if a lorry and driver are hired.

> In *Mersey Docks and Harbour Board* v. *Coggins and Griffith Ltd* (1947), the harbour authority hired a crane and driver to a firm of stevedores. The contract of hire provided that the authority should pay and have power to dismiss the driver, but that he should be regarded as the servant of the stevedores. The stevedores had power to direct the work, but had no power over the way the driver operated the crane. The House of Lords held that the harbour authority was vicariously liable for the driver's negligence.

The contract between the employers may provide which of them will ultimately bear the loss, but this will not affect the above rules regarding which of them is vicariously liable *to the injured third party*.

Two further matters merit comment. First, it is worth repeating that the vicarious liability of the employer is in addition, and not an alternative, to the personal liability of the worker who committed the wrongful act. The worker may be sued by the injured party if the latter so chooses. Moreover, if the the employer is successfully sued he may, under the Civil Liability (Contribution) Act 1978, be entitled to indemnity from the worker.

> In *Lister* v. *Romford Ice and Cold Storage Ltd* (1957), Lister was employed as a lorry driver. He reversed the lorry carelessly, and injured his father, a fellow employee, who recovered damages from the employer. The employer (at the insistence of the insurance company) sued for and obtained indemnity from Lister.

Secondly, a distinction must be drawn between an employer and a superior servant. Vicarious liability for the misconduct of a bank clerk will rest upon the bank itself and not upon the bank manager. The latter will be liable only if he himself has contributed to the wrongful act.

The torts of independent contractors

The person who engages an independent contractor is not, as a general rule, vicariously liable for the contractor's torts. In general, only the contractor himself is liable for torts which he commits while carrying out the contract.

There are, however, some exceptional situations where the principal and the contractor may both be liable. The principal is not vicariously liable for the *contractor's* torts, but he will be liable if *he himself* has also committed a tort, or if the law imposes on him a duty to ensure that care is taken if he should delegate performance to another.

80

Liability may arise in the following instances:

1. *Where the principal is negligent* in that he has engaged an incompetent contractor, or failed to give proper instructions.

   In *Robinson* v. *Beaconsfield Rural Council* (1911), the Council had a statutory duty to clear cesspools. The Council engaged a contractor to do the work, but gave him no instructions as to disposal of the filth, and he deposited it on the appellant's land. The Council was held liable.

2. *Where strict liability is imposed by law*, the person who bears the responsibility cannot escape liability by engaging an independent contractor to do the job. Strict liability may arise at common law, as under the rule in *Rylands* v. *Fletcher* (Unit 10), or it may be imposed by legislation, for example, some of the duties arising from factory legislation.

3. *Where a contractor is engaged to do work on or adjoining a highway.*

   In *Holliday* v. *National Telephone Co.* (1899), the defendants, who were laying telephone cables along a highway, engaged a plumber to solder joints. They were held liable when a passer-by was injured by the negligent use of a blow lamp by the contractor.

4. *Where a contractor is engaged to do ultra-hazardous acts* which by their very nature involve special hardship to others.

   In *Sumner* v. *William Henderson & Sons Ltd* (1964), a fire was caused in a department store by the defective installation of an electric cable, and 11 people were killed. The respondents were held liable for the negligence of the contractors who installed the cable.

5. *Where the person who engaged the contractor interferes with the work or actively participates in the wrong.*

It is possible for the principal to impose liability on the contractor by contract. While this will not affect the claim of a third party against the principal, it will give him a right to claim indemnity from the contractor later.

F. Liability for the acts of others in criminal law

The concept of vicarious liability does not generally apply in criminal law. Thus, if your employee, in the course of his employment, drives carelessly and injures someone, you will be vicariously liable for the driver's tort, but you will normally incur no criminal liability. Only the driver can be prosecuted. There are some statutory exceptions to this general rule, but these depend on the wording of the statutes concerned.

Problems arise where the offender is a corporation. As has been noted, a corporation has no physical existence, and can only act through its organs (such as the board of directors), agents or employees. For most offences, the corporation cannot be held vicariously liable for the crimes of its employees.

For the purposes of criminal law, however, certain human persons are treated as the 'mind' of the corporation. These normally include executive directors and very senior management. The acts and decisions of these individuals are treated as the acts of the corporation, and can render the corporation criminally liable. Other less senior employees and agents are treated as separate persons, for whose acts the company is not criminally liable. We have seen how, in *Tesco Supermarkets Ltd* v. *Nattrass*, mentioned earlier, the branch manager in a supermarket chain was treated as 'another person', for whose misdeeds in the course of his employment the company was not criminally liable.

To some extent this case turned on the particular wording of the Trade Descriptions Act, but it does reflect the general position. On the other hand, had the manager committed a *tort* in the course of his employment, there is no doubt that the company would have been vicariously liable for this.

G. Limitation of actions

The Limitation Act 1980 provides that in general no action in tort may be brought after six years have elapsed. There are exceptions to this period, in particular, 12 years is allowed for the recovery of land, whereas an action which includes a claim for damages for personal injuries or which arises from a fatal accident must be brought within three years.

The time is calculated from the date when the cause of action accrued, that is from the date when the action could first have been brought. In some cases of personal injuries, however, the harmful effects of the wrongful act may not become apparent until after the three-year period has expired. Therefore, it is provided that an action may be brought on an otherwise statute-barred claim for three years after the discovery of material facts of which the plaintiff had not previously been aware. There are also similar rules to those in contract for extending the period on account of a disability such as minority or insanity, or of fraud (Unit 16).

There is no equivalent period of limitation in criminal law and a prosecution may be brought at any time, even for an offence committed many years earlier. There are a few exceptions to this general rule, of which the most important is that prosecutions for summary offences must normally be brought within six months of their commission.

Examination questions

1. To what extent is fault necessary for liability
   (a) in criminal law, and (b) in tort?
2. (a) In general any person may sue or be sued in tort. Discuss.
   (b) Smith, aged 17, hired a car for one day. On the following day, he failed to return the car as he had agreed. Instead he drove the car on another journey and damaged it through careless driving. Advise Smith as to his liability, if any, to the car owners.

3. Explain the liability, if any, of:
    (a) an employer for the wrongful acts of his servant;
    (b) an employer for the wrongful acts of an independent contractor he has engaged.
4. Sparks is employed by Power & Co. as an electrician. While carrying out certain repairs at the department store of Harridges, Sparks lights a cigarette and throws away the lighted match. This badly damages the fur coat of Mrs Lamb, a customer. Can Mrs Lamb sue Sparks, or Power & Co., or Harridges? Would your answer be different if Sparks had been forbidden to smoke during the course of his work?
5. To what extent does the passing of time affect the institution of legal proceedings? In this respect, distinguish between a criminal offence, a tort and a breach of contract (Unit 16).

Unit 9. Negligence

A. The tort of negligence

Negligence is perhaps the most important of all torts, affecting many aspects of life. It arises when damage is caused to the person or property of another by failure to take such care as the law requires in the circumstances of the case. To succeed in an action for negligence, the plaintiff must prove three things:

1. that the defendant owed him a legal duty of care;
2. that the duty was broken;
3. that damage was suffered in consequence.

Each of these requirements will be discussed further.

1. The duty of care

There are many situations where a legal duty of care has long been recognized as existing, for example, the duty of one road user towards, another and of an employer towards his employees. These situations have been extended and added to by judicial decisions. In the case of *Donoghue* v. *Stevenson* (1932) (see below), Lord Atkin tried to replace this piecemeal approach to the law of negligence by suggesting a general duty of care which could be applied to all situations. His view was that reasonable care should always be taken to avoid injury to your 'neighbour', that is, to any person closely affected by your conduct, and whom you should *reasonably foresee* might be injured by it.

This 'neighbour' principle has been increasingly accepted and applied by the courts during the past 50 years, particularly in novel situations. It has now become the general test for determining whether or not a duty of care exists and perhaps the outstanding example of its application came in 1963.

> In *Hedley Byrne* v. *Heller and Partners* (1963), a firm of advertising agents gave credit to a client in reliance upon a banker's reference, and suffered loss when the client became insolvent. The reference had been given carelessly but, since the bank had expressly disclaimed liability when giving it, the action failed. Nevertheless, the House of Lords stated that, contrary to what had previously been believed, liability for negligence may extend to careless words as well as to careless deeds and that damages may be awarded for financial loss as well as for physical injury to persons and property.

It remains to be seen how these rules will develop. Since the *Hedley Byrne* case, it is clear that a professional man, such as a banker, solicitor or accountant, owes a duty of care not only to his own client who employs or pays him, but also to another whom he knows is relying on his skill. On the other hand, there are still situations where no duty is owed for statements, for example where the statement was made casually in circumstances where it is unlikely to be relied on, or if it is made by someone who could claim no special professional knowledge of what he was talking about.

> In *Mutual Life Assurance* v. *Evatt* (1971), the insurance company made negligent statements to Mr Evatt about the financial state of an associated company. In reliance on this, Mr Evatt invested money in the other company, and as a result suffered loss. It was held that he could not recover damages. The insurance company and its employees were not professional advisers on investment, and therefore owed no duty of care to Mr Evatt.

If the law of negligence has gradually been moving towards the establishment of a general duty of care in all situations, this stage has not yet been reached. There are still exceptions to the 'neighbour' principle where, although harm is foreseeable, no duty exists. Thus a barrister owes no duty towards those for whom he acts as advocate.

> In *Rondel* v. *Worsley* (1969), the plaintiff, who had been convicted of causing grievous bodily harm, brought an action against his barrister on the grounds that he would have been acquitted if his case had been conducted properly. The House of Lords held that, despite the decision in the *Hedley Byrne* case, no action lay against a barrister for professional negligence in the conduct of a case. It was said to be in the public interest that this immunity should be preserved, and the case illustrates also the further point that the decision on the existence or otherwise of a duty may be influenced by considerations of public policy.

The present attitude of the courts to this matter was summarized in *Anns* v. *Merton London Borough Council* (1977) by Lord Wilberforce who said that it was no longer necessary to bring the facts of the situation within those of a previous situation where a duty has been held to exist. Instead, there were two stages: to establish first whether the 'neighbour' principle applied and, if so, then to determine whether there are any considerations (of public policy) which ought to negative or limit the scope of the duty.

The plaintiff must further prove that the duty exists *towards him*.

> In *Bourhill* v. *Young* (1942), a pregnant woman heard a collision while alighting from a tram, and she suffered shock when she later saw blood on the road. Her action failed, for she was deemed to be too far away from the accident for a duty to be owed to her. In

nervous shock cases, it would seem that a duty of care is owed only where it is reasonably foreseeable that shock is likely to result.

In *McLoughlin* v. *O'Brian* (1982), one of Mrs McLoughlin's children was killed by a lorry and her husband and two other children were badly injured. At the time, she was at home, two miles away, but the shock of hearing of her child's death and the sight of the injuries to the others made her ill. She recovered damages because ensuing shock to a *wife and mother* was a reasonably foreseeable result of the lorry driver's negligence.

2. Breach of duty

The standard of care

In deciding whether or not the duty of care has been broken, the standard against which the defendant's conduct will be measured is that of the so-called 'reasonable man'. Negligence will be deemed to be present if the defendant did not act in a reasonable manner in the circumstances of the situation. What is reasonable will depend upon factors such as the magnitude of the risk involved, for the greater the risk the greater the care required.

In *Bolton* v. *Stone* (1951), a batsman hit a ball out of the ground during a cricket match. It struck and injured Miss Stone, who was in the street. The top of the fence surrounding the ground was 17 feet higher than the pitch at the point where the ball crossed, and Miss Stone was about 100 yards from the batsman. It was only proved that a cricket ball had been hit out of the ground on six occasions in 30 years, and there was evidence that the shot was exceptional. It was held that, in the circumstances, the cricket club had taken reasonable care, and was not liable. It would have been otherwise if balls had landed in the road frequently.

Greater care will be required if the person exposed to the risk possesses known characteristics which either increase the likelihood of injury or, if an injury occurs, make the consequences more serious. Thus greater care is generally expected towards children and blind persons.

In *Paris* v. *Stepney Borough Council* (1951), a fitter with only one good eye was employed on work which involved some danger to the eyes from fragments of metal. No goggles were provided. It was held that the employer acted unreasonably, and hence negligently, in not taking extra precautions.

It may sometimes be reasonable to take less care in an emergency, such as driving an urgent case to hospital.

In *Watt* v. *Hertfordshire County Council* (1954), a fireman failed to recover damages when he had been injured by the movement of a heavy lifting jack which was not properly secured on a lorry. The vehicle was not properly equipped to carry the jack, but it was the only lorry available to carry the jack to free a trapped woman in danger of losing her life. The defendants had taken a reasonable risk in the circumstances.

A major problem connected with breach of duty is the *onus of proof*. Normally it is for the plaintiff to show that the defendant did not act in a reasonable manner, and in the absence of reliable evidence his action will fail. This can sometimes occur when the plaintiff is unable to say what happened, and there is no other evidence.

> In *Wakelin* v. *London and South Western Railway Co.* (1886), the body of a man was found on the railway, near a level crossing, at night. He had been hit by a train, and it seemed quite possible that the railway company had been careless. On the other hand, it was equally possible that the accident was entirely the man's own fault. In the absence of evidence either way, the action failed.

There are, however, some situations where an accident happens of which the only or mostly likely cause must be negligence. Unattended cars do not normally run away, train doors do not normally fly open, nor do cakes contain stones. The court may then apply the maxim *res ipsa loquitur* (the thing speaks for itself) and, upon proof of the accident by the plaintiff, infer negligence from this fact, unless the *defendant* offers a reasonable explanation. The onus of proof, at this point, is reversed, and the defendant is left to prove that he was *not* negligent.

This rule of procedure can be of considerable assistance to the plaintiff in obviously negligent situations, which are normally those where the plaintiff knows little of why the accident occurred, but the defendant is (or should be) able to explain what has happened.

> In *Richley* v. *Faull* (1965), the defendant's car skidded violently, turned round, and collided with the plaintiff's car on the wrong side of the road. It was held that this, of itself, was sufficient evidence of negligent driving. Since the defendant was unable to give a satisfactory explanation of his skid, he was held liable.

3. Resulting damage

Types of loss

The plaintiff must prove that he suffered loss as a result of the defendant's breach of duty of care. Loss can include damage to property, personal injury and, in some circumstances, financial loss. Policy considerations may also apply here in determining whether the loss may be recovered.

At one time it was not clear whether personal injuries could include nervous shock, because of the problems of linking cause and effect. Medical and psychological advances have overcome this difficulty, and it is now established that nervous shock may be compensated if it gives rise to physical or mental illness, and it is just as much a form of injury as a broken leg.

Financial or economic loss is recoverable in only some circumstances. Since the *Hedley Byrne* case, it may be recovered if it follows from a negligent statement. It may be recovered as a result of a careless *act* if it is closely connected with physical harm which has occurred.

> In *Spartan Steel & Alloys Ltd* v. *Martin & Co (Contractors) Ltd* (1972), careless excavation during road work damaged an electricity cable and cut off the power supply to the plaintiff's factory for 14 hours. Metal currently melted in a furnace had to be removed to prevent it from solidifying. Damages were recovered for the physical damage to the metal, and for the financial loss of profit on *that* operation. (The court refused to award damages for possible loss of profits from future operations while the power remained off, because this was not directly connected with the physical loss of the 'melt' in progress. For the reasons given below, this part of the case might well be decided differently today.)

Today, pure financial loss may also be recoverable for negligent acts or omissions even where it is not directly linked to physical harm. Possibly this applies only if there was a sufficiently close connection between plaintiff and defendant, so that the defendant must clearly have foreseen the possibility of such harm to the plaintiff.

> In *Junior Books Ltd* v. *Veitchi Co. Ltd* (1982), JB engaged builders for a new factory. At JB's request, the builders sub-contracted laying the floor to V. (There was no contract between JB and V; only between JB and the builders, and between the builders and V.) Two years later the floor developed cracks. The House of Lords (1) confirmed that V had owed a duty to JB when laying the floor, and (2) held that this duty could involve responsibility for the purely financial or economic loss caused by the cracks.

Remoteness

Finally, the resulting damage must not be too remote. Since the *Wagon Mound case* in 1961 (Unit 10), this means that the type of damage should reasonably have been foreseen by the defendant at the time when he acted carelessly.

> In *Doughty* v. *Turner Manufacturing Co. Ltd* (1964), the plaintiff was injured by an explosion caused by an asbestos cement lid being carelessly knocked into a cauldron of molten metal. His action failed for, according to the state of knowledge at the time, an explosion was not to be expected, and his injuries were not therefore reasonably foreseeable. The decision could well have been different if his injuries had been caused by a foreseeable splash of metal.

B. Liability for goods

A person who hands over dangerous or defective goods owes a duty to the immediate recipient and, in some cases, to other persons into whose hands the goods may come.

> In *Donoghue* v. *Stevenson* (1932), a woman drank some ginger beer which had been bought for her by a friend. The beer was in an opaque bottle and, when the last of it was poured out, it was found to contain what was thought to be the decomposed remains of a snail. The woman suffered shock and became ill. The House of Lords decided that a manufacturer owes a duty of care to the consumer of his products when they are marketed in the form in which the consumer will receive them. The snail was in an opaque bottle, and there was no reasonable possibility of its being discovered between leaving the manufacturer and reaching the customer. The manufacturer was therefore liable.

This rule, which has become more important in recent years with the increasing number of pre-packaged goods, is now treated as part of the general principles of negligence. Its scope has been extended by subsequent decisions and the duty is now imposed upon any person who does some work upon the goods in question. It protects any person who is likely to be injured by carelessness in that work.

> In *Stennett* v. *Hancock* (1939), Mrs Stennett, a pedestrian who had been injured by part of a lorry wheel which had broken away, successfully claimed damages from the defendants who had not carried out repairs to the lorry in a proper manner.

It must be emphasized that injury to a person caused by a dangerous defect in goods is not enough. Proof is required that the defect arose through negligence, by failure to exercise reasonable care, and that the defect was unlikely to be discovered by any reasonably foreseeable subsequent examination. The customer is often in no position to know whether the manufacturer has been careless and the courts have sometimes, therefore, applied the maxim *res ipsa loquitur* and reversed the onus of proof.

> In *Steer* v. *Durable Rubber Co. Ltd* (1958), a girl aged six was scalded when a hot water bottle split soon after being bought. The Court of Appeal held that it was for the manufacturers to prove that they had *not* been negligent, which they were unable to do.

C. Employer's liability

This is another aspect of the general principles of negligence, which deserves special mention in view of the large number of actions which arise out of injuries suffered at work. An employer owes a duty to his employees to take reasonable care to provide a safe system of work. This includes an obligation to provide reasonably competent staff, to provide reasonably safe equipment, and to provide a reasonably safe method of working. As will be seen later, this duty of care has been reinforced by a number of statutory duties imposed in the interests of safety (Unit 25).

D. Dangerous premises

Lawful visitors

The duty owed by an occupier of premises towards people coming on to his premises was formerly based upon complex rules which had evolved from the general principles of the tort of negligence. This duty was simplified and restated by the Occupiers' Liability Act 1957 which now largely governs the position.

The Act imposes a duty of care upon those in physical occupation and control of premises, who may not necessarily be the owners. Even temporary control can be enough, as where a builder occupies part of a site during construction work. It is possible for the duty to be owed by two (or more) people in respect of the same premises, for example the occupier of a house and a builder working there, if both have some degree of control over the work being done.

The duty is owed to all lawful visitors who enter with the express or implied permission of the occupier. It covers also those who enter in exercise of a right of law, for example a police officer executing a search warrant. The Act does not apply to trespassers whose position is discussed below.

The duty concerns the state of the premises and things done or omitted to be done on them. The occupier's obligation, described as the 'common duty of care', is 'to take such care as in all the circumstances of the case is reasonable to see that the visitor will be reasonably safe in using the premises for the purposes for which he is invited or permitted by the occupier to be there'. The occupier can protect himself by warning the visitor of specific dangers but this warning must, in the circumstances, be enough to enable the visitor to be reasonably safe.

As under the previous law the occupier must be prepared for children to be less careful than adults. What constitutes adequate warning or protection for an adult may not be deemed so for a child. In addition, some dangerous things may attract a child and these traps or allurements must be guarded against.

> In *Glasgow Corporation* v. *Taylor* (1922), a boy of seven died after eating attractive looking poisonous berries in a park. The berries were within easy reach and it was held that the warning notice was insufficient so far as young children were concerned.

Conversely, the occupier may expect that experts, for example electricians entering to repair an electrical fault, will appreciate the special risks likely to arise from their work.

> In *Roles* v. *Nathan* (1963), two sweeps were killed by carbon monoxide fumes while cleaning the flues of a coke boiler. It was held that this was a risk of which they should have been aware, and that the occupier had discharged his duty under the Act by passing on a warning he had been given by an expert.

The duty imposed by the Act may not now be excluded or modified by contract in so far as death or personal injury is concerned (Unfair Contract Terms Act 1977). The occupier may limit his liability for other loss or damage, for example to property, provided that he can prove that it is reasonable to do so.

Trespassers

At common law, trespassers were deemed to take the premises as they found them and could not, in general, complain if they were injured. At the same time the occupier had to act in a reasonable and civilized manner and could not inflict intentional harm upon trespassers. Thus, while he could erect a fence of barbed wire as a reasonable means of deterring entry and would not be liable for any injury thereby caused, he could not set deliberate traps designed to cause injury after trespassers had obtained entry. In addition, if an occupier knew that trespassers were on his land or were likely to be there, he could not disregard their presence and endanger them by acting recklessly, for example by shooting where they were likely to be.

In recent years, the courts have given greater protection to trespassers, particularly children, on humanitarian grounds.

> In *British Railways Board* v. *Herrington* (1972), children regularly played in a field next to an electrified railway. The fence guarding the line was broken down in one place, and people were known to use the gap for a short cut across the line. The Board was held liable to a boy aged six, who wandered from the field on to the line, and was badly injured by a live rail.

The Occupiers' Liability Act 1984 replaces these common law rules and attempts to clarify the liability of occupiers towards unlawful visitors. An occupier now owes a statutory duty to a trespasser if he knows or should know that a danger exists, that the trespasser is or may be in the vicinity of the danger and that it is reasonable for him to offer some protection. The duty is to take such care as is reasonable in all the circumstances to see that the trespasser does not suffer *personal* injury. It may be reasonable in appropriate cases to discharge the duty by a warning or by some other way of discouraging would-be trespassers. Greater care will, therefore, be presumably required in the case of, for example, a hiker who has lost his way than a burglar.

Finally, acquiescence in a trespass may result in the trespasser being regarded as a lawful visitor. Again, this frequently applies to children.

> In *Lowery* v. *Walker* (1911), passengers had crossed a farmer's field regularly for the last 30 years on their way to the station. It was held that, although the farmer had never expressly given permission, he had acquiesced for so long that the people were no longer regarded as trespassers. The farmer could have built a large fence, or otherwise made it clear that he no longer acquiesced, but he did not do so. Instead he put a savage horse in the field, and was held liable to someone who was attacked.

Examination questions

1. (a) The plaintiff in an action for negligence must prove that the defendant failed to exercise reasonable care. What is meant by *reasonable care*?
   (b) Contractors Ltd is engaged in road repairs. One of its labourers carelessly fractures a main and cuts off gas supplies to a bakery. The baker's ovens are damaged by the sudden break in supply and bread in the ovens is ruined. His employees lose two days' benefits under the bakery's bonus scheme. What damages, if any, can (i) the baker, and (ii) his employees recover, and from whom?

2. Albert is the proprietor of a large garage. What is his liability, if any, in each of the following situations?
   (a) One of his employees is taking a car for a test drive when it skids out of control on to the wrong side of the road and damages another car coming in the opposite direction.
   (b) A car that has just been repaired is being driven away by a customer when the car door falls off and injures a pedestrian.
   (c) Albert suggests that a customer changes his vehicle insurance company in order to get better terms. The customer does so and suffers loss when the recommended company later fails and is unable to meet his claim.

3. Your firm is manufacturing a variety of corn cure which can have damaging consequences if it is allowed to come into contact with the more tender parts of a person's body. Draft a report explaining the legal liability of your firm if this should happen and suggest any ways in which this liability might be excluded or mitigated.

4. (a) To what extent will the occupier of a factory owe a duty of care to the employee of a contractor who is carrying out maintenance on the premises?
   (b) Tom, who is employed as an electrician by Super Builders Ltd, carelessly leaves a length of cable in the entrance to a partly built house. Dick, who is employed by Fine Scaffolds Ltd, a firm of sub-contractors on the site, is injured when he trips over the cable. Advise Dick.

5. Your company owns a sports field upon which children are accustomed to play during school holidays. On one occasion a guard dog is released to frighten them away. The dog savages Fred, aged nine, and John, aged ten, is injured by barbed wire surrounding the ground when he tries to escape. Mrs Smith, who is passing on the adjoining road, suffers nervous shock upon seeing the children's injuries. Advise your company as to its possible liability. Would your answer be different if Fred and John were adults?

Unit 10. Further Principles of Liability in Tort

A. Specific torts

The tort of negligence was discussed in detail in the previous unit because of its special importance. It is not possible to treat other torts in the same depth here, but the first part of this unit will be devoted to an outline of some other specific torts.

Torts against the person

Any direct interference with the person or liberty of another without lawful justification is actionable as a *trespass to the person*. This may take three forms: *assault*, where a person is threatened with violence; *battery*, where force is actually applied; and *false imprisonment*, where a total restraint is unlawfully placed upon the liberty of another. All forms may be present, for example, if a suspected shoplifter is wrongfully taken into custody by a store detective.

Torts against land

The tort of *trespass to land* is committed by *direct* interference with land of another. Trespass to land is only a tort, and trespassers cannot generally be criminally prosecuted, except in a few instances such as trespass upon railway or military property. Apart from its simplest form of entry upon land, it is trespass to use land for an unauthorized purpose, to remain on land when permission to be there has ended, or to dump or throw things on another's land. Thus it can be trespass to abandon a car on someone's field, or to dump other waste there without permission. 'Land' includes not only the surface and any buildings upon it, but also the air space above within the area of ordinary use and the ground (including minerals) beneath.

Someone expressly invited on to the land will not be a trespasser, nor will someone with implied authority to be there, for example, a sales representative entering business premises in the hope of selling something. In both cases, however, they must leave if asked to do so. Even against the wishes of the occupier, police officers have various powers of entry, and many officials such as public health inspectors and factory inspectors have statutory powers to enter certain premises. In addition to a remedy through the courts by way of damages or an injunction, an occupier has a right to ask the trespasser to leave and, if he refuses, to use such force as is reasonably necessary to remove him.

If the interference with a person's use or enjoyment of land is *indirect*, an action may lie for *private nuisance*. Indirect interference with the enjoyment of land can take many forms, such as noise, smoke, smells, vibrations, fumes, etc. Interference with specific rights over land, such as blocking a right of way or taking away a right of light, can also be nuisance. On the other hand, not all interference will be actionable; the law expects some 'give and take' and an action for nuisance will lie only if the interference is unreasonable. In an industrial area, for example, a certain amount of noise is accepted as inevitable. All circumstances, such as the locality and the duration and frequency of the alleged nuisance must be considered.

If the annoyance or harm affects the public generally, a *public nuisance* may have been committed. This is not a tort against land, but is mentioned here for convenience. It is primarily a crime but an action in tort is also possible if the plaintiff has suffered loss over and above that suffered by the public as a whole. Thus, a road-user cannot recover damages simply because of the smell from a factory which he passes, but he may do so if acid smuts from the factory damage his car.

Torts against goods

A third form of trespass, *trespass to goods*, arises when there is direct and unauthorized physical interference with goods in the possession of another. It usually arises when the goods are removed or damaged; strictly, the slightest interference will suffice, but an action is unlikely unless there is substantial damage. There can be liability without fault, and it is sufficient if the goods are removed by mistake; unlike the crime of theft, the tort can be committed when there is no intention to deprive the owner permanently of the goods.

If a wrongdoer deals in goods in such a way as wrongfully to deny another's *title* to them, an action will lie for *conversion*. The most common forms arise when someone wrongfully purports to sell goods which do not belong to him, or wrongfully refuses to return goods to their rightful owner. Thus, it would be conversion for the hirer of goods to try to sell them to someone else, or to refuse to return them when the hiring expires. Again, there can be liability without fault, and the tort can be committed by mistake or in ignorance of the true ownership.

By the Torts (Interference with Goods) Act 1977, the court may order the return of the goods in a successful action for conversion; or it can award damages, particularly if return is impracticable because the goods have been altered or resold; or the court can give the defendant the choice of either returning the goods or paying damages.

Torts against reputation

The publication of a (false) statement which tends to injure the reputation of another may constitute the tort of *defamation*. The test is whether, in consequence of the statement, right-thinking members of society might regard the plaintiff with hatred, ridicule or contempt. The statement must clearly refer to the plaintiff, either expressly or by necessary implication. Moreover, it must be published to a third party; a person's reputation depends upon the opinion of others.

Defamation in a permanent form, such as writing, is *libel*; in a temporary form, such as speech, it is *slander*. The distinction is important because slander is only actionable if the plaintiff proves that the statement caused him financial loss, whereas libel is actionable even without such loss. There are exceptional cases of slander where loss need not be proved, for example allegations that the plaintiff has committed a serious criminal offence, or that a person in any office, trade or profession is unfit to hold his position or practise his trade.

Several defences are available. If the defendant can show *unintentional defamation*, he may avoid liability by apologizing, publishing a suitable correction and paying any legal costs or other expenses that the plaintiff has reasonably incurred. It is always a defence to show that the allegations are *true*, for no one can fairly claim a reputation which he does not deserve. In the interests of free speech and criticism, opinions passed on matters of public concern may be defended if they constitute *fair comment on a matter of public interest*, and are made in good faith. Finally, statements made in some situations are *privileged*, and therefore not actionable. Statements in court or in Parliament have absolute privilege, and are completely protected. Some other situations attract only qualified privilege, where there is protection only in the absence of malice, for example, where the publisher has a duty to make the statement and the recipient has an interest in receiving it. Thus a reference or testimonial is protected if it is honestly, though mistakenly, made.

The rule in *Rylands* v. *Fletcher*

This rule takes its name from the case in which it was first formulated. It provides that, if a person brings on to his land and keeps there something likely to do damage if it escapes, he keeps it there at his peril and will be strictly liable for any damage which follows from an escape, even if there has been no negligence. In *Rylands* v. *Fletcher* (1868), the defendant was liable when water leaked from his reservoir and flooded a neighbour's mines. The rule applies only where keeping the dangerous thing constitutes a 'non-natural' use of the land, and more recently it has been suggested that some industrial processes are natural uses of land, and so not within the rule. On

95

the other hand, some industrial discharges, or the escape of toxic waste from private tips, may still come within the rule.

Breach of statutory duty

Many statutes impose duties on individuals, firms or public authorities, breach of which are primarily *criminal* offences. In certain cases, particularly where the purpose of duty is to protect people from physical danger, there may also be a further sanction: a person injured as a result of breach may be allowed to recover damages for the *tort* of breach of statutory duty. An important example is where someone is injured as a result of breach of the duty under the Factories Act to fence dangerous machinery (Unit 25).

The nature of the duty depends upon the wording of the legislation. Some statutory duties are *strict*, and there can be liability without fault (for example, under some sections of the Factories Act). Other provisions simply impose a statutory duty of reasonable care.

Deceit

In Unit 9 we examined how, in limited situations, liability can arise for negligent misstatements; the tort of deceit (fraud) is concerned with *intentional* or *reckless* falsehood. The tort has five main elements:

1. There must be a false statement of *fact*, not merely an expression of opinion.
2. It must be made fraudulently, that is knowingly, or without belief in its truth, or recklessly, not caring whether it be true or false.
3. The plaintiff must be intended to act on the statement.
4. He must actually act in reliance on it.
5. He must thereby suffer loss.

Where the maker of a deceitful statement thereby induces the plaintiff to make a *contract* with him, the plaintiff will also be entitled to recover damages under section 2(1) of the Misrepresentation Act 1967 (Unit 13). To this extent, there can be an overlap between misrepresentation and deceit, but the tort can also apply more widely.

B. Defences in tort

Many defences may be raised to an action in tort. In the first place, the defendant can argue simply that the alleged tort has not been committed; for example, in the tort of negligence, the defendant may claim (a) that he owed no duty of care, (b) that in any case he was not careless, and (c) that even if he was careless, his negligence did not cause the defendant's loss. Secondly, certain torts such as defamation have their own special defences. Finally, there are some 'general' defences which apply to almost all torts, and it is these which are discussed here.

Statutory authority

Nothing authorized by statute is unlawful. Much, therefore, depends upon the interpretation of the statute, which may sanction an act even though it involves what would otherwise be a tort. Thus British Rail, which has statutory authority to run the railways, could not be sued for making such noise as is an inevitable result of running a railway, even though, but for the statutory authority, this might constitute the tort of nuisance.

On the other hand, the courts are reluctant to hold that Parliament authorized a harmful act unless the statute is quite unambiguous. So, if the statute gives someone power to do something, the courts will assume that the power was given only on the understanding that it be exercised carefully.

> In *Fisher* v. *Ruislip–Northwood UDC* (1945), the local authority had, by statute, been given power to erect air-raid shelters on the highway. In the black-out, Fisher drove his motor cycle into such a shelter, and was injured. When sued for the tort of public nuisance, the Council pleaded that it had statutory authority to put up the shelter. The defence failed, because the Council could, even in the black-out, have put up small, shaded warning lights for motorists. The Council only had statutory authority on condition that it was exercised with care for the safety of others.

> Similarly, in *Metropolitan Asylum District* v. *Hill* (1881), the authority had statutory power to erect a smallpox hospital. It chose to put it in a residential part of Hampstead, and it was held that statutory authority was no defence. The authority could have exercised its powers so as to cause much less danger.

It is presumed that an act authorized by statute will be carried out with reasonable care, and statutory authority is rarely a defence if there is negligence. It should also be noted that when a statute takes away a right of action, it may at the same time make provision for some compensation to be paid.

Consent

If a person consents to suffer damage or run the risk of it, he cannot later bring an action. This defence is sometimes called voluntary assumption of risk, and expressed in the maxim *volenti non fit injuria*. The risk may be assumed by express agreement, for example, by giving consent to an operation, or may be implied from the circumstances, as by participating in a vigorous game.

> In *Hall* v. *Brooklands Racing Club* (1933), a spectator who was injured while watching a motor race was held to have agreed to take the risk of such injury.

1. It is not sufficient to prove merely that the plaintiff knew of the risk; there must be evidence of a willing consent to undergo it. For this reason the defence has normally failed when pleaded by employers in actions brought by employees for injuries suffered at work. The courts have demanded evidence of positive consent as opposed to mere acquiescence, and the nature of the employer–worker relationship has made this difficult.

In *Bowater* v. *Rowley Regis Corporation* (1944), a carter was injured by a dangerous horse which he took out under orders after protesting. It was held that he had not genuinely consented to run the risk.

In *Smith* v. *Charles Baker & Sons* (1891), a workman was injured by a falling stone when he worked under an overhead crane. He had not objected, even though he must have known that it was dangerous. He recovered damages nevertheless. His silence was evidence of acquiescence, not necessarily of consent.

2. This defence will also fail in 'rescue' cases where the plaintiff acted under a strong moral compulsion, if not a legal one.

In *Haynes* v. *Harwood* (1935), a policeman succeeded in his claim for damages when he was injured while stopping a runaway horse and cart which was endangering the safety of people, including children, in a crowded street. He would not have been injured if he had stayed out of the way, but he could hardly be said to have freely consented. The legal position would have been different if he had acted in a similar voluntary manner in a country lane with no people about.

3. *Volenti* will not be a defence to an action for breach of a strict statutory duty. Therefore, even if a factory employee consents to work an unguarded machine, he may still recover damages for any injury, if his employer is in breach of the Factories Act. The factory occupier cannot, in other words, persuade his workmen to consent to abandon their statutory protection.
4. Finally, the defence of consent may be excluded by statute on grounds of public policy. The Road Traffic Act 1972 prevents a car driver from relying upon this defence against a passenger who has suffered injury by reason of his negligent driving.

Contributory negligence

Although this defence is normally raised to actions for negligence, it is also applicable to most other torts, including breach of statutory duty, but not conversion. It arises when damage is suffered partly by the fault of the defendant and partly by the fault of the plaintiff. The defendant, therefore, attempts to reduce the damages by proving that the plaintiff was himself partly responsibe. The Law Reform (Contributory Negligence) Act 1945 provides that in such cases the court shall reduce the damages by an amount proportionate to the plaintiff's share of responsibility. Thus if damages are assessed at £100 and the plaintiff is 30 per cent to blame, he will receive only £70.

In *Sayers* v. *Harlow UDC* (1958), Mrs Sayers found herself locked in a public lavatory. Unable to summon help, she tried to climb out over the top of the door. She found this impossible and, when climbing back down, allowed her weight to rest on the toilet roll which 'true to its mechanical requirement, rotated'. Mrs Sayers fell and was injured. It was held that 75 per cent of her injury was the fault of the Council for providing a defective lock which jammed, and 25 per cent was her own fault.

In *Stapley* v. *Gypsum Mines Ltd* (1953), two miners who worked, in breach of instructions, under a dangerous roof were held 80 per cent contributorily negligent.

C. Causation and remoteness

Where liability in tort depends upon loss, the plaintiff must show that his loss was legally *caused* by the defendant's conduct. Various problems can arise.

No causal connection

The defendant cannot be held liable for something to which his conduct has not contributed. The plaintiff may be the sole author of his own misfortune.

> In *Mc Williams* v. *Sir William Arrol & Co. Ltd* (1962), a steel erector fell to his death. His employer had not provided a safety belt, but evidence was given that he would not have worn one even had it been provided. The employers were held not liable because, on this evidence, their failure was not the cause of death.

In some such situations, on the other hand, an employer may be held liable for breach of his duty to supervise and enforce the use of safety equipment (Unit 25).

Remoteness of damage

It is possible for a wrongful act to give rise to a succession of events ultimately terminating in injury to another. Although logically the damage would not have occurred but for the defendant's wrong, a break may have to be made somewhere in the long chain of consequences. Some damage is too remote, and the general rule is that only damage which was *reasonably foreseeable* at the time of the wrong is taken into account.

> In the *Wagon Mound Case* (1961), a ship negligently discharged oil while bunkering and the oil carried under a wharf. A piece of cotton waste floating on the oil was set alight by sparks from welding operations. The oil caught fire and the wharf was severely damaged. The action failed because the fire was not reasonably foreseeable, particularly since there was expert evidence that oil would not normally ignite under these conditions.

If, however, the type of damage is foreseeable, there will be liability for its full extent, even though the consequences are much more serious than could have been anticipated.

> In *Smith* v. *Leech Brain & Co. Ltd* (1962), a labourer was splashed and burned by a piece of molten metal and, because of an existing pre-malignant condition, died later of cancer. It was held that the damage was not too remote since the burn was foreseeable, even though the ultimate consequences were not.

It is sometimes said that the defendant must take his victims as he finds them, in the sense that if a (slight) injury was foreseeable and the victim has, for example, a thin skull, there will be liability for all the (serious) consequences.

The damage will be too remote if the chain of events is broken by some unforeseeable independent or new act intervening between the wrongful act and the resulting injury (*novus actus interveniens*) over which the defendant has no control. A defendant whose negligence caused a road accident will not normally be liable for further injury suffered by the victim which is caused by negligent hospital treatment. The intervening act must be a conscious and independent act. It must not be an instinctive, or even a reasoned, attempt to deal with the danger which the defendant has created.

> In *Sayers* v. *Harlow UDC*, mentioned earlier, the defendants pleaded that Mrs Sayers's attempt to climb over the door was a *novus actus interveniens*, so that it was this, and not the defective lock, which caused her injury. This defence failed.

D. Remedies

Damages

The principal remedy in tort is an award of *damages* to compensate the injured party for the loss he has suffered. The aim is to put the plaintiff back in his original position so far as money is able to do this. This can frequently be done satisfactorily where property has been damaged by assessing the value of the things destroyed or the cost of repairs.

Injuries to the person present more difficulties for much depends upon the individual in question. Fixed tariffs for compensation cannot be laid down and many things must be considered in attempting to arrive at an assessment of loss. These include pain and suffering, loss of ability to pursue previous activities or interests, loss of actual and prospective earnings, and medical expenses. By the Administration of Justice Act 1982, damages are no longer awarded for loss of expectation of life, although a plaintiff's knowledge that his life has been shortened may be relevant in assessing his pain and suffering. Payments received from other sources, such as national insurance benefits, may be set off against damages, and compensation for loss of earnings can take account of tax which would otherwise have been payable. The court can award interest on damages from the date when the cause of action arose, partly so as to deter defendants from trying to delay matters.

Although damages can still be assessed by a jury, this is usually done today by a judge sitting alone. Appeals may be made against the amount of damages awarded but the Court of Appeal is reluctant to interfere unless there has been an obvious error in the assessment.

Other remedies

In some situations, as with threatened or repeated trespass or nuisance, damages will not provide an adequate remedy. The court may then, at its discretion, grant an *injunction* ordering the defendant to refrain from committing or repeating the wrongful act. If the length of time before the case can come to trial might lead to irreparable damage being caused, it is possible to apply for an interlocutory or temporary injunction which will either be confirmed or discharged at the later trial.

E. The effect of death

At one time death effectively put an end to actions in tort by reason of two common law rules. One provided that the causing of death should not give rise to an action on the grounds that no one should profit out of another's death, and the second provided that a personal action died with the person. The effect of the first rule was the anomalous situation that a tort causing injury was actionable but not one causing death, so that it could be cheaper to kill than to maim. The resulting hardship to dependants and the increase in the number of deaths from railway accidents led to the Fatal Accidents Act 1846. This was amended several times, and replaced by a consolidating Act in 1976.

The Fatal Accidents Act 1976 now provides that, if the deceased could have sued had he lived, his dependants will have a right of action arising from his death. The right to sue is limited to certain classes of dependants, who can claim for monetary loss that they have suffered as a result of the death. Thus a wife may claim for the maintenance and support she could have expected from her husband, and a husband may claim if the death of his wife obliges him to incur expense by employing someone to look after his children.

There still remained the second rule, which prevented a claim for things such as pain and suffering which could have been claimed by the deceased had he lived. Furthermore, the death of the tortfeasor put an end to a plaintiff's claim. The increase in the number of road deaths led to the Law Reform (Miscellaneous Provisions) Act 1934 which provides that, on the death of any person, any causes of action existing in favour of or against him shall survive and exist in favour of or against his estate. Thus if *A* injures *B* and *B* dies, the estate of *B* may, in general, sue *A* for all that *B* could have claimed had he lived. On the other hand, if *A* were the one to die, his estate would be liable to *B* to the same extent as if he had lived. A few personal actions, in particular defamation, are excluded and are still brought to an end by the death of either party.

If the victim of a tort dies, there are, therefore, two possible claims, one by the dependants under the 1976 Act, as amended, and one by the estate under the 1934 Act. The two claims are quite distinct even though in practice they may be settled in the same action. If the same people are to benefit under both claims, an adjustment will be made to prevent duplication of damages. It can be to the advantage of the dependants to claim as much as possible under the Fatal Accidents Act, since these damages go directly to the dependants and not into the estate of the deceased, and are therefore not liable to capital transfer tax payable on death.

Examination questions

1. Explain, with reasons, what torts have been committed in each of the following circumstances.
    (a) Smoke from a factory chimney kills flowering plants in a nearby park.
    (b) An auctioneer sells *B*'s goods without *B*'s permission, believing that the goods belong to *A*.

(c) An office manager dismisses a clerk saying, in the presence of others, that he is a thief.

(d) An explosion in a nuclear power station releases radioactive material which kills animals on a neighbouring farm.

(e) A worker is injured by an unguarded machine.

2. *X*, who has only one arm, is injured when unroping a load of timber which has been delivered to his employer's factory. When sued for damages by *X*, the employer pleads:

   (a) that *X* was negligent in not waiting for an inspection by a competent person to see that the load was safe;

   (b) that *X* willingly accepted what he knew to be a dangerous job; and

   (c) that, but for *X*'s disability, he could have prevented the timber from falling upon him.

   Discuss the validity of each of these defences.

3. Explain the considerations which a court will take into account in fixing the amount of damages to be awarded if the following claims have been successful:

   (a) by an employee who has suffered personal injuries in an accident at work;

   (b) by the widow of an employee who has been killed in an accident at work;

   (c) by another firm whose delivery van has been damaged by the careless driving of an employee.

4. Tom carelessly drives his car into the back of Bill's car. The bumpers of the two cars are locked together, and Tom and Bill attempt to separate them. Bill is recovering from an operation and the effort causes serious injury. Advise Tom as to his liability.

5. Garish Garages Ltd overhauled a lorry belonging to Express Carriers Ltd. The work was carried out by Turner, an employee of Garish Garages Ltd. Shortly afterwards, while the lorry was being driven at an excessive speed by Driver, an employee of Express Carriers Ltd, the brakes failed because of Turner's negligent work. In the resulting accident injuries were suffered by Driver and by two pedestrians, Walker and Mort. Mort, before the accident, was in a very poor state of health and his injuries proved to be fatal. Nervy, an onlooker, fainted when he saw the accident and became seriously ill.

   Discuss the legal position.

Unit 11. The Nature of a Contract in English Law

A. Essential requirements

There are still misconceptions about this branch of law. For many people the word 'contract' suggests a visit to a solicitor's office and the signing of a formal document containing incomprehensible language. This is far from the truth. Most people make contracts every day of their lives, usually without realizing it. Every time they buy an article or pay for a service such as a haircut they are entering into a contract, while matters connected with their work, such as holidays, wages and hours, are governed in part by the contract which they have made with their employer.

Another popular belief is that a contract must be in writing. Apart from a few exceptional instances (see page 109), this is not so. Most contracts are made by word of mouth. It may be desirable to have a written agreement where a lot is at stake, or where the contract has to last for a long time, but this is only for practical purposes of proof, and is usually not legally necessary.

A contract is simply *an agreement which the law will recognize*. It is of vital importance in business life, and forms the basis of most commercial transactions, such as the sale of goods and land, the giving of credit, insurance, carriage of goods, formation and sale of business organizations, and, to some extent, employment.

What agreements will the law recognize?

The law will not recognize all agreements. The law of contract is concerned mainly with providing a framework within which business can operate; if agreements could be broken with impunity, the unscrupulous could create havoc. English law will intervene, therefore, and make the person who breaks an agreement pay compensation (damages) to the other party, but only if the agreement has the following essential features:

1. *Intention to create legal relations.* Unless the courts are satisfied that the parties intended the agreement to be legally binding, the courts will take no notice of it (see page 105).
2. *Agreement.* The courts must be satisfied that the parties had reached a firm agreement, and that they were not still negotiating. Agreement will usually be shown by the unconditional acceptance of an offer (Unit 12).
3. *Consideration.* English law will only recognize a *bargain*, not a mere promise. A contract, therefore, must be a two-sided affair, each side providing or promising to provide some consideration in exchange for what the other is to provide (see page 106). Consideration is a special feature of the common law and is not required by most European legal systems, including Scotland.
4. *Form.* Certain *exceptional* types of agreement are only valid if made in a particular form, for example in writing.
5. *Definite terms.* It must be possible for the courts to ascertain what the parties have agreed upon. If the terms are so vague as to be meaningless, the law will not recognize the agreement (Unit 12).
6. *Legality.* Certain types of agreements are so plainly 'contrary to public policy' that the law will have nothing to do with them. For example, the courts would not allow a hired murderer to recover damages if his principal refused to pay the agreed price (Unit 17).

Defective contracts

Discussion of essential requirements must also include situations where, although English law will recognize the agreement, the contract will only be given limited effect or no effect at all.

Some defects will render a contract *unenforceable*, so that although the contract does exist, neither party can *sue* the other. Certain contracts, for example, need not be *in* writing, but no party can be sued for breach in the absence of written evidence (see page 109). Goods or money which pass under an unenforceable contract are validly transferred and cannot be reclaimed, but the contract cannot be sued upon if one of the parties refuses to abide by its terms.

Other defects can render a contract *voidable*. Although English law will recognize the agreement, it will allow one of the parties to withdraw from it if he so wishes. Voidable contracts include most agreements made by minors or by persons incapacitated by drunkenness or insanity, and contracts induced by misrepresentation, duress or undue influence.

Finally, there are defects which can render a contract *void*, that is, destitute of all legal effect. The expression 'void contract' is really a contradiction in terms; if the contract is void it cannot be a contract. The expression is useful, however, to describe a situation where the parties have attempted to contract but the law will give no effect to their agreement at all. Thus a contract may be void if there is a common mistake on some fundamental issue, as where the parties agree to sell a cago which, unknown to both, has already been completely destroyed. Mistake as to the identity of the other party may also render a contract void (Unit 13).

The distinction between void and voidable contracts is important where the rights of third parties are concerned. If a contract of sale is void, ownership of the property sold will not pass to the buyer, and he cannot normally sell it to anyone else. The original seller will be able to recover the property from whoever has it. If the contract is merely voidable, it remains valid unless and until the innocent party chooses to terminate it; therefore, if the buyer resells *before* the contract is avoided, the sub-buyer becomes the owner, and can retain the property provided that he took it in good faith.

B. Intention to create legal relations

Many agreements are plainly never intended by the parties to be *legally* binding; there is no intention to take any dispute to a court of law.

In the case of agreements of a friendly, social or domestic nature there is a strong presumption that the parties did not intend to create a legal relationship. If friends agree to come to tea and they fail to turn up, or if a husband agrees to meet his wife and forgets, there can be no action for breach of contract, even though the complaining party may have incurred certain expenses.

> In *Balfour* v. *Balfour* (1919), a husband promised his wife an allowance before he left to take up a post abroad. When he stopped the payments, an action by the wife failed on the ground that this was not a binding contract but merely a domestic agreement with no legal obligations attached to it.

> Conversely, in *Simpkins* v. *Pays* (1955), three people sharing a house, the owner, her granddaughter and paying lodger, regularly entered a competition in a Sunday newspaper. The entries were sent in the name of the grandmother, but all three contributed. When an entry won, the grandmother refused to share the prize of £750. It was held that the others *were* entitled to share, because their agreement to this effect was, in the view of the court, intended to be legally binding.

On the other hand, there is a strong presumption that business agreements are intended to create legal relations. This presumption can be rebutted, but only by very strong evidence such as a clear statement in a written contract.

> In *Rose and Frank* v. *Crompton Bros. Ltd* (1925), an English company agreed to sell carbon paper in America through a New York firm. This marketing arrangement was for a renewable period of three years and provided that 'This arrangement is not entered into . . . as a form or legal agreement, and shall not be subject to legal jurisdiction in the Law Courts . . .'. Therefore, when the English company withdrew, it was not liable for breach of contract, although it was held liable to honour orders placed before withdrawal.

> Similarly, in *Appleson* v. *Littlewood Ltd* (1939), the plaintiff sued to recover money which he claimed to have won on a football pool. His action failed, because the printed entry form contained a statement that the transaction was 'binding in honour only'.

Most collective agreements between employers and trade unions as to wages and other terms of employment will not be legally binding. The parties are assumed to have intended the agreement to be no more than a broad working arrangement, not a binding contract to be subject to detailed scrutiny in the courts.

C. Consideration

As stated above, the English law of contract is concerned with *bargains*, not mere promises. Thus if *A* promises to *give* something to *B*, the law will not allow any remedy if *A* breaks his promise. On the other hand, if *B* promises to do (or does) something in return, so that *A*'s promise is dependent upon *B*'s, this reciprocal element, the *exchange* of promises, turns the arrangement into a contract. To use legal terminology, *A*'s promise (or action) is the 'consideration' for *B*'s, and vice versa. Thus the promise of the seller to deliver the car is consideration for the buyer's promise to pay the agreed price.

Consideration may, therefore, be described broadly as something given, promised or done in exchange. The act, forbearance or promise of each party is the price for which the promise of the other is bought.

Consideration can be *executory* or *executed*. Executory consideration is a promise yet to be fulfilled, and most contracts start in this way, with the consideration executory on both sides. Executed consideration is the completed performance of one side of the bargain.

The existence of consideration

Consideration must exist and have some value; otherwise there is no contract. The following have no value and cannot, therefore, constitute consideration so as to render a promise actionable:

1. *Past consideration*. Something already done and completed by *B* at the time when *A* makes a promise to him cannot operate as consideration. *A* already has the benefit of what *B* has done, and therefore receives nothing in exchange. Thus if, unasked, I paint my neighbour's house while he is away and, upon his return, he promises me £100 for doing so, I have no remedy if he later refuses to pay.

   In *Eastwood* v. *Kenyon* (1840), the plaintiff had been the guardian of a Miss Sutcliffe, and had spent money on her upkeep and education. When she came of age, the girl promised to repay her guardian, and her husband, Kenyon, repeated this promise when she married. It was held, however, that the guardian could not recover damages when these promises were broken, because the consideration for them was past. Any moral obligation to repay was irrelevant.

   Similarly, in *Roscorla* v. *Thomas* (1842), *after* Roscorla had bought a horse, the seller promised that it was sound and free from vice. It was held that Roscorla could not sue for breach of this undertaking, for which no new consideration had been given. (This would apply equally to promises made by a car salesman *after* the sale.)

A contrast must be drawn with those situations where, although the actual promise to pay a specific sum is made after the work has been carried out, there was an implied promise to pay (a reasonable sum) before the work was begun. If my neighbour *asks* me to paint his house, he may be impliedly promising to pay me for my work.

> In *Stewart* v. *Casey* (1892), Stewart, who was joint owner of some patents, asked Casey to promote them. *After* Casey had done so successfully, Stewart promised him a share in them. It was held that this promise was binding, and that the consideration was not past. The original request carried with it an implied promise to pay a reasonable amount for Casey's services. The subsequent promise to share in the profits merely put a figure to the original promise, which was given before Casey carried out his side of the bargain.

2. *A promise to perform an existing obligation.* This is usually not consideration, because the promisor is only giving what he was already bound to give.
   (a) This applies particularly if the promisor merely promises afresh to perform an existing contract *with the promisee*. Therefore, if a debtor promises to pay part of his debt in consideration of the creditor releasing him from the rest, the release is not binding. If *A* is owed £10 by *B* and agrees to take £9 in full satisfaction, *A* can still go back and demand the remaining £1. *B* gave no consideration for the promise to release him from the £1.

   > In *D & C Builders Ltd* v. *Rees* (1966), the defendant owed £482 to the building company for work carried out, and refused to pay. Eventually the builders agreed to take a cheque for £300 in full satisfaction of the debt. It was held that they were still entitled to demand the remaining £182, because there was no consideration for the earlier promise to settle for less.

   The promise to forgo part of the debt will be binding only if the debtor gives some *new* consideration, by doing or promising something which he was not previously bound to do: for example paying the debt earlier than he was bound to do, or at a place other than where he was bound to do. These rules apply equally to obligations other than debts.
   (b) The position is different as regards a promise to perform a contract which the promisor already has *with a third party*. This *can* be binding. The promisor is undertaking a new duty to the promisee in addition to the one which he has to the third party. He now has two obligations, not just one, and this is the consideration.

   > In *Pao On* v. *Lau Yiu Long* (1979), for example, the defendants gave Pao On a guarantee in consideration of Pao On promising to carry out a contract which Pao On had *with Fu Chip Ltd*. Pao On's promise was good consideration for the guarantee.

   (c) A promise to perform *an existing public duty* will not usually be consideration. For example, it would be contrary to public policy to allow a public official to take (and, therefore, possibly demand) private payment for carrying out his public duty. However, a promise to do *more* than his duty *can* be enough.

107

In *Glasbrook Bros. Ltd* v. *Glamorgan County Council* (1925), the police were offered £2200 to provide a special guard for a coal mine during a strike. It was held that they could recover this amount when the owners later refused to pay, because the special guard went beyond the ordinary police duty to protect property. (Similarly, police authorities receive payment from football clubs for providing officers inside the ground, and could sue for this sum if it were not paid.)

3. *A promise made to a third party.* Normally, only a person who has given consideration may sue on a contract. For example, *A* may promise to pay £1 to *B*, if *B* will give a book to *C*. If *B* refuses to deliver the book, *A* may sue, but not *C*, who has given no consideration and is not a party to the contract (Unit 16).

4. *Vague promises*, which are incapable of monetary value, will not be consideration. A promise to show natural love and affection or to behave as a good son should behave will be of no effect in the law of contract.

The adequacy of consideration

Provided that the consideration has some value in the monetary sense, the court will not concern itself with whether or not the value is adequate, for the value of a particular article or service is largely a matter of opinion and for the parties to decide. The court will not make a man's bargain for him. The price paid may be relevant in determining whether goods are 'merchantable' at that price (Unit 18), but this does not directly affect the existence of the contract. The fact that goods are sold for a very high or low price may also be evidence, but no more than evidence, of fraud.

Promises made by deed

There is one major exception to the rules relating to consideration. Where a person embodies his promise in a formal document called a *deed*, it can be enforced against him whether or not the promisee has given any consideration. A deed is a document signed by the person making the promise, and 'sealed' and 'delivered' by him. Promises made by deed are sometimes called *specialty* contracts, as opposed to *simple* contracts when a deed is not used.

Equitable estoppel

Although a promise made without consideration cannot be sued upon, and will not amount to a contract, it may have limited effect as a *defence*. If *A* promises not to enforce his rights against *B*, and the promise is intended to be binding, intended to be acted upon, and is in fact acted upon by *B*, then *A* may be estopped from later bringing any action inconsistent with his promise. This defence has been called promissory estoppel.

In *Central London Property Trust* v. *High Trees House* (1947), the lease of a block of flats proved unprofitable to the tenant because of the war, and the landlord made a written promise to reduce the rent while the war lasted. After the war, the landlord withdrew this promise and started to charge the full rent again. It was held that he was free to do this for the future, because no consideration had been given for the wartime promise. On the other hand, the court said, *obiter*, that the landlord could not have recovered the full rent for the period between making his promise and the end of the war since the tenant had relied on the landlord's promise.

This defence is limited, and only applies where it would be unfair and inequitable to allow the plaintiff to succeed in spite of his promise.

> In *D & C Builders Ltd* v. *Rees* (above), it was also suggested that the builders should be estopped from going back on their promise to take £300 in full satisfaction. This defence failed because it was not grossly unfair to demand the balance. If anyone it was Rees who was unfair, in failing to pay the full amount and putting pressure on the builders, who had financial difficulties, to settle for less. Certainly Rees had not been made to act to *his* detriment as a result of the promise.

D. Form

In general, the form in which a contract is made does not matter and will have no effect upon the validity of the contract. However, there are certain exceptions.

Some contracts must be by deed. Promises for no consideration, and some bills of sale (mortgages of goods), are void unless in this form. Conveyances of land and leases for over three years must be completed by deed.

Contracts which must be in writing, but not necessarily by deed, include bills of exchange, cheques and promissory notes, contracts of marine insurance, the transfer of shares in a company, and legal assignment of debts. Absence of writing will render such contracts *void*. Hire-purchases and other regulated agreements which come within the Consumer Credit Act 1974 may be *unenforceable* against the borrower unless made in writing and unless they include the information required under the Act.

There is another group of contracts which, although not required to be in writing, will be unenforceable in the courts unless there is written evidence of the essential terms. This requirement derives historically from the Statute of Frauds 1677, and affects only two main types of contract today: contracts of guarantee, and contracts relating to land. This second category is now covered by section 40(1) of the Law of Property Act 1925, which substantially re-enacted part of the Statute of Frauds. This section provides that:

> 'no action may be brought upon any contract for the sale or other disposition of land or any interest in land, unless the agreement upon which such action is brought, or some memorandum or note thereof, is in writing and signed by the party to be charged or by some other person thereunto by him lawfully authorized'.

The written 'note or memorandum' which must be produced as evidence can come from correspondence or any other papers, whether made at or after the time of the contract. The writing must contain the names of the parties, or otherwise identify them, identify the subject-matter, and in relation to land, state the price or other consideration. It must also have been signed by the party against whom the evidence is to be used or by his authorized agent.

The absence of written evidence does not affect the validity of the contract, but simply makes it unenforceable in the courts. A party can obtain rights under an unenforceable agreement so long as he does not have to *sue*; thus a vendor can keep the deposit paid by a prospective purchaser of a house should the latter default, whether or not there is any written evidence.

In relation to land, there is one important way of escaping this requirement of written evidence, namely through the equitable doctrine of part performance which is preserved by section 40(2) of the Law of Property Act 1925. The old Court of Chancery could not overrule a statute, but it would not allow it to be used as an instrument of fraud and could intervene if one party tried to take unfair advantage of the lack of written evidence. Where certain conditions are satisfied, the court may give the remedy of specific performance compelling the promisor to carry out his promise, notwithstanding that there is no written note or memorandum. The conditions are:

1. There must have been some act of part performance by the plaintiff, so as to carry out part of his side of the bargain.
2. The probable explanation of that act must be a contract such as is alleged to exist. What has been done must prove the existence of some contract and be consistent with the contract alleged.
3. It must, in effect, be fraudulent of the defendant to try to rely on the absence of written evidence to escape liability.
4. Specific performance must be possible.
5. There must be sufficient oral evidence.

> In *Rawlinson* v. *Ames* (1925), Rawlinson orally agreed to lease his flat to the defendant and, at her request, carried out alterations. There was evidence that she gave continuing instructions as to what should be done. It was held that the only reasonable explanation for this was the existence of a contract such as Rawlinson alleged, and he therefore obtained an order for specific performance of the agreement even though there was no written evidence.

It must be remembered that the only remedy which can be given in these circumstances is specific performance (Unit 15). In the absence of written evidence, damages will not be awarded in the case of contracts to which section 40 applies.

Examination questions

1. (a) What essential features must be present in order to constitute a valid contract?
   (b) Distinguish, with examples, between void, voidable and unenforceable contracts.
2. Explain whether or not Henry has a remedy in respect of each of the following agreements.
   (a) His daughter has a knitting machine upon which she makes jerseys in her spare time. Henry promises to sell these garments in his shop and advertises them accordingly. His daughter then gives up knitting and fails to deliver any.

    (b) He agrees to buy a consignment of socks from a wholesaler. The contract contains a clause excluding the jurisdiction of the courts. The wholesaler fails to deliver the goods.

    (c) He enters into an agreement with a trade union regarding a productivity bonus scheme for his shop assistants. The union fails to honour the agreement.

3. (a) 'The rules of consideration ensure that English law only recognizes agreements which have a business element in them.' To what extent is this true?

    (b) Simple asks his friend, Sharp, a car dealer, if he will sell his (Simple's) car. After Sharp has sold the car, Simple promises to pay him £20 for doing so. Simple later refuses to pay. Advise Sharp.

4. Explain whether Paul is required by the law of contract to fulfil his promises in the following situations:

    (a) He promises to sell an expensive car to Arthur for £10.

    (b) He returns home to find that his house windows have been cleaned by Bernard and he promises to pay Bernard £1 for his work.

    (c) He agrees to pay Charles £100 for painting his house within three weeks and he later promises a further £20 if Charles finishes the job on time.

    (d) He promises to deliver goods to David in return for a payment to him of £50 by Eric.

    (e) He promises to release Frank from a debt of £500 if Frank pays him £400.

5. (a) In what circumstances will the validity or enforceability of a contract depend upon the form in which it is made?

    (b) Lester orally agreed to lease a shop to Thomas for the latter to use for the sale of fresh fish. At the same time Lester promised to carry out some electrical work and install some refrigeration to make the premises suitable for the business in question. During these alterations, Thomas called in from time to time and made suggestions as to what should be done. Later, Lester received a better offer for the premises and told Thomas that the lease was cancelled. Advise Thomas.

Unit 12. Agreement

Unit 11 was concerned with some of the essential features which must be present in an agreement before English law will recognize it as a contract. This unit is concerned with how and when agreement is reached.

There is a difference between the situation where negotiations are in progress and the situation where a binding agreement has been reached. During negotiations, each side is free to withdraw without any sanction; after agreement has been concluded, withdrawal can amount to breach of contract. Agreement is usually shown in English law by the unconditional acceptance of an offer, and these elements will be examined in turn.

A. Offer

This is a statement of the terms on which the offeror is willing to be bound. If the offer is accepted as it stands, agreement is made.

An offer may be made to a specific person and only open to him to accept, as where *A* offers to sell his car to *B* for a stated price. An offer may be made to a class of persons, any one of whom may accept, as where the offer is only open to employees of a company or members of a particular club. An offer may, sometimes, be made to the whole world, as where the owner offers a reward to anyone who returns his lost canary.

The following are *not* offers in this legal sense:

1. *A mere invitation to treat.* This is an indication that a person is willing to enter into negotiations, but *not* that he is yet willing to be bound by the terms mentioned.

   In *Gibson* v. *Manchester City Council* (1979), Mr Gibson, a council tenant, received a letter from the Council saying that the Council '*may* be prepared to sell the house to you at the purchase price of . . . £2180'. Mr Gibson formally applied to buy at this price, but meanwhile Council policy was changed and it refused to sell. It was held that the Council's letter was only an invitation to treat, not an offer. Therefore, there was no contract.

Catalogues or circulars advertising goods for sale constitute mere invitations. The same applies when a large undertaking invites tenders for the supply of goods or services. A company prospectus which invites investors to buy its shares is also an invitation to treat and not an offer, because the company can still refuse to allot the shares to those who apply for them.

In many cases where a person indicates that he is willing to deal with anyone in the world, as in the examples just given, this will be treated as a mere invitation to treat; otherwise there would be an impossible situation if, for example, an advertisement to sell a car were held to be a firm offer, and 20 acceptances were received. Only in cases where the advertiser very clearly intended to be bound will an advertisement be treated as a firm offer.

Perhaps the best examples of invitations to treat are goods in a shop window, even with price tickets attached. The shopkeeper does not undertake to sell the goods. They are on display merely to invite customers to come in and offer to buy at the price shown. The shopkeeper can always refuse, although obviously he rarely does so. The same rule applies to the display of goods in a self-service store.

> In *Pharmaceutical Society of Great Britain* v. *Boots Cash Chemists* (1953), a criminal case, customers selected pharmaceutical goods from self-service counters, and paid later at the cash desk, where a pharmacist was in attendance with the cashier. It was held that the display on the shelves was a mere invitation to treat. The customer made the offer when he took the goods to the cashier, who could always refuse to sell. Therefore, the pharmacist was present where the sale took place.

2. *A 'mere puff' or boast*, which no one would take too seriously, such as a claim on the packet that 'Brand X washes whitest', will not be treated as a firm offer. There can, however, be a narrow borderline between mere boasts, and promises which a reasonable man would take seriously.

> In *Carlill* v. *Carbolic Smoke Ball Co.* (1893), the defendants advertised that they would pay £100 to anyone who caught influenza after using their smoke balls, and that, as evidence of their sincerity, they had deposited £1000 with a named bank. Mrs Carlill followed their instructions, but still caught influenza, and consequently claimed £100. One of the many defences put forward was that the advertisement was not an offer. It was held that, in the circumstances, it was an offer. A reasonable person would take the promise seriously, and assume that the advertiser intended to be bound on the terms stated.

3. *A declaration of intention* is, similarly, not intended to form the basis of a contract, and is not an offer.

> In *Harris* v. *Nickerson* (1873), an auction sale was advertised and later cancelled, and the plaintiff, who had travelled to the place of sale, claimed his travelling expenses as damages. His action failed, for the advertisement was not an offer which he could accept by making the journey.

113

4. *Merely giving information* is not an offer.

> In *Harvey* v. *Facey* (1893), the plaintiff telegraphed 'will you sell us Bumper Hall Pen? Telegraph lowest price', and the reply was 'lowest price for Bumper Hall Pen £900'. This was held to be merely an answer to a request for information, and not an offer which could be accepted.

An offer must be communicated to the other party

Unless the offeree is aware of the offer he is unable to accept it. If *X* finds a wallet and returns it to the owner, he cannot claim any reward that may have been offered if he had no previous knowledge of this.

> In *Taylor* v. *Laird* (1856), the captain of a ship resigned his command in a foreign port, but later helped to work the ship home. The owners were entitled to refuse payment for these services for, by the failure to communicate the offer to them, the owners had no option of either accepting or refusing.

Duration of the offer

An offer does not continue indefinitely. While the offeror may be content *at the moment* to deal on the terms of the offer, circumstances may change. Once an offer has come to an end, it can no longer be accepted. It can end in the following ways:

1. It is possible for the offeror to *revoke* or withdraw his offer at any time up to acceptance. He is entitled to do this even if he has promised to keep the offer open for a specified time, unless the offeree had paid a sum of money or given some other consideration in return for such a promise (sometimes known as 'buying an option'). Even then, the offer can be withdrawn before the agreed time, but withdrawal will be a breach of this subsidiary contract to keep open the negotiations.

> In *Routledge* v. *Grant* (1828), Grant offered to buy Routledge's house, and gave him six weeks to decide whether to accept his offer. Before six weeks had elapsed, Grant withdrew his offer. He was held entitled to do so at any time before acceptance.

Revocation is only effective if it is communicated to the offeree, either by express words or by conduct which shows a clear intention to revoke. Selling the goods elsewhere would be an example of such conduct, but this will only revoke the offer when the first prospective buyer learns of the sale. Communication can be by the seller himself, or by another reliable source.

> In *Dickinson* v. *Dodds* (1876), the defendant had offered to sell a house to the plaintiff. Before the plaintiff accepted, the defendant sold the house to someone else. The plaintiff learned of this from a friend, Berry. It was held that, since the plaintiff had heard of the revocation from a reliable source, the original offer to him was revoked, and he could not now accept it. (On the other hand, a mere rumour would be much less likely to amount to reliable communication of revocation.)

2. An offer will *lapse* if the offeror imposes a time limit for acceptance, and the other party does not accept within that time. If no express time limit is imposed, the offer

will lapse after a *reasonable* time. What is reasonable will depend on all the circumstances.

> In *Ramsgate Victoria Hotel Co.* v. *Montefiore* (1866), an investor offered in June to buy shares in the plaintiff company. He heard nothing until November, by which time he no longer wanted the shares. It was held that it was now too late for the company to accept his offer.

3. The *death* of either party before acceptance will normally terminate the offer, certainly from the moment when the other party learns of the death and, when the identity of the other party is vital, from the time of death.

4. Once the offeree has *rejected* an offer he cannot later go back and purport to accept it. A counter-offer will operate as a rejection.

> In *Hyde* v. *Wrench* (1840), an offer was made to sell a farm for £1000. A counter-offer of £950 was made and refused, whereupon the buyer tried to accept the original offer of £1000. It was held that the seller could refuse this, because the original offer had been rejected.

Acceptance subject to conditions will also be a rejection, because the offeree is trying to introduce new terms into the bargain.

> In *Neale* v. *Merrett* (1930), the defendant offered to sell land to the plaintiff for £280. The plaintiff 'accepted' this offer, sent a cheque for £80, and promised to pay the rest by instalments of £50. It was held that there was no contract; the purported acceptance introduced credit terms which the seller did not want.

Rejection, like offer and revocation, must be communicated, and is only effective from the moment when the offeree learns of it. If, therefore, the offeree sends a letter of rejection, but then changes his mind and telephones acceptance before the rejection arrives, there will be a valid contract.

5. An offer may be *conditional* upon other circumstances. If the conditions are not fulfilled, the offer will lapse. The conditions may be express or implied.

> In *Financing Ltd* v. *Stimson* (1962), a customer offered to take a car on hire-purchase from Financings Ltd. Before the offer was accepted, the car was stolen from the dealer's garage where it was being kept, and badly damaged. Unaware of this, Financings Ltd purported to accept the offer. It was held that the company could no longer do so. The customer's offer was subject to the implied condition that the car remain in substantially the same state between offer and acceptance.

6. *Acceptance*, by completing the contract, will bring the offer to an end. If an offer, capable of acceptance by only one person, is made to a group of people and one accepts, the offer then ceases to exist so far as the rest of the group is concerned.

B. Acceptance

This must take place while the offer is still open. It must be an absolute and unqualified acceptance of the offer, as it stands, with any terms that may be attached. As we have seen, anything else will amount to rejection.

On occasions, an acceptance may be made subject to a written or formal agreement. It is then a question of construction whether the parties intend to be bound by the initial agreement, and the writing is only for the purpose of recording this, or whether there is no intention to be bound until the more formal agreement is made. This arises frequently in contracts for the sale of land, where it is now well established that certain phrases, particularly 'subject to contract', denote the second of these alternatives. Since an agreement 'subject to contract' does not bind either party, its value may be questioned; it does, however, show that the parties are sufficiently interested to pursue the matter further.

Acceptance completes the contract, and the place where acceptance is made is, therefore, the place of the contract. This rule may be important in determining in which County Court an action for breach should be brought. If negotiations take place between parties in different countries, the rule may help to determine which system of law applies.

The manner of acceptance

Acceptance may take the form of words, spoken or written, or it may be implied by conduct, as where the offeree performs some specific act required by the offeror. Mere mental assent is insufficient, nor is it possible in English law to dispense with acceptance altogether. There must be some positive act of acceptance, and mere silence will never be enough.

> In *Felthouse* v. *Bindley* (1863), negotiations were taking place regarding the price of a horse. The plaintiff eventually wrote, 'If I hear no more about him, I consider the horse mine at £30 15s.' The defendant did not reply. It was held that, although he had intended to accept and sell at this price, his silence could not constitute acceptance, and there was therefore no sale.

Thus where unsolicited goods arrive through the post with a note saying that unless they are returned within a specified time the recipient will be bound to pay the price, this note can be safely ignored. So long as the recipient does not treat the goods as his, by using or deliberately destroying them, his silence will not amount to acceptance. Indeed, under the Unsolicited Goods and Services Act 1971, the recipient will become owner of the goods as against the sender, unless the sender collects them within six months; the recipient can, by notice to the sender, reduce this period to 30 days. (Where the seller is a dealer, it can also be a criminal offence for him to demand payment.)

Where two businesses contract, an interesting 'battle of forms' can sometimes arise.

> In *Butler Machine Tool Co. Ltd* v. *Ex-Cell-O Corporation* (*England*) *Ltd* (1979) the plaintiff offered to sell tools to the defendant and sent a printed copy of the plaintiff's standard terms. The defendant 'accepted' this offer, enclosing a copy of the *defendant's* standard terms, which differed slightly from the plaintiff's. The plaintiff acknowledged this acceptance by sending back a tear-off slip from the defendant's copy (which probably was not read). It was held that the defendant's 'acceptance' was really a counter-offer. The plaintiff had accepted this counter-offer by sending back the tear-off slip and going on to perform the contract. When a dispute later arose, the defendant's terms were, therefore, applied.

Communication of acceptance

As a general rule, acceptance must be communicated to the offeror. There is no contract until the offeror knows that his offer has been accepted. The acceptance must, moreover, be communicated by the offeree himself or his authorized agent. Unlike revocation, acceptance cannot be communicated by an unauthorized third party, however reliable.

> In *Powell* v. *Lee* (1908), the plaintiff had applied for a post as headmaster. The school managers decided to appoint him, and one of the managers, without authority, told him this unofficially. Later the managers changed their minds. It was held that they were free to do so; there was no contract with Powell, because acceptance had not been communicated by the managers.

There are two main exceptions to the rule that acceptance is only effective on communication:

1. *The offeror may dispense with communication*, and indicate that the offeree should, if he wishes to accept, simply carry out his side of the bargain without bothering to inform the offeror. Thus if a customer wrote ordering coal and, without further communication, the coal was delivered in accordance with the order, the delivery would be acceptance of the offer to buy.

   > In *Carlill* v. *Carbolic Smoke Ball Co.* (1893), another defence raised was that Mrs Carlill had not communicated to the company that she intended to use the smoke ball and catch influenza. This defence also failed; the nature of the offer made communication of acceptance inappropriate.

2. *Where the posting rule applies*, a letter of acceptance, properly addressed and stamped, is effective from the moment of posting, even if never arrives. Three points must be emphasized about the posting rule. In the first place, the rule applies only where it must have been in the contemplation of the parties that the post would be used as a means of communicating the acceptance. This will not always be the case; if all the negotiations have taken place by telephone, and the offeror clearly expects a reply by telephone, a letter of acceptance might not be effective until it arrived. Similarly, the posting rule would not apply if the offeror made it plain that he was only prepared to be bound when he *knew* of the acceptance.

   > In *Holwell Securities Ltd* v. *Hughes* (1974), an offer to sell required that acceptance be made 'by notice in writing to the intending vendor' within six months. Notice was posted but never arrived. It was held that there was no contract. The words of the offer showed that the offeror was not prepared to be bound until he *received* the written notice.

Secondly, there must obviously be some evidence of posting. It is not enough to give the letter to some other person to post, or even to hand it to a postman; it must be put into the hands of the postal authorities in the normal way. Finally, the posting rule applies only to acceptance; an offer, or a letter of revocation or rejection, will be effective only on arrival.

117

In *Byrne* v. *Van Tienhoven* (1880), a firm in Cardiff offered by letter to sell tin plate to a firm in New York. Later, the firm sent another letter revoking this offer, but while this was in transit and before its delivery, the New York firm posted a letter of acceptance. It was held that the parties clearly intended the use of the post to communicate acceptance, and posting the letter of acceptance, therefore, brought the contract into existence, since this was done before the revocation arrived.

These rules also applied to telegrams, but not to the use of the telephone or telex. In these latter cases, the communication is virtually instantaneous and is inoperative unless and until it reaches the other party.

In *Entores* v. *Miles Far East Corporation* (1955), an acceptance sent by telex from Amsterdam to London was held to be effective only when it arrived in London, so that the contract, being made in England, could be brought before the English courts.

C. Certainty of terms

Even where offer and acceptance are apparently complete, there may still be no agreement. There can be no contract at all if it is not possible to say *what* the parties have agreed upon because the terms are too uncertain. In particular, this will be the case where the parties have still left essential terms to be settled between them. They are still at the stage of negotiation, and an agreement to agree in future is not a contract.

In *Scammell* v. *Ouston* (1941), Ouston agreed to take a van 'on the understanding that the balance of the purchase price can be had on hire-purchase terms over a period of two years'. It was held that this contract was void for uncertainty, because no one could say *what* hire-purchase terms were envisaged.

In *King's Motors (Oxford) Ltd* v. *Lax* (1969), an option to renew a lease 'at such rental as may be agreed upon between the parties' was similarly held void.

On the other hand, this rule is subject to some qualifications:

1. The parties may be bound if the unsettled terms are only part of a larger agreement, the rest of which is already being or has been performed, and which is agreed to be binding. This is particularly so if there has been some provision for arbitration to settle potential disputes.

    In *Foley* v. *Classique Coaches Ltd* (1934), a garage sold land to the bus company on condition (*inter alia*) that the company buy all of its petrol from the garage 'at a price to be agreed between the parties . . . from time to time'. A later clause provided that any dispute as to the subject-matter or content of the agreement should be referred to arbitration. The land was conveyed, and the bus company duly bought its petrol for three years, but then claimed that it need no longer do so. It was held bound. A reasonable price could be settled under the arbitration clause.

    In *Sudbrook Trading Estate Ltd* v. *Eggleton* (1982), the plaintiff was tenant of some land, but had the right to buy it before his lease expired. The price was to be fixed by two arbitrators, one appointed by the landlord, the other by the tenant. The landlord refused to appoint an arbitrator. The House of Lords held that since the parties had clearly intended to be bound at the outset, and were already performing the lease, the *court* would make alternative arrangements to settle the sale price, and would order the transfer.

2. If the parties have agreed criteria according to which the price can be calculated, or have had previous dealings similar to the present transaction, the courts can use these matters to ascertain the terms of the contract.

> In *Hillas & Co. Ltd* v. *Arcos Ltd* (1932), an option to buy 100 000 standards of soft-wood goods in 1931, without mention of detailed terms, was held binding because it was assumed to be on terms similar to those agreed in previous dealings between the parties.

> In *Brown* v. *Gould* (1972), an option was given to renew a lease 'at a rent to be fixed having regard to the market value of the premises at the time of exercising this option taking into account . . . structural improvements made by the Tenant . . .'. This was held binding, because the court could, if necessary, discover the market price and the value of the improvements from independent valuers.

3. If only a fairly minor term is meaningless, it may simply be ignored, and the rest of the contract treated as binding.

> In *Nicolene Ltd* v. *Simmonds* (1953), the defendant agreed to sell 3000 tons of steel bars at £45 per ton, and added that he assumed that 'the usual conditions of acceptance apply'. There were no usual conditions. The court held that he was bound; the rest of the agreement made good sense, and the meaningless phrase could, therefore, be ignored.

Examination questions

1. (a) Explain and illustrate the distinction between an offer and an invitation to make an offer in the formation of a contract.
   (b) Brenda visits a self-service store and selects several articles which she places in the wire basket provided. She then changes her mind about some of these articles and replaces them on the shelves. The manager of the store claims that she has purchased the goods by placing them in the basket and that she must pay for them. Advise Brenda.

2. Outline the legal position of the parties and the principles of law involved in the following circumstances:
   (a) *A* offers to sell a lorry to *B* who states that he will accept the offer if *A* will undertake to pay for any repairs that may be necessary during the next three months. *A* refuses this condition. *B* then states that he will buy the lorry without insisting upon this requirement, but *A* replies to the effect that he no longer wishes to sell.
   (b) *C* offers to sell a van to *D* and states that he will give *D* a week to decide whether or not he wishes to buy. After three days, *D* is informed by *X* that *C* has sold the van to *E*. *D* writes to *C* accepting his offer.

3. (a) When may a contract be formed without the acceptance of the offer being specifically communicated to the offeror?

(b) Williams, a wholesaler, offered to sell a consignment of cheap tinned fruit to Roger, a retailer. Roger intended to accept this offer, but forgot to inform Williams. Roger did, however, arrange for the printing of leaflets advertising the sale of this fruit in his shop. Williams saw one of the leaflets when he happened to visit the printer. Williams now believes that he can obtain a better price for the fruit and has written to Roger withdrawing his offer. Advise Roger.

4. (a) Outline the rules applicable to the formation of contracts made by letters through the post. Do these rules apply equally to contracts made by telephone and telex?

(b) Martin telephones Nigel and offers to sell him a lorry. Nigel accepts the offer but Martin does not hear because of a bad line. Later, Nigel changes his mind and writes to Martin saying that he does not wish to buy the lorry. Advise Martin.

5. (a) To what extent, if at all, is it possible for parties to enter into a contract and leave some of the terms to be decided at a later date?

(b) Merchant bought the whole of Archer's 1984 potato crop at the prevailing market price. The contract also gave Merchant an option to buy the 1985 crop without mention of the price or any other terms. Merchant now wishes to exercise this option at the current market price. Archer, who has had a better offer from elsewhere, refuses to sell.

Discuss.

Unit 13. Matters which Affect the Validity of Contracts

Some contracts which appear perfectly valid may nevertheless be wholly or partly ineffective because of some defect when they were formed. The vitiating factors discussed in this unit are mistake, misrepresentation, duress, undue influence, and lack of capacity in the formation of the contract.

A. Mistake

The general rule is that mistake does *not* affect the validity of a contract. For example, if a man is mistaken as to the nature or value of what he buys, this is simply his misfortune. The law will not help him unless he has been misled by the other party (see Misrepresentation, page 124).

> In *Leaf* v. *International Galleries* (1950), a drawing was sold which both seller and buyer believed to be by Constable. In fact it was not. The contract was not affected by this mistake, because each side intended to deal with the physical thing sold; they were simply mistaken as to its quality and value.

A further preliminary point is that mistake of *law* will never affect the validity of contract. Ignorance of the law is no defence! In certain circumstances, mistake of *fact* may affect the contract and, if sufficiently serious, render the contract void.

Mistakes of fact which render a contract void

1. *Mistakes concerning the subject-matter of the contract*, for example the property sold, can render the contract void if sufficiently serious. A mere mistake as to the nature or value of the subject-matter will not be enough (see above).

121

A mutual mistake as to the identity of the subject-matter will render the contract void. A mutual mistake will occur where the parties are, unknown to each other, thinking about different things. Neither is right, neither wrong; they are simply at cross purposes, and have never really agreed.

In *Raffles* v. *Wichelhaus* (1864), a cargo of cotton was described as being on the *SS Peerless* from Bombay. There were in fact two ships of that name sailing from Bombay with an interval of three months between them. The seller intended to put the cargo on the second ship, while the buyer expected it on the first. The contract was held void.

A fundamental common mistake about the subject-matter will also render the contract void. A common mistake occurs where both parties are under the same misapprehension; both are wrong. The clearest instance of this is where, unknown to both parties, the subject-matter does not exist.

In *Couturier* v. *Hastie* (1856), a contract was made for the sale of a cargo of wheat which, unknown to both seller and buyer, no longer existed. The wheat had gone bad during the voyage, and the captain, in exercise of his powers, had re-sold it. The seller was not, therefore, liable for non-delivery.

Similarly, in *Galloway* v. *Galloway* (1914), a separation agreement between 'husband' and 'wife', disposing of property between them, was held void when it was discovered that they had never legally been married.

2. *Mistaken signing of written documents* may, exceptionally, be a nullity. Three elements must be present if the contract is to be void: the signing must have been fraudulently induced, the mistake must be fundamental, and the signer must prove that he or she has not been negligent. A person attempting to avoid liability under a contract on these grounds is said to plead *non est factum* (it is not my act).

In *Foster* v. *Mackinnon* (1869), a rogue induced Mackinnon, an old gentlemen with weak sight, to sign a document which Mackinnon thought to be a guarantee. In fact he was endorsing a bill of exchange for £3000 thereby incurring personal liability for this amount. It was held that, so long as he had not been negligent, he was not liable on the bill.

Conversely, in *Saunders* v. *Anglia Building Society* (1971), a Mrs Gallie intended to assign the lease of her house so as to enable her nephew to borrow money. The assignment was prepared fraudulently by a rogue, Lee, who had promised to arrange the loan. The document which she signed transferred the lease to Lee himself, who mortgaged it to the building society and departed with the proceeds. Mrs Gallie and her nephew received nothing. Mrs Gallie claimed that the original assignment was void for mistake; she had not read it because her glasses were broken, and she had not realized its effect. Her plea failed. She had intended to assign her lease, and her mistake as to the way in which she was assigning it was not so fundamental as to avoid the contract.

3. *A mistake by one party as to the identity of the other* may sometimes invalidate the contract. If *A* contracts with *B* under the impression that he is really dealing with *C*, the contract will be void if *A* can prove that his mistake was material; he intended to deal with *C* and would not have dealt with anyone else. It may be very difficult for *A* to prove this, particularly where the parties dealt with each other face to face.

In *Phillips* v. *Brooks* (1919), a rogue bought a ring in a jeweller's shop. He then persuaded the jeweller that he was Sir George Bullough, and was, therefore, allowed to take away the ring in return for a cheque. The cheque was dishonoured, and the ring was eventually traced to a pawnbroker. The jeweller claimed that his contract with the rogue was void for mistake, but his claim failed. The jeweller had dealt with the man facing him; the question of identity was only raised when it came to payment.

Again, in *Lewis* v. *Averay* (1972), Lewis sold and parted with his car to a rogue who pretended to be Richard Greene, the film actor. The rogue paid by cheque which was dishonoured, and then re-sold the car to Averay. The contract between Lewis and the rogue was not void; Lewis could not prove that he was willing to sell only to Richard Greene and to no one else.

Where the parties did not deal with each other face to face, it may be easier for *A* to prove that the mistake was material.

In *Cundy* v. *Lindsay* (1878), a rogue called Blenkarn ordered linen by post from Lindsay & Co. by pretending to be Blenkiron, a reputable dealer. Blenkarn re-sold the linen to Cundy. Lindsay & Co. were able to recover it because the contract with Blenkarn was void. They satisfied the court that they intended to deal only with Blenkiron.

In *King's Norton Metal Co. Ltd* v. *Edridge, Merrett & Co. Ltd* (1897), on the other hand, the plaintiffs sold goods to a firm called 'Hallam & Co.' which placed an order by post. Hallam & Co. turned out to be a complete fiction; the real buyer was a rogue called Wallis. The contract was not void. If the plaintiffs were willing to deal with an unknown company, without checking, then the identity of the buyer was clearly not sufficiently material.

It will be apparent that most of the cases on mistake of identity are actions between two innocent parties. *A* will have parted with the goods to a rogue, who will have re-sold to *X* and departed with the proceeds. If the contract between *A* and the rogue was void for mistake, *A* can recover the goods or their value from *X* by an action for the tort of conversion (Unit 10); otherwise *X* will normally be entitled to keep the property.

Other consequences of mistake

Where there is a mistake as to the subject-matter, but the mistake is not so fundamental as to render the contract void, the court *may* nevertheless allow one party the equitable remedy of *rescission*, that is, the right to have the contract set aside *if he so wishes*. The party claiming this remedy must show that he has not been at fault in any way, and the court may impose certain conditions on granting the remedy.

In *Cooper* v. *Phibbs* (1867), Cooper agreed to lease a fishery from Phibbs. It later turned out that, unknown to both, the fishery already belonged to Cooper. The court allowed Cooper to rescind the lease, on condition that he compensate Phibbs for improvements which the latter had made.

In *Grist* v. *Bailey* (1967), Grist contracted to buy Bailey's house for £850. Both parties believed that the house was occupied by a tenant protected under the Rent Acts. In fact, unknown to both, the tenant had died. This increased the value of the house to about £2250, and Bailey refused to carry out the contract, claiming that it was void for mistake.

The contract was held *not* to be void at common law, but the court exercised its equitable power to set the original contract aside on condition that Bailey would now sell for the true value.

Mistake by one or both parties may affect other equitable remedies. For example, specific performance of a contract may be refused if one party has made a mistake which renders it unfair to enforce the agreement against him.

Where, by mistake, the terms of a written document do not represent accurately what the parties agreed orally, the court may, at its discretion, order the rectification of the document so that it does express what was agreed.

B. Misrepresentation

The conclusion of a contract is often preceded by negotiations, in the course of which one party makes statements of fact intended to induce the other to enter into the contract. If any such statement is false, it is called a misrepresentation.

A misrepresentation, then, may be defined as a false statement of fact, made by one party to the contract to the other before the contract, with a view to inducing the other to enter into it. The statement must have been intended to be acted upon, and it must actually have induced the other party to make the agreement.

It must be a representation of fact, not law. A mere boast is not regarded as a statement of fact (otherwise advertisers might incur substantial liabilities). A distinction is also made between a statement of fact and a mere expression of opinion, although this can prove difficult. Statements about a car such as 'beautiful condition' and 'superb condition' have been held in criminal cases to be statements of fact, not mere expressions of opinion.

The statements must be by one party to the contract to the other. A statement by the manufacturer which induces a customer to buy from a retail shop will not give the customer any remedy for misrepresentation against either retailer or manufacturer.

The false statement must actually have deceived the other party and induced him to make the contract. Obviously it must be false, but even a misleading half-truth can be false.

> In *London Assurance* v. *Mansel* (1879), a person seeking life assurance was asked on the proposal form what other proposals for cover he had made. He answered, truthfully, that he had made two proposals the previous year, both accepted. He did not mention, however, that he had also had several proposals rejected. This half-truth was held to be a misrepresentation. (See also non-disclosure, page 126.)

Many misrepresentations also amount to promises which are actually incorporated into the contract. In this event, the party deceived will normally sue for breach of contract rather than for misrepresentation because once breach of contract is proved, damages will automatically be awarded. Where mere misrepresentation is proved, the person liable may still have a defence to an action for damages if he can prove that he reasonably believed himself to be telling the truth. The distinction between mere representations and contractual promises can be difficult, but in contracts of sale the court will normally hold that statements by a seller who is a *dealer* are contractual promises, whereas statements by a seller who is not a dealer are mere representations.

> In *Oscar Chess Ltd* v. *Williams* (1957), the defendant was a private car owner, trading in his vehicle in part-exchange for another. He falsely stated that it was a 1948 model, whereas in fact it was a 1939 car. This statement was quite innocent, because the registration book had been falsified by a previous owner. It was held that his statement was a mere representation, so that his innocence was a defence.

> On the other hand, in *Dick Bentley Productions Ltd* v. *Harold Smith* (*Motors*) *Ltd* (1965), a dealer sold a car which appeared from the instruments to have travelled only 20 000 miles. In fact it had done about 100 000. This was held to be breach of contract, not a mere misrepresentation, so that the buyer automatically was entitled to damages. A dealer, who knows more about the goods than his customers, is readily assumed to *promise* that his statements are true.

Remedies for misrepresentation

1. *Damages.* Under the Misrepresentation Act 1967, section 2(1), a party to the contract can recover damages for loss arising from a misrepresentation; but the other party has a defence if he can prove that, up to the time of the contract, he believed that his statements were true, and had reasonable cause so to believe. It should be noted that the onus of proving this is on the defendant.

   Under section 2(2), damages may also be awarded as an alternative to rescission at the court's discretion and, in this event, even the defendant's innocence may be no defence.

   If the misrepresentation was made fraudulently, the party deceived can, alternatively, sue for damages for the tort of deceit (Unit 10), but since the onus of proving fraud is on the plaintiff, this will rarely be done.

2. *Rescission.* Any misrepresentation, even innocent, will give the other party a right to *rescind* the contract, that is, to end it if he so wishes. Each party must be restored to his original position; for example, the property must be returned to the seller and the price to the buyer. The contract is said to be *voidable* (Unit 11).

   The right to rescind will be lost as soon as it becomes impossible to return the parties to their position before the contract. For example, if the property has been re-sold by the buyer, or has been destroyed by him, it will be impossible to return it to the seller.

   Since rescission is an equitable right, it must be exercised reasonably promptly. It is undesirable for a contract to remain voidable for too long, because this leads to uncertainty as to the ownership of the property. If he delays unduly, therefore, the innocent party will lose his right to rescind, and be left to sue for damages. What is a reasonable time is a question of fact, and may in some cases be only a matter of days or hours.

> In *Leaf* v. *International Galleries* (1950), which was mentioned earlier, the picture was sold in 1944. The plaintiff only discovered in 1949 that it was not by Constable. Although the contract was not void for mistake, the plaintiff claimed the right to

125

rescind for innocent misrepresentation. It was held that, after a lapse of five years, any right to rescind had been lost. (The plaintiff could have claimed damages for breach of contract, but did not in fact do so.)

Time may not run against the plaintiff, however, until he could with reasonable diligence have discovered the error.

Normally, rescission will only be effective from the moment when it is communicated to the party at fault. This would cause injustice, however, where the misrepresentation was fraudulent and the rogue has disappeared. In this event, therefore, the rule is relaxed.

In *Car and Universal Finance Co. Ltd* v. *Caldwell* (1965), Caldwell was persuaded by a rogue to part with his car in return for a cheque which was dishonoured. On discovering this, Caldwell immediately told the police, but could do no more to rescind the contract because the rogue could not be found. It was held that, in the circumstances, Caldwell had done everything possible to make public his intention to rescind, and the rescission was, therefore, effective.

Finally, the right to rescind will be lost if the innocent party 'affirms' the contract, that is, elects to go on with it knowing of the misrepresentation. He cannot blow hot and cold, and once he has decided to go on, he cannot change his mind.

Section 3 of the Misrepresentation Act makes it very difficult for a party to exclude his liability for misrepresentation (Unit 14). A term in the contract which would exclude any liability or remedy for misrepresentation will be of no effect unless the defendant can show that the clause is 'reasonable' within the meaning of the Unfair Contract Terms Act 1977.

C. Duty to disclose

There is, in general, no duty to *disclose* facts. Silence cannot normally constitute misrepresentation even when the silent party knows that the other is deceiving himself and does nothing about it. Each party must find out the truth as best he can, and in contracts of sale this rule is known as *caveat emptor*—let the buyer beware.

There is, however, a duty to correct statements which, although originally true, have subsequently become false before the contract was made. The facts have changed, and it would be unfair to let the original statement stand.

In *With* v. *O'Flanagan* (1936), at the start of negotiations for the sale of a doctor's practice, the seller stated, truthfully, that the annual income was £2000. The seller then fell ill, and by the time that the sale took place some months later, the profits had fallen drastically. It was held that the early statement should have been corrected, and the fall disclosed.

Silence is also not enough in contracts of the utmost good faith (*uberrimae fidei*). These are, for the most part, contracts where one party alone has full knowledge of the material facts, and, therefore, the law does impose on him a duty to disclose. The main examples are:

1. *Contracts of insurance.* There is a duty on the insured person to disclose to the insurance firm any circumstance which might influence it in fixing the premium or

deciding whether to insure the risk. Failure to do this will render the contract voidable at the option of the insurance firm.

2. *In contracts for the sale of land*, the vendor must disclose all defects in *title*, but not in the property itself.

3. *Contracts to subscribe for shares in a company.* A prospectus issued by a company, inviting the public to make an offer to buy shares in the company, must disclose various matters set out in detail under the Companies Act. If it does not, the contract may be rescinded.

4. *In contracts of family arrangement*, each member of the family must disclose all material facts within his knowledge.

D. Duress and undue influence

At common law, duress arose when a party was induced to enter a contract by force or the threat of force. His consent was not freely given. Today, economic coercion can also be duress.

> In *Universe Tankships Inc.* v. *ITWF* (1982), a trade dispute arose involving a ship, *The Universe Sentinel*. The union stopped it from leaving port, and eventually only allowed it to do so on condition that the owners paid money into a welfare fund. This agreement was held voidable for duress, and the owners recovered the money.

However, the economic pressure must be such that the courts regard it as improper. There can be a narrow line between economic duress and legitimate commercial pressure.

> In *D & C Builders Ltd* v. *Rees* (1966) (Unit 11), it was suggested, *obiter*, that even if there had been a valid contract, it would have been voidable for duress. Mr and Mrs Rees almost held the builders to ransom; the builders needed the money quickly, and the Rees family (who owed £482) said in effect, 'either agree to accept only £300 or we delay still further'.

> On the other hand, in *Pao On* v. *Lau Yiu Long* (1979) (Unit 11), the defendant was the major shareholder in Fu Chip Ltd. He was persuaded to give a guarantee to Pao On by the latter's threat to break his contract with Fu Chip Ltd. This could have harmed the defendant. Nevertheless the guarantee was held valid. The full facts were complex, and Pao On's threat was ultimately regarded as legitimate commercial pressure.

Equity has long recognized less direct pressures, particularly where confidential or professional relationships are abused. Generally, improper pressure has to be proved.

> In *Williams* v. *Bayley* (1866), a father was induced to give security for his son's debts to the bank by the bank's threats to prosecute the son. On proof of this, the father was held not to be bound.

In some instances equity goes further and *presumes* undue influence unless the contrary is proved. This will occur where the relationship between the parties was such that one had a dominant position over the other. The main examples include doctor and patient, solicitor and client, religious adviser and disciple, parent and child (but not husband and wife). The presumption of undue influence can only be rebutted in these cases by proof that the weaker party had independent advice or used his own free will. There are also situations where, although the *relationship* does not necessarily suggest undue influence, the *circumstances* do.

> In *Lloyd's Bank Ltd* v. *Bundy* (1975), a son was in financial difficulty. The bank manager visited the father and persuaded him to give the bank a guarantee of the son's debts and a mortgage of the father's house as security. The father was old and was given no warning or opportunity to seek independent advice (which might have been against the contracts). Undue influence by the bank was presumed from the circumstances, and the contracts were set aside when the bank could not rebut the presumption.

Where undue influence is deemed to exist, either by proof or presumption, the contract is voidable, but the right to rescind must be exercised within a reasonable time of the influence being withdrawn.

> In *Allcard* v. *Skinner* (1887), Miss Allcard joined a religious order and, in accordance with its rule of poverty, gave about £7000 to the head of the order during the eight years that she was a member. After leaving the order she waited six years and then sued to recover the money. It was held that, while the money had been obtained from her by undue religious influence, her action failed because she had waited too long before suing.

E. Lack of capacity

The general rule is that everyone is fully capable of entering into contracts, and that these contracts are enforceable both by and against him. However, there are certain classes of people whose contractual capacity is limited.

Minors (infants)

A minor or infant is a person under the age of 18. As a general rule, he will be entitled to avoid his contracts and damages will not be awarded against him. For example, he will not be bound by trading contracts which he makes.

> In *Cowern* v. *Nield* (1912), it was held that a minor who was a hay and straw merchant was not liable to repay the price of goods which he failed to deliver.

> In *Mercantile Union Guarantee Corporation Ltd* v. *Ball* (1937), an infant haulage contractor who took a lorry on hire-purchase was held not liable for arrears of instalments.

On the other hand, a minor *can* recover damages against an adult if the latter breaks the contract. The minor can *sue*, but cannot *be sued*.

There are two main exceptions to this rule:

1. A minor must pay a reasonable price for necessary goods sold and delivered to him. He need not pay the contract price if this is exorbitant, and in any event he can withdraw from the contract at any time before delivery. Furthermore, this rule applies only to 'necessaries', that is, goods suitable to the minor's condition in life and to his actual requirements at the time of sale and delivery.

In *Nash* v. *Inman* (1908), an undergraduate ordered expensive clothes from a tailor, including 11 fancy waistcoats. The minor's father was a prosperous architect, and it was argued that the clothes were suitable to the minor's station in life. Since he was already well supplied with clothes, however, these goods were not held to be necessaries.

2. Contracts of employment, apprenticeship and education which, *taken as a whole*, are for the minor's benefit. If as a whole the contract is beneficial, the court will enforce all of the clauses, even ones which, taken in isolation, are not beneficial.

In *Doyle* v. *White City Stadium* (1935), an infant boxer was held bound by a clause in his contract which provided for forfeiture of his prize money if (as happened) he was disqualified. The contract as a whole was similar to apprenticeship, and the forfeiture clause encouraged clean fighting.

The Infants' Relief Act 1874 declares certain contracts made by minors to be void, but this has been treated as meaning merely void *against* the minor. He can still acquire rights under the agreement, and sue for breach. The contracts covered are ones for goods supplied or to be supplied other than necessaries, for money lent or to be lent, and accounts stated, that is, IOUs or similar admissions of money due. There are two qualifications to this rule.

First, if money is lent to a minor specifically to enable him to buy necessaries, the lender can recover such part of the loan as is actually spent on necessaries at a reasonable price. The lender is said to be 'subrogated' to the rights against the minor of the supplier of the goods. Secondly, where the minor has acted fraudulently, for example, by falsely pretending to be of full age, he can be made to return goods which he still has in his possession. If, however, he has parted with the goods, the seller cannot get them back.

Special rules apply to contracts of a continuing nature which can last after the minor reaches 18. A contract such as a lease, a partnership or the holding of shares in a company will bind the minor after 18 unless he repudiates before or within a reasonable time after attaining this age.

Finally, as regards actions against the minor, the court will not hold him liable for damages in tort if this would merely be an indirect way of awarding damages for breach of contract (Unit 8).

There are also some exceptions to the rule that a minor can sue on his contracts. For example, since the remedy of specific performance will never be awarded *against* an infant, the court will not award it *to* an infant either (Unit 15). As another example, when a minor avoids the contract, as a general rule he can recover money or goods which he has handed over; but if he has received a benefit under the contract this will not be the case.

In *Valentini* v. *Canali* (1889), a minor leased a house and agreed to buy some furniture, paying part of the price. After several months the minor left, and avoided the contract as he was entitled to do. He could not recover the payments which he made for the furniture, however, because he had received some benefit from the contract.

Insane and drunken persons

A mental patient cannot validly enter into contracts. Contracts may be made on his behalf by the Court of Protection or receivers appointed for this purpose.

If a person makes a contract while temporarily insane, or drunk, the contract is voidable if he can prove that he was so insane or drunk at the time as to be incapable of understanding what he did, and the other party knew this. The contract will be binding unless it is avoided within reasonable time of regaining sanity or sobriety. An insane or drunken person must pay a reasonable price for necessary goods sold and actually delivered to him.

Examination questions

1. Explain whether or not the contract under which *B* buys a machine tool from *S* is valid in each of the following circumstances:
   (a) *S* believes that it is a cash sale. *B* believes that he is obtaining credit over a period of 12 months.
   (b) *S* believes that he is dealing with *X* and not with *B*.
   (c) Both *S* and *B* believe that the contract price of £5000 represents the true value. *B* discovers later that, because of a latent defect in its manufacture, it is only worth £3000.
   (d) *S* offers to sell for £500. *B* realizes that *S* has made a mistake and means £5000. *B* nevertheless accepts the offer.
2. Dullard, an elderly man with weak sight, has two cars for sale. Smart agrees to buy one and, by pretending to be a well-known local business man, is allowed to drive it away in return for a cheque. The cheque is dishonoured. Alec asks if he may hire the second car for a week and persuades Dullard to allow him to draw up a hire agreement which Dullard signs. The agreement in fact transfers the ownership of the car to Alec. Both Smart and Alec have now sold the cars and disappeared. Advise Dullard as to his rights to recover the cars from the subsequent purchasers.
3. (a) Under what circumstances may a person who alleges that he has been induced to enter into a contract by reason of a misrepresentation have a remedy? What remedies are available?
   (b) At the start of negotiations for the sale of a retail shop the seller makes a true statement regarding annual turnover and profits. While the negotiations are proceeding a supermarket opens a branch nearby and the trade of the shop declines considerably. After the sale is completed the purchaser discovers this. Advise the purchaser.
4. Distinguish between duress and undue influence and explain their effect upon the validity of a contract.
5. A company has been formed to establish and operate a chain of stores, known as 'Teenage Markets', offering goods and services specifically for young people.
   Draft a report outlining the legal problems which the company is likely to meet in dealing with minors.

Unit 14. The Terms of the Bargain

This unit deals with the rights and obligations which arise under a contract. It will also discuss one aspect of the idea of 'freedom of contract', that is, how far the parties can agree between themselves what their relations are to be, and how far the law determines their relations for them.

A. Express terms

Express terms are those specifically mentioned and agreed by the parties at the time of contracting, whether this be done in writing or by word of mouth. In simple agreements, such as small cash sales, the express terms may be very sketchy; the buyer will simply ask for what he sees before him at the price indicated, and the seller will agree to sell. There will be no need for detailed arrangements as to delivery or payment, because goods and cash will be handed over immediately.

Where the subject-matter is very valuable, where the agreement is complicated, or where the contract will last for some time, for example because credit is allowed, the parties are likely to be much more specific as to detailed terms. In these contracts, detailed terms will often be set out expressly, frequently in a written agreement. Thus, contracts of insurance, hire-purchase, or for the sale of land will be in writing and contain detailed express terms, whether or not this is required by statute or for the purpose of evidence (Unit 11).

Contractual terms, oral or written, differ in importance, and may be classified into conditions and warranties. A *condition* is an important term which is vital to the contract, so that non-observance will affect the main purpose of the agreement. Breach of condition will give the injured party a right to rescind or terminate the contract. Alternatively, the injured party may, if he so wishes, go on with the contract,

131

but recover damages for his loss. A *warranty* is a less important term, non-observance of which will cause loss but not affect the basic purpose of the contract. Breach of warranty will only give the injured party the right to sue for damages, not to repudiate the contract.

> In *Bettini* v. *Gye* (1876), an opera singer agreed to attend for rehearsals six days before the first performance. He did not arrive until two days beforehand. This was held to be only breach of warranty, which entitled the management to recover damages but not to terminate the contract.

> Conversely, in *Poussard* v. *Spiers & Pond* (1876), Madame Poussard, a singer, failed to turn up for the first few performances. This was held to be breach of condition, which entitled the management to end her contract.

Some express terms are difficult to classify so neatly in advance, and can only be classified by reference to the nature of the breach. A minor breach of the term might only be a breach of warranty, whereas a serious breach of the same term, or a breach which has serious consequences might be breach of condition.

> In *Hong Kong Fir Shipping Co. Ltd* v. *Kawasaki Kisen Kaisha* (1962), the plaintiffs chartered their ship to the defendants. The contract provided that the ship would be 'in every way fitted for ordinary cargo service'. This term could not be classified in advance as a condition or a warranty, because breach could be either a minor matter if the ship was slightly defective, or very serious if the ship was about to sink. In fact, the engines were old, the engine-room staff were inefficient, and the ship was delayed. This was held to be only a breach of warranty, which did not entitle the defendants to repudiate the contract.

The difficulty of such 'innominate' terms is that the parties may not know their rights and liabilities even after the contract is broken. One party may say that it was only a minor breach and that he is only liable to damages; the other may say that it was serious and that he can end the contract. The courts, and the parties themselves, often prefer that the remedies for breaking the term should be clear from the outset.

B. Implied terms

Terms implied by the courts

Where the parties have not made express provision on some point, the court will sometimes imply a term to cover the position. The court will impose such obligations as, in the court's view, the parties would reasonably have agreed had they thought of the matter

> In *The Moorcock* (1889), the owner of a wharf contracted to provide a berth for a ship. The berth was unsuitable for the vessel, which was damaged when it hit a ridge of hard ground at low tide. There was no express undertaking that the berth was suitable, but the court implied a term to this effect, and the shipowner recovered damages.

The implication of additional terms is usually justified on the grounds that it is necessary in order to give business effect to the intentions of the parties; the agreement makes commercial nonsense without it. If, at the time of the contract, someone had

132

said to the parties, 'What will happen in such a case?' they would both have said, 'Of course so and so will happen; we did not trouble to say that'.

> In *Liverpool City Council* v. *Irwin* (1977), the written tenancy agreements in a tower block of flats imposed no express duty on the landlord to keep the lifts and stairs in good repair! The court nevertheless implied such a term.

In some instances the courts have gone beyond this, and implied terms largely because this was necessary to achieve substantial justice between the parties. In a tenancy of a furnished house, the courts will imply a term that the premises will be reasonably fit for human habitation when the tenancy begins. Under a contract of employment, the employer owes an implied duty to take reasonable care for the safety of his employees, and the latter owe a duty to show good faith and to exercise reasonable care and skill in the exercise of their duties. (A careless employer may also be liable for the tort of negligence; Unit 9.) In contracts for the carriage of goods by sea, there are implied undertakings that the ship is seaworthy, that it will proceed on its voyage with reasonable dispatch, and that there shall be no unnecessary deviation.

It should be remembered that, as a general rule, the courts will only imply terms where the parties have made no express provision. Most implied terms can be excluded or varied by the parties.

Terms implied by statute

In some types of contract, detailed terms are implied by Act of Parliament. In many instances this has resulted from codification of the common law rules relating to such contracts. Some provisions aim simply to standardize the obligations of the parties; others go further and aim to do justice between the parties.

Perhaps the best example is the Sale of Goods Act 1979. The terms implied by this Act were first developed by the courts and then codified by statute in 1893. There were subsequent changes, and the 1979 Act is a consolidating one (Unit 2).

Some of the implied terms are general rules which can be freely altered by the parties if they so wish. Thus delivery of the goods and payment of the price are concurrent conditions, that is to say, the general rule is 'cash on delivery'; but there is nothing to stop the parties from varying this implied term and expressly contracting that the buyer can take away the goods on credit.

Some other sections operate differently. They impose duties which the seller owes to the buyer and, in *consumer* sales, govern the parties *whether they wish it or not*. The seller cannot exclude them. There are four main examples. By section 12, there is an implied condition that the seller has a right to sell the goods. By section 13, where goods are sold by description, there is an implied condition that they shall correspond with the description. By section 15, where goods are sold by sample, the bulk must correspond with the sample. By section 14, where the seller sells in the course of a business, the goods must be of merchantable quality, and reasonably fit for the buyer's purpose if he has made this known. These are discussed more fully in Unit 18.

Under the Supply of Goods (Implied Terms) Act 1973, obligations almost identical

133

to these are imposed on the owner of goods who lets them on hire-purchase. By the Supply of Goods and Services Act 1982, similar terms are implied into contracts of hire, and other contracts where possession or ownership of goods passes (Unit 18). Where the goods are supplied to a *consumer*, again, most of these implied terms cannot now be excluded; see the Unfair Contract Terms Act, later.

Other statutes which imply terms into certain types of contract include the Trading Stamps Act 1964, the Defective Premises Act 1972, and the Marine Insurance Act 1906.

C. Problems of unequal bargaining power

The law of contract, as we have seen it so far, has been based on the assumption that the parties freely negotiated the terms of their bargain. This is not always the case, particularly where one party is in a stronger economic position than the other.

The most obvious inequality arises where one of the parties enjoys a monopoly position. If someone wishes to acquire the goods or service which the monopolist supplies, he cannot genuinely negotiate terms to suit himself. He must either take the terms which the monopolist offers, or simply do without. Thus a passenger cannot haggle over the price of a railway ticket or the terms under which he will be carried; he must either accept the British Rail terms, or travel in some other way.

The position is very similar where there are only a few suppliers. The customer does not normally negotiate over the terms of an insurance contract, a hire-purchase agreement, or a mortgage. He contracts on a standard form prepared in advance by the company, which he can either take or leave. There will be little point in going to another company if all companies insist on more or less the same terms.

There may be other circumstances in which genuine bargaining is difficult. A borrower who has no money, for example, is in a weaker position than the lender who has. Even in contracts for the sale of goods, it may be difficult to negotiate where the goods are so technically complicated that the average buyer is not competent to judge the quality or fitness of what he buys.

The stronger party has sometimes used his position to impose heavy duties on the other, while attempting to limit or to exclude altogether his own possible liability. Hire-purchase agreements, for example, normally impose wide duties on the hirer, but often used to contain clauses excluding any liability of the finance company for defects in the goods. Other types of contract which contain exemption clauses will be seen from the cases mentioned later. The attitude of the courts and the legislature to such clauses will be discussed below.

D. Exemption clauses

While it may be acceptable for parties negotiating on an equal footing to exclude or limit their liability, both the courts and Parliament have been reluctant to allow exemption clauses which a stronger party has imposed on a weaker.

134

Such clauses can take various forms. They may exclude one party's liability altogether. They may accept possible liability, but limit the damages to, say, £1000. They may exclude or restrict any remedy (e.g., 'no refunds'); or impose onerous conditions ('complaints must be made within 24 hours'); or exclude or restrict rules of evidence or procedure ('receipt must be produced'). There are many possibilities.

The approach of the courts

1. *Is the clause part of the contract?* The courts will require the person relying on an exemption clause to show that the other party agreed to it at or before the time when agreement was reached. Otherwise it will not form part of the contract.

   (a) Where a contract is made by signing a written document, the general rule is that the signer is bound by everything which the document contains, whether he has read it or not.

   > In *L'Estrange* v. *Graucob Ltd* (1934), Miss L'Estrange signed a contract to buy an automatic machine. The document provided that 'any express or implied condition, statement or warranty . . . is hereby excluded', and the court commented that this clause was in 'regrettably small print'. Although Miss L'Estrange had not read the document, it was held that the clause bound her, and she had no remedy when the machine proved defective.

   (b) Where the terms are in an unsigned document, the person seeking to rely on them must show that the other party knew, or should have known, that the document was a contractual one which could be expected to contain terms. He must show that everything reasonable has been done to bring the terms to the notice of the other party. Most of the cases concern documents such as tickets, order forms and unsigned receipts.

   > In *Chapleton* v. *Barry UDC* (1940), the plaintiff hired a deck chair, and was injured when it collapsed. The ticket which he had received when paying contained a clause excluding liability, but he had put the ticket into his pocket without looking at it. The court decided that he was entitled to assume that a deck chair ticket was merely a receipt without conditions, and his action succeeded.

   > In *Thompson* v. *LMS Railway Co.* (1930), Mrs Thompson obtained a cheap excursion ticket with the customary wording referring the buyer to conditions in the company's timetables. One such condition excluded liability for injury. The court upheld the company's contention that a rail ticket, particularly a cheaper one, must reasonably be expected to contain terms. The fact that Mrs Thompson was illiterate was disregarded, and she recovered no damages.

   > In *Roe* v. *R. A. Naylor Ltd* (1918), a 'sold note' containing an exclusion clause was simply placed in front of the business buyer at the time of sale. This document clearly contained terms, and it was held that the buyer was bound by the clause even though he had not read it. As a prudent businessman he should have done, and the seller had done everything reasonable to bring it to his notice.

   (c) Any attempt to introduce an exemption clause *after* the the contract has been made will be ineffective. (Apart from anything else, the consideration for such a clause would then be past.)

135

In *Olley* v. *Marlborough Court Ltd* (1949), property was stolen from the plaintiff during her stay at a hotel. There was a notice in the bedroom that the proprietors accepted no responsibility for articles stolen, but this was held to be ineffective. The plaintiff only saw it *after* the contract had been made at the reception desk.

In *Thornton* v. *Shoe Lane Parking Ltd* (1971), the plaintiff made his contract with the car park company when he inserted a coin in the automatic ticket machine (at the latest). The ticket which he received referred to conditions displayed inside the car park, and which he could only see after entry. It was held that he was not bound by the conditions, which purported to exempt the company from liability for injury to customers.

(d) Exceptionally, a court may assume knowledge of an exemption clause from the course of past dealings between the parties. If they have contracted many times, always with the same exemption, it might only be natural to expect it in the present contract.

In *Spurling (J.) Ltd* v. *Bradshaw* (1956), Bradshaw deposited some barrels of orange juice with Spurlings, a warehouse firm. The parties had dealt with each other for many years and always the warehouse firm had excluded its liability for 'negligence, wrongful act or default'. On this occasion, the document containing the exclusion was not sent until several days after the contract. Nevertheless, the clause was held to be implied into the contract, because the parties had always previously dealt on this basis. Spurlings, therefore, were not liable when most of the barrels were found to be empty on collection by Bradshaw.

However, the past dealings must always have been on the same basis. If the terms have varied, or are different this time, then the court may assume that the exemption clause does not apply now.

2. *Construing exemption clauses*. Traditionally, the courts have construed exemption clauses *contra proferentem*, that is, in the manner least favourable to the person who put them into the contract. Any ambiguity or loophole in the drafting has been seized upon.

In *Wallis, Son & Wells* v. *Pratt & Haynes* (1911), the buyer of seed found when it grew that it was not what he had ordered. The sellers relied on a clause in the contract excluding all '*warranties*, express or implied, as to growth or description'. This did not protect them, because the term broken was a *condition*, not a warranty.

In *White* v. *John Warrick & Co. Ltd* (1953), the plaintiff hired a tricycle. The contract provided that '*Nothing in this agreement* shall render the owners liable . . .'. The plaintiff was injured when the saddle tilted forward. It was held that the clause only excluded liability *for breach of contract*; the owners might still be liable for the tort of negligence (Unit 9).

Moreover the courts have sometimes assumed that a clause was not intended to cover fundamental breach, where one party does something fundamentally different from what he contracted to do (supplying beans instead of peas). However, this is only a presumption and a sufficiently clear clause can cover even the most serious breach.

If the contract is between two businesses with equal bargaining power, the court will not even make the presumption. The clause will be examined in the context of the contract as a whole. Was the price kept low on the understanding that the supplier's liability was limited? Was it assumed that the buyer of the property or service would insure himself against any loss? Was the exemption clause simply one of a set of trading terms upon which both sides were apparently content to do business? If so, then the clause—if it is clear and comprehensive—can be upheld.

> In *Photo Production Ltd* v. *Securicor Transport Ltd* (1980), Securicor contracted to guard the plaintiff's factory where paper was stored. The patrolman deliberately started a fire, and it destroyed the premises. It was held that an exemption clause in the contract protected Securicor. Both parties were established businesses that had negotiated the terms freely. The price of the patrol was modest. Both parties were insured, the plaintiff against loss of the building, Securicor against liability. The court was satisfied that both sides had intended Photo Production (or its insurers) to bear the risk.

The courts have also made an important distinction between clauses *excluding* liability and clauses which merely *limit* liability to a particular sum. The courts will be less hostile to mere limitation clauses, especially where (as above) the limitation is reflected in the other terms.

> *Ailsa Craig Fishing Co. Ltd* v. *Malvern Fishing Co. Ltd* (1983), again involved Securicor, which were guarding a quay where ships were berthed. The patrolman went off for the celebrations on New Year's Eve, leaving the vessels unattended. The tide rose and a boat rose with it. Its bow jammed under a quay and it sank. Again the owner was insured against such an accident, and therefore plainly did not envisage Securicor taking the entire responsibility. A clause limiting Securicor's liability to £1000 was therefore upheld.

3. *Privity of contract.* The terms of a contract generally only affect the parties to that contract. Therefore, an exemption clause will normally not protect anyone who is not party to the contract; see *Adler* v. *Dickson* (Unit 16).

Unfair Contract Terms Act 1977

This is the most important piece of legislation affecting exemption clauses. Most of the Act applies only to 'business liability', that is, liability arising from things done or to be done by a person in the course of a business, or from occupation of premises used for business purposes. Certain contracts are excepted from the Act, principally those relating to land, patents, etc., shares, contracts affecting formation or internal management of companies, and insurance. The Act deals slightly differently with various situations.

1. *Negligence liability* is covered by section 2. No one acting in the course of a business can, either by contractual terms or by any notice given or displayed, exclude his liability, in contract or tort, for *death or bodily injury* arising from *negligence*. He can exclude or limit liability for mere financial loss or loss of property due to negligence, but only if he can prove that the exemption is reasonable. This will usually be difficult, although it may be possible where the two large businesses are concerned; the two *Securicor* cases above show the way in

which the courts approach this today (although the Act did not apply to them because both arose from things which happened before 1977).

2. *Liability under a contract* may also be affected by two further rules in section 3. Where a business contracts on its own written standard terms, it cannot exclude or vary its liability for breach of contract unless it can show that the exemption is reasonable. Secondly, the same rule applies whenever a business contracts with a *consumer*, whether or not on standard terms.

3. *Sale of goods contracts* are also governed by section 6, which can apply even to non-business liability. We have seen that the Sale of Goods Act 1979 imposes terms binding on sellers. By section 6, if the buyer is a *consumer*, these obligations cannot be excluded. A buyer is a consumer when he buys, for his private use, goods normally supplied for such use, from a seller selling in the course of a business. If the buyer is not a consumer (for example if he is a trader buying for re-sale) section 6 does allow the seller to exclude or restrict the Sale of Goods Act sections 13–15, but only if he, the seller, can show that the exemption is reasonable. Section 12 cannot be excluded.

The 1977 Act, Schedule 2, contains guidelines to help determine what is 'reasonable'. Regard may be had for various matters: (a) the relative bargaining strength of the parties; (b) whether the customer is given an inducement such as a price reduction to agree to the terms; (c) whether the customer should have known the existence and extent of the exemption clause, especially in the light of trade customs or past dealings; (d) whether it was reasonable to expect compliance with any condition imposed on the plaintiff (for example that complaints must be made within *x* days of delivery); and (e) whether the goods were made to the customer's special order.

> In *R. W. Green Ltd* v. *Cade Bros Farms* (1978), a farmer bought seed potatoes from a supplier. The contract provided, *inter alia*, that any complaint must be made within three days of the seed being delivered. The court had no difficulty in holding this part of the term unreasonable, because the defect was one which could not become apparent until the seed had had time to grow.

> In *Mitchell Ltd* v. *Finney Lock Seeds Ltd* (1983) a farmer bought cabbage seed from a supplier. When the cabbage grew, it proved inferior and of the wrong type. The seller relied on clauses in the standard form contract which purported to limit and/or exclude his liability. The House of Lords held these clauses unreasonable (partly because, in the past, the suppliers had negotiated settlements rather than try to rely on the clauses; therefore, even the suppliers may have had doubts about their reasonableness).

4. *Hire-purchase contracts* too are governed by section 6. We have seen that the Supply of Goods (Implied Terms) Act 1973 imposes obligations on the owner of goods who lets them on hire-purchase. These are basically the same as the seller's obligations under the Sale of Goods Act, and are subject to the same rules regarding exemption.

5. *In other contracts for the supply of goods*, such as hire, or 'work and materials' agreements, the Supply of Goods and Services Act 1982 imposes obligations on the

supplier. The 1977 Act, section 7, applies to these, and is limited to business liability. Again, the supplier's statutory obligations cannot be excluded or varied in consumer transactions. They can be excluded or limited—except for the obligations as to title—in non-consumer contracts, but only if the supplier can prove that the exemption is reasonable.

6. *Separate 'guarantees' of goods*, by manufacturers or suppliers, sometimes also contain exemption clauses. Such clauses can be caught by the 1977 Act, section 5. If the goods are of a type normally supplied for private use or consumption, then no term in the guarantee can exclude or restrict the supplier's liability for defects while the goods are in consumer use, if the loss results from the negligence of the manufacturer or a distributor.

Misrepresentation Act 1967

By the Misrepresentation Act, section 3, as amended in 1977, any term excluding or restricting liability for misrepresentation is void unless the person making the false statement proves that the exemption is fair and reasonable having regard to the circumstances which were, or ought reasonably to have been, known to or in the contemplation of the parties when the contract was made. This applies even to non-business liability.

> In *Walker* v. *Boyle* (1982), misrepresentations were made on behalf of the private seller of a house. When the buyer discovered this he rescinded the contract and recovered the £10 500 deposit which he had paid. An exemption clause in the condition of sale did not protect the seller, because she could not show that the exemption was reasonable.

Fair Trading Act 1973

This Act empowers the Secretary of State for Trade and Industry to make regulations prohibiting certain undesirable consumer trade practices. He can, for example, prohibit the inclusion in specified consumer transactions of terms or conditions purporting to exclude or limit a party's liability. Under these powers, the Minister could invalidate exemption clauses which at present are unaffected by legislation. He can also impose criminal sanctions: for example, by the Consumer Transactions (Restriction on Statements) Order 1976 it can be a criminal offence for a trader to use a void exemption clause or notice such as a 'no refunds' notice to consumers. (This was sometimes done by traders to deter consumers who did not know that the notice was ineffective.)

Examination questions

1. (a) Distinguish between conditions and warranties.
   (b) Jones agreed to hire a car for a week's holiday and called at the premises of the hire firm to collect it on the morning of his departure. Advise him in each of the following situations:
      (i) The car is an older model with a higher petrol consumption.

139

  (ii) The luggage capacity of the car is much smaller than the hire firm previously stated.

  (iii) Part of the bodywork of the car is in a very dangerous condition.

2. (a) In what circumstances will terms be implied into a contract in addition to those expressly stated by the parties?

 (b) *D* left his car in a car park. He paid the parking fee and was given a slip of paper which he put in his pocket without reading. The paper contained a note to the effect that the owners of the car park were 'not liable for any loss or damage however caused'. When *D* returned to his car he found that it had been badly damaged. Advise *D*.

3. (a) To what extent have the courts intervened to protect parties to a contract who would otherwise suffer from the presence of an exclusion clause in the contract?

 (b) William, a wholesaler, receives an urgent order for certain electrical goods. He, therefore, agrees to buy these goods from Martin, a manufacturer, who promises delivery in about two weeks' time. During the negotiations, Martin produces a catalogue of his firm's products which he leaves on William's desk. William does not look at the catalogue and places it in the waste paper basket after Martin has left.

  Martin does not deliver for two months and William loses his order. Martin then produces the goods and explains that labour trouble has upset production. When William refuses to accept delivery, Martin points out a clause in the catalogue which excuses late delivery for any reasonable cause.

  Advise William.

4. S. Cleaners Ltd offered 'to clean two garments for the price of one'. A notice was displayed in the shop to this effect but with the addition, in smaller print, of a statement that the customer must agree in return to accept full responsibility if anything should happen to the garments. A similar statement was printed on the back of the tickets which were handed to customers when they deposited the garments.

 Albert brought two jackets for cleaning. Because of poor eyesight he was unable to read the small print on the notice, and he put the ticket in his pocket without reading it.

 Some days later when Albert collected the jackets he saw that one had now been badly torn. After wearing the other jacket he contracted a skin disease which was caused by a chemical which the cleaner had used.

 Advise Albert.

5. There are a number of recent examples where Parliament has limited the right to exclude liability by a contractual term. What are these examples?

Unit 15. Performance, Breach and Remedies

A. Performance

The number of contracts broken is very small in relation to the number performed, but it is the broken contracts which attract attention. Since most contracts are made with the intention of performance, and most are so performed, this method of discharging the bargain will be discussed first.

The basic rule is that each party must perform completely and precisely what he has bargained to do.

> In *Re Moore & Co. and Landauer & Co.* (1921) the buyer ordered a consignment of canned fruit, to be packed in cases of 30 tins each. The correct amount was delivered, but about half was in cases of 24 tins each. It was held that the buyer was entitled to reject the whole consignment.

This rule is not always so inflexible as it seems. Difficult questions of interpretation sometimes arise as to exactly what the parties *did* promise to do, and the court will try to give a common-sense meaning to the terms agreed.

> In *Peter Darlington Partners Ltd* v. *Gosho Ltd* (1964), the seller agreed to supply a quantity of canary seed on a 'pure basis'. The seed delivered was 98 per cent pure, and evidence was given that this was the highest standard of purity which it was normally possible to obtain in the trade. The seller was held to have performed his obligation.

> In *Reardon Smith Line Ltd* v. *Hansen–Tangen* (1976), the contract involved building a ship. It specified details of the proposed vessel, and referred to 'yard no. 354' as the place for building. In fact a ship was supplied which met all of the requirements, but was built at another yard. The defendants rejected it on this pretext (but in reality because the market

had fallen and they no longer wanted a ship). It was held that the rejection was wrongful. The reference to 'yard no. 354' was merely an indication of what was intended, not a term in the contract that the vessel must be built there.

The courts will also ignore microscopic deviations, such as a few pounds in a load of thousands of tons.

If one party *has* broken his obligations, it will normally be no defence to him that the breach was not his fault. He has promised to perform his contract, and he will be liable if he does not. Only if some outside cause makes performance physically, legally or commercially *impossible* will he have an excuse for non-performance (Unit 16). The fact that he has taken all reasonable care will be no defence to him.

> In *Frost* v. *Aylesbury Dairy Co. Ltd* (1905), the dairy supplied milk infected with typhoid germs, and Mrs Frost died of the disease. It was held that, even if the dairy could prove that it had taken all possible precautions, it was still liable for breach of its implied duty to supply milk which was reasonably fit for drinking.

The consequences of non-performance will be discussed later. If the breach is a minor one, a breach of warranty, the contract will not be discharged. Both parties must go on with it, but the injured party can recover damages. If there has been a more serious breach, breach of condition, the injured party will have a right to discharge the contract and bring it to an end.

Special rules as to performance apply to an obligation to pay money. It is the duty of the debtor to seek out and tender to the creditor, at a reasonable time of day, payment of the correct amount of money in *legal tender*, without any necessity for the creditor to give change. Legal tender consists of those coins or notes which by law must be accepted in payment of a debt. It comprises bank notes up to any amount, 50p pieces up to £10, silver (or cupro-nickel) coins of 20p or less up to £5, and bronze coins up to 20p. A cheque is not legal tender, and the creditor need not take it in payment. If a cheque is taken, it will normally be treated as conditional payment, and the debt will not be discharged until the cheque is honoured.

If the creditor refuses to take the money when tendered, the debt is not discharged; the debtor must still pay, but the creditor must now come and seek him. If money is sent by post, the risk of loss lies upon the sender unless his creditor has authorized him to use the post. In this latter event, the risk passes to the creditor, provided that the sender takes reasonable precautions for care of the money in transit.

Where a debtor owes several debts to his creditor, and pays a sum insufficient to satisfy them all, it may be important to determine which debts the payment satisfies or reduces. The creditor will prefer to appropriate the payment to the oldest debts, because after six years they may become unenforceable. The rule, however, is that the debtor has a right to appropriate at the time of payment. Only if he does not appropriate then, can the creditor appropriate at any time thereafter. Exceptionally, in the case of current accounts, the rule is that first debts are paid first, for where money is being continually paid in and out it would be difficult to carry out specific appropriation with every payment.

B. Breach of contract

Breach of contract can occur in several ways. For example, one party may expressly repudiate his liabilities and refuse to perform his side of the bargain. This can happen either at or before the time when performance was due. If a party renounces his obligations in advance, this is known as *anticipatory* breach. A person can impliedly renounce his obligations by rendering himself incapable of performing them; for example, if he had contracted to sell a specific painting, he would renounce the contract by selling the painting elsewhere. Alternatively, one party may simply fail to perform the contract. He may fail altogether to perform his bargain or he may merely fail to perform one, or some, of his many obligations under the agreement. If the obligation broken was a major part of the contract, there will be *breach of condition*; if only a minor part, there will be *breach of warranty*.

Sometimes the courts have classified a breach according to whether or not it is 'fundamental', but this classification has been used mainly in relation to exemption clauses (Unit 14).

Effects of breach

1. Every breach of contract will give the injured party the right to recover damages (see below).
2. If the breach is sufficiently serious, it also gives the injured party a right to avoid the contract and bring it to an end. This right arises if the contract has been repudiated, or if there is breach of condition. It will not arise for breach of warranty.

The consequences of breach can be so serious that the injured party has no choice. He may have to treat the contract as ended if, for example, the property is destroyed. Subject to this, however, he need not end the contract unless he wants to. He can either avoid the agreement and no longer perform his side; or he can go on with it and either be content with defective performance from the other (but recover damages) or, sometimes, continue to press for performance. If he does wish to end the contract, he must do so reasonably promptly and, as with rescission for misrepresentation (Unit 13), the right is lost if he 'affirms' the agreement.

If a term is so wide that it is not possible to classify it in advance as a condition or a mere warranty, then the right to avoid the contract will depend upon the seriousness of the breach; see *Hong Kong Fir Shipping Co. Ltd* v. *Kawasaki Kisen Kaisha Ltd* (Unit 14). Often, however, commercial requirements demand that terms should be classified in advance, so that the parties will be sure of what their rights are in the event of breach.

> In *Bunge Corporation* v. *Tradax Export SA* (1981), the seller contracted to deliver goods to the buyer's ship provided that the buyer gave at least 15 days' notice that the ship was ready. This notice requirement was held to be a condition, which the buyer then broke by giving shorter notice. The seller could, therefore, refuse delivery.

Terms implied by statute are almost invariably classified in advance. For example, the terms implied by sections 13 to 15 of the Sale of Goods Act are all conditions, and breach entities the buyer to withdraw from the contract. On the other hand, late payment does not entitle the seller to avoid, unless the parties had specifically agreed otherwise. A time set for delivery of the goods is almost invariably a condition, and lateness entitles the buyer to reject the goods and end the contract. The buyer can, alternatively, waive failure to deliver on time, but impose a new deadline, breach of which will again entitle him to set the contract aside.

> In *Charles Rickards Ltd* v. *Oppenheim* (1950), the buyer ordered a new car body, to be ready in seven months' time. It was not, but the buyer agreed to wait a further three months. When it was still not completed, he indicated that he would cancel the order unless it was ready within a further four weeks. He was held entitled to do so, and to refuse the car body when it was finally tendered months later.

3. If one party renounces his obligations and commits an anticipatory breach, the injured party may have two possible courses of action. He may treat the contract as at an end and bring an action immediately, either for damages for breach or for reasonable remuneration for the work which he has performed.

> In *Hochster* v. *De La Tour* (1853), the defendant agreed in April to employ the plaintiff as a courier on a European tour as from 1 June. In May, the defendant repudiated this agreement, and the plaintiff was held entitled to commence proceedings immediately, before waiting for 1 June.

The plaintiff may, in fact, be forced to adopt this course if the defendant has made it impossible to go on with the contract, perhaps by destroying the subject-matter. In any event, when the contract ends, the plaintiff must try to mitigate his loss immediately, for example, by seeking another job.

Alternatively, since renunciation does not generally discharge a contract automatically, the injured party can often continue to press for performance until the due date arrives. If this is done, the contract continues to exist, for the benefit and at the risk of both parties, until the final date for performance. If, before that date, performance becomes impossible, this will discharge the contract without the party who renounced it having to pay damages.

> In *Avery* v. *Bowden* (1855), a ship arrived at Odessa for a cargo of wheat and was met by a refusal to load. This renunciation was not accepted and, before the last date for performance arrived, war broke out between England and Russia. This discharged the contract, and the shipowner was unable to recover damages.

C. Damages for breach of contract

Whenever one person has broken a contract, the other can recover damages which are assessed according to the following principles:

1. The basic rule is that the plaintiff should be *compensated*, but no more than compensated, for loss which he has suffered as a result of the breach. Loss can be financial, damage to property, personal injuries or even distress to the plaintiff, as where a holiday firm defaults on its obligations; see *Jarvis* v. *Swans Tours Ltd* (1973). Where no loss has been suffered, as where a seller fails to deliver the goods

but the buyer is able to purchase elsewhere at no extra cost, the court may award *nominal* damages, a nominal sum, perhaps of £2, to mark the breach.

Exemplary or *punitive* damages, which exceed the actual loss suffered by an amount intended to punish the offending party, are not normally awarded for breach of contract, although they have been awarded in the past against banks who have dishonoured traders' cheques when the account had sufficient funds to meet them.

2. The plaintiff, however, cannot be compensated for *all* of the consequences which might logically 'result' from the defendant's breach, otherwise there might be no end to liability. Some loss, therefore, will be too remote.

> In *Hadley* v. *Baxendale* (1954), a mill owner entrusted a broken crankshaft to a carrier, for delivery to an engineer who would replace it. Delivery was delayed through the fault of the carrier, and the mill stood idle longer than was necessary. The mill owner recovered damages against the carrier, but a claim for loss of profits was disallowed, because it was not shown that the carrier knew that the mill would have to stand idle.

The court suggested two tests which still form the basis of the rules covering remoteness of damage. The damage or loss treated as resulting from the breach should only include:

(a) such damage as may fairly and reasonably be considered as arising naturally, that is, according to the usual course of things, from the breach; and

(b) such other loss as may reasonably be supposed to have been in the contemplation of both parties at the time they made the contract, so that the defendant in effect accepted responsibility for it.

The working of these rules can best be illustrated by some of the cases which have arisen.

> In *Horne* v. *Midland Railway Co.* (1873), Horne had a contract to manufacture boots for the French army at a price higher than the normal market price, provided that he could deliver by a certain date. The boots were consigned to the railway company, which was informed of the importance of the delivery date but not the special price. Delivery was delayed, the boots were rejected and had to be sold elsewhere at below the normal market price. Horne only recovered the difference between his re-sale price and the *market* price. His claim for the difference between the *contract* price and the price on re-sale failed, because the carriers did not know of the original contract price.

> In *Victoria Laundry (Windsor) Ltd* v. *Newman Industries Ltd* (1949), a laundry firm ordered a new boiler which arrived late. The firm was held entitled to recover damages for *normal* loss of profits, because the supplier should have anticipated this. It was not, however, entitled to recover for further losses due to losing an exceptionally profitable contract of which the suppliers did not know.

> In *The Heron II* (1969), a shipowner was late in delivering a cargo of sugar to Basrah, and by the time of delivery the market price had fallen. It was held that the loss of profits could be recovered, because this possibility must reasonably have been in the contemplation of the parties.

3. At least when the contract is ended, the injured party must try to *mitigate* or minimize his loss, that is, take all reasonable steps to reduce it. A worker who is wrongly dismissed must attempt to find other work; a seller whose goods are

rejected must attempt to get the best price for them elsewhere; a buyer of goods which are not delivered must attempt to buy as cheaply as possible elsewhere. Loss arising from failure to take such steps will not be recovered. On the other hand, only *reasonable* steps need to be taken to mitigate; the buyer, for example, need not tour the globe looking for the cheapest alternative supplier.

4. In some cases, the parties, foreseeing the possibility of breach, make an attempt in the original contract to assess in advance the damages which will be payable on breach. Such a provision for *liquidated* damages will be perfectly valid if it is a genuine attempt to pre-estimate the likely loss. If it is not a genuine pre-estimate, however, but an attempt to impose punitive damages where none would otherwise be awarded, then the liquidated damages clause will be void as a *penalty*. The essence of a penalty is that it was inserted *in terrorem*, to frighten the potential defaulter. Such clauses often used to appear in hire-purchase agreements, so that if a hirer returned the goods after paying only one instalment, he might have to bring his payments under the agreement up to half or more of the original hire-purchase price. The courts held such clauses to be void and, where the Consumer Credit Act 1974 applies, such penalties are invalidated by stature.

> In *Bridge* v. *Campbell Discount Co. Ltd* (1982), Bridge agreed to take a vehicle on hire-purchase for £482. He paid a deposit of £105 and one instalment of £10, but then repudiated the agreement because he could afford no more. He was sued for a further £206, under a clause in the agreement requiring him to bring his total payments up to two-thirds of the hire-purchase price of £482 'by way of agreed compensation for depreciation of the vechicle'. Bridge had only had the vehicle for a few weeks, had returned it in good condition, and had already paid £115. The clause was held void as penalty.

Contracts for the sale of goods and building contracts sometimes provide that, in the event of late performance, a specified sum shall be payable for each day of delay. Minimum price agreements have sometimes contained similar provisions to apply in the event of breach.

> In *Dunlop Ltd* v. *New Garage Ltd* (1915), the defendants had agreed that damages of £5 should be payable for each tyre sold below Dunlop's listed price. The clause was held valid, because even the smallest breach of the pricing arrangements could lead to widespread undercutting and severely damage Dunlop Ltd.

> On the other hand, in *Ford Motor Co. Ltd* v. *Armstrong* (1915), a promise to pay £250 for each car sold below the listed price was held void as a penalty.

D. Other remedies for breach

1. *Claims on a* quantum meruit. In some situations a claim for damages may not be the appropriate financial remedy. This may happen where the plaintiff is prevented from completing his side of the bargain by the defendant's conduct and repudiation. The plaintiff may have done a lot of work, but not yet earned any fee. He may be entitled to claim on a *quantum meruit* basis (for so much as he deserves) for what he has done.

> In *Planché* v. *Colburn* (1831) the plaintiff was commissioned by a publisher to write a book for £100. After he had done the necessary research and written part of the book, the publisher repudiated the contract. It was held that the plaintiff could recover £50 on a *quantum meruit*.

A claim on this basis may also be made where work has been done under a void contract. The plaintiff cannot recover damages for breach, because no contract exists, but he may recover on a *quantum meruit*.

> In *Craven-Ellis* v. *Canons Ltd* (1936), the plaintiff recovered reasonable remuneration for work which he had done as managing director of the company, when it transpired that his appointment was void.

> In *British Steel Corporation* v. *Cleveland Bridge & Engineering Co. Ltd* (1984), BSC supplied steel to the defendants while still negotiating terms. Negotiations failed and there was, therefore, no contract. BSC was entitled to a *quantum meruit* payment for what it had supplied and Cleveland had used.

2. *A decree for specific performance* is an equitable remedy which is sometimes granted where damages would not be an adequate remedy. It is an order of the court directing the party in breach to carry out his promises, on pain of penalties for contempt of court. Since it is equitable, it is discretionary (Unit 1); in particular, it will not be granted in the following circumstances:

(a) It will not be awarded where damages would be enough and, for this reason, it will rarely be granted in commercial transactions. Monetary compensation will usually enable a disappointed buyer to obtain similar commodities elsewhere. In a sale of goods, the seller will normally only be ordered to hand over the article specifically where it is unique, such as an original painting.

> In *Cohen* v. *Roche* (1927), the court refused to order specific performance of a contract to sell some Hepplewhite chairs which were rare, but not unique. Similar chairs could be bought elsewhere, albeit with difficulty.

On the other hand, each piece of land *is* unique, and the main use of the remedy today is in contracts for the sale of land; see *Rawlinson* v. *Ames* (Unit 11). The remedy may also be granted in contracts to sell or allot shares.

(b) The court must be sure that it can adequately supervise enforcement. Therefore contracts of a personal nature, such as employment, which depend upon good faith which the court cannot ensure, will not be specifically enforced. Similarly, building contracts will not be enforced.

(c) Specific performance will not be awarded either to or against a minor.

(d) The court may exercise its discretion to refuse specific performance in any other situation where it is not felt just or equitable to grant it.

> In *Malins* v. *Freeman* (1837), the remedy was refused where a bidder foolishly bought property at an auction in the belief that he was bidding for an entirely different lot. It would have been harsh to compel him to take the property; the seller could still sue for damages if he so wished.

3. *An injunction* is an order of the court directing a person *not* to break his contract. It is normally appropriate to enforce a negative provision in the agreement and,

being an equitable remedy, is only awarded on the same principles as specific performance. It can, however, be awarded to enforce a negative stipulation in a contract for services or employment.

In *Warner Brothers Pictures Incorporated* v. *Nelson* (1937), an actress had contracted with the film company not to work as an actress for anyone else during her present contract. It was held that she could be restrained by injunction from breaking this undertaking.

On the other hand, an injunction will not be granted in contracts of employment if it would operate as an indirect way of specifically enforcing the agreement; thus, Nelson could only be restrained from working elsewhere *as an actress*, otherwise she might be faced with the alternatives of either working for Warner Brothers or starving. An employer, however, may *temporarily* be restrained from dismissing an employee; this is not tantamount to specific performance, because the employer can usually suspend the man on full pay if the employee's presence is an embarrassment.

In Hill v. *C. A. Parsons & Co. Ltd* (1972), the plaintiff was dismissed with inadequate notice as a result of trade union pressure to maintain a 'closed shop'. The court granted an injunction restraining Parsons Ltd from dismissing Hill until adequate notice had been given.

As will be seen, injunctions are sometimes granted to enforce lawful restraints on trade; see cases such as *Home Counties Dairies Ltd* v. *Skilton* (Unit 17). The remedy may be granted to enforce negative promises in contracts relating to land; for example, a purchaser may be restrained from breaking his contractual promise not to build on the land sold. In exceptional circumstances, injunctions may even issue to order the seller of goods not to withhold delivery.

In *Sky Petroleum Ltd* v. *VIP Petroleum Ltd* (1974), the parties made a 10-year agreement in 1970 that VIP would supply all Sky Ltd's petrol requirements. In November 1973 a dispute arose between the parties, and VIP withheld supplies. In the oil crisis then existing, Sky Ltd could not get supplies from any other source (contrast *Cohen* v. *Roche*, page 147). The court granted a temporary injunction restraining VIP from withholding reasonable supplies, even though this was equivalent to a temporary order of specific performance.

Examination questions

1. (a) It is said that each party to a contract must perform completely that which he had agreed to do. Discuss this statement.
   (b) PCM Ltd buys photocopying machines from the manufacturer, and hires them to firms. Your firm hires such a machine from PCM Ltd for one year. The following problems arise:
      (i) the machine is delivered two hours after the agreed time;
      (ii) the 'stop' button, which should light up when pressed, does not do so, although it does stop the machine;
      (iii) the machine overheats badly when operated.

PCM Ltd proves that each problem was solely the manufacturer's fault. Discuss whether any of the above problems entitles your firm to any remedies, and if so what, against PCM Ltd.

2. Advise B in both of the following situations, explaining the relevant principles of law:

   (a) B agrees to buy a second-hand car from S for £1000; the profit of S from the transaction would be £200. B then refuses to go through with the purchase. S sells the car to X for £1000 but claims £200 loss of profit from B on the grounds that X would have bought another car from him and he has thereby lost another sale. Would your advice differ if the car had been a new one and S had a number of cars of this model for sale?

   (b) B agrees to buy a consignment of coffee from S for £1000 and then refuses to accept the goods. By this time the market price has fallen to £900. S turns down a sale at this price as he feels that the price will rise again. The market price continues to fall and the coffee is eventually sold for £800. S claims £200 from B.

3. (a) What action is open to the injured party when a contract is repudiated by the other party before the date of performance?

   (b) Under what circumstances is (i) a decree for specific performance, and (ii) an injunction likely to be awarded for a breach of contract?

4. (a) M agrees to build an extension to N's factory at a cost of £8000, this sum to be paid upon completion. After M has committed work and materials to the project to the extent of £5000, N claims that the workmanship is defective and refuses to allow M on to the site to complete the work. Advise M.

   (b) P, a well-known musician, agrees to give a performance at Q's club and promises that he will not give another performance in the same town for one month before or after the date in question. Q later hears that R, a rival club owner, has engaged P for a much larger fee to appear at R's club the following night. Advise Q.

5. Better Builders contracts to reconstruct a laundry and to complete the work within eight weeks. The work in fact takes ten weeks and the laundry is now claiming damages for the loss of normal profits during the two additional weeks and also for the loss of a particularly valuable contract which it could not accept because its plant was out of action.

   (a) Advise Better Builders.

   (b) To what extent would your advice differ if the contract had contained a clause under which Better Builders agreed to pay £200 by way of penalty for each week late in completing the work?

Unit 16. Discharge, Limitation and Privity

A contract may be discharged, that is, come to an end, in four main ways. Two of these, namely performance and discharge as a result of breach, arise directly out of the terms of the original contract, and were discussed in the last unit. The present unit is concerned with methods of discharge which do not necessarily arise out of what was originally agreed, but from extraneous events. These methods of discharge are new agreement and frustration.

Two other matters which affect the right to sue on a contract will also be discussed here, namely the time limits affecting *when* actions must be brought, and the rules of privity affecting *who* can sue or be sued.

A. Discharge by agreement

There are three main ways in which a contract can be discharged by agreement.

1. The parties may have made provision for discharge in their original contract. For example, the parties may have agreed at the outset that the contract should end automatically on some determining event or on the expiration of a fixed time. Thus goods may be hired, premises may be leased, or a person employed for a fixed term. On the expiration of the term, the contract will cease.

   Alternatively, the contract may contain a provision entitling one or both parties to terminate it if they so wish. Thus a contract of employment can normally be brought to an end by either party on reasonable notice to the other (subject only to statutory minimum periods of notice laid down by the Employment Protection (Consolidation) Act 1978). Hire-purchase contracts usually give the hirer a

150

contractual right to end the agreement and return the goods at any time; where the Consumer Credit Act 1974 applies, there is also a statutory right to do this.

Discharge in these ways does arise out of the terms of the original agreement.

2. Discharge can also arise, not out of the original agreement, but by reason of a new, extraneous contract. In order that the new agreement should discharge the old one, however, the new contract must be valid; for example, there must be consideration.

Where neither side of the original contract has yet been performed, there will be no difficulty; each side still owes duties, and the consideration for one party waiving his rights is the waiver of rights by the other. Thus the buyer and seller may agree to cancel an order; the seller need no longer supply the goods, and the buyer no longer has to pay.

The position is more complicated where one party has completely performed his original obligations. The agreement for discharge will only be binding if, in return for the release, the other party does or promises something which he is *not* already bound to do, such as paying earlier than he was bound to do. In the absence of such new consideration, the agreement for release will not be binding, and the original contract will stand; see *D & C Builders Ltd* v. *Rees* (1966) (Unit 11). For this reason discharge by new agreement is sometimes called discharge by accord (agreement) and satisfaction (consideration).

3. Finally, one party can release the other unilaterally, without consideration, but only if he does so by *deed*.

B. Discharge by frustration

Until the last century, the obligation to perform a contractual duty was absolute. If it became physically impossible for a party to perform his bargain, he nevertheless had to pay damages for breach, and if extraneous events took away the whole purpose of the contract without the fault of either party, the parties still had to continue with the agreement.

> In *Paradine* v. *Jane* (1647), a lessee was evicted during the Civil War. It was held that he still had to pay the rent; the fact that he could not enjoy the property because of events beyond his control was of no concern to the lessor, and was no excuse.

Starting with the case of *Taylor* v. *Caldwell* in 1863 (see below), the courts have developed the doctrine of frustration as an exception to this absolute rule. If some outside event occurs, for which neither party is responsible and which makes total nonsense of the original agreement, then the contract will be discharged by frustration. A radical change in circumstances can sometimes, therefore, be pleaded by a party as a valid excuse for not performing his side of the bargain. This doctrine must be approached with caution, however, because the courts have understandably been reluctant to accept anything but the most fundamental changes as frustrating events. The following are the main examples:

1. *Subsequent physical impossibility*. This will occur where, *after* the contract was made, it becomes physically impossible or impracticable to perform it. (If this was

151

already impossible when the contract was *made*, the agreement would be void from the outset.)

> In *Taylor* v. *Caldwell* (1863), a music hall hired for a series of concerts was burnt down before the date for the first performance. This was held to frustrate the contract, because there was no longer any hall to hire. The hirer, therefore, no longer had to pay.

> In *Robinson* v. *Davison* (1871), a pianist, who was engaged to give a concert on a specified date, became ill and was incapable of appearing. It was held that this frustrated the contract.

2. *Subsequent illegality*. This will occur where, *after* the contract was made, a change in the law or in the circumstances renders it illegal to perform the agreement.

> In *Avery* v. *Bowden* (1855), the contract to load a cargo at Odessa was eventually discharged by the outbreak of the Crimean War, which made it thenceforth an illegal contract of trading with the enemy.

3. *Basis of the contract removed*. The contract may be frustrated where both parties made it on the basis of a future event which does not take place.

> In *Chandler* v. *Webster* (1904), the contract was for the hire of a room in Pall Mall for the day of Edward VII's coronation procession. The rent was over £140, because the procession would pass directly beneath the window. Unfortunately the coronation was postponed when the King became ill. This was held to frustrate the contract.

4. *Frustration of the commercial purpose of the contract*. A change may occur which makes a total nonsense of what was originally agreed, so that what the parties would have to perform bears no relation to what was originally intended. This change must be radical; an event which merely makes it more difficult or expensive for a party to perform the contract will be no excuse. It is rare that a contract will be frustrated on this ground.

> In *Metropolitan Water Board* v. *Dick, Kerr & Co.* (1918), a firm of contractors agreed in 1914 to build a reservoir. In 1916, under wartime emergency powers, the Government ordered the contractor to stop work and sell the plant. This was held to frustrate the contract. Although it might eventually be possible to start work again after the war, the enforced hold-up for an indefinite period made nonsense of the contract.

> On the other hand, in *Tsakiroglou Ltd* v. *Noblee & Thorl G.m.b.H* (1962), the sellers agreed to deliver groundnuts from Port Sudan to the buyers in Hamburg, and to ship them in November or December 1956. In November 1956, the Suez Canal was closed, and the sellers would now have had to ship the goods round the Cape of Good Hope, a much longer and more expensive journey. It was held that this did *not* frustrate the contract, but merely made it more difficult to perform.

If a seller wishes to protect himself against liability to the buyer for delays due to such matters as strikes or non-delivery of raw materials, he should make special provision for this in the contract. If one party makes a promise which he fails to perform, the court is reluctant to allow him to say, in effect, 'Oh, but it's not my fault'.

The effects of frustration

Frustration automatically brings the contract to an end and renders it void. As a general rule, all sums paid by either party in pursuance of the contract before it was discharged are recoverable, and all sums not yet paid cease to be due.

> In the *Fibrosa Case* (1943), an English company agreed in 1939 to make some machinery for a Polish buyer at a price of £4800. The buyer paid an initial sum of £1000. When war broke out, Poland was occupied by the German army, and the contract was, therefore, frustrated by subsequent illegality. It was held that the London agent of the Polish buyer had no further liability, and could recover the £1000 already paid.

This was rather harsh on the seller, who had already done considerable work and incurred expense in manufacturing the goods. The Law Reform (Frustrated Contracts) Act 1943, therefore, restated the general rule, but introduced two exceptions to it.

1. If one party has, before the time of discharge, incurred expenses in performing it, the court may in its discretion allow him to keep or recover all or part of sums *already paid or due* under the contract.
2. If one party has, by reason of anything done by the other, obtained a valuable benefit (other than the payment of money), then the other may recover such sum as the court considers just.

The Law Reform (Frustrated Contracts) Act applies to all contracts except (a) contracts for the carriage of goods by sea, (b) contracts of insurance, (c) contracts containing special provisions to meet the case of frustration, and (d) contracts for the sale of specific goods where the agreement is frustrated because the goods perish before risk passes to the buyer. This last category is covered by the Sale of Goods Act 1979, section 7 (Unit 19).

C. Limitation of actions

Contractual obligations are not enforceable for ever. Apart from other considerations, evidence becomes less reliable with the passage of time, and therefore, after a certain period, the law bars any remedy.

The Limitation Act 1980 lays down the general periods within which an action must be brought. These are as follows:

1. Actions based on a *simple* contract will be barred after six years from the date when the cause of action accrued.
2. Where the contract is made by *deed*, actions can be brought up to 12 years from the date when the cause of action accrued.
3. Actions to recover *land* can be brought up to 12 years from the date when the cause of action accrued.

A right of action 'accrues' when breach occurs. Thus, if a loan is made for a fixed time, the right will accrue when this time expires. If no time is agreed it will be when a written demand for payment is made.

153

If, when the cause of action accrues, the plaintiff is under a disability by reason of infancy or unsoundness of mind, the period will not run until the disability has ended or until his death, whichever comes first. Once the period has started to run, subsequent insanity will have no effect.

If the plaintiff is the victim of fraud or acts under a mistake or if the defendant deliberately conceals relevant facts, the limitation period will not begin until the true state of affairs is discovered or should reasonably have been discovered.

> In *Lynn* v. *Bamber* (1930), some plum trees were sold in 1921 with an undertaking by the seller that they were of a particular type. Not until they matured in 1928 was it discovered that they were of inferior quality. It was held that an action for damages could still be brought, since the fraudulent misrepresentations by the seller had postponed the operation of the period of limitation.

Provided that the limitation period has not already expired, the period may be extended where the party in breach either acknowledges his liability in writing, signed by him or his agent, or makes part payment in respect of the debt or claim. Time will then begin to run afresh from the date of acknowledgement or part payment. Property obtained by theft may be recovered at any time unless it has passed to a bona fide purchaser who is protected after six years.

Equitable remedies, such as specific performance or an injunction, are not covered by the ordinary limitation periods, but will almost invariably be barred much earlier under general equitable principles. An equitable remedy must be sought reasonably promptly, because 'equity aids the vigilant, not the indolent'. A short delay, of weeks or even days, may bar the remedy.

D. Privity of contract

As a general rule, the legal effects of a contract are confined to the contracting parties. An agreement between *A* and *B* cannot confer any legally enforceable benefit on a stranger, cannot impose any obligations on a stranger, and cannot take away the rights of a stranger. Only *A* can sue *B* for breach, and vice versa.

> In *Tweddle* v. *Atkinson* (1861), a young couple were about to marry. The husband's father and the bride's father agreed between themselves that each would make payments to the couple. It was held that the husband could not sue for breach of this contract when the bride's father failed to pay.
>
> In *Adler* v. *Dickson* (1955), a passenger on board ship was injured by the negligence of the master and boatswain. Her ticket from the shipping company provided that 'passengers are carried at passengers' entire risk'. Nevertheless she successfully sued the master and the boatswain; the exclusion clause was in a contract between the passenger and the company, and could not protect employees.

This rule is of great importance in English Law. A customer who buys a new car from a garage cannot sue the manufacturer for breach of contract, because the customer contracted only with the garage. If the car breaks down and a passenger is injured, the passenger has no contract with either the manufacturer or the garage. The plaintiff can only sue in tort in these cases, and must, therefore, prove that the defendant has been negligent (see *Donoghue* v. *Stevenson* in Unit 9). Similarly, a shareholder cannot take the benefit of a contract made by the company, because the company is a separate legal person (Unit 6).

There are exceptions to this general rule. For example, where an agent contracts with a third party on behalf of a principal whose existence he does not disclose, the latter may step in and sue or be sued on the contract. If two people contract with the intention of creating a trust in favour of a third person, the latter, although unable to enforce the contract, may take action as a beneficiary for breach of trust if any of the contractual obligations are broken. A lease of land may create rights and obligations which attach to the land, and bind not only the landlord and the tenant, but also future assignees of the lease.

In other situations the parties to a contract may change by operation of law or by agreement. Thus, in the case of bankruptcy, rights of action pass to the trustee in bankruptcy. In the case of death, rights pass to the personal representatives.

> In *Beswick* v. *Beswick* (1968), Peter Beswick, a coal merchant, sold his business to his nephew, John, in return (among other matters) for an undertaking by John to pay £5 per week to Peter's widow after Peter's death. Although the widow could not sue John in her own right, because she was not a party to the contract, she was able to recover payment *on Peter's behalf*, as administratrix of his estate.

Contractual rights may be assigned, in which case someone other than the original promisee may sue or be sued. Rights are easier to transfer than obligations, for if a debt is owed it matters little, to the debtor, to whom this is paid. Who is to pay does matter considerably to the creditor, and his permission to a transfer is, therefore, required.

An important situation where a third party can take the *benefit* of a contract made between two others is in connection with liability insurance, which includes compulsory motor insurance. The contract is between the insured, that is to say the driver in motor policies, and his insurance company, which promises to indemnify the driver against possible liability to third parties whom he may injure. As a general rule only the insured can demand payment from the insurance company on this contract, not the third party. Where the insured has become bankrupt, however, the Third Parties (Rights Against Insurers) Act 1930 allows the injured party to claim directly from the insurance company; otherwise the money would go to the insured's trustee in bankruptcy, and the third party might get nothing. Moreover in relation to motor insurance, the Road Traffic Act 1972 provides other exceptions to the privity rule: thus, a person driving with the owner's consent may be entitled to cover even though not a party to the insurance agreement and, in respect of compulsory third party risks, the person injured can recover directly from the insurance company under section 149.

The *burden* of a contract can be imposed on a stranger where a restrictive covenant is imposed on land at the time of sale, for example a covenant prohibiting its use as an inn or alehouse; this can bind all future occupiers of the land, even though not parties to the original contract of sale.

155

In *Tulk* v. *Moxhay* (1848), the owner of land which included Leicester Square in London sold the Square itself but retained some land round it. The buyer contracted not to build on the Square, but later sold the land and, after it had passed through several hands, an ultimate purchaser did propose to build. It was held that the original seller could restrain the present purchaser from building even though there was no privity of contract between them. The present purchaser had taken with notice of the restrictive covenant, and equity restrained him from breaking it.

Another example is the Resale Prices Act 1976, which still allows a supplier, with the consent of the Restrictive Practices Court, to impose a minimum re-sale price which will bind anyone who takes the goods with a view to re-sale, and who has notice of the restriction.

Examination questions

1. (a) Discuss the circumstances in which a contract may be discharged by agreement before all the contractual obligations have been performed.
   (b) *L*, a builder, contracted to build two houses for *M* and *N*, each house to cost £30 000. When the houses were finished, *M* said that he could not afford to pay the full price and offered *L* £25 000 in full settlement; *L* accepted this amount. *N* said that he would only pay if *L* landscaped the garden; *L* did this at a cost of £1000.

   Discuss whether *L* may now recover £5000 from *M* and £1000 from *N*.
2. A builder agrees to erect a factory within one year. Discuss the validity of the following defences if he has failed to complete the work on time and is being sued for breach of contract.
   (a) The Government imposed building restrictions which prevented him from continuing with the work.
   (b) The cost of building materials increased, obliging him to buy in smaller quantities because of a shortage of working capital.
   (c) An influenza epidemic led to the illness of a number of his specialist workers.
   (d) Some building materials on the site were damaged by a fire.
3. Advise Bernard whether he may begin legal proceedings in 1983 in respect of the following:
   (a) He bought a case of wine from Charles in 1976, and when the first bottle was opened in 1981 he discovered that it was of an inferior quality to that ordered.
   (b) He sold goods to David in 1974. When pressed for payment in 1978, David admitted the debt and promised to pay but has not done so.
   (c) He agreed in writing to buy land from Eric in 1978 and now seeks specific performance of the contract.
   (d) He lent money to Fred in 1975 without fixing a date for repayment. The first of many demands for the return of the money was made in 1978.
4. Explain the applicable principles of law and advise Weaver in both of the following cases:
   (a) Weaver bought a small textiles factory from Spinner. As part of the agreement, Weaver promised to pay Spinner a weekly pension for life and to continue

paying this pension to Mrs Spinner after Spinner's death. Spinner has now died and Weaver wonders whether he is still obliged to pay the pension to the widow.

(b) Merchant owed Weaver £1000 for goods supplied. Merchant said that he was in serious financial difficulties and he offered Weaver £600 in full satisfaction of the debt. Weaver accepted this but has now heard that Merchant's business is flourishing. Weaver enquires whether he may claim the balance of the debt.

5. (a) To what extent is it true to say that only a person who is a party to a contract may sue or be sued in respect of its breach?

(b) A contract for the sale of goods includes a provision that the seller will deliver but only at the purchaser's risk. The goods are entrusted to a carrier for delivery and are damaged by the carrier's negligence.

Advise the purchaser.

Unit 17. Contracts and Public Policy

Earlier units have dealt with those agreements which English law will recognize as contracts, and the nature, effect and discharge of such agreements. This unit refers to another aspect of the concept of freedom of contract. From the earliest days of this branch of the law, freedom of contract has been subject to overriding considerations of public policy. Some agreements have been completely *illegal*, and the courts will normally do nothing to help parties who rely on them. Other agreements, while not being illegal, have been held *void*, so that the courts will give no remedy for breach, but will allow money paid under the contract to be recovered. Various statutes have added to the list of contractual provisions which are void or illegal as contrary to public policy at common law.

A. Contracts which are illegal at common law

1. *An agreement to commit a criminal offence or a tort* is probably the oldest example of an illegal contract. An agreement to do something in a friendly foreign country which will be an offence in that country will also be illegal in England under this head.

   In *Allen* v. *Rescous* (1676), the plaintiff paid the defendant 20 shillings to assault *X* and evict him. It was held that the plaintiff was not entitled to recover his money when the defendant failed in this illegal purpose.

   In *Foster* v. *Driscoll* (1929), an English partnership, formed to smuggle whisky into the United Stated at a time when liquor was prohibited there, was held to be illegal in English law.

2. *A contract to defraud the revenue* will be illegal for similar reasons.

   In *Miller* v. *Karlinski* (1945), an agreement between employer and employees to disguise part of the salary as expenses, so as to evade income tax, was held to be illegal.

158

As a result, the employee was not entitled to reclaim arrears of salary from the employer.

3. *Contracts to corrupt public life*, such as contracts to bribe officials, to sell public offices, or to procure a title or honour are similarly illegal.

> In *Parkinson* v. *College of Ambulance Ltd* (1925), the secretary of the College, which was a charity, promised that he could obtain a knighthood for the plaintiff in return for a suitable donation. Parkinson donated £3000 but did not obtain a knighthood. His action for the return of the £3000 failed.

4. *Immoral contracts*. This category is limited to contracts for a sexually immoral purpose, such as a contract between a man and a woman for future cohabitation. Any contract clearly connected with an immoral purpose will be illegal.

> In *Pearce* v. *Brooks* (1866), the owner of a coach of unusual design was unable to recover the cost of hire from a prostitute who, to his knowledge, had hired it to attract clients.

A promise to pay money for past illicit cohabitation could not be sued upon since the consideration is past.

5. *Contracts for trading with the enemy*. These include all contracts with a person or firm voluntarily residing in enemy territory in time of war. If war breaks out after the contract was made but before it is performed, the contract is frustrated by subsequent illegality; see *Fibrosa Case* (Unit 16).

6. *Contracts to impede the course of justice*. These include agreements to prevent or hinder the prosecution of a serious criminal offence, for example, by paying the victim not to report the offence or not to cooperate in the prosecution.

   Contracts of maintenance, where a person with no legal interest in the proceedings gives financial assistance to another to enable him to bring or defend the proceedings, and contracts of champerty, where a litigant is assisted in return for a share in the proceeds if he wins, are also illegal under this head.

Effects of illegality

An illegal contract is void. Furthermore, contrary to the general rules applying to void contracts, any money that has passed cannot be recovered. Thus in *Parkinson* v. *College of Ambulance Ltd*, Parkinson could not recover his donation. Any contract closely connected with the illegality, so as to be tainted by it, will also be void; thus the contract of hire in *Pearce* v. *Brooks* and the partnership in *Foster* v. *Driscoll* were illegal. There are, however, some exceptions to these rules:

1. Where one party was innocent of the illegality, he will be entitled to sue on the contract, although the other party cannot. This will occur where the contract appears perfectly innocent, but one party is performing it for an illegal purpose without the other's knowledge. For example, in *Pearce* v. *Brooks*, had the owner of the coach not known the purpose for which his customer was using it, he *would* have been entitled to recover his hire.

159

2, Where one party repents of the illegal purpose before carrying it out, the court may allow him a remedy. On the other hand, his repentance must be genuine; if he withdraws simply because it becomes impossible to carry out the illegal purpose, the court will not believe his repentance.

3. The ownership of goods can pass as a result of an illegal contract, at least to the extent that the original owner cannot reclaim them once they have been delivered. On the other hand, he may sometimes be able to claim damages for the tort of conversion from someone equally at fault who subsequently deals wrongfully with the goods.

B. Contracts which are illegal by statute

The nature and effects of statutory illegality vary with the terms of the Act concerned. Some statutes expressly declare the whole contract illegal, with the same consequences as illegality at common law. An example of this is the Life Assurance Act 1774, under which a contract to insure a life in which the proposer has no 'insurable interest' will be illegal. In spite of its title, the Act also applies to insurance of buildings, and liability insurance. The temptations which might be raised if the proposer were free to insure the life or buildings of a stranger are obvious. A proposer will normally have an insurable interest in his own life, the life of his wife, and the lives of debtors and others whose death would financially affect him.

> In *Harse* v. *Pearl Life Assurance Co.* (1904), it was held that the plaintiff has no insurable interest in the life of his mother, whose life he had insured. The policy was illegal, and the plaintiff was not entitled to recover the premiums which he had paid.

Another example is section 1 of the Resale Prices Act 1976, which declares unlawful all agreements between the suppliers of goods to 'blacklist' retailers who sell below the minimum re-sale price agreed by the suppliers.

Some difficulty arises from statutes which, while not expressly making a contract illegal, provide that it shall only be carried out by someone who has a licence to do so. For example, licences are required by those who sell alcoholic drinks, or carry goods by road. Someone who acts without a licence commits a criminal offence, but does this render his contracts illegal? The answer depends on the purpose of the legislation in question. If, in the view of the courts, the Act was designed to forbid contracts of this type by unlicensed dealers, so as to protect the public, then the contract will be illegal. If the purpose of licensing was only to raise revenue or to help in the administration of the trade, contracts will not be affected.

> In *Cope* v. *Rowlands* (1836), an unlicensed broker in the City of London was held not to be entitled to sue for his fees, because the purpose of the licensing requirements was to protect the public against possible shady dealers.

> On the other hand, in *Archbolds (Freightage) Ltd* v. *Spanglett Ltd* (1961) a contract by an unlicensed carrier to carry goods by road was held valid, because the legislation was only designed to help in the administration of road transport.

Similar problems arise where a statute requires that certain contracts be carried out in a particular manner, with penalties in the event of breach.

> In *Anderson Ltd* v. *Daniel* (1924), the seller of artificial fertilizers was required by statute to state in the invoice the percentages of certain fertilizers. Failure to do this was held to render the contract illegal, and the seller was unable to recover the price of goods which he had delivered.

> On the other hand, in *Shaw* v. *Groom* (1970), a landlord who let furnished premises without a proper rent book did recover arrears of rent. The court took the view that the rent book requirements were not central to the contract as a whole, and that the Act did not intend the landlord to lose more in unpaid arrears than could have been imposed by way of fine.

Finally, some statutes declare certain *terms* in a contract to be illegal, without thereby affecting the rest of the contract. An example is found in the Truck Acts 1831–1940, which apply to contracts of employment. This legislation is designed to ensure that the wages of manual workers are paid in cash and not, as sometimes happened in the last century, in goods or by vouchers which could only be exchanged for goods at the company store. The Acts also prohibit certain deductions from wages by employers. A term which infringes these provisions is void and illegal, but this does not invalidate the contract of employment as a whole. The requirements as to payments in cash are now modified by the Payment of Wages Act 1960, which allows payment by cheque or through a bank if the workman requests this in writing and the employer agrees (Unit 23).

C. Contracts in restraint of trade

It is a long tradition of the common law that all agreements or provisions in agreements which tend to restrain trade are contrary to public policy and therefore *void* (although not generally illegal). Most restraints are still governed by the rules of common law. Some, such as price-fixing agreements, are also governed by statute (see later).

Restraints take many forms, but the following are the main types:

1. Contracts of employment sometimes provide that the employee, after leaving his present employment, may not compete against his present employer either by setting up in business on his own or by working for a rival firm.
2. On the sale of a business, the buyer will often require the seller to promise that, in future, he will not carry on a similar business in competition with the buyer. (Otherwise the seller might set up in business nearby and attract all his old customers away from the buyer.)
3. Suppliers of goods and services sometimes agree between themselves to fix prices, restrict output, regulate the methods of supply, or otherwise influence the market for their products.
4. Retailers sometimes make solus or similar agreements with suppliers, under which the retailer promises to sell only that supplier's brand of goods. The main cases have involved agreements between garages and petrol companies.

161

Except under the third head above, the restraint will normally be only one clause in a much wider agreement, such as a contract of employment or a sales agreement. In these circumstances, the bulk of the agreement will not be affected; the only clause in question is the one which attempts to impose the restraint.

The rules relating to covenants in restraints are basically the same for all types. Every restraint is *presumed void* unless it can be proved otherwise. It can be proved valid if it can be shown to be reasonable in the interests of both parties *and* in the interests of the public at large.

Reasonableness between the parties depends upon whether the person for whose benefit the covenant was made had any legitimate interest in imposing it, that is, whether he had anything to lose, such as trade secrets or contact with customers. The restraint must then be measured against this interest. The nature of the restraint, its geographical area, the time for which it is to operate, and all other features must be no more than is reasonable to protect the interest in question.

Reasonableness in the public interest affects restraints which have a wide economic effect, particularly restraints under the third and fourth heads above. This is less likely to be important in restraints on employment.

Restraints on employment

In the main, the courts have not been sympathetic to restraints of this kind, which attempt to restrict the right of a person to earn his living where and with whom he likes. Futhermore, the worker may have been 'persuaded' to agree to the restraint because the employer was in a stronger bargaining position. The following cases will illustrate the rules.

In *Home Counties Dairies Ltd* v. *Skilton* (1970), a milk roundsman had to agree in his original contract of employment that, for one year after leaving his present job, he would not sell milk to customers of his present employer. The restraint applied both to setting up a rival business himself, and to working for any rival firm. The restriction was held valid, and necessary to protect his employer against potential loss of customers. Skilton was restrained by injunction from breaking his undertaking.

In *Forster & Sons Ltd* v. *Suggett* (1918), the works manager of a glass-making company had agreed not to work for any rival firm for five years after leaving his present job. This was held valid, because the manager knew of secret manufacturing processes which would be of value to a rival.

On the other hand, in *Eastham* v. *Newcastle United Football Club* (1964), the Football Association's retain and transfer rules, whereby a player could not transfer to any other club without the consent of his present one, were held invalid as being wider than necessary to protect the clubs.

In *Mason* v. *Provident Clothing Co. Ltd* (1913), the clothing company had imposed a term restraining Mason, a collector and canvasser, from working for any similar business within 25 miles of London for three years after leaving. The House of Lords held that the onus was on the company to prove that such a wide restraint was reasonable to protect them, and that they had failed to do this.

Any attempt by an employer to impose restraints by indirect means will be subject to the same tests.

> In *Bull* v. *Pitney-Bowes Ltd* (1966), a rule in the pensions scheme of the defendant company provided that employees should lose their pension rights if they left to work for a competing company. Bull did leave after 26 years, and went to work for a competitor. It was held that this rule in the pension scheme was void as an attempted restraint on trade.

> In *Kores Ltd* v *Kolok Ltd* (1959), an agreement between two employers that neither would employ anyone who had worked for the other in the last five years was held invalid.

Restraints on the seller of a business

The courts have been much more ready to uphold restraints imposed in these circumstances, because the buyer plainly has an interest to protect and the seller is a free agent. The restriction must, however, be no more than is necessary to protect the business which the buyer has acquired; he cannot validly prevent the seller from competing with other businesses which the buyer already owns elsewhere. The restriction must also be reasonable as to time and area.

Agreements to fix prices, regulate supplies, etc.

The common law rules described above apply to these agreements, but most are also governed by statute today.

The Restrictive Trade Practices Act 1976 requires that most such agreements affecting goods or services be registered with the Director-General of Fair Trading. The agreements are then presumed *void* unless the parties can prove to the Restrictive Practices Court that the agreement is beneficial and in the public interest. The 1976 Act sets out various 'gateways' which the parties can use to help convince the court that the agreement is acceptable; for example, that the restrictions are reasonably necessary in order to protect the public from injury from defective products. These provisions are supplemented by the Competition Act 1980.

As regards goods, attempts by suppliers to restrict the minimum prices at which the *buyer* may *re*-sell are affected by the Resale Prices Act 1976. Generally such a restriction is *unlawful*, not merely void. It is also usually unlawful to withhold supplies from a dealer who has, or is likely to, undercut the supplier's minimum price. The Restrictive Practices Court can exempt certain goods from this general rule, but at present only books and medicaments have been exempted. As regards these, we have seen in Unit 16 that it is possible to impose a minimum re-sale price which binds any dealer who takes the goods with a view to re-sale and with notice of the restriction.

Restrictive trading agreements may also now be invalid in English law if they contravene Article 85 of the Treaty of Rome. This provides that all agreements between firms which may affect trade between member states, and which operate to prevent, restrict or distort competition within the Common Market, shall be automatically void.

163

'Solus' and similar agreements

In *Esso Petroleum Co. Ltd* v. *Harper's Garage Ltd* (1968), the garage company agreed to sell only Esso petrol for the next four years, and to keep its garages open at all reasonable hours. In return, it received a discount on the price of the petrol. This agreement, although it restricted the garage company's freedom to sell whatever petrol it wished, was held as being reasonable in the interests of both parties and the public at large. An agreement affecting another of Harper's garages, however, tied the garage to sell only Esso for 21 years, in return for a loan of £7000. This was held to be too long a restraint, and, therefore, against the public interest and void.

Interpretation of restraint clauses

1. The court will not alter or re-write the words of a restraint clause. If it is void, it is totally void. The court will not cut down a 25-mile or a 21-year restraint to a more acceptable figure; if this is too wide, the person restrained can ignore it and set up business next door and tomorrow.

2. On the other hand, if the clause restricts several different activities, it may be possible to sever the void restrictions from the valid ones. The court does not alter the restriction; it merely deletes—puts a 'blue pencil' through—one of the several restraints.

   In the *Nordenfelt Case* (1894), an inventor and manufacturer of munitions sold his business to a company and agreed not to engage in munitions business, or in any other business liable to compete in any way with that for the time being carried out by the company, in any part of the world for the next 25 years. The House of Lords held that this was really two restrictions. The munitions restraint was valid, notwithstanding its time and extent, because of Nordenfelt's importance as an inventor and the world-wide scope of the business. The second restriction, covering competition with any other activity of the company, was too wide and, therefore, void.

3. The court will sometimes give a common-sense meaning to the words actually used, again without altering them.

   In *Littlewoods Organisation Ltd* v. *Harris* (1978), *H* was employed by Littlewoods. A clause in his contract restrained him from working for GUS (Littlewoods' rival) for 12 months after leaving. Littlewoods only operated a *mail-order* business *in this country*, whereas GUS had branches or subsidiaries in many types of business throughout the world. *H* claimed that the restraint was, therefore, void as being wider than necessary to protect Littlewoods. The court held that the restraint had plainly been intended to apply only to mail-order in the UK, and, therefore, issued an injunction against *H* limited to this.

D. Other contracts which are void

Contracts prejudicial to the institution of marriage

The courts will not recognize contracts which interfere with marriage or the proper performances of marital or parental duties. A promise never to marry is deemed to be against public policy and void, though a promise not to marry a particular person or not to marry for a short period of time may be valid.

So far as parental duties are concerned, a parent cannot by contract deprive himself of the custody, control and education of his children, except by certain clearly defined legal procedures such as adoption and separation agreements.

Gaming and wagering contracts

Wagering contracts are void under the Gaming Acts, and no action may be brought to enforce payment of the bet, either directly or indirectly. On the other hand, the contract is not illegal; a partnership formed to carry on a wagering business will be valid, whereas a partnership to smuggle whisky is illegal and void. Wagering contracts, where neither party has an 'interest' in the event concerned other than the amount of the bet, must be distinguished from insurance contracts. If X insures his own goods against theft, this is valid, because X has an insurable interest in the goods; if X insures someone else's goods, the contract will be void, because X's only interest in the goods is the amount of his bet that they will be stolen. (Note that the Life Assurance Act 1774 does not apply to insurance of goods, and so the contract is not illegal.)

Gaming contracts involve the playing of a game of chance for winnings in money or money's worth. They can be valid if they comply with certain statutory requirements, for example that all players must have an equal chance.

Clauses excluding certain statutory requirements

Frequently an Act will expressly prohibit and declare void any attempt to contract out of its requirements. Examples include the Employer's Liability (Defective Equipment) Act 1969 (section 2), the Consumer Credit Act 1974 (section 173), the Road Traffic Act 1972 (section 148), and the Employment Protection (Consolidation) Act 1978 (section 140).

Examination questions

1. (a) To what extent may an employer impose a restraint upon a worker so far as the latter's future employment is concerned?
   (b) Sidney is a cost accountant employed by a large brewery company. He agrees that, if and when he leaves his present post, he will not work for any concern making beer or similar products in the United Kingdom for a period of three years. He has now been offered a better paid appointment with a company which makes mineral waters.
   Advise Sidney.
2. (a) Compare the principles governing the validity or otherwise of a contract restraining an employee in respect of his future employment with those

applicable to a restraint upon the vendor of a business in respect of his future business activities.

(b) Antonio sold his hairdressing business to Marcel and promised that he would not open a hairdressing shop or solicit customers within 10 miles of the business he had sold for a period of three years. Is this promise binding upon Antonio? Give reasons for your answer.

3. Your company is about to market on a large scale a new and inexpensive brand of paint. It is intending to do this principally through existing retail shops, but is prepared to give financial assistance towards the opening of new shops in localities where there would otherwise be no retail outlets.

Advise the company whether it may, by contract, ensure:

(a) that retailers stock only this particular brand of paint and none other; and

(b) that the jurisdiction of the courts be excluded from any dispute arising with a retailer.

4. Explain the meaning of the following expressions:
   (a) Subject to contract;
   (b) Buying an option;
   (c) *Solus* agreement;
   (d) *Quantum meruit.*

5. Explain, with reasons, whether the following agreements are valid and enforceable.
   (a) A partnership agreement under which whisky is to be smuggled into a country where its import is forbidden.
   (b) Two life assurance policies effected by a wife on the lives of her husband and her brother respectively.
   (c) An agreement between two manufacturers fixing a minimum price below which they will not sell their products.
   (d) A promise by a retailer that he will not sell below a price fixed by a manufacturer.

Unit 18. Sale and Supply of Goods: Obligations of Parties

The law affecting contracts for the sale of goods was largely codified by the Sale of Goods Act 1893. This was later amended several times, and has now been replaced by a consolidating Act, the Sale of Goods Act 1979 which, for convenience, will be called simply 'the Act' in this unit and the next. The Act covers the obligations and remedies of the parties, and the transfer of ownership and risk. Other matters, however, such as offer and acceptance, and consideration, are still governed by the ordinary law of contract (Units 11–17).

The contract need not be in writing. The vast majority of *cash* sales are made orally, as where goods are sold over the counter in a shop or pub, or in a restaurant, or where a car is sold for cash. Only where credit is allowed *may* the contract have to be in writing, e.g., under the Consumer Credit Act 1974.

The Act covers contracts 'whereby the seller transfers or agrees to transfer the property in goods to the buyer for a money consideration called the price'. This applies both to a '*sale*', where ownership passes immediately to the buyer, and to an '*agreement to sell*', where the parties agree now that ownership ('property') shall pass later.

The Act does not apply to barter or exchange, because there is no 'price' in money, although it does apply to part-exchange. It does not apply to hire, because no ownership passes to the hirer. It does not apply to contracts for 'work (or skill) and materials', where the goods supplied form only a fairly small part of the consideration. Therefore, the Act would not apply to the vaccine provided by a vet as a small part of his treatment of the animals. What the customer principally paid for was the vet's skill. The vaccine was only an incidental to this, as with the material which a dentist actually puts into a tooth which he fills. Contracts to supply and fit double

167

glazing or cental heating are probably 'work and materials' contracts rather than sales of the goods.

All of the above contracts which are not sales are now governed by the Supply of Goods and Services Act 1982. This imposes obligations on the supplier almost identical to those in the Sale of Goods Act, sections 12–15 (below). If the goods supplied are defective, therefore, the rules are now the same both for sales and for contracts such as hire or 'work and materials'.

A. Obligations of the seller

Section 27 sets out the principal obligations of the parties:

> 'It is the duty of the seller to deliver the goods, and of the buyer to accept and pay for them in accordance with the contract of sale.'

What the seller delivers, therefore, must accord with his express or implied obligations under the contract of sale. The Act sets out various implied obligations, as to title, description, quality, quantity, time and place of delivery, etc., some of which the parties are free to vary, some not. The main implied terms are as follows:

Title

By section 12(1) of the Act there is:

> 'an implied *condition* on the part of the seller that in the case of a sale, he has a right to sell the goods, and in the case of an agreement to sell, he will have such a right at the time when the property is to pass'.

If the seller has no right to sell the goods (because he had stolen them, or only held them on hire or hire-purchase, for example), then he will be liable to the buyer for breach of condition. The buyer can recover the full price which he paid, even if he has had the use of the goods for some time.

> In *Rowland* v. *Divall* (1923), the buyer of a car used it for about three months, but then found that it was stolen and had to return it to the true owner. He was held entitled to recover from the seller the full price which he had paid even though, when he had to part with it, the car was probably worth rather less. He had paid to become owner, he had not become owner, and he was, therefore, entitled to the return of his money.

It will be noticed that, if the buyer obtains no title, he will be bound to return the goods to the true owner, or be liable to him in conversion (Unit 10).

Section 12(2) also implies two *warranties* into contracts of sale: that the goods are free from any encumbrance (such as a mortgage) not disclosed or made known to the buyer before the contract is made, and that the buyer will enjoy quiet possession of the goods. These overlap with section 12(1), but they can sometimes be useful.

> In *Microbeads A. G.* v. *Vinhurst Road Markings Ltd* (1975), shortly *after* the sale, a third party obtained a patent which interfered with the buyer's right to use the machines (i.e., with his quiet possession). There had been no breach of section 12(1), because the seller had had a right to sell. However, the buyer was entitled to recover damages for breach of section 12(2).

Sections 12(3)–(5) do provide limited rights for the seller to contract out of his obligations as to title, if it is made quite clear in the contract that the seller's title may be defective, so that the buyer knows the risk he may be taking. In this event, there is no condition that the seller has a right to sell, only various warranties to the effect, for example, that all *known* encumbrances have been disclosed, and that the buyer's quiet possession will not be disturbed *by the seller*.

Description

Section 13(1) provides that:

> 'Where there is a contract for the sale of goods by description there is an implied condition that the goods shall correspond with the description.'

Goods ordered through a catalogue, or a new car ordered from the manufacturers through a dealer, will always be sold by description, because this is the only way to identify what is required. Even goods seen and specifically chosen by the customer can be sold by description, and a customer is entitled to expect, for example, that goods which he chooses from the shelf in a supermarket will correspond to the description on the tin or packet.

> In *Beale* v. *Taylor* (1967), a car was advertised as a 'Herald Convertible, white, 1961'. The buyer saw the vehicle before buying it, but only discovered some time later that, while the rear part had been accurately described, the front half had been part of an earlier model. The seller was held to be in breach of section 13.

The word 'description' covers a wide variety of matters. Statements as to quantity, weight, ingredients and even packing have been held to be part of the description.

> Thus in *Re Moore & Co. and Landauer & Co.* (Unit 15), the buyer described in the contract how he wished the consignment of canned fruit to be packed. When the seller supplied fruit which was not packed as stipulated, the buyer was entitled to reject the goods.

We have seen in Unit 15 that compliance with the description must be complete and exact.

> In *Arcos* v. *E. & A. Ronaasen & Son* (1933), the contract was for half-inch wooden staves. Some of the staves supplied were as much as nine-sixteenths of an inch thick, and it was held that the buyer was entitled to reject the consignment.

On the other hand, we have seen in cases such as *Peter Darlington Partners Ltd* v. *Gosho Ltd* (Unit 15) that the courts will usually try to give a common-sense meaning to any descriptive terms agreed and that, in any event, microscopic deviations may sometimes be ignored.

Quality

Unlike the obligations imposed by sections 12, 13 and 15, which apply to all sales of goods, section 14 applies where the seller sells *in the course of a business*. As a general

169

rule, a seller owes no obligation as regards the quality or suitability of his goods but, where section 14 applies, there are three important exceptions to this general rule.

1. *Merchantable quality*. Section 14(2) provides that:

> 'Where the seller sells goods in the course of a business, there is an implied condition that the goods supplied under the contract are of merchantable quality.'

By section 14(6), 'merchantable' means 'as fit for the purpose or purposes for which goods of that kind are commonly bought as it is reasonable to expect having regard to any description applied to them, the price (if relevant) and all the other relevant circumstances'. The quality which the buyer is entitled to expect, therefore, can depend upon many factors. If he buys cheap goods, he must reasonably expect lower quality than if he pays more. Similarly, goods sold second-hand may be merchantable as such, even though they would not be satisfactory if sold new in that condition.

> In *Bartlett* v. *Sidney Marcus Ltd* (1965), a second-hand car was sold with a defective clutch. The seller had warned the buyer of the defect, and the price took account of this. The car was held to be of merchantable quality in the circumstances, even though repair cost more than the buyer expected.

This obligation regarding merchantable quality does not apply (a) as regards defects specifically drawn to the buyer's attention before the contract is made, or (b) if the buyer examines the goods before the contract is made, as regards defects which that examintion ought to reveal. The second of these exceptions is often misunderstood; there is *no* obligation on the buyer to examine the goods, and if he chooses not to do so, he is entitled to the full protection of section 14(2).

2. *Reasonable fitness for the purpose made known*. Section 14(3) provides that:

> 'Where the seller sells goods in the course of a business and the buyer, expressly or by implication, makes known . . . to the seller . . . any particular purpose for which the goods are being bought, there is an implied condition that the goods supplied are reasonably fit for that purpose, whether or not that is a purpose for which such goods are commonly supplied, except where the circumstances show that the buyer does not rely, or that it is unreasonable for him to rely, on the skill or judgment of the seller. . . .'

This subsection only applies, therefore, if the buyer has expressly or impliedly made known to the seller the purpose for which he requires the goods. Where the goods only have one or two obvious uses, it will readily be assumed that the buyer has impliedly indicated that he wants them for their normal purpose. Thus, if someone buys food, he will be taken to indicate that he wants it to be reasonably fit for eating.

> In *Grant* v. *Australian Knitting Mills* (1936), a customer bought underpants from a shop. The garment still contained a chemical substance which had not been removed after manufacture, and this caused dermatitis. It was held that the buyer had impliedly made known that he intended to wear the underpants, which were not reasonably fit for that purpose. Furthermore, the garment was not of merchantable quality.

The goods supplied need only be *reasonably* fit, however, and then only for the purposes made known.

> In *Griffiths* v. *Peter Conway Ltd* (1939), a lady with abnormally sensitive skin suffered dermatitis from contact with her new tweed coat. The garment would not have affected normal skin, and the lady's action against the seller, therefore, failed. The garment was reasonably fit for normal purposes, and the buyer had not made known her special circumstances.

The subsection contains one exception to this implied condition, namely, where the circumstances show that the buyer does not rely, or that it is unreasonable for him to rely, on the seller's skill or judgment. This may apply, for example, where the buyer is an expert in such goods, and gives detailed specifications as to what he requires. On the other hand, even partial reliance on the seller is enough, and several important cases have held that it can be reasonable for one dealer or expert to rely partly on the skill or judgment of another.

Many buyers need credit. Section 14(3) also applies, therefore, where the owner does not sell directly to the buyer, but only indirectly, via a finance house or other consumer credit business. The owner sells the goods for cash to the finance house, which then re-sells the goods on conditional sale or credit sale to the buyer, who pays by instalments (page 205). In this event, the original owner is called a 'credit-broker' because he introduces the would-be buyer to the finance house. It is sufficient for section 14(3) if the would-be buyer makes known to the original owner or 'credit-broker' the purpose for which the goods are being bought.

3. *Terms implied by usage.* Section 14(4) provides that implied conditions and warranties as to quality or fitness may be annexed by usage.

Two final points must be made about section 14 as a whole. First, the section applies to all goods *supplied* under the contract, so that even if the goods sold are in order, there can be breach if the packaging is defective.

> In *Geddling* v. *Marsh* (1920), mineral water was sold by the manufacturer to a retailer in bottles which had to be returned to the manufacturer. The buyer was injured when a defective bottle burst. He recovered damages under section 14 because, even though the bottles were not *sold* under the contract, the section applies to all goods supplied.

There will also be breach if dangerous extraneous matter is supplied with the goods sold.

> In *Wilson* v. *Rickett, Cockerell & Co. Ltd* (1954), the plaintiff ordered 'Coalite' from the seller. The consignment contained a detonator, which exploded when put on the fire. When sued, the seller pleaded that the detonator was included by mistake, was not part of the goods *sold*, and, therefore, was not subject to section 14. The Court of Appeal rejected this defence; the detonator had been *supplied* under the contract, albeit erroneously.

Secondly, compliance with section 14 must be strict.

> In *Frost* v. *Aylesbury Dairy Co. Ltd* (1905), a dairy supplied milk which contained typhoid germs. The dairy showed that it had taken all reasonable care to prevent this. It was held that this was no defence (Unit 15).

171

Sample

By section 15, if goods are sold by sample, there are implied conditions (a) that the bulk will correspond with the sample in quality, (b) that the buyer will have a reasonable opportunity of comparing the bulk with the sample, and (c) that the goods will be free from any defect, rendering them unmerchantable, which would not be apparent on reasonable examination of the sample.

A sale will be by sample if there is an express or implied term to this effect. Fitted carpets are normally bought by sample, for instance, as is the material for made-to-measure clothes. A retailer ordering goods in bulk from a supplier will often order in this way.

> In *Godley* v. *Perry* (1960), a boy bought a plastic catapult from a retail shop. The catapult broke almost immediately, and the boy lost an eye. The retailer had bought his catapults by sample from a wholesaler. The retailer had tested the sample by pulling back the elastic, and no defect was apparent at that stage. It was held that (a) the boy could recover damages from the retailer for breach of sections 14(2) and (3), and (b) the retailer could recover damages from the wholesaler for breach of section 15(2)(c).

Delivery

The mechanics of delivery (as opposed to *what* is delivered) are covered by a series of sections later in the Act. By section 28, delivery and payment are concurrent conditions, so the seller can retain the goods until payment is tendered. Section 29(1) provides that, in the absence of agreement to the contrary, it is for the buyer to collect the goods from wherever the seller has them, not for the seller to dispatch them to the buyer. Where the seller does agree to dispatch the goods, he must do so within a reasonable time and, in any event, demand or tender of delivery must be at a reasonable time of day. By section 3(1), the buyer is entitled to delivery of all the goods at once, and need not accept delivery by instalments.

Exclusion of the seller's obligations

Although as a general rule the parties can make whatever bargain they please, we have seen in Unit 14 that any clause purporting to exclude sections 13 to 15 above will be void as against a person buying as a *consumer*; it may be void even against a non-consumer unless the *seller* can show that the exclusion is reasonable under the Unfair Contract Terms Act 1977. Section 12 of the 1979 Act can never be wholly excluded.

On the other hand, the parties are quite free to exclude or vary provisions such as section 28, 29 or 31 if they so wish.

B. Remedies of the buyer

Where a seller breaks one of his express or implied obligations under the contract, the buyer may have the following remedies.

Damages for breach of contract

Damages can always be claimed as of right, although where no real loss has occurred the amount may be nominal. The measure of damages and the question of remoteness are the same as in contract generally; sections 51 and 53 provide rules very similar to those put forward in *Hadley* v. *Baxendale* (Unit 15), the basic rule being that 'the measure of damages is the estimated loss directly and naturally resulting, in the ordinary course of events, from the seller's breach of contract'. The second rule in *Hadley* v. *Baxendale* is preserved by section 54.

An action for damages may be commenced at any time within the normal limitation period of six years.

Rights to reject the goods and end the contract

Where the term broken by the seller is a *condition* (not a mere warranty), the buyer has rights to reject the goods and treat the contract as repudiated. It will be noted that most of the terms implied by sections 12 to 15 are conditions; similarly, the courts have held that late delivery by a seller is a breach of condition which entitles the buyer to reject the goods and end the contract.

Since these remedies derive from equity, the limitation period can be very short. Section 11(4) provides that, where the contact of sale is non-severable, the rights to reject the goods and treat the contract as repudiated are lost as soon as the buyer has *accepted* the goods, or part thereof. Section 35 provides that the buyer is deemed to have accepted the goods:

1. when he intimates to the seller that he has accepted them; or
2. (except where section 34 provides otherwise) when the goods have been delivered to him and he does any act in relation to them which is inconsistent with the ownership of the seller; or
3. when, after the lapse of a reasonable time, he retains the goods without intimating to the seller that he has rejected them.

These rules are based on the ordinary equitable ones whereby a party who 'affirms' the contract thereby loses his right to rescind it. The first and third rules are fairly simple; the remedies are lost if the buyer expressly accepts the goods, or if he retains them for more than a 'reasonable' time, this being a question of fact. The right to reject perishable goods, for example, may be lost within hours. The second rule arises when the buyer treats the goods as belonging to him, for example by consuming or re-selling them. This rule is subject to section 34, which provides that the seller must give the buyer a reasonable opportunity of examining the goods to see whether they conform with the contract, and that the buyer is not deemed to have accepted the goods unless and until he has had a reasonable opportunity of examining them. Therefore, if a buyer acquires goods which are pre-packed so that he cannot examine them, re-sells them, and is then told by the sub-buyer that they are defective, the goods can still be rejected as against the original seller, provided that only a reasonable time has elapsed.

173

Section 30 covers tender of a wrong quantity, or of mixed goods.

1. Where the seller delivers too small a quantity, the buyer can either reject the consignment, or he can accept the lesser amount, the price being reduced rateably.
2. Where the seller delivers too large a quantity, the buyer may reject the whole, accept the contract amount and reject the rest, or accept the whole and pay a price increased rateably.
3. Where the seller delivers goods, some of which accord with the contract description, some of which do not, the buyer may accept those which do accord with the contract and reject the rest, or he may reject the whole.

Section 31(2) deals with instalment contracts. It will be recalled that section 11(4) applies only to 'non-severable' contracts. Where the goods are to be delivered by instalments, each to be paid for separately, the contract is treated as severable. In this event, where only one or two of many instalments is defective, each defective delivery can be *rejected*, notwithstanding that earlier instalments have been accepted. The difficulty arises, however, over whether one defective instalment entitles the buyer to treat the whole contract as *repudiated*, and refuse all future deliveries, satisfactory or not. The tests to determine this are the relation which the size of the breach bears to the contract as a whole, and the likelihood or otherwise of the breach being repeated.

> In *Munro Ltd* v. *Meyer* (1930), a first delivery of 611 tons of defective bone meal out of a contract to supply 1500 tons did entitle the buyer to refuse further deliveries.

> In *Maple Flock Co.* v. *Universal Furniture Ltd* (1934), a defect in one instalment of rag flock, the 16th out of 20 deliveries made, did not entitle the buyer to avoid the whole contract.

Finally, it should be noted that all of these rules affect only the buyer's rights to reject the goods and end the contract. Where the buyer has lost these rights, *he can still sue the seller for damages* within the six-year limitation period.

Specific performance

Section 52 preserves the remedy of specific performance in contracts for the sale of goods but, as noted elsewhere, this will only be awarded where the article sold is unique, such as an original painting. Mere rarity is not normally enough; see *Cohen* v. *Roche* (Unit 15).

C. Other sanctions against suppliers of goods

Actions in tort

Sections 12 to 15 of the Sale of Goods Act merely imply terms into the contract between seller and buyer and, therefore, because of the privity of contract rules, have serious weaknesses as a means of protecting consumers. Thus, where the goods have passed through several hands, the Sale of Goods Act only gives remedies against the immediate seller, not previous owners or the manufacturer. If the immediate seller is not worth suing, the buyer's only right of action may be in tort if he can, for example, prove negligence by the manufacturer. Similar problems arise where dangerous goods (such as a defective car) injure someone other than the buyer himself; the person injured cannot sue on a contract to which he is not a party, and the Sale of Goods Act is, therefore, of no help. Cases such as *Donoghue* v. *Stevenson* and *Steer* v. *Durable Rubber Co. Ltd* (Unit 9) arose in this type of situation.

Criminal liability of seller

A second problem arises because few buyers have the energy or initiative to pursue claims against the sellers of defective goods. Moreover, many buyers are inhibited by the likely cost of proceedings.

Consumers are protected, therefore, by the criminal law, which prohibits certain practices by sellers. The main provision is section 1 of the Trade Descriptions Act 1968.

> 'any person who, in the course of a trade or business . . . (a) applies a false trade description to goods; or (b) supplies or offers to supply goods to which a false trade description is applied; shall . . . be guilty of an offence.'

This section has fairly limited scope: it applies only where the sale is in the course of a business, and it covers only false *descriptions*. The section does not prohibit the supply of defective goods, so long as the seller makes no false claims about them. Criminal sanctions as to the *quality* of what is sold only exist over a few types of goods; for example, the Road Traffic Act makes it an offence in some circumstances to sell a vehicle in a dangerous condition, and the Food Act 1984 creates offences for selling unfit or adulterated food.

Administration and enforcement of these criminal controls is by various public officers: trading standards inspectors in the case of trade descriptions, public health inspectors for food, police in the case of vehicles. These controls, therefore, are not dependent upon the initiative of the buyer.

The sanctions are the normal criminal ones of fines and, exceptionally, imprisonment. These do not directly benefit the buyer, but a Magistrates' Court can now, under the Powers of Criminal Courts Act, as amended, award limited compensation, up to £2000, to a person affected by the offence, and such compensation orders are quite frequently made for trade descriptions offences.

D. Obligations of the buyer

The buyer must accept the goods and pay for them in accordance with the contract.

Payment

The amount of the price is normally fixed by the contract. Alternatively, it may be determined by the course of earlier dealings between the parties, or may be left to be fixed by a valuer or referee.

175

The time for payment is on delivery of the goods. A later date or dates may be agreed where credit is allowed. Section 10 provides that, unless otherwise agreed, delay in payment is only a breach of warranty, not condition.

Acceptance

This is largely self-explanatory; a buyer, having ordered goods, breaks his contract if he then refuses to take them. He can only validly reject the goods if the seller is in breach of condition.

E. Remedies of the seller

Action for the price

Where the ownership of the goods has passed to the buyer, or where a specified date for payment was set and has passed, the seller can sue for the contract price.

Damages for non-acceptance

Moreover, where the buyer refuses to accept or pay for the goods the seller may claim damages, the measure being 'the estimated loss directly and naturally resulting, in the ordinary course of events, from the buyer's breach of contract' (section 50). Where, between the contract and the date for delivery, the market price of such goods has fallen, so that the seller will get less on a re-sale, the damages will, prima facie, be the difference between the contract price and the market price at the time when the goods should have been accepted.

Unpaid seller's rights over the goods

A common reason for non-payment is because the buyer has no money. In these circumstances, the seller's rights to sue for the price or damages may be worthless, and he will often prefer simply to keep the goods. The Act, therefore, gives him certain rights.

1. Under sections 41 and 39(2), an unpaid seller has a *lien* or *right to withhold delivery* until he is paid. These rights exist while the goods are still in the seller's possession and no credit has been allowed to the buyer. The rights are lost as soon as the seller parts with possession; he has no right to re-take them from the buyer. Note also that the lien gives the seller no right to *re-sell* the goods yet, only to retain them.
2. By section 44, if an unpaid seller has parted with the goods to a carrier, he still has a *right of stoppage in transit* if, during the transit, the buyer *becomes insolvent* (not otherwise). The seller can order the carrier to re-deliver the goods to the seller or his agent, so that the buyer will not get possession.

176

3. By section 48, if an unpaid seller still has the goods, he will have a *right to re-sell* them in three circumstances: (a) where the goods are perishable; or (b) where the unpaid seller gives notice to the buyer of his intention to re-sell, and the buyer still does not pay or tender the price within a reasonable time; and (c) where, in the contract, the seller expressly reserved a right to re-sell should the buyer default.

   Where re-sale is at a profit, so that the seller gets more than the original contract price, the seller can keep the profit. If an unpaid seller re-sells wrongfully, e.g., without giving reasonable notice, the new buyer gets a good title but, in this event, the seller must account to the old buyer for any profit as compared with the original contract price.

4. In addition to these statutory rights, some sellers of valuable industrial goods have, in recent years, used '*reservation of title*' clauses for further protection.

   In *Aluminium Industrie Vaassen BV* v. *Romalpa Aluminium Ltd* (1976), AIV sold some aluminium foil to Romalpa. The written contract provided that ownership of the foil would only pass to Romalpa when the latter paid all that it owed to AIV. If Romalpa made a new object with the foil, or incorporated or mixed it with other goods, AIV would become owner of this other object. Romalpa could sell the new object, but only on condition that its rights against the sub-buyer were handed over to AIV. When Romalpa later became insolvent, AIV successfully claimed (a) the proceeds of re-sale of some foil by Romalpa, and (b) that the foil still held by Romalpa belonged to AIV, and should be returned.

   Such '*Romalpa*' clauses do give rise to legal difficulties, and have come before the courts several times in recent years. They can be very valuable to the seller if the buyer is insolvent, but must be very carefully drafted. In particular, the part dealing with *mixed* goods will rarely be valid.

Examination questions

1. Simple wishes to buy his son a car as a birthday present. He approaches Wheeler, a retailer of car spares, who he knows sells cars for his customers from time to time. Wheeler offers to sell Simple a second-hand car, explains that the brakes require attention and reduces the price to take account of this. He also says that he will take no responsibility for this or any other defect. Simple accepts the offer without examining the car. If he had done so he would have seen that the tyres were badly worn.

   Simple drives away the car but, because of its defects, fails to negotiate a bend in the road. The car strikes a wall and is damaged beyond repair.

   Advise Simple of his rights, if any, against Wheeler.

2. A company operating a chain of retail wine shops sells a considerable amount of wine which is imported in bottles. It is not possible for the company to ensure that the wine will always comply with the label on the bottle or that the wine is free from harmful substances.

   Draft a report explaining the legal liability which might arise towards a customer and whether or not this liability might be avoided. (Do not consider the effect of the Trade Descriptions Act 1968 or any other possible criminal liability.)

3. Section 27, Sale of Goods Act 1979, states, 'It is the duty of the seller to deliver the goods, and of the buyer to accept and pay for them, in accordance with the terms of the contract of sale'.

   Explain the meaning and the effect of this section. In particular, describe the seller's duties in connection with delivery and indicate what constitutes acceptance by the buyer.

4. Advise H in the following cases, explaining the relevant principles of law:
   (a) J sold to H 2000 lb of fruit, to be delivered in 10 lb tins. J delivered the total quantity in 20 lb tins.
   (b) J sold to H 1000 tins of biscuits. J delivered 1500 tins.
   (c) J sold to H 600 blue shirts. J delivered 400 blue shirts and 200 brown shirts.

5. Explain what action may be taken by the seller in respect of each of the following transactions:
   (a) Goods are sold on credit terms and dispatched by rail. While the goods are on rail the seller hears that the buyer is having difficulty in paying his debts.
   (b) Goods are sold and the buyer then asks if the seller will grant him credit terms and dispatch the goods. The seller is unwilling to do this in spite of the fact that the goods are of perishable nature.

Unit 19. Sale of Goods: Ownership and Risk

A. Transfer of property between seller and buyer

The purpose of a contract of sale is to transfer ownership of the goods from seller to buyer, and the Act contains rules for determining precisely when this happens. This is important mainly because of the question of risk; by section 20, any loss, prima facie, falls on the party who is owner at that time. In this unit the words 'property' and 'ownership' mean the same thing.

To determine when ownership passes, it is important first to distinguish between specific and unascertained goods. *Specific* goods are 'goods identified and agreed on *at the time a contract of sale is made*'. Thus a buyer may point to a specific car in the showroom as the one which he wants. All sales in self-service shops, and most over-the-counter sales will be of specific goods. All goods which are not specific are *unascertained*. If a buyer orders a new car which is yet to be delivered from the manufacturer, it is not yet possible to point to which specific car is to become his. Almost all orders in bulk (e.g., 100 tons of wheat) will be of unascertained goods, as will most orders by post.

In a contract for unascertained goods, the subject-matter will, at some stage, be 'appropriated' to the contract. Thus, 100 tons of wheat from the seller's stock will, at some stage, be set aside for the buyer. The 100 tons is then said to be *ascertained*. The 100 tons do not become specific goods, however, because they were not identified at the time of the contract; unascertained goods cannot become specific ones under the same sale.

179

Passing of property in specific goods

Section 17 provides that the property in specific goods passes whenever the parties intend it to pass. They can make their own provision (as in the *Romalpa* case). To ascertain the intention of the parties, 'regard shall be had to the terms of the contract, the conduct of the parties, and the circumstances of the case'. This is the overriding rule, and section 18, below, must always be read subject to it.

Where the parties do not expressly or impliedly indicate when they want ownership to pass, section 18 sets out various rules to ascertain their presumed intention:

> *Rule 1* 'Where there is an unconditional contract for the sale of specific goods, in a deliverable state, the property in the goods passes to the buyer *when the contract is made*, and it is immaterial whether the time of payment or the time of delivery, or both, be postponed.'

In spite of the last words of this rule, the courts are still free under section 17 to hold that, where both payment and delivery are postponed, the parties did not intend ownership to pass yet.

> In *Ward (R. V.) Ltd* v. *Bignall* (1967), the seller unconditionally sold a specific car to the buyer, but retained possession until the buyer could pay for it. In the Court of Appeal, Diplock L. J. indicated (*obiter*) that he would, if necessary, be willing to treat the car as still belonging to the seller, in spite of the wording of Rule 1. It was arguable that both parties regarded the car as being the seller's until the buyer paid or was allowed to take delivery, and the court could assume that this was their real intention.

It should be noted that Rule 1 applies only where the goods are already in a 'deliverable state'; if they are not, then the second rule may apply:

> *Rule 2* 'Where there is a contract for the sale of specific goods and the seller is bound to do something to the goods for the purpose of putting them into a deliverable state, the property does not pass until the thing is done, and the buyer has notice that it has been done.'

Goods are only in a deliverable state 'when they are in such a state that the buyer would under the contract be bound to take delivery of them' (section 61(5)). If, therefore, the seller still has things to do to the goods under the contract, the ownership will not pass yet. For example, if the seller agrees in the contract to fit new tyres to the car, the car will remain in the seller's ownership and at his risk until the tyres are fitted *and* the buyer has notice of this.

The third rule is self-explanatory:

> *Rule 3* 'Where there is a contract for the sale of specific goods in a deliverable state, but the seller is bound to weigh, measure, test, or do some other act or thing with reference to the goods for the purpose of ascertaining the price, the property does not pass until the act or thing is done and the buyer has notice that it has been done.'

The fourth rules covers the situation where a buyer asks for goods, such as a new book or machine, on approval. Note that this rule applies only where the buyer has *agreed* to take the goods on this basis; it does *not* apply where a would-be seller sends unsolicited goods to someone (Unit 12).

Rule 4 'When goods are delivered to the buyer on approval or on sale or return or other similar terms, the property in the goods passes to the buyer:
(a) when he signifies his approval or acceptance or does any other act adopting the transaction (for example, by re-selling the goods);
(b) if he does not signify his approval or acceptance to the seller but retains the goods without giving notice of rejection, then, if a time has been fixed for the return of the goods, on the expiration of that time, and, if no time has been fixed, on the expiration of a reasonable time.' (What is a reasonable time is a question of fact.)

Passing of property in unascertained goods

Section 16 provides that:

'Where there is a contract for the sale of unascertained goods, no property in the goods is transferred to the buyer unless and until the goods are ascertained.'

This is simply a rule of common sense; while goods remain unascertained, it is impossible to point out which car or bag of wheat is to belong to the buyer. It should be noted, however, that the section is phrased negatively; even when the goods are ascertained, they do not necessarily become the buyer's (see the *Romalpa* case again). Passing of property is, prima facie, governed by section 18 again:

Rule 5 'Where there is a contract for the sale of unascertained . . . goods by description, and goods of that description and in a deliverable state are unconditionally appropriated to the contract, either by the seller with the assent of the buyer, or by the buyer with the assent of the seller, the property in the goods then passes to the buyer; and the assent may be express or implied, and may be given either before or after the appropriation is made.'

Ownership can only pass, therefore, when goods are 'appropriated' to the contract, that is, set aside or otherwise identified, labelled, etc., with the firm intention that these are the goods covered by the contract. Delivery of the correct amount to a carrier for transport to the buyer will be appropriation for this purpose.

Moreover, ownership does not pass to the buyer unless and until the goods are in a deliverable state.

In *Philip Head & Sons* v. *Showfronts Ltd* (1970), the seller agreed to deliver and lay fitted carpets. A carpet was delivered, but left overnight to be laid next morning. It was held that the carpet was still at the seller's risk, so that when it was stolen overnight, the seller bore the loss.

B. Risk

'Risk' can cover a multitude of mishaps, from slight damage to theft or total destruction. The basic rule to determine on whom the loss should fall is in section 20 of the Act:

'Unless otherwise agreed, the goods remain at the seller's risk until the property in them is transferred to the buyer, but when the property in them is transferred to the buyer, the goods are at the buyer's risk whether delivery has been made or not.'

The Act also contains more detailed rules. There are three possible times when loss can occur.

1. Loss occurring before the contract is made

This obviously falls on the seller. He may not only lose the goods, but also be liable to the buyer for damages if he contracts to deliver goods and then cannot do so. Where *unascertained* goods are sold, for example, it is up to the seller to find supplies and, if his own stocks turn out to be damaged, stolen or destroyed, this is his misfortune; he must find alternative supplies or face damages for non-delivery.

Where *specific* goods are sold, however, the seller may be protected from liablility to the buyer by section 6:

> 'Where there is a contract for the sale of specific goods, and the goods without the knowledge of the seller have perished at the time when the contract is made, the contract is void.'

This section has limited scope: it applies only where the goods have *perished*, that is, ceased to exist either physically or commercially, and it applies only where this has happened wihout the seller's knowledge. (A seller who tries to sell goods which he knows have perished will be guilty of fraud.) Goods can 'perish' without being totally destroyed.

> In *Asfar & Co. Ltd* v. *Blundell* (1896), a cargo of dates which had sunk in the harbour and, when raised two days later, was 'simply a mass of pulpy matter impregnated with sewage and in a state of fermentation', was held to have 'perished' although still physically in existence.

> In *Barrow, Lane & Ballard Ltd* v. *Phillips & Co. Ltd* (1929), the sellers sold 700 *specific* bags of Chinese nuts. Unknown to the sellers, 109 bags had already been stolen. It was held that the specific consignment of 700 bags had perished, because a substantial part of it had gone.

Section 6 is based on the common law rules of mistake, and on cases such as *Couturier* v. *Hastie* (Unit 13). If the contract is void, the seller still bears the loss, but has no liability to the buyer.

2. Loss occurring between contact and the passing of property

Property will pass immediately on making the contract only when section 18, Rule 1 applies. Loss occurring after the contract but before ownership passes will be subject to rules similar to those discussed above; prima facie the loss falls on the seller and, moreover, the buyer may recover damages for non-delivery if the seller does not get other supplies.

Where *specific* goods are sold, however, section 7 may protect the seller against liability to the buyer:

> 'Where there is an agreement to sell specific goods and subsequently the goods, without any fault on the part of the seller or buyer, perish before the risk passes to the buyer, the agreement is avoided.'

This is based on the common law rules of frustration and, like section 6, applies only where specific goods have 'perished'. Where the specific goods are only slightly damaged, section 7 may not apply, and the seller may face liability to the buyer, even though the damage was not the seller's fault.

When section 7 applies, the Law Reform (Frustrated Contracts) Act 1943 does not; all moneys payable, therefore, cease to be due, and all moneys paid under the contract must be returned. If the seller has incurred expenses under the contract, he can neither recover these from the buyer, nor keep part of any deposit which the buyer may have paid.

3. Loss occurring after the passing of property

Under section 20, this falls on the buyer, even if the goods are still in the seller's possession.

> In *Tarling* v. *Baxter* (1827), a farmer sold a haystack, which remained on his farm, to be collected in the spring. Before collection, the stack was destroyed. It was held that, on the facts, ownership had passed to the buyer, and, therefore, he bore the loss.

There are, however, two provisos. First, section 20(2) provides that where delivery has been delayed through the fault of either seller or buyer, the goods are at the risk of the party at fault as regards any loss which might not have occurred but for the delay.

> In *Demby Hamilton & Co. Ltd* v. *Barden* (1949), the seller agreed to send 30 tons of apple juice by weekly consignments to the buyer. The buyer delayed taking delivery of some of the juice which, as a result, went bad. The buyer was still held liable to pay, because the delay was his fault.

Secondly, by section 20(3), 'nothing in this section affects the duties or liabilities of either seller or buyer as a bailee of the goods of the other party'.Thus, if the seller remains in possession after ownership has passed to the buyer, the seller must take reasonable care of the goods.

Finally, section 20 applies only in the absence of contrary agreement, and the parties can always agree that the risk is to pass before the ownership, or vice versa.

> In *Inglis* v. *Stock* (1885), the buyer bought an unascertained part of a large cargo of sugar. The contract validly provided that risk should pass when the cargo was put aboard ship, although, under section 16, ownership could not pass until the buyer's part of the cargo was ascertained.

C. Transfer of title by a non-owner

As a general rule, only the owner of goods or his agent can validly sell them. This is often expressed in the phrase *nemo dat quod non habet* (no one can give what he does not have), and the rule is embodied in section 21:

> '. . . where goods are sold by a person who is not their owner, and who does not sell them under the authority or with the consent of the owner, the buyer acquires no better title to the goods than the seller had. . . .'

When the buyer obtains no title, he must return the goods on demand to the true owner, or face an action for the tort of conversion. In turn, the buyer can recover damages from the seller for breach of section 12 of the Act, but by this time the seller may have absconded.

This rule can, therefore, be hard on buyers, who often have no means of knowing whether the seller is the owner. The issue is often between an innocent true owner and an innocent ultimate buyer, both of whom are victims of a rogue who has departed. There are other situations discussed below where the *nemo dat* rule would also be harsh to buyers, and a number of exceptions to the general rule have, therefore, developed.

Sale by an agent

An agent acting within his actual authority can pass a good title to his principal's goods. Even if the agent exceeds his actual authority, he may still pass a good title if he is acting within his implied or apparent authority, so that the buyer has no reason to suspect that the agent has no right to sell.

The Factors Act 1889 puts these rules into statutory form as regards *mercantile agents*. A mercantile agent is one having, in the course of his business as an independent agent (*not* merely as an employee of the principal), authority to sell goods or otherwise deal with them. Section 2(1) of the Factors Act provides that:

> 'Where a mercantile agent is, with the consent of the owner, in possession of goods or of the documents of title to the goods, any sale, pledge or other disposition of the goods, made by him when acting in the ordinary course of business of a mercantile agent, shall . . . be as valid as if he were expressly authorized by the owner of the goods to make the same, provide that the person taking under the disposition acts in good faith, and that he has not at the time of the disposition notice that the person making the disposition has not authority to make the same.'

The operation of the section can be seen in the case of:

> *Folkes* v. *King* (1923), where an agent had authority to sell his principal's car for not less than £575. In breach of these instructions, he sold for only £340. The buyer obtained a good title, because the agent was clearly in possession with authority to sell, and the buyer had no reason to suspect the limitation which the principal had imposed.

The section applies only where the person who sells was in possession *as agent to sell*. If a car is left with a garage for repairs, and wrongly sold by the garage, the Factors Act will not apply, because the garage was not in possession as agent to sell. The agent must, moreover, have obtained possession with the owner's consent, although consent induced by fraud can be enough.

Sale by the mercantile agent must be in the ordinary course of business, and the buyer must take in good faith. These requirements are often connected, because if there are unusual features surrounding the sale, so that it is not in the ordinary course of business, then the buyer should be suspicious and, if he makes no enquiries, his good faith is in doubt. The owner of a car can, therefore, protect himself when entrusting the vehicle to a dealer for sale, by retaining the registration book. If the dealer sells a second-hand car without the registration book, this should make the buyer enquire further, and the buyer will get no title under the Factors Act if the dealer exceeds his authority.

Estoppel

Section 21 of the Sale of Goods Act itself provides an exception to the *nemo dat* rule, where 'the owner of the goods is by his conduct precluded from denying the seller's authority to sell'. This may occur where the owner deliberately gives someone else the appearance of having a right to deal with the goods.

> In *Eastern Distributors Ltd* v. *Goldring* (1957), a car owner gave a dealer documents which made the dealer appear to be the owner, as part of a scheme to enable the car owner to borrow money without adequate security. The scheme fell through, but the dealer went ahead and sold the car to a finance company. It was held that the finance company obtained a good title because, although the dealer had no right to sell, the owner's conduct estopped him from asserting this.

Sale in market overt (section 22)

> 'Where goods are sold in market overt, according to the usage of the market, the buyer acquires a good title to the goods, provided he buys them in good faith and without notice of any defect or want of title on the part of the seller.'

A market overt is an open, legally constituted public market which is recognized as such by statute, Royal Charter, or simply prescription from long use. Furthermore, all sales in the public part of the shop in the City of London, of goods usually sold in the shop, in daylight, by the shopkeeper to the customer, are in market overt. Note that the sale must be according to the custom of the market, must be of goods usually sold there, and that the buyer must take in good faith.

> In *Bishopsgate Motor Finance Corporation Ltd* v. *Transport Brakes Ltd* (1949), a seller who only held the car on hire-purchase, sold it privately at Maidstone market. It was held that the buyer obtained a good title, because Maidstone market had been recognized as a market overt by long usage, private sales were customary in the market, and the buyer took in good faith.

Sale under voidable title (section 23)

We have seen in Unit 11 that if a buyer obtains goods under a contract which is voidable (e.g., for misrepresentation or breach of condition), he can pass on a good title to someone who buys from him in good faith without notice of the defect in title, provided that the re-sale takes place before the original contract is rescinded (see cases such as *Lewis* v. *Averay* (1972). On the other hand, if the original contract is *void* (e.g., for mistake), no title can pass under section 23, although other exceptions to the *nemo dat* rule might apply in some circumstances.

185

Re-sale by seller in possession (section 24)

Where a person who has sold goods remains in possession of them, or of documents of title to them, any re-sale by him to a buyer who takes the goods in good faith without notice of the previous sale will give a good title to the new buyer as soon as the latter *takes physical delivery* of the goods or documents of title. The old buyer is left to sue the seller for damages for non-delivery. A similar rules applies if the seller in possession pledges the goods or disposes of them in any other way.

Re-sale by buyer in possession with the consent of the seller (section 25)

Where a person who has bought or agreed to buy goods obtains possession of the goods or documents of title *with the seller's consent*, any sale and delivery by the buyer to a person who takes in good faith, without notice of any rights of the original seller to the goods, shall have 'the same effect as if the person making the delivery . . . were a mercantile agent in possession . . . with the consent of the seller'.

Because of the words quoted, this section has very limited effect. It applies only where the original buyer re-sells *in the ordinary course of business*, as if he were a mercantile agent, or at least where the circumstances are such that the ultimate buyer could assume that he was buying from a mercantile agent or dealer.

> In *Newtons of Wembley Ltd* v. *Williams* (1965), a rogue bought the seller's car with a cheque which was dishonoured. Meanwhile the rogue had taken the car to Warren Street, which was an established street market for second-hand cars, and sold it to an innocent buyer for cash. It was held that the buyer obtained a good title, because the rogue was a buyer in possession with the consent of the owner and, although the rogue was not himself a mercantile agent, he had sold the car in a place where car dealers ordinarily did business.

The first buyer must have obtained possession with the consent of the seller, but consent induced by fraud can be enough. Notice also that, as under section 24, title passes only to the new buyer when the goods are actually delivered to him, not before. Section 25 will not apply to 'conditional sale' agreements within the Consumer Credit Act 1974 (see Unit 21).

Motor vehicles on hire-purchase

Under the Hire-Purchase Act 1964, Part III, if a *vehicle* on hire-purchase is sold by the hirer to a *private* purchaser, who takes in good faith and without notice of the hire-purchase agreement, a good title will pass. A 'private' purchaser is one who is not a 'trade' purchaser (e.g., a garage) or a 'finance' purchaser (e.g., a hire-purchase company). If the hirer sells to a garage, the garage gets no title under these provisions. Moreover, a garage which buys and re-sells a vehicle in these circumstances commits the tort of conversion against the true owner. On the other hand, although the garage is not protected, the first innocent private purchaser to acquire the goods thereafter does get a good title.

Once the goods have become the property of an innocent private purchaser, the title is cured, and a *subsequent* trade or finance purchaser does get a good title. The onus of proof favours the buyer, who is presumed an innocent private buyer unless the contrary is proved.

Finally, it sometimes happens that the first private person to take the vehicle acquires it on hire-purchase. This can happen if the original hirer wrongly sells to a garage, which then disposes of the vehicle to a new hirer through a finance company. The new hirer is protected provided that he takes the car on hire-purchase in good faith.

Sale under common law or statutory powers

Various powers of sale by non-owners exist at common law or under statute. A pledgee has common law powers to sell unredeemed goods pledged with him. Innkeepers, and bailees such as shoe repairers, may have statutory powers to sell their customers' goods to satisfy unpaid charges, and landlords can in some circumstances sell tenants' goods for arrears of rent. An unpaid seller of goods may have power to re-sell under section 48(2) of the Act (see page 177).

Sale under a court order

The High Court has wide powers to order the sale of goods which are affected by some dispute, and which are perishable or likely to deteriorate if kept, or which it is desirable to sell immediately for any other reason.

The legal position regarding transfer of title was summarized by Denning, L.J., in *Pearson* v. *Rose and Young* (1950):

> 'In the early days of the common law the governing principle of our law of property was that no person could give a better title than he himself had got, but the needs of commerce have led to a progressive modification of this principle so as to protect innocent purchasers. . . . The cases show how difficult it is to strike the right balance between the claims of true owners and the claims of innocent purchasers.'

Examination questions

1. A furniture dealer agreed to sell two pieces of furniture to *B*:
   (a) an antique commode which *B* had chosen in the shop; the dealer agreed to replace one of the handles before delivery;
   (b) a new bureau of a standard design, as soon as the dealer could obtain one from the manufacturer; the dealer again agreed to fix new handles to match those on the antique commode.
   When both pieces of furniture were in the shop, with the handles fitted, and ready for collection by *B*, the dealer's shop and furniture were accidentally destroyed by fire. Explain whether *B* still has to pay for the furniture.
2. In April, *B* agreed to buy 1000 rare 'Dutch Uncle' tulip bulbs from *S* Ltd. *B* paid a deposit of 5 per cent of the price, and agreed to pay the balance on 1 September

when the bulbs were to be delivered. In July, all the 'Dutch Uncles' in the world were destroyed by a fungus disease. Advise *B*:

(a) whether he still has to pay for the bulbs; and

(b) alternatively, whether he can get back his 5 per cent deposit.

Would it make any difference whether or not *B* had chosen the specific bulbs which he wanted from *S* Ltd's stock?

3. Advise *BTV* Ltd, which retails television sets, on its legal position in respect of each of the following transactions:

   (a) A set was sold to *L* but not removed from the store. It was subsequently sold and delivered to another customer.

   (b) A set was delivered to *M* on approval for a 10 days' free trial. *M* has now retained the set for one month.

   (c) A particular set was sold to *N* but received slight damage during the course of delivery. *N* thereupon refused to accept delivery.

4. (a) *H*, who held a van on hire-purchase from *F* Finance Ltd, wrongfully traded-in the vehicle to *G* Garages Ltd in part-exchange for a new car. *F* Finance now demand the return of the van from *G* Garages. Explain the rights of each of the parties against each of the others.

   (b) Explain the position of each of the parties, if, before *F* Finance discovered the van's whereabouts, *G* Garages had sold it to Mr *X*, who bought it in good faith.

5. 'In the development of our law, two principles have striven for mastery. The first is for the protection of property: no one can give a better title than he himself possesses. The second is for the protection of commercial transactions: the person who takes in good faith and for value without notice should get a good title' *per* Denning, L.J., in *Bishopsgate Motor Finance Corporation* v. *Transport Brakes Ltd* (1949). Discuss.

Unit 20. Agency

An agent is a person authorized or empowered by another (the 'principal') to bring the principal into legal relations with a third party. Most commonly, the agent's task is to bring about a contract between his principal and a third party. Thus, an estate agent is engaged by the householder to find a buyer for the house, and a travel agent brings about contractual relations between the would-be holidaymaker and the airline and hotel companies.

An agent may be an employee of his principal, as where a firm employs salesmen or buyers, or the agent may be an independent contractor such as an estate agent. There are other possible relationships between principal and agent; for example, a company director may have authority to make contracts on behalf of the business, and a partner may have power to act on behalf of his fellow partners. A corporate body, having no physical existence, can *only* act through its organs or agents.

Normally there will be a contract between principal and agent, and the agent will be paid by way of salary, commission or fees. This is not always the case, however; the man who acts for a friend as a favour, and the wife who buys goods on her husband's account, are none the less agents. As a general rule, an agent can be appointed orally or in writing, with no formal requirements, and anyone, even a minor, can validly be an agent.

This unit is concerned with the creation, effect and termination of the agency relationship, and with the rights and duties of principal and agent to each other.

A. Creation of agency

The concept of 'authority'

An agent's acts can bind his principal if, and only if, the agent has authority to do so. The word authority, however, can be used in at least two different senses, and the subject can perhaps best be tackled with this as a first step.

As between principal and agent, 'authority' means what the principal has expressly or impliedly instructed the agent to do. 'Authority', therefore, means what the agent has been given a *right* to do.

As between principal and third party, the issue is slightly different. The third party wants to know what the agent has *power* to do. The important question is: 'Will the principal be bound by what the agent does?' The third party cannot be expected to know everything that has gone on between principal and agent.

The third party is, therefore, normally entitled to rely on appearances. So long as the agent is doing what he *appears* to have the right to do, then the third party need usually enquire no further. An agent may have 'ostensible' or 'apparent' authority even if (unknown to the third party) he is exceeding or disobeying his principal's instructions. In this sense, therefore, 'authority' means what the agent has *power* to do, whether or not he has a *right* to do it.

Actual authority

This is what the principal expressly or impliedly gives the agent the *right* to do on the principal's behalf. It is important chiefly between principal and agent, because if an agent exceeds his actual authority then he will be liable to his principal.

Express authority arises from the express instructions given by the principal. If these are ambiguous, the agent must seek clarification but, if he cannot contact the principal, he is justified in acting in good faith on a reasonable interpretation of his instructions, even if this turns out not to be what the principal intended.

Implied authority. An agent is impliedly authorized to do such things as are normally incidental to carrying out his express instructions. Thus he may impliedly be authorized to incur postal, telephone and travelling expenses. More importantly, where by ordinary business usage it is *usual* for a particular type of agent to carry out certain functions, the principal, by appointing the agent, will be taken impliedly to have authorized this. There are cases below on the 'usual authority' and powers of people from pub managers to solicitors. Most of the problems, however, have arisen from undisclosed restrictions on usual authority; see below.

Apparent or ostensible authority

This is important between principal and third party because, as explained above, sometimes an agent can have power to do things which he has no right to do. If an agent appears to the third party to be within his authority, then the principal may be bound, even if the agent was in reality breaking or exceeding his instructions.

1. This can occur where there have been undisclosed restrictions on an agent's 'usual' authority. The principal can restrict the usual authority (rights) of a particular type of agent simply by telling the agent not to do what he would normally expect to do. If the agent then disobeys his instruction, *he* is liable to the principal (see page 197). However, this restriction will not affect a third party who deals with the principal

through the agent in good faith and without notice of the restriction. The principal has placed the agent in a position where he appears to the world to have the powers usual to such an agent. If there are no suspicious circumstances, the principal is bound to the third party.

> In *Waugh* v. *Clifford & Sons Ltd* (1982), solicitors were acting for a building firm in a dispute concerning property. The other side suggested a compromise involving an independent valuer. The solicitors sought their client's instructions. In fact their client did not want to settle on these terms, but his instructions to this effect were not passed on by the firm of solicitors to the partner dealing with the case. Therefore, he did agree the compromise. It was held that the builder was bound by it. It was within the usual authority of a solicitor to agree such a compromise, and the other side could rely on the solicitor's ostensible powers.

We saw the effect of undisclosed restrictions on the usual authority of a mercantile agent in *Folkes* v. *King* (Unit 19), and of a partner in a garage business in *Mercantile Credit* v. *Garrod* (Unit 6).

2. A third party can also rely on an agent's 'usual' and apparent authority when the agent has misused his position.

> In *Panorama Developments Ltd* v. *Fidelis Furnishing Fabrics Ltd* (Unit 7), the company secretary hired cars in the company's name but used them for his own purposes. The company still had to pay the bill.

3. Sometimes ostensible authority can arise from estoppel. The principal has 'held out' another as being his agent and, as a result, a third party has been deceived, as in *Freeman and Lockyer* v. *Buckhurst Park Properties Ltd* (Unit 7). A similar rule applies where the owner of property allows another to appear to have power to deal with it, as in *Eastern Distributors Ltd* v. *Goldring* (Unit 19).

4. Something similar can occur even if the principal is undisclosed. If the principal allows the agent ('*A*') to appear to be acting for himself (*A*), whereas in reality *A* is only acting for the principal, then *A* may have all of the usual powers of a person in this position. Restrictions on *A*'s apparent rights will not affect a third party who has been allowed to believe that he is dealing solely with *A*, and who, therefore, cannot know of the restraints.

> In *Watteau* v. *Fenwick* (1893), Mr Humble ran a public house. His name appeared as licensee, and he appeared to be dealing for himself. He ordered cigars from a supplier, *W*, for re-sale in the bar. In fact he had been forbidden to order cigars by Fenwick, the owner, but there was nothing to make *W* suspect this. Fenwick was, therefore, liable to *W* for the price.

> On the other hand in *Kinahan & Co. Ltd* v. *Parry* (1910), the licensee of a *tied* public house, who again appeared to be acting for himself, was bound to buy drinks only from the owners. He ordered whisky from another supplier, *who knew that it was a tied house*. The supplier was involved in the trade and should, therefore, have suspected that the licensee's freedom to buy drinks was limited. The supplier could, therefore, not recover the price from the real owners.

In all of the above situations it must be remembered that if there are suspicious circumstances then ostensible or apparent authority will not apply. The third party can only rely on a *genuine* appearance of authority.

In *Reckitt* v. *Barnett, Pembroke and Slater Ltd* (1929), an agent who could draw cheques on his principal's bank account used such a cheque to pay his private debts. It was obvious from the cheque that this was not the agent's own money. The principal could, therefore, recover the money from the creditor, who should have been suspicious.

In *Overbrooke Estates Ltd* v. *Glencombe Properties Ltd* (1974), the catalogue given to bidders before an auction made it clear that the auctioneer had no authority to make representations about the property. The seller was, therefore, not bound by statements which the auctioneer did make.

Agency of necessity

Exceptionally, a person (the 'agent') may acquire authority from the pressure of necessity. Four conditions must be satisfied:

1. The 'agent' must have been placed in control of the principal's property.
2. A genuine emergency must have arisen, which threatens the property. This may occur, for example, where the property is perishable, and storage or transport facilities break down.
3. It must be impossible for the 'agent' to seek the owner's instructions in time.
4. The 'agent' must be acting in good faith in a genuine attempt to protect the property.

In *Great Northern Railway Co.* v. *Swaffield* (1874) the railway company, through no fault of its own, was unable to deliver a horse consigned by rail. Unable to contact the owner, the company paid to put the horse in livery stables, and was held entitled to recover the cost from the owner.

Agency of necessity will rarely arise today because, due to improved communications, it should normally be possible to seek the owner's instructions quickly.

Ratification

In some situations, a principal can choose to adopt and ratify transactions which were made quite without his authority. Where someone has pretended to be his agent and used his name, the principal can subsequently ratify the transaction so as to obtain the benefit and undertake the obligations agreed. Four conditions must be satisfied before this is possible:

1. The 'agent' must have used the principal's name and claimed to act on the principal's behalf.

In *Re Tiedemann and Ledermann Frères* (1899), an agent who periodically bought and sold wheat on behalf of a principal, also used the principal's name, for financial reasons, in a transaction which he made on his own behalf. It was held that the principal could ratify and adopt this transaction.

Conversely, in *Keighley, Maxted & Co.* v. *Durant & Co.* (1901), an agent agreed to buy wheat in his *own* name. The agent intended this to be on behalf of the principal, but the seller did not know this. The principal, having purported to ratify, later refused to take delivery. He was held not bound to do so. The seller had been content to deal with the agent, and the principal's 'ratification' was inoperative.

2. The principal must have existed and had contractual capacity at the time when the agent acted. A principal cannot ratify something which he could not himself have done or authorized at the time when it happend.

> In *Kelner* v. *Baxter* (1866), three promoters of a company bought goods on the company's behalf *before it was incorporated*. When it *was* formed, the company purported to ratify the transaction, but was held not entitled to do so.

In this situation, by the Companies Act 1985, section 36(4), the company promoter will be *personally* bound by the contract.

3. The principal must have been aware of all material facts at the time when he ratified; otherwise his ratification will not bind him.

> In *Marsh* v. *Joseph* (1897), a rogue purported to be acting on behalf of a solicitor in transactions which turned out to be fraudulent. He then gave a partial account of what he had done to the solicitor who, believing the transactions to be legitimate, ratified the rogue's action. The ratification was held inoperative.

4. An illegal or totally void act cannot be ratified. Thus forged signatures, or things done by a company *ultra vires*, are total nullities which cannot be cured by ratification.

Effect of ratification

Ratification *relates back* to the time of the agent's act, so that the position is the same as if the agent had had authority in the first place. The effect of ratification is *retrospective*. This may have startling results.

> In *Bolton Partners* v. *Lambert* (1889), Lambert made an offer to an agent of Bolton Partners which the agent, acting without authority, purported to accept on behalf of Boltons. Lambert then sought to revoke his offer. *After* this, Boltons ratified the agent's act. It was held that Lambert was bound by the contract, because the ratification related back to the agent's acceptance, so that Lambert's revocation was too late.

The main limit on 'relation back' is that vested rights cannot be divested, so that ratification cannot affect a third party who has acquired rights to the property before ratification.

> In *Bird* v. *Brown* (1850), goods were in transit from seller to buyer when the seller's agent heard that the buyer was insolvent. The agent, without authority, sent a notice of stoppage in transit. By the time that the seller ratified this, however, the goods had been delivered to the buyer's trustee in bankruptcy. The ratification was held ineffective, because it would defeat the rights over the goods which the trustee had now acquired.

B. Effect of the agent's acts

The contract between principal and third party

> As a general rule, *the agent simply drops out* as soon as the contract (or other legal relationship) comes into existence between principal and third party. The agent incurs no personal liability, nor can he sue the third party.

There are a few exceptions to this rule.

1. *Where the third party knows that he is dealing with an agent*, the general rule almost invariably applies, although it can be overriden by special custom in some trades that the agent takes personal responsibility for performance by principal or third party.

   If an agent *signs a document* in his own name, without indicating that he merely does so as agent, then a court may be reluctant to admit oral evidence that a document, which appears to bind the agent, in fact only binds someone else, the principal. This is simply a question of admissibility of evidence; an agent who wishes to escape personal liability should always add words like '*as* agent' or '*as* director' after his signature.

2. *Where the principal is undisclosed*, so that the agent gives the impression of acting on his own behalf, the general rule does *not* apply, and the agent does not automatically drop out. The third party has an option to sue *either* the agent (with whom he thought he was contracting) *or* the principal. However, he cannot sue both. He can *ask* both for a remedy, but if he receives no satisfaction he must choose which to sue, and if the one whom he sues cannot pay, he cannot then sue the other.

   Conversely, the undisclosed principal *can* sue the third party on the contract, unless this would work injustice. Where the terms of the contract are inconsistent with agency, or where the agent expressly contracts as sole principal, it may be unjust to allow the undisclosed principal to come in.

   > In *Humble* v. *Hunter* (1848), Hunter chartered a ship from *X*, who described himself in the contract as 'owner'. In fact *X* was not the owner. It was held that *X*'s undisclosed principal could not sue on the contract.

   Secondly, an undisclosed principal cannot come in where the nature of the contract renders the identity of the parties important. Thus, if an employee accepted a job and then stepped aside and revealed that he was only doing so on behalf of his younger brother, the employer would not be bound to employ the younger brother.

   > In *Said* v. *Butt* (1920), a critic who had quarrelled with the theatre management was unable to get a ticket for the first night of a play. A friend, therefore, bought a ticket in his own name, and gave it to the critic, who appeared on the night. The management was held entitled to refuse admission, because the critic was claiming to step in as undisclosed principal in circumstances where identity was material.

   Finally, if an undisclosed principal is allowed to sue, he can be met with any defence or set-off which the third party had against the agent before he discovered the principal's existence.

The agent's warranty of authority

A person who acts as agent is taken to promise that he does have authority, and that his principal will be bound. If the agent lacks authority, or exceeds his powers so that the principal is not bound, the third party can sue the agent for damages for breach of warranty of authority. Notice that it is the *third party* who can sue for breach of warranty of authority; the principal may also seek a remedy against the agent, but this is another matter.

The warranty of authority is strict, and the agent may be liable even though he acted in all innocence, and genuinely believed that he did have authority.

> In *Yonge* v. *Toynbee* (1910), solicitors, acting for their client, defended proceedings started by Yonge, and thereby put him to considerable expense. Unknown to the solicitors, their client had become insane, thereby ending their authority. Yonge was held entitled to recover his legal expenses from the solicitors personally since these were incurred because of their unauthorized defence.

Finally, the third party must have been deceived by the agent's warranty of authority. If the third party knows that the agent is exceeding his authority, he has no remedy against either principal or agent.

Payment via the agent

1. *By the principal.* When the principal owes money to the third party, it is not enough merely to hand the money to the agent. If the agent fails to pass it on, the principal is still liable to the third party. The only exception is where the third party has, by his own conduct, induced the principal to entrust the money to the agent, for example, by giving the impression that the agent has already paid over the money.
2. *By the third party.* A debt owed by the third party to the principal is not prima facie discharged by payment to the agent. On the other hand, when the agent has express, implied or apparent authority to receive payment on his principal's behalf (as may often be the case), then the third party's debt *is* discharged, and the principal is left to sue the agent if the money is not handed over.

Liability of principal for the agent's torts

A principal is liable to the victim for torts committed by his agent *in the course of his authority.* Thus the principal will be liable where his agent, acting within his authority, makes fraudulent statements to a third party so as to commit the tort of deceit. The agent will be liable as well, if he knows that the statement is false or acts recklessly. If the agent is acting innocently, however, merely passing on false information given him by the principal, he will escape liability unless, perhaps, he has been negligent in not checking.

C. Termination of agency

Agency can come to an end in the following ways:

1. *Performance.* If the agent is engaged for a specific task, his authority ends as soon as his task is completed. Thus, an estate agent engaged to find a buyer for the house has no further authority once the sale is completed.

2. *Withdrawal of authority.* In general, the principal can withdraw his agent's authority at any time, although he may have to pay damages to his agent if this involves breach of a contract between principal and agent (for example, if the agent is employed by the principal and is wrongly dismissed from his employment without notice).

In two exceptional situations the principal cannot revoke his agent's authority. First, powers of attorney may be rendered irrevocable under the Powers of Attorney Act 1971. Secondly, authority 'coupled with an interest' may be irrevocable. This could arise where a principal who owes money to his agent gives the agent authority to collect the principal's debts and keep the money. The agent has an interest in the subject-matter, and his authority is irrevocable.

3. *Death of either party* ends the agency.

4. *Bankruptcy* of the principal ends the agency, as will bankruptcy of the agent if (as is usual) this renders him unfit for his duties.

5. *Insanity* can end the agency: the agent's insanity if it renders him unfit for his duties, the principal's if it renders him incapable of making the transactions contemplated.

6. *Frustration* of the agency can occur in other ways: supervening illegality can end it, for example, where the agent becomes an enemy alien; illness of either party might frustrate it if the illness makes commercial nonsense of the agency.

Effect of termination

As between principal and agent, the agency is terminated for the future, but existing rights, such as the agent's rights to commission already earned, are not affected.

As between principal and third party, it depends largely upon the manner in which termination occurred. Where the principal consciously withdraws his agent's authority, this does *not* affect a third party unless and until he knows of the termination or of circumstances which should make him suspect this. He can still rely on the agent's ostensible or apparent authority. On the other hand, where termination occurs involuntarily, by operation of law, the authority may end automatically, whether or not the third party knows or ought to know of the termination. Thus in *Yonge* v. *Toynbee* (page 195) the principal's insanity automatically ended the agent's power to bind the principal, even though the third party knew nothing of it. Death of the principal can have the same effect. The third party is left to sue the agent for breach of warranty of authority.

However, if the agent has been consciously 'held out' by the principal, so as to raise an estoppel, the agent's power to bind his principal will be lost only when the third party learns of the terminating event.

In *Drew* v. *Nunn* (1879), a husband had held out his wife as having authority to pledge his credit, and had always previously paid her bills. He then became insane. His wife continued to pledge his credit to tradesmen who did not know of the insanity. He was held liable for these bills when he recovered.

196

D. Duties of principal and agent to each other

Principal and agent owe certain implied duties to each other, and have corresponding rights.

Duties of agent

1. *Obedience.* An agent must obey his principal's instructions; if he fails to do so he will be liable for damages.
2. *Personal performance.* An agent cannot validly delegate his duties to a sub-agent, although he may have implied authority to entrust mere secretarial and routine administrative tasks to employees. He may also delegate with the authority of the principal, or in the case of necessity, or in accordance with trade custom. In this event, the sub-agent normally acts on behalf of the *agent*, not the principal, so that the sub-agent must look to the agent, not the principal, for his fees; conversely, it is the agent who can sue the sub-agent for disobedience, carelessness or failure to show good faith.
3. *Care and skill.* An agent must use such care and diligence as is reasonable in all the circumstances. Moreover, if he has professed some special skill, he must show the degree of care and skill ordinarily expected in his profession.
4. *Duties of good faith.* An agent must never permit an undisclosed *conflict of interest*, that is, he must never allow his own interests to conflict with those of his principal. Examples include:

   (a) An agent must not personally buy from or sell to his own principal without full disclosure.

   > In *Lucifero* v. *Castel* (1887), the principal authorized his agent to buy a yacht for him. The agent found an attractively priced boat, bought it himself, and then offered to sell it to his principal at a higher price, without disclosing the earlier transaction. He was held entitled to recover from his principal only the price which he had *paid* for the boat.

   > In *Armstrong* v. *Jackson* (1917), a stockbroker was engaged to buy certain shares for his principal. The stockbrocker held some such shares himself and, without disclosing this, transferred his own shares to his principal. It was held that the principal could rescind the contract, and recover what he had paid for the shares (even though they had since fallen in value).

   (b) An agent must not act for both sides without full disclosure.

   > In *Fullwood* v. *Hurley* (1928), an agent was engaged by the owner to sell a hotel. The agent found someone who wanted a hotel and, without disclosing his connection with the owner, arranged the sale and claimed commission from both. He was held not entitled to claim commission from the buyer.

   (c) An agent owes strict duties of disclosure to his principal, but secrecy towards others. He must not use, for his own or another's benefit, confidential information obtained on his principal's behalf. Conversely, during the course of his agency, any information relevant to his duties which the agent obtains must be disclosed to his principal.

197

In *Keppel* v. *Wheeler* (1927), Keppel engaged Wheeler, an estate agent, to sell his house. Wheeler received an offer of £6150, which Keppel accepted 'subject to contract' (so that neither party was yet bound). Five days afterwards Wheeler received another offer of £6750, but his principal did not learn of this until much later, after the first contract had become binding. Wheeler was held liable to Keppel for damages of £600, the difference between the offers.

(d) An agent must account to his principal for all moneys received in the course of the agency, and must take care not to mix his own money and property with that of the principal.

(e) An agent must not make any secret profit from an unauthorized use of his position.

In *Mahesan* v. *Malaysia Government Officers' Housing Society* (1978), M was engaged by the Society to find building land. He found a cheap and suitable site, but accepted a bribe from a property speculator to keep silent about it. This enabled the speculator to buy the site cheaply, and then re-sell it to the Society at a huge profit. The Society was entitled to recover the bribe and the speculator's profit from M.

In *Hippisley* v. *Knee Bros* (1905), an advertising agent obtained discounts from printers with whom he regularly dealt. It was held that the discounts had to be passed on to the principal. On the other hand, the agent had not been fraudulent, and was still entitled to his commission.

(f) An agent must not take a bribe, that is, any payment or gift to induce him to act in favour of the donor.

Principal's remedies

The agent must account for profits improperly made, and must compensate for any loss caused by his misconduct. In the event of serious breach, the principal may end any contract, of employment or otherwise, with the agent without notice or compensation.

If the agent acted fraudulently, the principal can rescind any contracts made through the agent, and can refuse any commission. If there is bribery, both agent and donor commit criminal offences; moreover, the principal can recover damages both from agent and donor, but not now double damages. Sums recovered from one would be set off against sums recovered from the other.

Duties of principal

1. *Payment of commission.* Agency can be gratuitous, without payment, but *if* commission or other payment is agreed (expressly or impliedly) the principal must pay the agreed amount. If the agent is in business, and would not ordinarily act gratuitously, there may be an implied obligation to pay a reasonable sum, normally by reference to usual commercial or professional rates.

The agent must, however, have *earned* his commission, that is, the event for which he was engaged must have occurred, and occurred through his actions.

Thus, as a general rule, an estate agent does not earn his commission until the sale is completed, and no commission is payable if the vendor finds a buyer privately, not through the agent.

When the agency is terminated, the agent is entitled to payment for transactions which he brought about before termination, but not (unless otherwise agreed) for transactions thereafter, even with continuing customers whom he initially introduced. Similar problems arise when the principal ends his business, thereby depriving the agent of further opportunities. The general rule again is that the agent has no redress unless there was an express or implied term in the agency agreement that the principal would so conduct the business as not to deprive the agent of commission for a given period.

> In *Turner* v. *Goldsmith* (1891), Turner was engaged *for five years* to sell shirts manufactured or sold by Goldsmith on a commission basis. Within the five years, Goldsmith's factory was burnt down. Turner was held entitled to damages for commission lost for the rest of the five-year term.

2. *Indemnity*. The principal must indemnify his agent for expenses properly and legally incurred in exercising his duties.

Examination questions

1. (a) Under what circumstances may a principal ratify the act of his agent who has entered into a contract without authority?

   (b) Albert is authorized by Peter to buy a quantity of carpeting at a price not exceeding £4 per square yard. The type of carpet specified is difficult to obtain and Albert agrees to buy from William for £4·20. Albert states that he is acting as an agent, and, although he does not disclose the name of his principal, William is aware of the person for whom he purports to act. Albert's intention at the time is to buy for himself, with the object of selling at a profit elsewhere, but he later abandons this plan. When Peter learns of the transaction, he agrees to pay the higher price but, when Albert's double dealing subsequently comes to light, he refuses to take delivery of the carpet from William. Advise William.

2. (a) Explain what is meant by the apparent or ostensible authority of an agent and how this may differ from an agent's actual authority. What is the effect of such difference upon (i) the agent's ability to bind his principal, and (ii) the agent's personal liability under the contract?

   (b) *X* is a clerk in the site office of a firm of building contractors, and it is normal practice for him to give a receipt for incoming materials. His employers are concerned about faulty deliveries from Goodbricks Ltd and inform him that all future deliveries from his supplier are to be accepted only by the site foreman after careful checking. *X* disregards these instructions and signs for the next delivery which is again faulty, whereupon his employers refuse to accept any responsibility to the supplier. Advise Goodbricks Ltd. Would your advice be different if the lorrydriver who made the delivery knew that *X* had no authority to give a receipt?

3. (a) In what ways may the authority of an agent be brought to an end?
   (b) Paul borrowed £10 000 from Arthur to finance the expansion of his business. It was further agreed that Arthur should act as Paul's sole agent for the distribution of Paul's goods in the United Kingdom for a period of 10 years. Receipts were to be remitted to Paul monthly, less a deduction for commission and a further deduction in respect of repayment of principal and interest on the loan. After two years Paul wishes to withdraw from the agreement since he feels that Arthur is unsuccessful in promoting the sale of his goods. Advise Paul.

4. (a) What are the duties owed by an agent to his principal?
   (b) *A* is employed as your firm's representative for Leeds. You have learned that he has accepted a gift of £50 from *C* on the understanding that he will use his influence with the firm to secure a valuable contract for *C*. This contract has recently been concluded. What action may your firm take?

5. Paul engages Arthur as his agent to sell three cars for the best price possible but for not less than £2000 each. The agent's commission is to be 10 per cent. Arthur informs Paul that he has found a buyer for the first car for £2000 and, after deducting his commission, remits £1800. In fact, Arthur has bought this car himself. There are two potential buyers for the second car, offering £2200 and £2400 respectively. Arthur carelessly loses the address of the second buyer and, to avoid extra work, sells the car for £2200 and again remits the money to Paul, after deducting his commission. Arthur cannot find a buyer for the third car and, therefore, sends it to his friend, Terry, who lives in another town, asking Terry if he will attempt to sell the car. Terry is unable to sell and returns the car to Paul who then discovers that Terry's carelessness has caused damage to the car to the extent of £2000. Advise Paul.

Unit 21. Credit and Security

Money may be lent and credit may be given in many ways, and on many different terms. A specified sum may be lent for a fixed term at a stated rate of interest. The whole sum may be repayable on a fixed date, or the loan may be repayable by instalments. The creditor may allow the borrower to draw varying sums on a current account up to a stated limit, as on a bank overdraft. The borrower may have a credit card which he can use to pay bills, on an arrangement that he will repay the lender (often a company controlled by his bank) in due course. Some credit is for a specific purpose, as where the supplier of goods allows his customer to pay for them by instalments, or where a building society lends money to a house buyer in return for a mortgage on the house. In other instances there may be no arrangement between lender and borrower as to how the money is to be used, as where a company issues debentures to the public.

Frequently the lender will require some *security*. We shall see later how property such as goods and land can be used in various ways as security. Other forms of property too, such as shares, can be mortgaged or charged.

The legal problems and rules can vary according to many things. The nature of the borrower may be important: the Companies Acts apply to borrowing by companies, while the Consumer Credit Act applies only to borrowing by *non*-corporate bodies. The rules can vary according to the amount owed: the Consumer Credit Act applies only where the credit does not exceed £15 000. Differences also arise according to who is the lender: an individual may lend money to a corporation (by opening a savings account at a building society, for instance), or a corporation may lend to an individual (a finance company letting a car on hire-purchase). This unit deals with some of the possibilities.

For as long as loans have existed, some creditors have abused their stronger bargaining position to impose harsh and unfair burdens on debtors, and many of the rules discussed below are attempts to prevent such injustices. On the other hand, creditors too need protection against debtors who will not pay. In more recent times, an added factor has been public interest in the economy, and at times national economic circumstances have been felt to demand credit restrictions.

A. Consumer credit

The Consumer Credit Act 1974 applies to personal credit agreements by which the creditor provides the debtor with *credit not exceeding £15 000*. Credit is 'personal' when the borrower is an individual or partnership, not a corporate body. The purpose for which the money is required is immaterial; a loan for an individual's business is still 'personal'. The 'credit' is the amount *borrowed*, not necessarily the amount to be repaid. Therefore, if someone borrows £14 000 but, with interest, has to pay back £16 000, the agreement is within the Act. The interest is a 'charge for credit'. There are, therefore, two limits on the operation of the Act: (a) as to the amount borrowed; and (b) as to the nature of the borrower.

Some agreements are 'exempt' from most provisions of the Act. The following are the main examples:

1. Loans by building societies, local authorities, and many other corporate bodies, if the loan is secured by a mortgage of land.
2. Fixed sum loans to finance the purchase of goods, services or land, if the credit is repayable by four or fewer instalments; but hire-purchase and conditional sale agreements are *not* exempt, however many instalments are payable (see later).
3. 'Running-account' credits, where the whole credit *for a period* is to be repaid by a single payment; (a running-account credit is one where no specific sum is borrowed, but credit up to a certain amount is allowed). Credit card accounts, and accounts with the local greengrocer, where the bill comes and is payable, say, monthly, are usually exempt under (2) and/or (3).

The 'extortionate bargain' provisions (see later) can apply even to exempt agreements and to personal credit outside the financial limits.

Controls over lenders and advertising

Any person wishing to carry on consumer credit business must first obtain a licence from the Director-General of Fair Trading, who must be satisfied that the applicant is a fit person to engage in such activities. This can apply not only to potential creditors, but also to credit brokers such as retailers who have arrangements to introduce customers requiring credit to a particular finance company. Regulations govern the ways in which a licensee must conduct his business. Loans by unlicensed creditors are criminal offences, and are enforceable against the borrower only at the Director's discretion.

The Department of Trade has made regulations controlling advertisements by credit dealers, to ensure that a fair picture is given as to the nature of the credit offered, and the true rate of interest, etc. There are similar controls over quotations by dealers as to the terms on which they offer credit. Canvassing people other than on business premises to persuade them to borrow, sending unsolicited credit tokens (credit cards), and activities persuading minors to borrow are prohibited. Breach is usually a criminal offence.

Information

In *commercial* consumer credit agreements, i.e. where the creditor acts in the course of his business, the Act aims to ensure that a prospective debtor knows what he is letting himself in for.

Before the agreement is made, the creditor must give written details of terms such as the charge for credit.

The agreement itself must be in writing, signed by the debtor personally and by or on behalf of the creditor. Signature of a form in blank, leaving it to an agent or the creditor to fill in the blanks, is not enough. Regulations cover the type, size, and in some instances colour of the print, and the document must give details of the debtor's rights as well as his duties (see later). If these requirements are not met, the agreement is unenforceable against the debtor without a court order, and the court has powers to refuse to allow the creditor to recover arrears or, e.g., to vary the terms of the loan.

Copies of the agreement must be given to the debtor. He must always receive, immediately, a copy of the form which he signs. If the form then has to be sent away for completion by the creditor, the debtor must be given a second copy, of the completed agreement, within seven days of its completion, so that he can check that no alterations have been made since his signature. Non-compliance can similarly render the agreement unenforceable without a court order.

Later, while a fixed-sum credit is being repaid, a debtor is entitled to information about how much he has currently paid and still owes, and to further copies of the agreement.

Rash or hasty agreements

A prospective debtor can withdraw his offer at any time before the creditor accepts it. Therefore, if the debtor's proposal has to be sent away for acceptance by the creditor (as in many hire-purchase transactions), the debtor has a short interval in which to think again. He can withdraw his offer by informing the lender or any agent. The offer may also end for other reasons, as in *Financings* v. *Stimson* (Unit 12).

Second, if a credit agreement has been induced by the creditor's misrepresentations, the debtor has a reasonable time in which to rescind the contract (see Unit 13).

Third, if a commercial consumer credit agreement, within the 1974 Act, is signed by the debtor other than on the trade premises of the creditor or any dealer with whom the debtor originally negotiated, the debtor has a statutory *right of cancellation*. This gives a 'cooling off' period, and particularly protects people who are persuaded by door-step salesmen to sign credit or hire-purchase agreements at home. In cancellable transactions, the debtor must receive a copy of the agreement as soon as he signs, and a second statutory copy must be sent to him *by post* within seven days of its completion. He then has until the end of the fifth day following receipt of his second statutory copy in which to cancel the agreement. Cancellation must be in writing, but posting it is sufficient. Both copies of the agreement must inform him of his right to cancel.

Terms of the agreement and enforcement by the creditor

Various provisions in the Consumer Credit Act protect the debtor during the credit period. For example, the *debtor* under a regulated agreement is entitled *at any time* to pay off what he owes, on giving notice to the creditor that he intends to do so. He may also be entitled to a rebate of interest if the creditor is getting his money earlier than originally contracted for.

Second, before the *creditor* can terminate the agreement or take other action for the debtor's breach, he must serve a 'notice of default'. This must specify the alleged breach, give at least seven days in which to remedy it or pay compensation, and explain the consequences of failure to comply. If the debtor complies with the notice, 'the breach shall be treated as if it had never occurred'. Similar seven day notices must be served if the creditor wishes to enforce any of his rights in the agreement, even if there has been no breach.

Only if the debtor fails to comply with a notice of default can the creditor ask the court for an enforcement order, and even at this stage the court can give the debtor additional time to pay or grant other relief.

Third, if at any time a court finds a personal credit bargain to be *extortionate*, it may re-open the agreement so as to do justice between the parties. This can be done under sections 137–140, either in proceedings brought by the debtor or as a defence to an action by the creditor. A bargain is extortionate if it requires the debtor, or any relative of his, to make payments which are exorbitant or grossly contravene 'ordinary principles of fair dealing'. The court can have regard to (i) interest rates prevailing at the time, (ii) the debtor's age, experience, business capacity and health, and whether he was under financial pressure at the time, and (iii) the degree of risk accepted by the creditor, his relationship with the debtor, and whether a 'colourable' (i.e., inflated) cash price was quoted for goods or services so as to make the interest rates seem less.

The court has powers to set aside the whole or part of the debtor's obligations, to require the creditor to repay all or part of what the debtor has paid, and/or to alter the terms of the credit agreement.

In *Barcabe Ltd* v. *Edwards* (1983), a low-paid man with four children had answered an advertisement, and been persuaded to borrow £400 at interest totalling 100 per cent per year. There was no evidence that he had defaulted on earlier debts, or otherwise was a bad security risk. The court reduced the interest to 40 per cent.

B. Goods as security

Conditional sale and hire-purchase

When customers seek goods they often need credit, which can be given in various ways. If the seller allows payment by instalments, and makes no provision for when ownership is to pass, the contract is a *credit sale*. Ownership normally passes as soon as the buyer takes possession, and the seller has no right to re-take them if the buyer defaults. Some sellers, therefore, use the goods as security, by stipulating that ownership is not to pass to the buyer until he satisfies some condition (usually payment of the last instalment). This is a *conditional sale*. The goods remain the seller's, and he can reclaim possession until the condition is met. Again, the supplier may simply hire the goods to the customer but, on payment of a specified number of hire 'instalments', the hirer will have option to buy the goods for a nominal sum of, say £1. This is *hire-purchase*.

Frequently, the garage or retailer supplying the goods will prefer payment immediately and will, therefore, have arrangements with a finance house. In one common 'triangular' transaction of this sort, the dealer will have a stock of the finance company's hire-purchase forms. If the customer wants credit, the dealer asks him to fill in his part of such a form which constitutes an offer, addressed to the finance house, to take the goods on hire-purchase *from the finance house*. The dealer forwards this form together with his own offer to sell the goods for cash to the finance house. If the latter accepts both offers, it pays the dealer the cash price, becomes owner of the goods, and lets them on hire-purchase to the customer (the hire-purchase price being higher than the cash price). The customer collects the goods from the dealer, and the finance house rarely sees them.

Hire-purchase and conditional sale to individuals or partnerships are governed by the Consumer Credit Act within the financial limits. Notice again that, for the Consumer Credit Act, it is the amount of *credit* which matters. If someone acquires a car on hire-purchase for £20 000 but pays a £5000 deposit, the amount of credit is only £15 000 and, therefore, within the Act (see also page 202 above).

Some of the protections given by the 1974 Act have already been described. The controls over lenders, information to debtors, rash 'door-step' agreements, and harsh terms apply to hire-purchase and conditional sale in the same way as to other agreements under the Act. There are also additional protections.

1. By section 99, a hire-purchaser or buyer on conditional sale can *terminate* the agreement at any time. He must give notice to the creditor, return the goods, and pay off any arrears of instalments currently due. He is then no longer liable to complete his payments under the agreement. This right to terminate the agreement and surrender the goods is in addition to his right, discussed earlier, to pay off the whole balance early (in which case he keeps the goods).

2. The Act protects against harsh 'minimum payment' clauses. If the hirer terminates the contract early and returns goods which have drastically depreciated, the creditor might suffer loss. Many agreements, therefore, required the debtor to bring his

205

payments up to, say, 75 per cent of the hire-purchase price if the agreement ended early. Such clauses were often in reality more attempts to penalize the debtor than to compensate the creditor and, even at common law, could probably be struck out as in *Bridge* v. *Campbell Discount Ltd* (Unit 15), whether or not the hirer was in breach.

When the 1974 Act applies, section 100 imposes statutory limits on minimum payment clauses. If there is such a clause, the payment must not exceed the amount, if any, by which one-half of the total price exceeds the aggregate of the sums paid and due immediately before termination. If the creditor's actual loss is less than this, the court may order payment of his actual loss only. On the other hand, if the debtor has not taken reasonable care of the goods, the debtor's payment will be increased, if need be, to compensate the creditor.

3. Hire-purchasers and conditional sale buyers are also protected against 'snatch-back'. At common law, if the hirer or buyer was late with *any* instalment, the creditor could rescind the agreement and take back the goods. This could work injustice.

> In *Cramer* v. *Giles* (1883), the hirer took a piano at a hire-purchase price of 60 guineas. After paying more than 50 guineas (probably more than the piano's cash value), the hirer was late with his last two instalments. He tendered payment shortly afterwards, but this was refused. Instead, the creditor sued for return of the piano, and was held entitled to it, leaving the hirer with nothing for the instalments which he had paid.

Many creditors did not trouble to sue, but simply took the goods back summarily at the slightest default. The contract often gave the creditor right of entry to the hirer's premises for the purpose. The process often gave the creditor a considerable profit.

If the Act applies, it protects the hirer against this. We have seen that a creditor must give at least seven days' notice of default before taking any steps against the debtor. Moreover, a creditor must not now enter any premises to take back the goods without first obtaining a court order. Even more important, by section 90, when one-third of the hire-purchase or conditional sale price has been paid, the goods become 'protected goods', and must not be taken back without a court order unless the debtor himself ended the agreement. If the debtor pays the whole balance of the price before the court order, the goods become his. Even if he does not do this, the court can give him additional time to pay.

If a creditor does take back protected goods without a court order, the agreement and the debtor's liabilities end, and the latter can recover *all* that he has previously paid.

> In *Capital Finance Ltd* v. *Bray* (1964), a finance company took back, without a court order, a car which Bray had on hire-purchase. The car was protected goods and, when the company realized its mistake, it returned the car immediately. Bray used it for several months, refusing all requests for payment. Eventually, the company sued for possession, and this was granted. The company could not, however, recover payment for Bray's use of the car after its return to him. Moreover, Bray recovered everything which he had paid.

A creditor can only recover protected goods without a court order if the debtor voluntarily returns them, or if the debtor has abandoned them.

4. Finally, finance houses and other suppliers of goods on hire-purchase owe obligations as regards title to the goods, description, fitness, and quality under the Supply of Goods (Implied Terms) Act 1973. This applies to all hire-purchase, irrespective of the amount borrowed or the nature of the borrower. The obligations implied are almost identical to those imposed on the seller by the Sale of Goods Act, with the same limits on exclusion. Where a triangular transaction takes place, the finance company is liable for representations or promises made by the dealer.

Other uses of goods as security

When credit is needed in order to buy goods, another more drastic means by which the seller can protect himself is by a 'retention of title' (*Romalpa*) clause (Unit 18). This is often used where the buyer is a large company.

If someone who *already owns* goods wishes to use them as security, different problems arise. First he can *transfer ownership* to the creditor, but retain possession. The creditor will undertake to re-transfer ownership when the loan is repaid. In practice this 'mortgage' of goods will be in writing, to provide the proof needed to prevent an unscrupulous borrower from abusing his retention of the goods. Such a document is known as a *bill of sale*. It must be in a form laid down by statute, and the bill must be registered at the Central Office of the Supreme Court.

Alternatively, the borrower can *transfer possession* of the goods to the lender while retaining ownership, the reverse of the situation with a bill of sale. This is known as *pawn* or *pledge*. The goods are redeemed by repayment and, in the event of default, the lender may sell the goods either after lapse of an agreed time or, if no time has been agreed, by giving reasonable notice to the borrower of intention to sell. There are again statutory protections, imposed now under the Consumer Credit Act.

Goods may also be subject to a *lien* when the creditor has a right to *retain possession* until a debt has been discharged. Thus a garage may retain a car as security for the cost of repairs carried out, and a hotel or dry cleaners may hold a customer's goods until the bill is paid.

C. Land as security

Mortgages

The most common method of using land as security is the mortgage. The borrower (*mortgagor*) transfers an interest in the land to the lender (*mortgagee*), and the lender may realize his interest if the loan is not repaid. The most familiar example is a loan from a building society to buy a house. The loan is repaid by the purchaser, with interest, by periodic payments.

A legal mortgage may be created today in two ways. The first is to grant a legal estate to the mortgagee in the form of a very long lease, with a proviso that the lease shall come to an end on repayment of the loan. If the property is leasehold, then a sub-lease is granted for a slightly shorter period than the original lease. The mortgagee does not take possession of the property; this remains with the mortgagor, who retains his legal estate.

An alternative and more usual method is by the execution of a deed which declares that a legal charge has been created. This is a more simple method, applicable to both freehold and leasehold, introduced by the Law of Property Act 1925. The mortgagee has the same protection as if a lease had been created.

A more informal mortgage may arise when, in return for a loan, the landowner deposits the title deeds with the lender as security. Without the title deeds, the owner would find it extremely difficult to sell or mortgage the land to another person. Deposit of the deeds only creates an equitable mortgage, over which a subsequent legal mortgage would take preference if the legal mortgagee had no knowledge of this equitable interest. Legal mortgages normally take priority according to the date of creation. The problem of priority may arise when a mortgagor defaults after raising several loans on the security of his land to a total amount which exceeds the value of the land.

If the mortgagor defaults, the lender has various remedies. He may sue for the money due. He may take possession of the land, either personally or by appointing a receiver, and recoup himself from any income arising from management of the property. He may ask the court for a foreclosure order which transfers the land to him if the mortgagor does not repay within a specified time. The most usual action is to exercise the mortgagee's power of sale, and recoup himself from the proceeds of the sale; any surplus must ultimately be returned to the borrower.

From early times, the courts have protected mortgagors from harsh and unconscionable terms. For example, they have not permitted terms which make it impossible for the borrower to redeem his mortgage for an *unreasonable* time.

In *Fairclough* v. *Swan Brewery Co. Ltd* (1912), a 20-year lease was mortgaged on terms which made redemption impossible until six weeks before the 20 years expired. These terms were held void, and the borrower could redeem earlier.

Similarly, the courts have sometimes held void terms which give collateral advantages to the lender, but only if the advantages are unreasonable. A loan by a brewery making the mortgaged property a 'tied' public house until redemption could well be reasonable. Too long a restraint, however, might be void as an unlawful restraint of trade today, as in *Esso Petroleum* v. *Harper's Garage* (Unit 17).

If the mortgagor is an individual or partnership, the 'extortionate bargain' provisions of the Consumer Credit Act can apply to it now, with the consequences described earlier. Apart from this, however, the Act does not apply to loans secured by mortgages of land, if the lender is a building society, local authority or other body which gives loans to buy land.

Equitable liens

Equitable liens, unlike legal ones, are not merely rights to *keep* possession of property, but can exist over property in the possession of someone else. One example is that the vendor of land has an equitable lien over the property sold, even after the buyer takes possession, as security for any unpaid part of the purchase price.

D. Borrowing by companies

We have seen in Unit 7 that companies raise their capital by issuing shares. They can also raise money by borrowing it, and this can have advantages. In particular, if the company is doing well, the existing shareholders may not want to dilute their prospects by introducing new members. Moreover, although the loan will have to be repaid (unlike share capital), at least the cost of the loan, including interest, is a deduction from profits, which can save tax.

Any document issued by a company as evidence of a loan or debt is called a *debenture*. Debenture holders are, therefore, merely creditors of the company, not members.

Debentures can be secured or unsecured. Obviously many are secured in order to attract lenders, and various types of security can be offered. Some are secured by a *fixed charge*, the loan being charged on a specific asset of the company. A mortgage of one of the company's buildings is a debenture of this kind. If the company is wound up, the proceeds of sale of the asset are applied in paying that creditor in full, even if this means that other creditors go short. The disadvantage of a fixed charge is that it ties up the asset charged, which cannot now be dealt with without the consent of that debenture holder. Companies can, therefore, issue *floating charges*, where the loan is charged on such property as the company has from time to time. If the company sells one asset and buys another, the charge ceases to attach to the old asset, and automatically attaches to the new. It is only when the company defaults in repayments, or starts to wind up, that the floating charge 'crystallizes' and attaches permanently to the assets at that time.

In order to protect those dealing with the company, registers of debentures must be kept, so that outsiders can see what the company's debts are. At the registered office, a company must keep a register of charges, including floating charges, on its property. Often the company secretary will also keep a register of debentures of all kinds, including unsecured, although not strictly bound to do so. Most charges on the company's property must also be registered with the Registrar of Companies. Again this includes both fixed and floating charges. Charges affecting land must also be registered with the Land Charges Registry, otherwise the charge is void. These registers are open to public inspection.

On default by the company, debenture holders can have the following rights.

1. If so permitted by the terms of issue, they may appoint a receiver, who will take over management of the company from the directors so as to ensure that holders are paid.

209

2. Holders may bring an action for the sale of the asset(s) charged.
3. In some circumstances, debenture holders can petition for the company to be wound up.

Examination questions

1. Rash enters into a loan agreement under which he agrees to borrow £2000, and repay the creditor by 24 monthly instalments of £130 each. Soon after making the agreement, he has second thoughts and wishes to escape from this liability. Advise him.

2. A hirer takes goods on hire-purchase from Finance Ltd, paying a deposit of £500, and agreeing to pay the balance, namely £912, by equal monthly instalments over two years. The agreement provides that, in the event of it being terminated in any way at any time during the two-year period, the hirer shall make up his total payments under the agreement to 60 per cent of the hire-purchase price. Explain the possible liability of the hirer to Finance Ltd should the hirer terminate the agreement after (a) two months, or (b) 12 months.

3. A buyer takes goods on conditional sale from a dealer for £16 000, paying a deposit of one-third and agreeing to pay the balance by monthly instalments over two years. After two months, the buyer defaults in paying instalments. Advise the dealer as to his rights, if any, to recover possession of the goods, including the consequences of failure to observe any legal requirements.

4. A salesman in Dealer Ltd's shop, talking to a customer, describes a washing machine in the showroom as being 'in perfect condition'. The customer agrees to take the machine, but wants credit. Dealer Ltd has an arrangement with a finance company, under which Dealer Ltd sells the machine for cash to the finance company, which then lets it on hire-purchase to the customer. The machine proves seriously defective, and the customer wishes to know whether he has any remedies against either the finance company or Dealer Ltd. Advise him.

5. Explain briefly the meaning of
   (a) Bill of sale
   (b) Floating charge
   (c) 'Triangular' transaction
   (d) Equitable lien
   (e) Protected goods.

Unit 22. The Employment Relationship

A. The nature of employment

The employment relationship arises when one person (the employee, worker or servant) supplies his skill and labour to another (the employer or master) in return for payment. The arrangement must be close and continuing, to distinguish it from situations where an independent contractor contracts only for a particular job, whereupon he leaves and sells his services elsewhere. Employment can be for a fixed or indefinite period, long or short, or merely until a particular piece of work is completed; but in all cases the parties are more closely bound than, say, a householder and the plumber engaged as an independent contractor to repair the sink (see later).

A person can be both employed by, and have other legal relations with, his employer. For example, since a company has separate legal personality, it can employ some of its own directors, so that the latter are both directors and employees.

> In *Boulting* v. *ACTAT* (1963), the Boulting brothers, who were managing directors of a film company, also had employment contracts. As 'employees' they were, therefore, held eligible for trade union membership.

On the other hand, partnerships have no separate legal personality, and even a salaried partner is, therefore, not an employee.

Employees are often also agents for the employer if, as commonly occurs, they deal with third parties on behalf of the employer. Thus, a salesman may be both employee and agent.

Employment is a contract, and the express and implied terms of this contract are still

211

the basis of the relationship between employer and employee. On the other hand, for social, economic and political reasons, there has been increasing governmental intervention in employment in the last 150 years (see Unit 1). As will be seen, many of the rights and duties of the parties are imposed by legislation today, and to regard employment *solely* as a contract would be very misleading.

B. Employees and independent contractors

Tests to distinguish employees from contractors

For various purposes, mentioned later, the courts have had to distinguish between employees and independent contractors, and the following tests used by the judges help to explain the nature of employment.

1. *The control test*. This relatively simple test was evolved in the nineteenth century: a contract of employment exists when the employer has control over the manner in which the employee does his work. The employee can be told not only *what* to do, but also *how* to do it. In contrast, the independent contractor is paid for the completed job, and *how* he does it is his concern.

   This test, by itself, is not satisfactory today. The size of many organizations and the complex skills involved make detailed control impossible. A partial solution is to substitute 'right of control', but even this is unsatisfactory. It is unrealistic, for example, to suggest that a health authority should control how its doctors treat their patients.

   Gradually the single 'control' test evolved into a *series* of tests indicating control. The courts would look at matters such as (a) the power to select the servant, (b) the right to control the method of doing the work, and (c) rights of suspension and dismissal. The notion of a series of matters developed into the two tests mainly used today, the 'integration' test, and the 'multiple' or 'economic reality' test.

2. *The organization or 'integration' test*. In *Stevenson, Jordan and Harrison Ltd* v. *Macdonald and Evans* (1952), (Unit 23), Denning, L.J. said:

   > 'It is often easy to recognize a contract of service when you see it, but difficult to say wherein the distinction lies.' After giving a number of examples, he continued, 'Under a contract of service, a man is employed as part of a business, and his work is done as an integral part of the business; whereas under a contract for services, his work, although done for the business, is not integrated into it but is only accessory to it.'

   This statement summarizes the 'organization' or 'integration' test. If a man is an integral part of an organization, he is an employee; if he performs work for the organization but remains outside it, he is an independent contractor. The test is particularly helpful in determining the position of professional people where there is obviously no right of control over the method of performance.

   > In *Cassidy* v. *Ministry of Health* (1951), patient suffered injury to his hand as a result of the negligence of full-time medical staff at a hospital. The hospital authority was held vicariously liable for the acts of these members of staff. (There would have been no vicarious liability had the medical staff been held to be independent contractors.)

212

The test was also applied in *Whittaker* v. *Ministry of Pensions and National Insurance* (1967), where a claim for industrial injuries benefit depended upon the existence of a contract of employment. The claimant was engaged by a circus as a trapeze artist but was also required to spend part of her time as an usherette. It was held that her work was an integral part of the circus and a contract of employment existed.

3. *The 'multiple' or 'economic reality' test*. Although both the right of control and the extent of integration are relevant, neither provides the complete answer. In recent years the courts have taken a wider view and tried to consider *all* factors. These have included powers to appoint, suspend and dismiss; the method of payment, and whether deductions are made for PAYE income tax and national insurance; whether the worker has received sick pay; the nature of the work and the degree of independence as to hours of work; whether the worker provides tools and equipment, and/or works at his own premises; and the general 'economic reality' of the relationship. What they call themselves ('employee' or 'contractor') may be evidence, particularly if there is a written contract, but even this is not conclusive.

In *Ready-Mixed Concrete Ltd* v. *Ministry of Pensions and National Insurance* (1968), the company engaged owner-drivers to deliver concrete and arranged for them to buy their lorries from the company on hire-purchase. The lorries were in the company's colours and drivers had to wear the company's uniforms. Payment was on a piecework basis subject to a guaranteed minimum. The drivers were responsible for maintaining the lorries and buying the fuel. It was held that, in spite of some control, the lack of integration into the business and the other circumstances meant that the drivers were independent contractors, not employees.

In *Hitchcock* v. *Post Office* (1980), a sub-postmaster who used his shop as a sub-post office was held to be self-employed, even though he had to carry out the Post Office's instructions and advise the head postmaster if he was absent for three days or more. However, he could delegate his duties to assistants, and he bore the risk of profit or loss.

The importance of the distinction

It is important to determine whether or not a contract of employment exists for the following reasons:

1. An employer is normally liable vicariously for torts committed by his employees in the course of employment, but not for torts by independent contractors (Unit 8). In limited circumstances an employee's acts may even involve the employer in criminal liability.
2. A employee has statutory protection not given to independent contractors, for example, minimum periods of notice, compensation for redundancy and remedies for unfair dismissal, under the Employment Protection (Consolidation) Act 1978 as amended.
3. Social security provisions for statutory sick pay, sickness benefits, disablement benefits, etc., differ for employees and independent contractors.
4. An employer must deduct income tax from wages and salaries to employees under

213

Schedule E (PAYE). An independent contractor pays his own income tax under Schedule D and may claim more generous allowances.

5. If the employer's business fails and he is insolvent, an employee has certain preferential rights over other creditors in respect of unpaid wages and redundancy payments.

6. The terms of a contract of employment include implied rights and duties of both employers and employees. These do not apply to the same extent with independent contractors (Unit 23).

Labour-only sub-contracting

For many years now, some businesses which formerly *employed* workmen have engaged 'labour-only sub-contractors' instead. The employer provides the materials, and hires the workmen, either individually or as members of a gang, as independent contractors for the job in hand. This is particularly common in the building industry, where gangs of craftsmen are hired as contractors for the bricklaying or joinery work on a particular site. In this context, sub-contracting was popularly called 'the lump'.

The practice has several advantages to the employer. He does not need to keep a large workforce to meet fluctuating demand; he can avoid administrative complications such as deducting income tax from wages or paying statutory sick pay; and the workmen cannot claim employment protection rights such as redundancy payments. The employer's duties regarding safety are now similar for both employees and sub-contractors, but he may still escape vicarious liability for the torts of sub-contractors. The sub-contractors themselves sometimes unlawfully evaded income tax and national insurance contributions altogether, but various Finance Acts since 1971 have controlled this.

C. Formation

The general principles of contract apply to the formation of employment contracts. There must be agreement on the essential terms. Consideration is principally the undertaking to work in return for the undertaking to pay the agreed wage or salary. Capacity to contract is important here chiefly in relation to minors and, as discussed in Unit 13, a minor can be bound. On the other hand, children must attend school full-time until the statutory leaving age, and part-time employment of school children can be strictly controlled by regulations under the Employment of Children Act 1973. Even after leaving school, they are protected by, for example, the Factories Act, which imposes maximum hours of work for minors.

Mistake, misrepresentation, duress or undue influence can vitiate a contract of employment. On the other hand, a worker seeking a job need not disclose past misdeeds unless asked, even criminal convictions, because the relationship is not one *uberrimae fidei*. Sometimes he need not disclose the truth even if asked, but this is exceptional.

In *Property Guards Ltd* v. *Taylor* (1982), two applicants for jobs as security guards were asked if they had any previous convictions. They had both been convicted of offences involving dishonesty many years ago, but these convictions were 'spent' under the Rehabilitation of Offenders Act 1974. They, therefore, answered, 'No'. When the employer discovered the truth and dismissed them, the dismissal was held unfair.

Failure to disclose may be relevant if this is a contributory cause of an accident.

In *Cork* v. *Kirby MacLean Ltd* (1952), the plaintiff suffered injury partly because of breach of statutory duty by his employer and partly because of a fall due to an epileptic fit. The damages were reduced by half for his contributory negligence in not informing the employer that he suffered from epilepsy.

Finally, certain terms in contracts of employment may be illegal or void as contrary to public policy. Terms in unreasonable restraint of trade have already been considered in Unit 17. Terms by which an employee purports to surrender statutory rights such as redundancy payment or compensation for unfair dismissal are void by statute except in certain fixed-term contracts. Terms which contravene race relations or sex discrimination legislation are void and, in some instances, illegal; likewise, terms which contravene the Truck Acts (Unit 23).

Written notification of terms

Section 1 of the Employment Protection (Consolidation) Act 1978 provides that, not later than 13 weeks after the beginning of the employment, the employer shall give the worker a written statement. This statement must, first, outline the scope of the contract. It must:

1. identify the parties;
2. specify the date when the employment began;
3. state whether service with any previous employer counts towards the employee's period of continuous employment (see Unit 26) and, if so, when the continuous employment began; and
4. if the contract is for a fixed term (say, two years), specify the date when the contract expires.

Secondly, the statement must give particulars of the following terms:

1. the scale or rate of remuneration, or the method of calculating it;
2. the intervals at which remuneration is paid;
3. any terms and conditions relating to hours of work;
4. any terms and conditions relating to holidays and holiday pay, incapacity for work and sick pay, and (normally) pension rights;
5. the length of notice which the employee must give, and is entitled to receive, to end his employment; and
6. the title of his job.

Thirdly, the statement must include a note:

1. specifying any disciplinary rules applicable, or referring to a reasonably accessible document setting out such rules; and
2. specifying a person to whom the employee can apply if he is dissatisfied with a disciplinary decision affecting him; also a person to whom he can apply to seek redress for any grievance relating to his employment; specifying the manner in which any such applications should be made; and explaining any further steps necessary on such an application.

The employer must give written notice of any change in the above particulars within one month.

These provisions apply only where the hours of work are at least 16 per week as a general rule. However, a break of up to 26 weeks in which the hours are at least eight per week will not prejudice the employee's entitlement. Moreover, someone continuously employed for five years or more for at least eight hours per week, becomes entitled to the above statement (and to the statutory minimum notice of dismissal described in Unit 23).

Registered dock workers, merchant seamen, and employees working wholly or mainly outside Great Britain (unless temporarily) are not covered by these provisions; nor is the statutory notification necessary if, as sometimes occurs, there is a *written* contract of employment which covers all of the above matters, with a copy given to the worker or otherwise made reasonably accessible to him.

Apart from these exceptions, the matter may be referred to an industrial tribunal which has power to determine what the missing particulars shall be even if the employer fails to comply with the above.

It should again be emphasized that an employer can comply with the above requirements without including all the material in one document, or even directly handing over a list of the particulars to the employee. As regards the particulars, it is sufficient if the statement refers to other documents which are made reasonably accessible to the employee. In practice, it is usual for statutory statements to refer to documents such as works' handbooks or collective agreements.

Itemized pay statements

By the Employment Protection (Consolidation) Act 1978, section 8, all employees have the right to an itemized pay statement, in writing, on or before each payment of wages or salary. The statement must show:

1. the gross amount of wages or salary;
2. the amounts and purposes of all deductions from the gross amount;
3. the net amount of wages or salary payable; and
4. where different parts of the net amount are paid in different ways, the amount and method of each part-payment.

D. Sources of terms

As suggested earlier, the rights and duties of parties come from a number of sources. Some terms are expressly agreed, in writing or orally; other terms may be implied; other rights and duties are imposed by statute. It should be remembered that a contract of employment need not be, and rarely is, a single written document. We have seen that written *notice* must be given of certain terms, but where the terms come from is a different matter.

Express terms

Some terms will be expressly negotiated between the parties, either orally or, for example, in correspondence, when the employee is offered and accepts the job. Details of the terms agreed may be set out in a number of places: the employer's works' handbook, for example; in many instances, the terms of a collective agreement form an important part of the contract (see later); even obligations displayed on notices at the place of work may be incorporated.

Exceptionally, the parties may set out the main terms in one document which is signed by the parties when the contract is made, but this occurs mainly in senior managerial appointments (e.g., some football managers).

Implied terms

In a contract of employment, there are implied common law duties on both employer and employee, which apply in the absence of any express term to the contrary. These will be dealt with in Units 23 and 27. Terms may also be implied from long and well-known usage in the trade or industry concerned.

> In *Sagar* v. *Ridehalgh (H.) & Son Ltd* (1931), for example, Lancashire weavers were held to be employed on a customary term that their rate of pay varied with the quality of work produced.

Statutory terms

Important examples of these appear in the Employment Protection (Consolidation) Act 1978, and are examined in Unit 23.

Collective agreements

Collective agreements are made between an individual employer or an employers' association on the one hand, and a trade union on the other. An individual employee will not normally be party to such an agreement and, because of the rules of privity of contract, the terms are not directly binding upon him. Nevertheless, collective agreements do govern the terms of employment of many workers today. The reason is that the terms of the collective agreement have become incorporated as terms of the *individual* contract.

1. There may be express incorporation, in which event no problem arises. Thus it may be expressly agreed that the worker shall be paid at the prevailing union rates. The worker will receive notice of this in the statement given him under the Employment Protection (Consolidation) Act 1978.
2. Where there is no express reference to the collective terms, there may be implied incorporation if, for example, the parties have known of and constantly observed the terms of collective bargains over a reasonably long time.

> In *National Coal Board* v. *Galley* (1958), the contracts of employment of colliery deputies contained a clause expressly incorporating national and county agreements currently in force. These agreements provided for work on such days in each week as the employer might reasonably require. Furthermore, the deputies had worked in accordance with these agreements for some time past. Following a dispute, some deputies refused to work on Saturdays, and the National Coal Board successfully sued them for breach of contract. It was held that the collective agreements formed part of the individual contracts of employement.

> In *Gray, Dunn and Co. Ltd* v. *Edwards* (1980), the employer negotiated a detailed agreement with a recognized union over a disciplinary code of practice. The Court of Appeal held that the employer was entitled to assume that all members of the union knew of and were bound by the code.

3. In the past, Fair Wages Resolutions of the House of Commons required that clauses be inserted in contracts between Government departments and outside contractors, requiring the contractors to employ people on terms at least as good as those recognized generally in the industry concerned. This was felt to have an inflationary effect and was rescinded with effect from September 1983.

Wages councils and statutory joint industrial councils

In certain trades collective bargaining is almost impracticable, for example in the catering industry where there are many small firms and employment is fragmented. Various Acts, therefore, empowered the Government to set up wages councils for industries where no effective bargaining machinery exists. The Wages Councils Act 1979 consolidates earlier legislation, and under it the Secretary of State for Employment, either on his own initiative or following an application by representative organizations of employers and workers, can establish wages councils where appropriate. Certain prescribed procedures must be followed in making a wages council order so that any objections can be considered. At present there are over 40 wages councils regulating wages and terms of employment of workers.

Members of wages councils are appointed from three sources: representatives appointed by nominated employers' associations; representatives appointed by nominated trade union(s); and not more than three independent members appointed directly by the Secretary of State, one of whom must be chairman. Decisions are by a majority so that, since employers' and workers' representatives will normally be equal in number, the independent members may sometimes have deciding votes.

Once established, a wages council may, since 1975, order the remuneration, holidays *and other terms and conditions of employment* for all or any of the workers in relation to whom it operates. In spite of the name, therefore, a wages council is no longer concerned only with wages and holidays. Before making an order, a council must carry out any necessary investigation, follow a prescribed procedure of giving notice to persons affected, and consider representations made to it. When made, an order may relate to wages and terms generally in the industry, or be restricted to particular types or grades of worker, or particular parts of the country. The order must be publicized, and wages inspectors are engaged by the Secretary of State to ensure compliance by employers. Any defaulting employer is liable to criminal prosecution, and can also be ordered, either (within limits) at the prosecution, or in separate County Court proceedings, to pay arrears to employees. Exemptions from the order may be granted for handicapped persons who can only find employment at a lower wage and, in any event, normal deductions for PAYE income tax and social security contributions are allowed.

For farm workers, wages and other terms of employment can be fixed in a similar manner by Agricultural Wages Boards, under the Agricultural Wages Act 1948 as amended.

In some industries where there are no wages councils, there have for many years been permanent bodies set up by the industry itself to help negotiate wages and conditions. These 'joint industrial councils' (in footwear manufacture for example) consist of representatives of workers and employers. Their orders have no binding force, and are not 'policed' by the wages inspectors, but they are a valuable channel for negotiation.

In an attempt to move gradually away from statutory regulation and towards voluntary bargaining machinery, the Employment Protection Act 1975 empowers the Secretary of State to change any wages council into a *statutory* joint industrial council. This would be composed of equal numbers of employers' and workers' representatives, but without any independent members. No statutory councils have yet been established.

Variation of terms

From time to time either party may wish to vary the terms of employment. If the other expressly accepts the changed conditions, there is no difficulty. If there is no express agreement, but the other party continues with the employment, it is a question of fact whether or not the new terms have been accepted by implication.

In *Marriott* v. *Oxford and District Co-operative Society Ltd* (1970), the plaintiff was informed that, because of a reduction in the size of his department, he would lose his status as foreman and his wages would be reduced. After protest, he continued to work for three or four weeks under the new conditions while seeking another job. Marriott's claim for redundancy payment succeeded, because it was held that the facts did not amount to an acceptance of the variation of terms of employment.

The length of notice for any variation should always correspond with the notice period required to terminate the contract. It will then be argued that there has been, in effect, a termination and an offer to re-engage on the new terms, to be accepted by continuing the relationship after the notice period has expired.

219

Examination questions

1. (a) *T* is engaged as an instructor by a driving school. The school finds the pupils, supplies and maintains the instruction car, and pays for the petrol. *T* has undertaken not to work for any other driving school while still engaged here. However, he is not paid a wage, only commission on the fees which he brings in. How many pupils he takes and how many hours he works are up to him. There are no directions as to how, where or when he teaches.

   Discuss whether he is an employee or an independent contractor. What other questions might you ask him if he sought your advice on the matter?

   (b) Would it make any difference whether or not there was a written agreement between *T* and the driving school?

2. (a) What tests are applicable to determine whether or not a contract of service exists?

   (b) Better Builders Ltd are building a number of houses and sub-contract the work of roofing to Tidy Tilers Ltd. While employees of Tidy Tilers Ltd are carrying out this work under the supervision of a foreman employed by Better Builders Ltd, a tile falls upon the head of Charles who is walking along the highway. Advise Charles regarding his possible claim for compensation.

3. Your employer, a construction company, has secured a valuable contract to build a new factory. On previous projects of a similar nature, trouble has been experienced with the electrical installations. Instead of sub-contracting this part of the work as in the past, your employer is considering the employment of a sufficient number of electricians to do the work. Draft a report explaining the legal implications of such a decision.

4. Advise your company regarding both of the following situations:

   (a) An accounts clerk serves a term of imprisonment for stealing money from a former employer. He is now employed by your company and his criminal record has just been discovered.

   (b) A labourer falls over a packing case which has been carelessly left in a dark passage by another worker. It is felt that the labourer's injuries were caused partly by his poor eyesight about which the labourer said nothing until after the accident.

5. (a) An employee of your company claims that he is being underpaid. What sources would you examine to ascertain the validity of this claim?

   (b) Your company decides that it would be less costly to close the factory for a third week's annual holiday and to maintain production by working an extra three-quarters of an hour on each Monday evening througout the remainder of the year. Advise on the legal considerations affecting the means by which this proposed change in the terms of employment could be introduced.

Unit 23. Terms of Employment

Unit 22 dealt with the nature of employment, how the terms are agreed, where they are to be found, the statutory provisions aimed to ensure that employees know the terms. This unit aims to set out what some of the normal terms *are*, and to describe the rights and duties of the parties.

A. Wages

The amount of the wage

We have seen that the amount may be fixed by negotiation, may depend upon a collective bargain, may be implied from the custom or practice of the trade, or stem from a combination of these. Exceptionally, in the absence of any agreement, there is an obligation to pay a reasonable amount.

In two respects there has been Government intervention. First, we have seen that in order to protect workers disadvantaged by inferior bargaining power, wages councils were introduced. Secondly, and particularly in the last 10 years, there has been intervention as part of Government economic policy. From time to time, wages generally have been 'frozen', increases allowed only within limits, and/or notification has been required of increases. Wider issues are involved here, beyond the scope of this book.

The Equal Pay Act 1970, which aims to ensure equal pay for men and women doing the same work, will be discussed later, as will 'guarantee payments' for workers where no work is provided.

Finally, the Government makes provision for families living with children, where a parent (the man if a couple live together) is employed full time but on low pay. If the family's income falls below a certain level, the parent(s) will be entitled to social security 'family income supplement', which is normally one-half the amount by which the income falls below the specified level.

Wages during illness

Any question of entitlement to wages during illness will normally be answered in the particulars given to employees under the 1978 Act, section 1 (Unit 22). Even if no notice is given, an industrial tribunal can decide what the provision ought to be, having regard to the circumstances and what the parties appear to have assumed. Each case today will depend upon its own facts.

In *Mears* v. *Safecar Security Ltd* (1982), *M* was engaged as a security guard. A few months later he became ill and was absent for a long time. His particulars under section 1 did not mention whether he was entitled to wages during illness, but he was told by his workmates that he would not be paid and he did not claim at the time. When he did apply later, the Court of Appeal held that he was not entitled.

In *Orman* v. *Saville Sportswear Ltd* (1960), the production manager in a skirt factory was paid a basic rate of about £30 per week, plus a production bonus which was normally another £20. When he was absent ill, the firm paid him his basic £30. There was no express provision in the contract of employment, and it was held in the circumstances that the manager was entitled not only to his basic rate, but also to the bonus which he could reasonably have expected.

The Employment Protection (Consolidation) Act 1978 provides for payment during statutory suspension due to occupational disease, and payment of women absent during pregnancy and confinement; see later in this unit.

In addition to (or more usually instead of) the wages to which he is entitled under his contract of employment, a worker will usually be entitled during illness to receive *statutory* sick pay. This *must* be paid by the employer during the first eight weeks of absence. Under the Social Security and Housing Benefits Act 1982, the employer can usually recover this amount from the Government by deducting it from the statutory national insurance contributions which, as employer, he has to pay for each employee. (To prevent illness from becoming profitable for the employee, it is normally agreed in the contract of employment that statutory sick pay, while it lasts, will be deducted from any contractual sick pay which may be due.)

Method of payment

Legislation has been necessary in the past to protect the wages of workers from doubtful practices by unscrupulous employers. These included payment of wages in the form of goods (or truck), requirements that wages be spent at the employer's shop, and excessive deductions for bad work or for minor benefits provided by the employer.

There are four principal statutes of general application, usually referred to as the Truck Acts 1831–1940. They apply only to workmen engaged in *manual* labour, and there has been considerable litigation as to what work may be considered as manual. The Acts provide that, for manual workers, wages must be paid in notes or coins, and that there must be no restrictions upon how or where the wages are spent. If goods are supplied in purported payment of wages, the worker may retain the goods and still claim the wages.

Deductions from wages for benefits provided by the employer may only be made with the written consent of the worker, and then only for a limited number of goods or services. The rent of an employer's house occupied by the worker, and the cost of food prepared and consumed on the premises are the only things of practical importance today.

Fines for disciplinary purposes and deductions for bad work or damaged material are also controlled. The deduction must be fair and reasonable having regard to the loss caused to the employer, and there must either be the written consent of the worker or a notice in the workroom clearly explaining the basis upon which deductions are made. If a bonus is paid regularly, so that it becomes regarded as part of the wages, the withholding of it without good reason would constitute an unlawful deduction.

Deductions in favour of a third party such as a trade union are permissible with the consent of the worker. There are also a number of deductions required by statute where consent is not necessary, for example PAYE income tax deductions, national insurance contributions, and payment under a court order in pursuance of the Attachment of Earnings Act 1971. The Shop Clubs Act 1902 deals with deductions in favour of clubs run in connection with the firm, and prescribes certain conditions, of which perhaps the most important is that the club shall not be controlled by the firm.

The rules still apply today although the need for them has decreased. Some recognition of changing conditions was made with the Payment of Wages Act 1960. With the written consent of the worker, his wages may now be paid into a bank account, by postal order, by money order or by cheque. If the worker is absent due to illness or injury, or if he is working away from the place where wages are normally paid, his consent to this form of payment is not required. A written statement must be supplied to the worker giving details of deductions, and the worker retains the right to withdraw his consent to this method of payment by written notice to the employer.

B. General duties of employers

Duties of employers are, for the most part, rights of employees. In addition to payment of wages, employers owe various common law obligations to employees, which constitute implied terms in the contract of employment in the absence of express agreement to the contrary.

Duty to provide work

This duty can apply in many instances today, particularly when it is vital for the employee actually to have the work.

223

In *Collier* v. *Sunday Referee Publishing Co. Ltd* (1940), the chief sub-editor of the *Sunday Referee* was engaged on a long-term contract. Before this expired, the *Sunday Referee* was transferred to another proprietor. Collier was still paid his salary, but was no longer provided with work. He was awarded damages for breach of contract, because the lack of opportunity to exercise his skills and build his reputation could prejudice his future career. (Similar reasoning might apply to an actor, for example.)

In *Turner* v. *Goldsmith* (1891), a commercial traveller had been paid solely on a commission basis. When he was deprived of work, therefore, he could no longer earn anything. He was held entitled to damages.

In *Breach* v. *Epsylon Industries Ltd* (1976), it was suggested that a senior engineer, who would need to keep up to date with rapid technical change, was entitled to be given work to enable him to do so.

A connected problem is whether employees are entitled to be paid while laid off or on short time. To remove doubt, some collective agreements specifically guarantee a minimum wage in these situations, for hourly-paid as well as for piece-workers. This is now supplemented by the Employment Protection (Consolidation) Act 1978, section 12, which provides for 'guarantee payments' on days when an employee is not provided with work because (a) the business does not need his services on that day, or (b) any other occurrence affects normal working. This right is limited, however: guarantee payments are only available for a maximum of five days in any period of three months (i.e., for a maximum of 20 days in any year); there are detailed rules for calculating amounts, but this is subject to a ceiling of £10.50 per day; the employee must not have unreasonably refused an offer of suitable alternative work; and he must have complied with any reasonable requirement by his employer with a view to making work available. He is not entitled during a stoppage due to a trade dispute involving workers of his employer or of an associated employer. Most seasonal workers whose employment is expected to last three months or less are excluded. Finally, only employees who have been continuously employed (Unit 26) for a qualifying period of one month are covered.

If there is a *contractual* right to a guarantee payment, for example under a collective agreement, payments under this go towards satisfying the worker's statutory entitlement, and vice versa, so that section 12 may add nothing for a worker who already has the benefit of a negotiated guaranteed wage scheme.

Reasonable management

Employers today owe an implied contractual duty to behave reasonably and responsibly towards their employees. It is suggested that there are implied duties of mutual respect. Arbitrary and inconsiderate action by the employer can amount to breach of contract. If sufficiently serious, this can be an implied dismissal.

In *Donovan* v. *Invicta Airways Ltd* (1970), a pilot was, three times in rapid succession, put under pressure by management to take abnormal risks on flights. On two occasions, there were passengers aboard. He refused each time. Relations with management deteriorated, and he left the company. Although the decision to leave was his, he was held to have been dismissed, and received £900 damages for breach of contract.

In *Cox* v. *Philips Industries Ltd* (1976), C sent a reasonable and moderate protest to his superiors about his salary. Soon afterwards he was demoted, although there was no suggestion of incompetence. Thenceforth his duties were vague, and nobody told him what he was supposed to do. He became depressed and ill. His employer was held to have broken the contract by treating him in this way, and he received £500 damages for distress and illness. (He was also dismissed, but the damages were not for this.)

What amounts to breach varies with circumstances and the nature of the job.

In *Wares* v. *Caithness Leather Products Ltd* (1974), an employer who abusively reprimanded a woman employee, in foul language, was held to have broken his contract. Such language would not necessarily be breach of contract on a building site.

Duty to provide a reasonably safe system of work

The employer owes a common law duty to take reasonable care for the safety of his employees, and to comply with all statutory safety provisions (Units 24 and 25).

Duty to indemnify

If a worker reasonably and necessarily incurs liabilities and expenses in the performance of his duties, he may claim reimbursement from his employer. It is submitted that this duty has limited application and should be narrowly construed.

Statements in references

Employers normally have *no* duty to give a testimonial or reference for a worker by answering enquiries from another employer who is considering whether to engage him. Any employer who does, voluntarily, give a reference must be careful and honest. If the reference is falsely unfavourable, the worker may be entitled to damages for defamation (Unit 10). If it is falsely favourable, then a new employer who engages the worker as a result might possibly recover damages for deceit (Unit 10) or negligence (Unit 9) if he suffers loss. An employer who falsely gives a good reference in the hope of getting rid of an employee might run internal risks as well.

In *Haspell* v. *Rostron & Johnson Ltd* (1976), the employer who gave a favourable reference was estopped from relying on inconsistent allegations when he later tried to justify dismissing the employee.

C. Special statutory rights of employees

In recent years, legislation has given increasing rights to employees. Some rights apply generally, such as those to written notification of terms and itemized pay statements (Unit 22), and to minimum periods of notice (Unit 26). Other rights apply only to particular types of employee, or in special situations.

Women employees

The Sex Discrimination Act 1975 renders it unlawful for employers to discriminate on grounds of sex in advertising a post ('foreman', 'salesgirl'), engaging employees, or in the terms offered. It is also unlawful to discriminate in promotion, training, transfer, or other benefits, facilities or services; or in selection for dismissal, short-time or other detriments. Discrimination as to membership of trade unions or other bodies which can affect employment prospects is also covered.

These provisions mainly protect women, but apply equally to discrimination against men, or against any person on grounds that he or she is married. The rules are discussed for convenience mainly in terms of discrimination against women. A person discriminates against a woman if, because she is a woman:

1. he treats her less favourably than he would a man; or
2. he applies some requirement or condition which men are more likely to meet than women (for example, 'must have a beard') unless he can show that the job really demands this special requirement.

Discrimination is only permissible, therefore, if being a man (or woman) is a genuine occupational qualification for the job. For example:

1. Some jobs demand authentic male characteristics (for example, actor rather than actress). Physical courage, hardiness, and even strength are not regarded as exclusively male qualities, however, so that discrimination against female steel erectors, pilots, welders or labourers can be unlawful.

   > In *Shields* v. *Coomes Ltd* (1979), male counter-hands in a betting shop were paid more than women doing the same work, allegedly because it was the men who would have to deal with trouble or violence. This was held to be discrimination, because the men had no special training and, in any event, properly trained women could deal with violence equally well. The Court of Appeal upheld this finding.

   On the other hand some jobs might more effectively be carried out by a man because of the relationships involved: boys' club leader in a tough district, or negotiating in a country where sex equality is not accepted, for example. In such instances, discrimination might be justified.

2. Decency or privacy might require selection, for example because of physical contact (trainer at a football club), or living together (lighthouse keepers).

   > In *Wylie* v. *Dee & Co.* (*Menswear*) *Ltd* (1978), an employer refused to employ a woman as sales assistant in a menswear shop. This was held to be unlawful discrimination. It could not be justified on decency grounds, because customers could change in a private cubicle. Contact such as inside-leg measurement was rarely required, and could be carried out by one of the other seven assistants, all male, if need be.

3. It is illegal to employ women in certain jobs, such as underground in coal mining, or on overnight shift-work in factories. Some of these rules date from exploitation of cheap female labour in the last century, and such provisions can now be reviewed by the Equal Opportunities Commission (below).

There are special provisions for ministers of religion, police, prison officers, probation officers and mineworkers. For most purposes, employment in a private household, or where not more than five people work for the employer, is not covered; nor are terms about retirement or death. Moreover, minor distinctions can be ignored.

In *Peake* v. *Automotive Products Ltd* (1977), men and women worked the day shift on equal pay. A male employee alleged discrimination because women were allowed to leave five minutes earlier than men to avoid a rush at the factory gates. The Court of Appeal treated this as too trivial to be unlawful. It was chivalrous and safer.

However, in *Jeremiah* v. *Ministry of Defence* (1979) chivalry was held immaterial, as was safety unless there were dangers solely to women. Men were sometimes required to work with dusty and unpleasant dyes. Women were not. The Court of Appeal held this to be discrimination which, unlike in *Peake's* case, was not trivial. Even the men's extra pay for this work was no excuse; one cannot buy the right to discriminate.

The Equal Opportunities Commission was set up in 1975 to keep this Act and the Equal Pay Act (below) under review and to promote equal opportunity. It has wide powers of investigation. If satisfied that there is discrimination, it may issue a non-discrimination notice after giving the employer the chance to defend himself, with a right of appeal to an industrial tribunal. If the notice is contravened within five years, the Commission may seek a County Court injunction against the employer.

Subject to this, complaints are heard by industrial tribunals. Any person may complain, within a normal limitation period of three months. A conciliation officer of the Advisory, Conciliation and Arbitration Service (ACAS) will first try to promote a settlement. If this fails, it is for the employer to justify any differences. Unless he does so, the tribunal may (a) declare the rights of the complainant, (b) order the employer to pay compensation, and (c) recommend that the employer remedy the cause of complaint, under the potential sanction of increased compensation. Compensation for hurt feelings can be included.

In *Gubala* v. *Crompton Parkinson Ltd* (1977), Mrs Gubala was selected for redundancy ahead of a male colleague. Their length of service was similar, and the employer admitted being influenced by the fact that the man was older and had a house and mortgage, whereas Mrs Gubala's husband worked. She was offered a job at a lower grade which 'was women's work'. She refused, and was compensated for unfair dismissal plus £400 for unlawful discrimination, including recompense for hurt feelings.

Equal pay is governed by similar legislation. By the EEC Treaty, Article 119, member states must 'ensure and subsequently maintain the application of the principle that men and women should receive equal pay for equal work'. This became binding on this country in 1973. At that time there already was an Equal Pay Act 1970, but it was not yet in force. The 1970 Act was amended and brought into force with the Sex Discrimination Act 1975.

However, the story did not end there. In several cases, claimants who were unsuccessful under the Equal Pay Act successfully applied to the European Court of Justice under Article 119 and a *Directive* of 1975 which supplemented it.

In *Macarthy's Ltd* v. *Smith* (1981), a male stockroom manager was paid £60 per week. He left and, after four months, was replaced by Mrs Smith, paid only £50 per week. Her claim under the Equal Pay Act failed, because the Act applied only to differences in pay for like work *at the same time*. However, the European Court held that Article 119 had been broken. This binds the English courts and, for this reason, Mrs Smith's claim finally succeeded.

Eventually, in *Commission of the European Communities* v. *United Kingdom* (1982), the European Commission successfully sued the UK Government in the European Court for a declaration that the Equal Pay Act did not yet comply with Article 119. The Government, therefore, has amended the Act again, as from the beginning of 1984.

The Equal Pay Act provides that the contracts of women employees shall contain an 'equality clause', under which the woman's terms of employment shall be no less favourable than those of a man in the same employment doing 'like work' or 'work rated as equivalent'. The job is 'like work' with a man's if it is the same or broadly similar. It is 'rated as equivalent' if a job evaluation study has given equal value to the woman's and a man's job with the employer, at the same establishment or, where common terms are applied, elsewhere in Britain. The job's value is assessed in terms of the demands made on the worker under headings such as effort, skill and decision. The equality clause also allows a woman to claim that her job is of 'equal value' *before* a job evaluation study has been made. In this event, the tribunal itself may ask an independent expert to prepare a report. Despite its name, the Act also covers matters such as hours, holidays and sick pay.

> In *Hayward* v. *Cammell Laird Ltd* (1984), a female cook was awarded equal pay on the grounds that her job was rated of equal value to those of a shipwright and a plumber.

Complaints are heard by industrial tribunals as under the Sex Discrimination Act. The procedure can be slightly different, and claims must be within six months of the claimant leaving the relevant employment. Arrears of wages can be awarded to cover past inequalities, but only for times within two years before the start of proceedings.

The Employment Protection (Consolidation) Act 1978, amended in 1980, gives women rights in the event of maternity. By section 60, it is usually unfair to dismiss a woman simply because of pregnancy (Unit 26). A woman who has had two years of continuous employment by the start of the eleventh week before the expected birth, and who works until then, is entitled to return to her job within 29 weeks beginning with the week of birth. She must tell her employer, at least three weeks before leaving, that she will be away because of pregnancy, that she intends to return, and the expected date of birth. She is also allowed up to six weeks 'maternity pay' (nine-tenths normal pay less social security maternity allowance) while absent. Her employer can claim full rebate from the Government. There are detailed provisions for notice of intended date of return. Failure to allow her to return *may* be treated as dismissal as from that date, although there are now exceptions. Pregnant employees may also, now, become entitled to reasonable time off for antenatal care.

Race relations

Under the Race Relations Act 1976, it is unlawful for an employer to discriminate against employees on grounds of colour, race, ethnic or national origins. This covers advertisements, recruitment, terms, promotion, and dismissal. The Commission for Racial Equality keeps the Act under review and works to promote good race relations. It can investigate, and issue non-discrimination notices enforceable in the same way as those of the Equal Opportunities Commission.

Apart from this, complaints of racial discrimination in employment are heard by industrial tribunals. A conciliation officer engaged by ACAS can try to promote a settlement but, subject to this, tribunals have the same powers as under the sex discrimination legislation above.

The Commission has issued a code of practice on race relations at work and this, although not binding, must be admitted in evidence in any proceedings (see Unit 2).

Trade union membership

Under the Employment Protection (Consolidation) Act 1978, as amended by the Employment Acts 1980 and 1982, it is unlawful to discriminate against an employee because he *joins* an *independent* trade union, takes part in its activities, or because he *refuses* to join a union, independent or not. An independent union is one not controlled by the employer. Dismissal for any of these reasons is unfair, and the person has three months in which to claim reinstatement, re-engagement and/or compensation through an industrial tribunal. This is dealt with in detail in Unit 26. Two matters can perhaps be mentioned here. First, the person can, within seven days, apply to an industrial tribunal for *temporary* reinstatement or re-engagement, pending hearing of the unfair dismissal claim. Secondly, if action *short of* dismissal is taken against the employee on the above grounds, he can complain to a tribunal within three months, and compensation can be awarded.

Sometimes there is a 'closed shop' or 'union membership' agreement between an employer and one or more unions, under which the employer agrees to employ only members of the union or unions concerned. If so, it *may* be lawful for an employer to dismiss a worker for refusing to join the union. However, there are many employees to whom even a valid closed shop agreement would not apply today. For example, it would still be unlawful to discriminate against a worker who 'genuinely objects on grounds of conscience or other deeply held personal conviction to being a member of any trade union whatsoever, or of a particular trade union' (again see Unit 26).

Furthermore, relatively few such closed shops are binding today. The agreement is only valid if it has been approved within the last five years by a secret ballot of employees. A majority of 80 per cent of those entitled to vote is needed for a new closed shop, and this must be confirmed at not more than five-year intervals by majorities of either 80 per cent of those entitled to vote, or 85 per cent of those actually voting.

Under the Employment Act 1980, employees who work in a closed shop, or who are seeking to work in one, are entitled to a remedy from the union if they are unreasonably expelled or excluded.

Time off work

The Employment Protection (Consolidation) Act allows time off for various purposes.

1. Section 27 entitles union officials to reasonable time off work, with pay, for union duties or training in industrial relations. Ordinary members may also be allowed reasonable leave, normally unpaid, for union activities. Codes of practice issued by ACAS give guidance as to what is reasonable.
2. By section 29, employers must allow reasonable leave, not necessarily paid, for service as a magistrate, or as a member of a local authority, health or water authority, or statutory tribunal.
3. By section 31, when an employee is given redundancy notice he must, if he has been continuously employed for two years, be given reasonable paid leave (with a two-day minimum) during the notice period, to look for new work or to arrange for retraining.
4. Section 31(A) (added in 1980) can entitle pregnant employees to reasonable time off for antenatal care.
5. Under various Acts, people working with dangerous materials such as radioactive substances or lead may be temporarily suspended from work on medical grounds. By section 19, such an employee must normally get full pay for up to 26 weeks, unless he unreasonably refuses his employer's offer of suitable alternative work, or disregards his employer's requirements imposed with a view to making his services available. Someone totally incapable of work because of disease or disablement is not entitled, but should qualify for social security benefits. Section 19 applies after four weeks' continuous employment.
6. Under the Safety Representatives and Safety Committees Regulations 1977, safety representatives must be allowed reasonable paid leave for training (Unit 24).

Other statutory provisions

Young persons
Various Acts prohibit employment of children; also employment of young persons on dangerous work or in excess of specified hours.

Disabled persons
The Disabled Persons (Employment) Act 1958 requires employers of more than 20 workers to employ a 3 per cent quota of disabled persons if suitable work is available. Non-compliance can be a criminal offence.

D. Duties of employees

As well as rights, employees obviously have duties. More detailed examples appear in Unit 26, because *serious* breach by an employee may justify his dismissal. The main implied duties are as below.

To render personal service

The worker must be prepared to work within the terms of his contract. The work must be carried out personally and cannot be delegated to a substitute.

To take care and exercise reasonable skill

A worker must take reasonable care in exercising his duties. He must take reasonable care of his employer's property, and be careful that his conduct does not harm fellow workers or outsiders so as to impose vicarious liability on his employer. Negligence may entitle the employer to dismiss the worker, and also to be reimbursed by him (see *Lister* v. *Romford Ice and Cold Storage Co. Ltd*, Unit 8). The degree of care expected may vary with the position held by the employee and the responsibility entrusted to him.

He must also exercise such skill as he has professed, and examples of dismissal for incompetence or lack of capability appear in Unit 26.

To obey instructions

All reasonable and legitimate orders which are within the terms of the employment must be obeyed. Disobedience is justified only if the order is illegal, likely to prove dangerous to the employee, or wholly unreasonable.

In *Ottoman Bank* v. *Chakarian* (1930), an Armenian employee of the bank was dismissed for refusing a transfer to Constantinople. It was shown to the satisfaction of the court that there would be real danger to his life in Constantinople, and it was accordingly held that his dismissal was wrongful.

In *O'Brien* v. *Associated Fire Alarms* (1969), an electrician who had worked and lived in Liverpool for many years justifiably refused to move 120 miles to work for his employer in Barrow-in-Furness at short notice.

In *Morrish* v. *Henlys (Folkestone) Ltd* (1973), a driver was sacked for refusing to obey his manager's order to make false claims for petrol expenses. Disobedience was held justified, and his dismissal was unfair.

To give loyal and faithful service

A number of important applications may be given of this rather vague expression.

1. An employee must carry out his duties at work in an honest and responsible manner. Even conduct in the worker's own time may, exceptionally, be breach of his contract of employment; for example, an accountant found guilty of fraud unconnected with his employment might, in some cases, legitimately be dismissed.
2. An employee indulging in 'moonlighting' (working in his own time either for himself or for another employer) may break his contract if the other work competes with and damages that of his employer. A remedy may also be granted against the other employer.

In *Hivac Ltd* v. *Park Royal Scientific Instruments Ltd* (1946), the appellants manufactured midget valves for hearing aids. Certain of their highly skilled workers began to work on Sundays for the respondents, a competing business which had been set up nearby. It was held that the workers were in breach of good faith, and an injunction was granted restraining the respondents from employing them.

3. If a worker makes an invention then, as a general rule, the patent rights and other benefits belong to him. This may be so even if he makes the invention in the course of his employment. By the Patents Act 1977, the invention belongs to the employer in two circumstances only: (a) if the invention arose from normal duties, or from some special job, which might reasonably be *expected* to produce an invention; or (b) if the employee had a *special obligation* at the time to further the employer's undertaking.

Even if the invention is lawfully patented by the employer, the employee can still apply to the Patents Court for a fair share of the moneys derived from a patent which proves to be of 'outstanding benefit' to the employer. In short, the 1977 Act tries to ensure that employees have a fair reward (and incentive) for inventions. If the employee himself owns and patents the invention, he can sell it freely. If he sells or licenses it to his employer, he can still claim statutory compensation later if it transpires that he sold it too cheaply.

On the other hand, *copyright* of written work produced in the course of employment normally belongs to the employer; see the Copyright Act 1956. Even if the work was not produced during employment, the employer may restrain publication if information is disclosed which may be considered the employer's property.

> In *Stevenson, Jordan and Harrison Ltd* v. *Macdonald and Evans* (1952), an accountant 'sold' to publishers the copyright of his manuscript on business management. Part of the book was based upon public lectures which he had given, and part was derived from a particular assignment which he had carried out for his employer. It was held that the employer could only restrain publication of the latter part.

4. The worker must not disclose or misuse trade secrets or confidential information which he has acquired during the course of his employment.
5. The worker owes other duties of good faith similar to those owed by an agent to his principal (Unit 20). In particular, he must account for any unauthorized benefit which accrues to him by reason of his position or employment. Thus he must not accept a bribe or secret commission although, where it is customary to do so, he may retain a 'tip' and, possibly, a Christmas present.

> In *Reading* v. *Attorney General* (1951), an Army sergeant serving in Egypt used to accompany lorries which were smuggling liquor. Because he was wearing uniform, the lorries were not searched. It was held that the 'profits' accruing to him from this enterprise (some £20 000) belonged to the Crown.

Duties of ex-workers

Some duties may continue even after the employment has ended. If there is an enforceable restraint clause in his contract of employment, for example, a worker may be restrained from future employment within the time and distance limits imposed. The principles governing validity of restraint clauses were considered in Unit 17.

The duty of secrecy may also continue even in the absence of a specific clause in the contract, although it may be prudent for an employer to insert such a clause. An ex-worker may be restrained from using confidential information obtained during the employment, but not the general knowledge or skill which he then acquired.

> In *Printers and Finishes Ltd* v. *Holloway* (1964), an injunction was granted against the use by a former works manager of secret documents which he had copied while in employment. On the other hand, he was not restrained from using more general information which he had retained in his mind regarding his former employer's business.

Examination questions

1. The payment of wages is a matter for agreement between each employer and worker. To what extent is this statement correct in view of (a) collective bargaining, and (b) statutory intervention?

2. (a) Outline the common law duties owed by an employer to his employee in the absence of any specific provisions in the contract of service.

   (b) Robert is a representative employed to sell washing machines. In each week he earns about £90 of which £50 is his basic wage and the remainder is commission on sales. The employer cuts back production in order to retool for a new model and informs Robert that his supply of machines, and hence his commission, will be halved. Robert claims that not only will his present earnings be reduced considerably but that he will lose his contacts and the chance of increasing his commission when production becomes normal again. Advise Robert.

3. Outline the duties owed by a worker to his employer in the absence of any agreement to the contrary in the contract of employment.

4. Your company operates a large television hire business. It has a training scheme for mechanics but much of the value of this is lost because a number of employees are using their acquired skills to compete with the company. In some cases this takes the form of spare-time work, and in other cases it arises after employees have terminated their employment. Draft a report explaining the legal position and the extent to which this competition may be restrained.

5. Thomas is the owner of a television retail shop to which is attached a workshop where repairs are carried out. He wishes to do the following:

   (a) withhold a bonus from Albert, the driver of a delivery van, who has been involved in an accident;

   (b) deduct 50p weekly from the wages of Bernard, a television mechanic, for a midday meal which is supplied to him daily in the workshop;

   (c) deduct a small fine from the wages of Clara, a shop assistant, for frequent unpunctuality;

   (d) pay the wages of David, a television mechanic, by cheque. David services sets in outlying areas and frequently receives instructions by telephone without attending at the shop.

   Advise Thomas of the circumstances under which he may take any of the above actions and explain the legal principles involved in each case.

Unit 24. Occupational Safety

A. General legislative controls

The common law is not directly concerned with *preventing* occupational accidents and diseases. The law of torts comes into operation only when the accident has already occurred, and the civil courts are concerned with compensating the victims of such occurrences. A heavy award of damages might operate as a deterrent to a defaulting employer, but even the deterrent effect is limited when the employer is indemnified against such liability by compulsory insurance (Unit 25).

From the early years of the nineteenth century, therefore, the legislature has concerned itself with trying to prevent occupational injury and disease, and with promoting better working conditions. The problems arose from the industrial revolution, when the growth of factory employment and powered machinery created working conditions previously unknown.

The first controls were in the cotton industry, where women and young children were employed in appalling conditions for very long hours. An Act in 1802 limited working hours for apprentices, and imposed minimum standards of lighting, heat and ventilation. This legislation was ineffective because of lack of enforcement, but gradually, during the next century and a half, legislation was extended to cover all factories, all persons employed in them, and a wide range of occupational risks and health hazards. Safety and working conditions in factories are now governed mainly by the Factories Act 1961, and the controls are administered through HM Factory Inspectors.

Safety legislation in mining developed independently. In 1842 an Act forbade the employment of women and children underground. Since then, legislation has been enacted to cover safety and working conditions generally in mines. The principal Act today is the Mines and Quarries Act 1954, administered through HM Inspectors of Mines and Quarries.

In agriculture, there were hardly any controls until the Agriculture (Poisonous Substances) Act 1952 and the Agriculture (Safety, Health and Welfare Provisions) Act 1956, administered largely by inspectors appointed by the Ministry of Agriculture.

The Offices, Shops and Railway Premises Act 1963 introduced the first occupational safety controls in offices, and extended the limited provisions then applying to shops and railway premises. This Act is administered largely by local authorities except as regards certain premises, in particular those occupied by the local authority itself, in which the Act is administered by factory inspectors. Most local authorities have exercised their functions through public health inspectors.

Finally, controls have been introduced in other types of employment by Acts such as the Mineral Workings (Offshore Installations) Act 1971.

As will be seen, this development has been fragmented and piecemeal, with no integrated administrative structure, and with no one having general, overall responsibility for occupational health and safety.

The Health and Safety at Work, etc., Act 1974

In 1970 the Government set up the Robens Committee on Safety and Health at Work, which reported in 1972. As a result of the Committee's recommendations, the 1974 Act was enacted to tidy up the fragmented controls, and to coordinate the administrative machinery. The Act also seeks to change the approach to occupational safety by the increased use of codes of practice. It does not repeal existing legislation such as the Factories Act and the Mines and Quarries Act, but these will only continue in force until they are gradually replaced by regulations under the 1974 Act in years to come. The Act does, however, introduce additional statutory obligations as regards safety which, for the first time, apply uniformly in almost all work situations.

1. *General duties of employers to their employees.* By section 2(1) of the Act, it is the duty of every employer:

> 'to ensure, so far as is reasonably practicable, the health, safety and welfare at work of all his employees'.

In particular, by section 2(2), the duty extends to:

(a) the provision and maintenance of *plant and systems of work* that are, so far as is reasonably practicable, safe and without risks to health;

(b) arrangements for ensuring, so far as is reasonably practicable, safety and absence of risks to health in connection with the *use, handling, storage and transport of articles and substances*; this can include matters such as the transport of heavy or flammable materials, or the handling or use of dangerous substances ranging from asbestos (which can cause cancer and leukaemia) to glue (which can cause dermatitis);

(c) the provision of such *information, instruction, training and supervision* as is necessary to ensure, so far as is reasonably practicable, the health and safety at work of his employees;

(d) so far as is reasonably practicable as regards any *place of work* under the employer's control, the maintenance of it in a condition that is safe and without risks to health and the provision and maintenance of means of access to and egress from it that are safe and without such risks;

(e) the provision and maintenance of a *working environment* for his employees that is, so far as is reasonably practicable, safe, without risks to health, and adequate as regards facilities and arrangements for their welfare at work.

An employer must normally prepare a written statement of his policy as regards safety and health at work, and bring it to the attention of his employees. This should serve to emphasize the importance which an employer must now place upon occupational safety. He must regularly update this.

It will be noticed that the above duties are not strict, but only require the employer to ensure the various matters mentioned *so far as is reasonably practicable*. The more detailed duties contained in the Factories Act and similar specialized legislation (as regards fencing of dangerous machinery in factories, for example) are much stricter. These stricter duties will, in due course, be contained in regulations under the 1974 Act to supplement the more general obligations.

Another difference between the above duties and those under the Factories Act is that the present ones are owed specifically by the employer, whereas those under the Factories Act are owed, for the most part, by the *occupier* of the factory who, although normally also the employer, need not necessarily be so. The 1974 Act goes on to impose obligations on other persons involved in the work situation.

2. *General duties of employers and the self-employed to persons other than their employees.* By section 3, every employer owes a duty so to conduct his undertaking as to ensure, so far as is reasonably practicable, that persons *not* in his employment, but who may be affected by it, are not thereby exposed to risks to their health or safety. A self-employed person owes a similar duty to others who may be affected by his activities.

> In *R.* v. *Swan Hunter Shipbuilders Ltd* (1982), the shipyard failed adequately to warn workmen employed by independent contractors on the vessel about the dangers of too much oxygen in an enclosed space. A workman did leave oxygen turned on, and an area became a fire risk. The shipyard was held guilty under section 2 as regards the consequent risk to its own employees, and under section 3 as regards the contractors' workmen. (In fact a fire killed eight people.) The shipyard owed duties to give information, training and supervision to the employees of independent contractors as well as to its own workmen.

3. *General duties of persons concerned with premises to persons at work.* By section 4, a person who has any control over premises where persons other than his employees work owes duties to those working there. He must take such measures as are reasonable for a person in his position, to ensure, so far as is reasonably practicable, that the premises are safe and without risks to health. The same duties

236

are owed as regards means of access and egress, and as to any plant or substance in the premises. (See also Occupiers' Liability Acts as to civil liability, Unit 9.)

Those in control of certain prescribed premises where dangerous processes take place owe an additional duty, under section 5, to use the best practicable means to prevent the escape of noxious or offensive substances into the atmosphere outside.

4. *General duties of manufacturers, designers, suppliers and importers as regards things for use at work.* By section 6, a person who designs, manufactures, imports or supplies any article for use at work must ensure, so far as is reasonably practicable, that the article is so designed and constructed as to be safe and without risks to health when properly used. He must carry out or arrange any necessary testing, and ensure that any necessary instructions as to safety or how the article should be used are made available. Designers and manufacturers must, furthermore, take responsibility for carrying out any necessary research to discover and, so far as is reasonably practicable, eliminate or minimize risks to health or safety from the design.

Identical duties are owed by those who manufacture, import or supply any *substance* for use at work.

5. *General duties of employees at work.* By section 7, it is the duty of every employee, while at work:

(a) to take reasonable care for the health and safety of himself and of other persons who may be affected by his acts or omissions at work; and

(b) to cooperate with his employer or others owing statutory safety obligations so far as is necessary to enable the duty or requirement to be complied with.

In addition to these duties, section 8 provides that no person shall intentionally or recklessly interfere with or misuse anything provided in the interests of health, safety or welfare in pursuance of any of the statutory provisions. Section 9 forbids the employer to charge employees for anything (such as safety equipment) which specifically has to be provided or done under the Acts.

Where any of these statutory duties is to do something 'so far as is reasonably practicable', the onus of proving impracticability is on the defence. It is presumed that safety measures *would* have been possible unless the *accused* can prove otherwise. This applies to duties under the 1974 Act above, and to duties under the Factories Act and similar statutes below.

Breach of the above duties, or of sections 8 or 9, is a criminal offence punishable, on summary conviction before the magistrates, by a fine of up to £2000. Alternatively, the offence may be tried before the Crown Court, which can impose heavier penalties. Breach does *not*, however, give any right of civil action for the tort of breach of statutory duty. Anyone seeking damages must either sue for the tort of negligence, or for breach of one of the more specialized duties imposed by legislation such as the Factories Act (Unit 25).

Regulations and codes of practice

The Robens Committee recommended that detailed duties such as those in the Factories Act should, in future, not be contained in an Act of Parliament. Instead, Parliament should simply set out general obligations such as those discussed above, and then give the appropriate Minister delegated power to make more detailed rules. The 1974 Act adopts this pattern, and the Minister accordingly has very wide powers under section 15 to make regulations which will eventually replace the factories, mines and quarries, offices and shops, and other legislation.

Section 16 implements another Robens recommendation. It gives the Health and Safety Commission, with the Minister's consent, power to approve codes of practice 'for the purpose of providing practical guidance with respect to the requirements of sections 2 to 7, or of health and safety regulations, or of any of the existing (e.g., factories) legislation'. The provisions of such codes must be admitted as evidence in criminal proceedings under the Acts, and will have an effect similar to that of the Highway Code in road traffic law (see Unit 2).

B. The Factories Act 1961

The Factories Act 1961 applies to factories. This is by no means so simple as it sounds. 'Factory' for this purpose is defined by section 175(1) of the Act as meaning any premises in which persons are employed in *manual labour* in any process for, or incidental to:

1. making any article or part of any article; or
2. altering, repairing, ornamenting, finishing, cleaning, or washing or breaking up or demolishing any article; or
3. adapting any article for sale; or
4. slaughtering animals or confining them prior to slaughter;

being premises in or within which the work is carried on *by way of trade or for purposes of gain* and to or over which the employer of the persons therein has the right of access or control.

Section 175(2) specifically includes certain premises, about some of which there might otherwise have been doubt. Examples include shipyards, dry docks and ship-breaking yards, bottle-filling plants incidental to the purposes of a factory, locomotive building or repair shops, printing works, and film studios (except as regards performers).

Various points in the definition should be emphasized:

1. The Act applies only to premises where some employees engage in manual labour. The word 'labour' suggests some strenuous physical effort, but this is not an easy test to apply; a girl working a sewing machine has been held to be within the category, a professional footballer has not.
2. The premises must be used for trade or gain. Engineering workshops in colleges

are, therefore, not within the Factories Act, although they are now covered by general duties in the Health and Safety at Work, etc., Act.

3. Factory processes include adapting articles for sale. This has been held to include processes necessary to prepare the items for sale or to render them more saleable, such as arranging flowers into a wreath or bottling beer.

4. By section 175(6), where a place within a factory 'is solely used for some purpose *other than* the processes carried on in the factory, that place shall not be deemed to form part of the factory' (although it might, where appropriate, form a separate factory). On the other hand, a place used for some purpose *incidental* to the main processes of the factory, including a works canteen, does form part of the factory. This can be so even if the incidental activity is in a separate building.

> In *Thurogood* v. *Van Den Berghs and Jurgens Ltd* (1951), a separate building used for oiling and repairing the machinery used in a margarine factory was held to be part of the factory.

General health provisions

Part I of the Act imposes detailed duties on the occupiers of factories as regards cleanliness, overcrowding, temperature, ventilation, lighting, drainage of floors, sanitary conveniences and medical supervision. Some of the provisions are quite detailed; for example, section 3 provides that:

> 'in every workroom in which a substantial proportion of the work is done sitting . . . a temperature of less than 60 degrees shall not be deemed, after the first hour, to be a reasonable temperature . . .'

Most of the sections, however, also contain powers for the Minister to make regulations specifying in more detail the standards required. There are almost identical provisions in the Offices, Shops and Railway Premises Act 1963.

General safety provisions

Part II of the Factories Act 1961 imposes very important obligations on the factory occupier.

1. *Fencing provisions.* By section 12, every flywheel directly connected to any *prime mover* must be securely fenced.

By section 13, every part of the *transmission* machinery shall be securely fenced unless it is in such a position or of such construction as to be as safe to every person employed or working on the premises as it would be if securely fenced.

Section 14 imposes a more general duty:

> 'every *dangerous part* of any machinery . . . shall be securely fenced unless it is in such a position or of such construction as to be as safe to every person employed or working on the premises as it would be if securely fenced'.

239

Whether a part is 'dangerous' for the purposes of this section is a question of fact; it is dangerous if it is a reasonably foreseeable cause of harm.

> In *Carr* v. *Mercantile Produce Co. Ltd* (1949), a girl operator suffered injuries when, in cleaning the machine, she put her hand inside it, through a narrow opening, while the machine was in motion. There was held to be no breach of section 14. The section did not cover parts which 'it is not only not difficult to avoid, but which it is actually difficult to get near'.

On the other hand, duties under sections 13 and 14 are owed towards 'every person employed or working on the premises', and machinery can be dangerous even to persons who have no business to be near it.

> In *Uddin* v. *Associated Portland Cement Manufacturers Ltd* (1965), a workman climbed an iron ladder to a platform where he had no permission to be. He leaned across a dangerous revolving shaft to catch a pigeon sitting behind it. His clothing became caught on one of the studs, and he received serious injuries. There was held to have been breach of section 14. (The case was a civil one, and Uddin's damages were substantially reduced for contributory negligence.)

The standard of guarding is set out in section 16: 'fencing and other safeguards shall be of substantial construction, and constantly maintained and kept in position while the parts required to be fenced or safeguarded are in motion or use'. The fencing must be secure, and sufficient to guard against all foreseeable situations in which the employee might make contact with the machine. By section 17, a person who sells machinery or lets it on hire for use in a factory owes duties to see that it is safely constructed and/or guarded.

The risk at which the fencing provisions are aimed is limited. The guard must be sufficient to prevent any employee from making contact with the machine, but need not be sufficient to prevent things from flying out, whether parts of the machinery or material being worked in the machine. Most of the cases are civil actions for damages.

> In *Nicholls* v. *Austin* (*Leyton*) *Ltd* (1946), a workman was injured when a piece of wood was thrown out by a circular saw. The fencing was inadequate to prevent this, but the accident was held not to be the 'mischief' against which the fencing provisions were aimed, and the workman could not recover damages.

> In *Kilgollan* v. *William Cooke & Co. Ltd* (1956), the fencing on a stranding machine making wire rope did not prevent pieces of wire from flying out. It was held that no action lay for breach of section 14, although the workman injured did recover damages for negligence.

> In *Close* v. *Steel Company of Wales Ltd* (1961), it was part of the machine itself which flew out. The bit of an electric drill shattered and entered the operator's eye. It was again held that there was no breach of section 14.

The duties to fence are strict. Unlike the duties under the Health and Safety at Work, etc., Act, which only apply 'so far as is reasonably practicable', the fencing provisions apply irrespective of practicability. If machinery cannot be used unfenced, it should simply not be used; see *John Summers and Sons Ltd* v. *Frost*

(Unit 25). If matters rested there, however, certain work on lathes, grinding wheels, circular saws and similar machines, where the very process involves contact with moving (and therefore dangerous) parts, could not legally be carried on. The Minister, therefore, has power under section 76 to make regulations excluding or varying the fencing provisions as regards certain parts of such machinery.

2. *Other provisions.* Part II goes on to deal with a wide variety of other safety hazards, including hoists, lifts and cranes, dangerous fumes, boilers and fire. Some of the duties imposed are strict, some not. Two sections, 28 and 29, may illustrate the varying standards demanded.

By section 28(1):

> 'all floors, steps, stairs, passages and gangways shall be of sound construction and properly maintained and shall, so far as is reasonably practicable, be kept free from any obstruction and from any substance likely to cause persons to slip'.

The first part of this subsection is quite strict, but the later part is plainly not.

> In *Jenkins* v. *Allied Ironfounders Ltd* (1969), pieces of scrap metal often became embedded in sand on the foundry floor. A workman walking backwards supporting one end of a hot casting was injured when he tripped over such an obstruction. It was held that there was no breach of section 28(1), because it was impracticable to keep the sand continuously raked.

Section 28(5), on the other hand, imposes a very strict duty: 'all ladders shall be soundly constructed and properly maintained'. Section 28(4) is somewhere between the two in strictness: 'all openings in floors shall be securely fenced, *except* in so far as the nature of the work renders such fencing impracticable'.

By section 29(1):

> 'there shall, so far as is reasonably practicable, be provided and maintained safe means of access to every place at which any person has at any time to work, and every such place shall, so far as is reasonably practicable, be made and kept safe for any person working there'.

This duty, again, is *not* strict.

> In *Levesley* v. *Thomas Firth & John Brown Ltd* (1953), a workman returning from the canteen tripped over a piece of metal packing which must have fallen from a lorry into the gangway. The object had not been there when he left, and it was held that section 29(1) did not cover transient sources of danger which it was not reasonably practicable to remove instantly.

Welfare and other provisions

Many other matters are covered in some detail in the Factories Act and/or in health and safety regulations. Part III of the Act makes general welfare provisions for things like drinking water and cloakrooms. First aid facilities are now governed by regulations. Part IV of the Act provides for special risks such as dust or fumes, or lifting of heavy weights. The Minister has made regulations for the protection of eyes in certain processes. Part IV contains detailed controls over the employment of women and young persons in factories.

Sanctions and penalties under the Factories Act

The main approach of the factory inspectors is to persuade, educate and advise factory occupiers and workers as to the best ways in which to meet their statutory requirements. When all else fails, however, the main teeth behind the Act are criminal sanctions. Prosecution is normally by a factory inspector, and it is brought before a Magistrates' Court.

1. *Occupiers of factories* may be prosecuted for breach of any of their obligations under the Act. The main penalty is a fine under, now, the Health and Safety at Work, etc., Act.

    Since most factory occupiers are limited companies, provision is made to make the individuals 'behind' the company criminally liable in appropriate circumstances. Where an offence by a body corporate

    > 'is proved to have been committed with the consent or connivance of, or to have been attributable to any neglect on the part of, any director, manager, secretary or similar officer of the body corporate . . . he as well as the body corporate shall be guilty of that offence'.

    Where the occupier is convicted, the court may, instead of fining him, simply order him to take specified steps to remedy the breach within a stated time. If he does so, he will not be fined; if he does not, the court may impose a continuing fine for each day while the default lasts.
2. *Offences by employees.* By section 143, no person employed in a factory shall wilfully and without reasonable cause do anything likely to endanger himself or others. Moreover, he has a duty to use safety appliances provided under the Act, and not wilfully to interfere with or misuse such appliances. Employees in breach may be prosecuted and fined. This section overlaps with sections 7 and 8 of the Health and Safety at Work, etc., Act above.
3. *Prohibition.* Under sections 54 and 55 of the Factories Act, the Magistrates' Court can prohibit the use of specified machinery in a factory, or even close down the premises where there is imminent risk of injury. These powers are being replaced by the powers of inspectors under the Health and Safety at Work, etc., Act, sections 21–25, to issue improvement and prohibition notices. An improvement notice will inform a defaulter of his misdeeds and require him to remedy the contravention within a stated period. Where an inspector believes that a breach of any of the statutory requirements involves a risk of serious personal injury, he may serve a prohibition notice ordering the addressee to cease certain activities until the breach is remedied. In the event of imminent danger of injury, an inspector also has power to seize dangerous articles or substances and, if necessary, destroy them.

C. Administration

Under the Health and Safety at Work, etc., Act 1974, new statutory bodies have been created with overall responsibility for health and safety in *all* work situations.

The Health and Safety Commission

This is the principal body, and is charged with assisting and encouraging those affected to carry out the purposes of the Act. It can undertake or sponsor research, disseminate information, make proposals to the Minister for regulations, approve codes of practice, and order investigations into particular accidents or situations. The Commission has a chairman appointed by the Minister, and between six and nine other members representing employers, employees and other bodies such as local authorities or professional associations. It must report to the Minister from time to time on what it proposes to do to carry out its functions, and submit an annual report on its activities in the past year.

The Health and Safety Executive

This body will exercise on behalf of the Commission the more detailed administration of the safety and health provisions. In particular, it has direct responsibility for enforcing the 1974 Act, and other safety legislation such as the Factories Act, although some responsibilities are left with bodies such as local authorities. Inspectors who operate the specialized factories, mines and other legislation will be appointed by and responsible to the Executive. It consists of a director and two other members appointed by the Commission subject to the Minister's approval.

Inspectors appointed by the Executive have very wide powers indeed. They can enter premises and direct that the premises remain undisturbed while investigations take place. They can take measurements, photographs and samples, and even dismantle or confiscate articles or substances felt to be dangerous. An inspector may question anyone who may have relevant information, and require him to sign a declaration of the truth of his answers. He may inspect or take copies of any relevant books or documents of the firm. The powers to issue improvement and prohibition notices are mentioned above.

Safety representatives and safety committees

The Minister may, by regulations, provide for internal safety committees in particular firms or industries. More generally, the Safety Representatives and Safety Committees Regulations 1977 allow an independent trade union recognized for the purpose of collective bargaining by the employer to nominate safety representatives. If two such representatives so request, the employer must set up a safety committee within three months. There are detailed provisions entitling representatives to investigate potential hazards, consult with inspectors, and have reasonable time for training.

Registers

The various Acts require that registers and similar records be kept. Regulations under the 1974 Act require that registers of accidents causing death or certain serious injuries be kept at places of work generally, and that particulars of any such accident be notified to the relevant inspectors. As regards factories, the 1961 Act requires that the occupier also keep registers recording matters such as testing hoists, lifts, cranes, boilers, etc.; also particulars of young persons employed and various other matters. Some of the other special Acts have similar provisions.

Examination questions

1. Difficulties have been encountered in ensuring the safety of people at work. What are these difficulties and what steps have been taken recently in an attempt to overcome them?
2. Outline the general duties regarding safety which have been imposed by the Health and Safety at Work, etc., Act 1974.
3. State, with reasons, whether you consider the following premises fall within the scope of the Factories Act 1961:
   (a) an engineering workshop in a technical college;
   (b) a works canteen used by all employees;
   (c) the stock room of a departmental store;
   (d) a laundry attached to the factory for the purpose of washing workers' overalls.
4. Explain, with examples, the ways in which the courts have interpreted the provisions of the Factories Act 1961, relating to the fencing of dangerous machinery. What legal consequences are likely to follow a failure to discharge these duties?
5. What authorities are responsible for the administration and enforcement of the Health and Safety at Work, etc., Act 1974? Outline the powers and duties of these authorities.

Unit 25. Compensation for Industrial Injuries

When a worker is injured at work, he may have a claim for compensation against his employer if he can prove that the employer was either negligent in not exercising reasonable care for his workers' safety or had broken a duty imposed upon the employer by statute. The claim may be pursued either as an action in tort or as an action for breach of an implied term in the contract of employment.

The liability of the employer may arise from a personal act or omission on his part or it may be the act or omission of another worker for whom the employer is vicariously responsible. If the injury is fatal, the employer may then be liable to the dependants and the estate of the deceased worker (Unit 10).

Irrespective of any fault by the employer, he may also have to make statutory sickness payments to the employee for the first eight weeks of absence due to illness or injury. This is a separate means of compensation which has no connection with the employer's liability in tort or contract, except that it may result in a slight adjustment of the damages. The employer can usually recover this statutory sick pay from the Government by deducting the amount from the social security contributions which he must pay to the Government for other employees (see Unit 27). After the eight weeks, the employee can claim social security payments ('sickness benefit') directly from the Department of Health and Social Security (DHSS).

If the worker's injury is permanent or long term, he may also be entitled to a disablement pension or gratuity from the state under the Social Security Act 1975. If he is killed, the widow can claim a death benefit (see later).

A. The employer's liability for negligence

This is an important application of the tort of negligence which was considered in some detail in Unit 9. The principles of the tort will not be repeated but consideration will be given to special aspects which arise when negligence occurs in the employment situation.

The duty of care

It is well established that an employer owes a duty of care towards his worker and the extent of this duty is often classified for convenience under three headings—to provide competent staff, to provide safe equipment and premises and to provide proper coordination to ensure a safe system of working.

While an employer does not give any guarantee as to the competence and skill of his workers, he must take reasonable care in their selection, give them proper instructions and dismiss anyone whose behaviour is likely to cause danger to others.

> In *Hudson* v. *Ridge Manufacturing Co. Ltd* (1957), the plaintiff's wrist was broken when he was tripped by a fellow worker who was well known for his 'skylarking'. It was held that the employer was liable since the culprit had repeatedly made a nuisance of himself with his practical jokes and nothing had been done to check him.

Care is required in respect of the premises where work is done and in the supply of materials, tools, machinery and other equipment. Proper maintenance must be carried out.

> In *Latimer* v. *AEC Ltd* (1952), a factory was flooded because of heavy rainfall and a combination of water and oil left the floor in a slippery state. All available sawdust was spread over the floor before work began but the plaintiff slipped on an untreated part and injured himself. It was held that the employer was not liable. All practicable precautions had been taken and the risk of injury was not sufficient to justify closing the factory.

> In *Bradford* v. *Robinson Rentals Ltd* (1967), the employer was held liable for the plaintiff's frost-bite. It was deemed unreasonable to send an elderly worker on a long journey in exceptionally cold weather in an unheated van.

At common law, it was difficult for a worker to recover compensation if he was injured by a defect in equipment which could not have been discovered by reasonable inspection. The employer would have discharged his duty by obtaining the equipment from a reputable supplier. The Employers' Liability (Defective Equipment) Act 1969 now enables the worker to sue the employer in these circumstances. The employer is liable if the worker is injured in the course of his employment by equipment provided by the employer for the purpose of the business. The employer can then claim an indemnity from the supplier, but may face practical difficulties if the equipment was imported, or, much worse, if the supplier is now insolvent.

Finally, the employer is under a duty to combine staff and equipment to provide a reasonably safe system of working. Whether or not this has been done can be determined only with reference to the facts of each particular case. It will be affected, for example, by the physical layout of the job, the sequence of operations and the necessity for warnings or other special instructions.

Breach of duty

The duty of an employer is not absolute in the sense that an accident automatically entitles an injured worker to compensation. The employer is expected to conform to the standard of a reasonable and prudent employer in the circumstances of the particular case.

Thus it would be deemed reasonable to take greater care in situations where the consequences of an accident would be especially severe. Greater care would be expected where dangerous substances are being used, where a worker with a known disability is at risk (*Paris* v. *Stepney Borough Council*, Unit 9), or where young and inexperienced workers are involved.

> In *Kerry* v. *Carter* (1969), an apprentice on a farm, aged 18, badly injured his hand while operating a circular saw. He had had little experience of working with a saw and the farmer was held liable for failing to check properly on the young man's competence before allowing him to use it.

The risk must also be measured against the cost and practicability of the safety precautions for, as in *Latimer's* case, it may be unreasonable to stop production if the risk of injury is very slight. In some circumstances, a worker may be assisted in proving his case by the application of the maxim *res ipsa loquitur*.

If the duty is to be discharged by the provision of safety equipment, it is normally enough if the equipment is made freely and conveniently available at the place where it is to be used. Once this has been done and instructions have been given as to its use, it is not normally reasonable to expect an employer to go further and stand over experienced workers to ensure that the equipment is used on every occasion. On the other hand, with inexperienced workers the mere provision of the equipment may not be enough, and the employer must also take further steps to supervise its use.

> In *Finch* v. *Telegraph Constructions and Maintenance Co. Ltd* (1949), safety goggles had been provided for grinding work but were kept in the works office and the plaintiff had not been told where they could be obtained. He was injured by a piece of metal in the eye. It was held that the employer had not taken reasonable precautions.

> On the other hand, in *Woods* v. *Durable Suites Ltd* (1953), barrier cream had been made conveniently available as a safeguard against dermatitis for workers using a synthetic glue. Instructions had been given that the cream was to be used but there was no compulsion. The plaintiff's action failed since he was an experienced worker and it was held that the safety measures were reasonable and adequate.

It may sometimes be possible for the employer to escape liability when he provides no safety equipment at all if he can show that, even had such equipment been provided, the workmen would not have used it. The employer's failure would not now be recognized as the 'cause' of the worker's injury (*McWilliams* v. *Sir William Arrol & Co. Ltd*, Unit 10).

Consequential loss

The third requisite for a successful claim in negligence is that loss was suffered by the worker in consequence of the employer's breach of duty. The damage must not have been too remote (Unit 10).

In *Robinson* v. *Post Office* (1974), the plaintiff lacerated his leg in a fall when descending an oily ladder. He was given an anti-tetanus injection to which he was allergic and which caused severe brain damage. The Court of Appeal held that it was foreseeable that the dangerous ladder would give rise to medical treatment and there was liability for all the consequences of that treatment.

Conversely, in *Hogan* v. *Bentinck Collieries Ltd* (1949), a miner suffered a fractured thumb in an accident. Acting on bad medical advice, he had the thumb amputated. He was not entitled to recover from his employer for the loss of his thumb because it was not foreseeable that the accident would lead to *negligent* medical treatment.

The loss will be compensated in accordance with the general principles applying to the assessment of damages (Unit 10). In the past, many employers have insured against this liability and the Employers' Liability (Compulsory Insurance) Act 1969 made it compulsory for all to do so. The insurance must be contained in approved policies with authorized insurers, and regulations have been made covering the details of the policies and the issue of insurance certificates. The Act does not apply to local authorities or the nationalized industries.

Defences

In addition to pleading that there was no negligence since all reasonable precautions had been taken, the two principal defences of the employer are contributory negligence and *volenti non fit injuria*. The former attempts to reduce the amount of damages awarded, while the latter seeks to defeat the claim entirely.

On most occasions, the defence of *volenti* has failed because the worker has been the weaker party in the employment relationship and the court has not accepted that he was a true volunteer. In 1965, however, the House of Lords held that, contrary to some views, the defence was still available in appropriate situations.

In *Imperial Chemical Industries Ltd* v. *Shatwell* (1965), two experienced shotfirers were injured when they set off charges contrary to safety regulations. No negligence or breach of statutory duty attached to the employer since the regulations applied to the shotfirers personally. The action against the employer was based upon alleged vicarious liability for the negligence of the other worker. Since the injured worker was well aware of the risks he was taking and freely accepted them, the defence of *volenti* was accepted. (The defence might have failed if the other worker had held a supervisory position and 'persuaded' the injured worker to take the risk.)

B. Breach of statutory duty

In the previous unit, consideration was given to the more important statutory provisions which have been imposed in the interests of occupational safety and to some of the problems of interpretation which have faced the courts. While a breach of one of these safety provisions by the offending employer or factory occupier may be punished criminally, a further question arises as to whether or not a worker injured by the breach may claim compensation.

Since safety legislation is intended to protect workers, the courts have held in most cases that the legislature must have intended a civil action to lie for breach of Acts such as the Factories Act. (No civil action lies for breach of the Health and Safety at Work, etc., Act, however.) In practice, an injured worker will sue for both negligence and breach of statutory duty in the alternative in the hope of succeeding with one of those claims. It will not, of course, affect the amount of damages if he succeeds with both.

The plaintiff must first prove that the statute applies, that the defendant is the person on whom the duty is imposed and that he, the plaintiff, is a person entitled to the benefit of this duty.

> In *Groves* v. *Lord Wimborne* (1898), a boy working in an iron works was badly injured when his arm was trapped in unfenced cog-wheels. Under the legislation then in force, the factory occupier owed a statutory duty, similar to that under the Factories Act 1961, to fence all dangerous machinery. The boy recovered damages for breach of this duty, which was clearly intended to protect people such as himself.

> In *Longhurst* v. *Guildford, Godalming and District Water Board* (1961), the plaintiff's action under the Factories Acts failed because the pump house of the water board was held not to be part of a factory. It was not, therefore, covered by the legislation pleaded.

> In *Hartley* v. *Mayoh & Co. Ltd* (1954), a fireman called to a fire in a factory was electrocuted because the occupier had failed to comply with regulations regarding electrical wiring. The regulations referred to a 'person employed' in a factory and this was held to exclude the plaintiff.

The plaintiff must next show that the statutory duty has been broken. This again involves problems of interpretation to ascertain the nature and extent of the duty placed upon the defendant employer or occupier. In *Close* v. *Steel Company of Wales Ltd*, for example, it was held that the 'mischief' at which the fencing provisions were aimed was the worker coming into contact with the machine, and that no action lay for injuries suffered when pieces flew out (Unit 24). There must then be a decision on the particular facts as to whether the duty has been discharged. If the statute describes the standard of care required by the use of words such as 'reasonable' or 'reasonably practicable', the position differs little from the common law action for negligence. On the other hand, many duties are much stricter, depending always upon the precise wording of the section concerned. If the duty is sufficiently strict, and this applies particularly to the guarding of dangerous machinery, the mere fact that the prohibited thing has happened may be enough. It may be no defence for the defendant to plead that he took all reasonable safety precautions.

> In *John Summers & Sons Ltd* v. *Frost* (1955), the respondent injured his thumb on a revolving grinding wheel which had only been partly guarded. It was held that the duty to fence dangerous machinery was strict and that it was no defence that fencing would make it impossible or impracticable to operate the machine. (Note, however, the power of the Minister to make regulations providing for such situations; see Unit 24.)

The final step is to prove that the breach caused the injury. The court will then proceed to assess the damages following the principles which normally apply to personal injury claims.

In an action for breach of statutory duty the employer may seek to reduce the amount of damages by putting forward the defence of contributory negligence. The defence of *volenti non fit injuria*, however, will not apply; to permit this would be to permit the worker to waive or contract out of the statutory provisions imposed for his protection. Likewise, where a statutory duty is imposed upon an employer, he may not escape his obligations by delegating to another. If he delegates, he remains liable if a breach occurs.

C. Industrial injuries benefits

The law of tort by itself has weaknesses as a means of providing for the victims of occupational accidents and diseases. It requires initiative, which a sick or injured workman might not find easy; the collection of evidence and the conduct of proceedings can take a long time during which the plaintiff remains uncompensated; the technical nature of some of the rules of tort discussed earlier may make the outcome of proceedings uncertain; and the financial limits on legal aid can make proceedings expensive for the plaintiff.

In order that victims should be compensated without having to prove fault, the Workmen's Compensation Acts around the turn of the century provided that employers should automatically compensate workers for all injuries arising out of and in the course of employment. Employers could, and usually did, cover their liability by insurance. This scheme too had weaknesses; in particular, compensation was only for loss of earnings up to a fairly low ceiling, not all employers insured and litigation was too frequently necessary to establish, for example, whether the accident arose out of the employment. Some workmen settled claims on modest terms in order to avoid this last possibility.

In 1948, the state assumed responsibility with the introduction of a compulsory national insurance scheme. In general, both employers and employees pay regular contributions to the state, in return for which the employees are insured *by the state* against two eventualities: (1) personal injury caused by accident arising out of and in the course of employment, and (2) *prescribed* occupational diseases and personal injuries *not* caused by accident.

Contributions are collected from employers and workers in the same way as income tax, but then go into the National Insurance Fund, which is used to provide the benefits and meet administrative costs. Benefits do not depend upon the amount of contributions paid or the contribution record. Cover starts from the moment when work commences, as it normally would with a private insurance policy.

Benefits

From 1948 until 1983, the chief benefit received by the employee from this compulsory insurance scheme was a weekly payment during his absence from work.

This was bigger than and instead of sickness benefit while it lasted. This 'injury benefit' was abolished by the Social Security and Housing Benefits Act 1982 under which, from April 1983, those injured at work receive only statutory sick pay, followed by sickness benefit, in the same way as other employees absent because of ill health.

However, the other possible benefits to workers under the 1948 scheme remain.

If the occupational injury or disease has lasting effects, the insured may claim a *disablement benefit* from the state. This is payable to the worker after six months as compensation for his physical loss, and it is paid whether or not he resumes work. He must appear before a medical board which examines the lasting physical or mental effects of the injury or illness, and assesses the worker's loss of faculty. This is done on a percentage basis: for example, both eyes is 100 per cent, the loss of four fingers 50 per cent, and the loss of a small toe 3 per cent. Less serious injuries, below 20 per cent, qualify for a lump sum or gratuity varying with the assessed loss. More serious cases give entitlement to a pension on a sliding scale ranging from a 20 per cent loss up to a maximum for a 100 per cent loss.

Supplements may be paid in addition to a disablement pension. If the claimant is unlikely to be able to earn more than a certain sum each year he will qualify for an unemployability supplement. If he is able to work, but not either in his regular employment or in suitable employment of an equivalent standard, he may be granted a *special hardship allowance*. During treatment in hospital his pension will be increased to 100 per cent and in cases of serious disability a *constant attendance allowance* is paid. *Dependants' allowances* are also paid while there is unemployability or during treatment in hospital.

A *death benefit* is payable to widows and dependent widowers if the injury is fatal. This takes the form of a pension, supplemented by children's allowances. A widow's benefit ceases on re-marriage, when she becomes entitled to a lump sum payment equal to one year's pension.

The risks covered

As mentioned above, disablement and death benefits are payable by the state if either of the two risks covered by the scheme occurs. These are as follows.

1. *Personal injury caused by accident arising out of and in the course of employment.* 'Personal injury' includes both physical and mental harm. 'Accident' has been described as an unlooked-for mishap or an untoward event which is not expected or designed. Thus self-inflicted injuries are excluded, but the wilful act of a third party may be an accident so far as the victim is concerned. The injury must have followed from some identifiable event or occurrence, as opposed to arising gradually from a *process*. The line between 'accident' and 'process' is a difficult one. A series of unconnected occurrences, or a *briefly* protracted event such as a leakage of gas over a few hours, can still amount to an accident. The distinction is

important because injury caused by a process is only within the scheme if it is so prescribed by regulations (see below).

'In the course of employment' means that the accident must have happened during the *time* while the claimant was at work. This can include tea breaks or even meals in works canteens, but it does not normally include accidents off the premises on the way to or from work.

'Arising out of' employment means that the accident must also have been *caused* by or closely connected with the employee's work. He is only covered if it was a risk arising from the job, and not a risk to which the public generally are subject. Thus a wasp sting while at work would not be an industrial injury unless, perhaps, the victim worked in a jam factory. The Social Security Act 1975, which still governs this, does help claimants in some respects. First, it is presumed that all accidents *during* employment are *caused by* it, unless the insurance officer proves otherwise. Secondly, the Act deals with three special situations.

(a) Things done without authority, in contravention of specific orders or of statutory regulations *are* covered, provided that the accident would have been deemed to arise out of employment if there had been no such contravention, and the worker was acting for the purposes of and in connection with his employer's business.

(b) Actions taken by the worker in an actual or supposed emergency to 'rescue, succour or protect' persons thought to be imperilled or injured, or to avert or minimize serious damage to property, are covered if the worker is at the time on or about premises where he is supposed to be for the purposes of his job.

(c) Injury during employment is covered even if it was caused by another person's misconduct, skylarking or negligence, or by the behaviour or presence of an animal, bird, fish, or insect, or is caused by or consists in the victim being struck by any object or by lightning; but in these cases the claimant must not himself have induced or contributed to the accident, directly or indirectly.

2. *Prescribed diseases and personal injuries not caused by accident.* Not all occupational injuries or diseases are caused by accident. Some, particularly diseases, are caused by a long process and, therefore, are not covered by the above provisions. The Minister, therefore, has power by section 76 to extend insurance to such diseases or injuries as he may prescribe. He must be satisfied that:

(a) the disease or injury ought to be treated, having regard to its causes and incidence and any other relevant considerations, as a risk of the workers' occupations and not as a risk common to all persons, and

(b) it is such that, in the absence of special circumstances, the attribution of particular cases to the nature of the employment can be established or presumed with reasonable certainty.

The claimant must, therefore, show (i) that he suffers from the disease, and (ii) that he has been engaged in one of the types of work associated with the disease in the regulations, currently the Social Security (Industrial Injuries) (Prescribed Diseases) Regulations 1980. Otherwise he is not covered.

In *Roberts* v. *Lord Penrhyn* (1949), a workman suffered a diseased hip due to work on a pneumatic drill over a long period. This was not a prescribed disease for such work and, since it occurred due to a process, not accident, he was not entitled to benefit.

Administration

The industrial injuries scheme is administered by the DHSS, as is the statutory sick pay scheme mentioned at the beginning of this unit. A claim for disablement or death benefit is made to a local insurance officer. There is a right of appeal to a local tribunal, and a further appeal may be made, either by the claimant or the insurance officer, to a Social Security Commissioner, a barrister or solicitor of at least 10 years' standing. Medical matters may be referred to a local medical board, with a right of appeal to a medical appeal tribunal.

If an employer refuses statutory sick pay to an employee, the latter may ask a local insurance officer for a formal written decision as to his entitlement. There are the same rights of appeal as those described above.

D. Alternative remedies

An injured worker may at the same time bring a civil action for damages against his employer for negligence or breach of statutory duty and also claim social security benefits. If both claims are allowed, he is likely to be over-compensated for his injury. On the other hand, it may be argued that the two claims are quite separate and that, so far as the national insurance benefits are concerned, he is only receiving that to which he is entitled by reason of his contributions.

A compromise was sought in the Law Reform (Personal Injuries) Act 1948. In any action for personal injuries a deduction is made from damages awarded for loss of earnings or profits in respect of statutory sick pay, sickness benefit or disablement benefit. The amount deducted is one-half of the value of these benefits that the plaintiff has received or is likely to receive for the five years beginning when the cause of action accrued. The proportion of one-half represents the approximate proportion of the benefits due to the employer's contribution which should, therefore, be deducted from the damages paid by the employer.

If damages are to be reduced also for contributory negligence, this adjustment is to be made *after* the adjustment for insurance benefits. This provision favours the injured worker.

Examination questions

1. Smith has been injured at work by an unguarded machine and seeks advice on his possible rights to recover compensation. Advise him, explaining the distinction between:
   (a) an action against the employer based upon negligence and one upon breach of statutory duty; and

(b) an action against the employer under (a) and a claim for social security benefits.

2. Charles, a laboratory assistant, receives serious injuries to his eyes when splashed by a chemical with which he is working in the course of his employment.

    (a) Outline the employer's liability in each of the following alternative circumstances:

     (i) protective goggles were provided by the employer but Charles did not use them;

     (ii) protective goggles were worn by Charles but were defective and failed to prevent the injury.

    (b) What difference, if any, would arise in the above situations if Charles had only one eye?

3. A group of apprentices are wrongfully playing football in the training workshop which is attached to a factory. The ball becomes lodged on top of a machine, and, in an attempt to retrieve it, Tom, one of the apprentices, slips and injures himself on the machine. The supervisor had previously been explaining how the guard was fixed and had not replaced the guard after the period of instruction.

    The employer, when sued by Tom, pleads:

    (a) that there was no breach of statutory duty since the Factories Act 1961 did not apply to the training workshop; and

    (b) that there was no negligence in that all reasonable care had been taken and the accident was entirely due to the fault of Tom.

    Discuss the validity of these two defences.

4. Explain whether or not a worker who was injured in the following circumstances would be able to claim that the injury arose out of and in the course of employment:

    (a) while cycling to work along a road owned by the employer but outside the factory gates;

    (b) while attending a trade union meeting on the firm's premises during a meal break;

    (c) while taking part in a snowball fight on the premises during a meal break;

    (d) while attempting to save the employer's property following an outbreak of fire;

    (e) while operating a machine after having removed a guard.

5. (a) Explain the social security benefits which may be payable following an industrial accident.

    (b) A worker succeeds in an action for negligence against his employer on the grounds that injury was suffered by reason of the employer's failure to provide a safe system of work. To what extent, if at all, will the court take into account social security benefits to which the worker is entitled when awarding damages?

Unit 26. Notice and Dismissal

A. Qualifying periods of continuous employment

Most of the statutory rights in the unit, particularly rights to notice and to remedies for unfair dismissal, are only available for workers who have been *continuously employed* by their employer for a qualifying period. Similarly, the statutory rights in Unit 22 (e.g., written notification of terms), Unit 23 (e.g., guarantee payments, rights during maternity), and Unit 27 (redundancy payments) all depend upon qualifying periods of service. The phrase 'continuously employed' is, therefore, extremely important and, for all of these purposes, the period is computed according to the Employment Protection (Consolidation) Act 1978, Schedule 13, as amended.

Weeks of employment

Continuous employment is built up from week to week and, today, part-time employment is enough. As the basic rule, any week in which the employee's contract requires at least 16 hours' work counts as a week of employment. Secondly, once his continuous service is sufficient to qualify him for any right (e.g., two years for redundancy payment), the worker remains so qualified unless and until his contract ceases to require at least eight hours per week and, in such a week, he actually works for less than 16 hours. Thirdly, if a worker is continuously employed for *five years* under a contract which normally requires at least eight hours per week, these years then count.

Generally, any week not within the above rules breaks the continuity, and the worker has to start afresh to accumulate qualifying weeks. The Act provides, however, that a worker is still employed during the following gaps.

1. A break of up to 26 weeks in which the employee's contract requires at least eight hours' work.
2. Absence for maternity, so long as the woman has either followed the correct procedure for statutory absence, or the absence is no more than 26 weeks.
3. A temporary stoppage other than a strike; or absence in such circumstances that the worker is considered by arrangement or custom to be still employed by his employer; for example, sabbatical leave.
4. Absence due to illness or injury does not necessarily break or end the contract at all (see later), so that such absence may be immaterial. Even if illness does end the contract, a gap of up to 26 weeks still counts as employment if the worker then resumes.
5. Where an employee successfully claims to have been unfairly dismissed, and he is reinstated, continuity of employment is preserved and includes the time between dismissal and reinstatement.

Stoppage due to a strike will not affect the continuity of employment, but time spent on strike does not, unlike the above weeks, count towards the qualifying periods.

Change of employer

Continuous employment must all be with the same employer. There can easily be changes which are outside the control of employees, however, and so legislation gives some protection.

1. The 1978 Act provides that if a trade, business or undertaking is transferred from one owner to another, the period with the old owner still counts with the new owner, so long as the new owner takes over and carries on the business as a going concern. This is supplemented by the Transfer of Undertakings (Protection of Employment) Regulations 1981, which were made in compliance with an EEC Directive. When these Regulations apply, the new owner of a commercial undertaking, in effect, buys the contracts of employment of existing workers from the old owner, so that the employments do not end.

   In these cases, the employees may or may not do the same work as hitherto, but this is not the main issue. The important point is that both the Act and the Regulations only apply if it is the 'undertaking' or 'trade or business' which is transferred, not merely its assets.

   > In *Dallow Industrial Properties Ltd* v. *Else* (1967), a business in Luton sold its *premises* and moved to Bristol. The premises remained empty, but a caretaker, Else, remained, working now for the new owner. It was held that Else's continuous employment had been broken. He was still caretaker, but not for the same *business*.

   > In *Crompton* v. *Truly Fair Ltd* (1975), a children's clothing company sold its factory to a firm which made clothes for men. Mrs C continued to work at the factory for the new firm. The work was similar; but the new firm was a different business or 'undertaking', and the old firm, TF, continued in business elsewhere. Mrs C was entitled to a redundancy payment from TF.

These provisions can apply to both large and small employers: for example, they might apply if an individual employer died but his children took over, or if one partner left a firm but the others carried on as a new firm (Unit 6).

2. A simple takeover of shares in a company does not interrupt the contracts of employees. The company has a separate legal personality (Unit 6), and employees are still employed by the same company, albeit controlled by different shareholders. Most takeovers in the UK are of this sort.

3. However, the 1978 Act does provide one limit to the separate legal personality of companies: transfer of an employee from one company to another *associated* company in the same group shall not break continuity of employment.

4. An employee can always make an agreement with his new employer that service with an earlier employer shall still count for redundancy or similar purposes. If the worker accepted his new job only on this understanding, then the agreement is for consideration, and it is binding on his new employer. However, it might not bind third parties such as the Redundancy Fund; see *Secretary of State for Employment* v. *Globe Elastic Thread Ltd* (Unit 27).

Presumption of continuity

A period of employment is presumed continuous unless the employer can prove otherwise. The only exceptions are for notice of termination (later) and notification of terms (Unit 22); for these purposes, the *worker* must prove continuity.

B. Termination by notice

A contract for a fixed term or a particular piece of work normally ends automatically on the expiration of the time or completion of the work. If, as is more usual, employment is for an indefinite period, either party may end it by giving notice to the other, and the length of notice required is frequently an express term in the contract. Even in a fixed period contract, there may be a term entitling one or both parties to terminate earlier by notice. If there is no prior agreement on the notice period, *reasonable* notice must be given.

At common law, what is reasonable notice will depend upon such matters as trade practice, the length of service, periods by which wages or salary are calculated, and the seniority of the position held. As a general rule, the more important the post, the longer would be the period; see *Hill* v. *C. A. Parsons & Co. Ltd* (Unit 15).

These common law rules are subject to statutory *minimum* periods of notice set out in the Employment Protection (Consolidation) Act. Where there has been continuous employment for one month, the *worker* then has a right to at least one week's notice. After two years' employment he is entitled to at least two weeks and, thenceforth, at least one week's notice for each year of continuous employment up to a maximum statutory entitlement of 12 weeks. The *employer* has a corresponding right to at least one week's notice from the worker after continuous employment of one month, but there is no sliding scale thereafter; however long the employment, one week is the maximum *statutory* notice which the worker need give.

It should be noted again that these periods are statutory *minima*. The individual contract of employment can expressly or impliedly provide for longer periods of notice, but never less. On the other hand at any time, for example on leaving or dismissal, either party can waive his right to notice. Moreover, since an employer may have no general duty to provide work, it may be sufficient for him to tender wages in lieu of notice (if, for example, he no longer wants the employee on his premises, but has no grounds for summary dismissal).

The Act contains detailed provisions safeguarding rights of workers during notice. In brief, he is entitled to be paid at the normal rate.

It should be emphasized that, even if proper notice is given, an employee may still be entitled to redundancy payment or statutory compensation for unfair dismissal.

C. Unfair dismissal

At common law an employer could sack an employee at any time, without giving reasons, provided that appropriate notice was given. Only dismissal *without* adequate notice could be wrongful, and then the burden of proving that the dismissal was wrongful rested upon the worker.

The new concept of unfair dismissal was introduced after 1971, and is now governed by Part V of the Employment Protection (Consolidation) Act 1978 (sections 54–80), as amended by the Employment Acts 1980 and 1982.

Qualifying period of continuous employment

Generally, an employee is protected from unfair dismissal only after employment for a qualifying period of two years (but in firms with more than 20 employees, the qualifying period is still only one year for those who were in their present job before 1 June 1985). A worker wrongfully dismissed without notice after 103 weeks may be covered, because the week's statutory notice which he should have received is added to his actual service.

Workers dismissed merely because of statutory medical suspension from work (Unit 23), are covered after only one month's qualifying employment.

Employees dismissed for reasons to do with union membership or activity may be protected from the outset, without any qualifying period at all.

Dismissal

A person complaining of unfair dismissal must obviously have been dismissed. He is treated as dismissed if:

1. the contract under which he is employed is terminated by the employer, with or without notice; or

2. he is employed for a fixed term which expires without being renewed under the same contract; or
3. the *employee* leaves voluntarily, with or without notice, in circumstances such that he is entitled to do so because of the employer's misconduct.

An employee who is given notice of dismissal, but leaves voluntarily with proper notice (perhaps to start another job) before the employer's notice expires, is still treated as dismissed for the reasons given for the employer's notice.

Refusal to re-engage a worker after a lock-out or to allow a woman to exercise her statutory right to return after pregnancy can be dismissal, although there are exceptions.

If employment ends because the contract is frustrated by some outside event, however, there is no dismissal (Unit 16). Thus in *Morgan* v. *Manser* (1948), military conscription for an indefinite period automatically ended the employee's contract. The onus is on the employer to prove that the contract is frustrated, and this may not be easy. Self-induced absence by the employee, such as imprisonment for a criminal offence, probably does not frustrate the contract today, but merely gives the employer the option to dismiss the employee, which he must justify.

Illness may or may not frustrate the contract. The tests generally used today are from the case of *Egg Stores (Stamford Hill) Ltd* v. *Leibovici* (1976). It depends upon matters such as the length of the absentee's previous employment; the expected length of his future employment; the nature of the job; the nature, length and effect of the illness; need for a replacement; risk to the employer of the replacement qualifying for unfair dismissal or redundancy rights; whether the absentee still receives wages; whether the employer has given the impression that he still regards the worker as employed; and whether a reasonable employer could be expected to wait any longer. Illness may *eventually* frustrate the contract; but *when*?

> In *Storey* v. *Fulham Steel Works Co.* (1907), the five-year contract of a works manager was not frustrated by an absence of four months after he had worked for two years.

> In *Hart* v. *A. R. Marshall Ltd* (1977), a 'key' worker, one of two service fitters who worked weekly night shifts alternately, was away ill for nearly two years, during which time his employer had to make other arrangements to cover his shift. His contract was held to have been frustrated, so that it was not dismissal when his employer refused to re-engage him.

Reasons for dismissal

An employer who dismisses a worker with six months or more of service must, within 14 days of a request by the worker, give him a written statement of the reasons. This is then admissible as evidence in any proceedings. If an employer unreasonably refuses, or gives inadequate or untrue reasons, the worker can complain to an industrial tribunal which (a) may declare what it considers to be the true reasons, and (b) must order the employer to pay the worker a sum equal to two weeks' wages.

If the employer discovers further reasons after giving notice but before the dismissal takes effect, these *may* be admissible in later tribunal proceedings; but reasons discovered only after the employment ends are not now admissible in unfair dismissal proceedings; see *Devis & Sons Ltd* v. *Atkins* (1977) below.

Unfair reasons

1. By the 1978 Act, section 58(1) (as re-enacted and amended in 1982), dismissal is automatically unfair, and no 'qualifying period' of employment is required, if it was because the employee:

   (a) was, or proposed to become, a member of an independent trade union (i.e., a union not controlled by the employer); or

   (b) had taken part, or proposed to take part, in the activities of an independent trade union at an appropriate time (i.e., out of working hours, or during time allotted by arrangement with the employer); or

   (c) *was not* a member of any trade union, or of a particular trade union or unions; or was because he refused or proposed to refuse to become or remain a member.

   In short, therefore, it is generally automatically unfair to sack a worker merely for being a union member. Equally it is normally unfair to sack him for *refusing* to join a union, even if the employer has a 'closed shop' agreement with a union or unions; but see below.

2. Dismissal is unfair under section 59 if a worker is declared redundant while others in a similar position are retained, and this selective dismissal is either to do with union membership or activities, or non-membership, or contravenes a customary arrangement or agreed procedure without good reason.

3. Dismissal of a woman on grounds of pregnancy is automatically unfair unless (a) her pregnancy renders her incapable of adequately doing her work, or (b) it would be illegal for a pregnant woman to do the work, *and* (c) the employer has offered suitable alternative work if any is available.

Fair reasons: problems of the 'closed shop'

In one situation, dismissal is stated by section 58(3) to be fair, namely if there is a valid 'closed shop' agreement under which the employer promises to employ only members of a specified union or unions on this work, and the worker is dismissed because he fails or refuses to join the union. There are now, however, many limits on this. For example:

1. The 'closed shop' agreement must be valid. This means that it must have been approved by the appropriate ballots of workers, which must be renewed at five-yearly intervals (see Unit 23).

2. Even if the closed shop is valid, it does not affect workers who have been employed there since before the 'closed shop' was agreed upon, and who have not been union members since it started.

3. In any event, an employee is legally entitled to refuse union membership if he 'genuinely objects on grounds of conscience or other deeply held personal conviction to being a member of any trade union whatsoever or of a particular trade union'. This does not only cover religious or similar objections.

In *Home Delivery Services Ltd* v. *Shackcloth* (1984), it was held that 'deeply held personal conviction' can be based on dissatisfaction with the union's affairs and with the way in which it has (not) looked after the claimant's interests in the past.

For these and similar reasons, it will very rarely be fair today to dismiss a worker for refusing to join or stay in a trade union. If the dismissal is not fair under section 58(3), then it is automatically unfair under section 58(1) above.

Other reasons

By section 57, all other reasons are *presumed* unfair, but the employer can prove otherwise if two requirements are satisfied. First, the employer must show that the reason, or the principal reason, for dismissal:

1. is related to the capability (e.g., relevant aptitude, skill, health, etc.) of the worker for the employment in question; or
2. is related to the conduct of the employee; or
3. was that the employee was redundant; or
4. was some other substantial reason justifying the dismissal of a worker in the position which he held.

Secondly, the tribunal must go on to decide whether, in the circumstances, having regard to equity and the substantial merits of the case, the employer acted reasonably in dismissing the worker. Since 1980, the *onus* is no longer on the employer to *prove* reasonableness. The tribunal now enquires for itself, and for this purpose the codes of practice issued by ACAS under the Employment Protection Act 1975 are relevant. The codes are designed to contain 'such practical guidance as would be helpful for the purpose of promoting good industrial relations', and one code recommends, for example, that a worker should normally be given a warning before dismissal for misconduct (although not necessarily for things like theft or violence at work).

Unless both of these requirements are satisfied, the dismissal is unfair. An ex-employee who claims that the reasons are unfair under section 57 must first, of course, have served the one-year (or two-year) qualifying period of continuous employment described above.

Where an employee is told in writing on entering the employment that the job is temporary, to fill a gap during (a) the absence of a woman for pregnancy, or (b) statutory suspension of a worker due to occupational illness, then dismissal of the temporary worker on return of the woman or the suspended employee can be fair, but only if it is shown to be reasonable under the second requirement above. Claims by temporary workers will rarely arise today, because such workers will not often have served the one- or two-year qualifying period now required.

Special situations

In two situations, special directions are given to the tribunal by the 1978 Act. First, if a Minister of the Crown certifies that dismissal was to safeguard the national interest, the tribunal shall dismiss the complaint.

Secondly, if an employer dismisses or refuses to re-engage *all* of the workers involved in a strike, lock-out or other industrial action, the tribunal 'shall not determine whether the dismissal was fair or unfair'. By the 1982 Act, if the employer has dismissed all of his workers, he can even choose to re-engage some but not others, so long as he does not re-engage anyone within three months of that employee's dismissal. Again the tribunal cannot intervene.

The tribunal, therefore, can act only if (a) *some* are singled out for dismissal, or (b) *some* are re-engaged *within three months* of their dismissal, and others are not. In these cases, if the dismissal or refusal to re-engage the unlucky ones contravenes section 58 (e.g., it was because of union membership or activity), or if it breaks a customary arrangement or agreed procedure without special reason, then the dismissal is unfair. Otherwise it is *presumed* unfair under section 57, but the employer can rebut this presumption under the above rules.

> In *Cruickshank* v. *Hobbs* (1977), four stable lads went on strike in support of a union wage claim. During the strike, work at the stables fell off for other reasons, and only one of the strikers was re-engaged afterwards. The other three alleged unfair dismissal, but their claim failed. Dismissal was due to redundancy and, although the employer had selected the three whom he regarded as most troublesome, this of itself was not unfair.

Complaint to an industrial tribunal

Complaint of unfair dismissal must normally be presented to an industrial tribunal before the end of three months beginning with the effective date of termination. The tribunal can extend this period if satisfied that it was not reasonably practicable to present the claim in time.

The tribunal sends a copy of the papers to the ex-employer, who has 14 days in which to send back his defence. If the complaint seems arguable, copies of the papers are then sent to a conciliation officer designated by ACAS. He may (*must* if requested by either party) try to negotiate a settlement. In particular, he can be required to promote reinstatement or re-engagement of the employee, or to try to negotiate agreed compensation.

If no conciliation is attempted, or if it fails, then the tribunal has power to *order* the employer to reinstate (give back the job to) or re-engage (give a comparable job to) the employee, if this would be practicable and just having regard, for example, to the employee's past conduct. If a reinstatement of re-engagement order is disobeyed, an additional award of compensation can be made (below).

Subject to this, the tribunal must award compensation to a worker unfairly dismissed. The amount is calculated in several stages.

1. First, the complainant is entitled to a *basic award*, calculated by length of service in exactly the same way as a redundancy payment (Unit 27), to a present maximum of £4560. Where the dismissal is unfair under section 58 (because of trade union membership or activities or non-membership), there is now a *minimum* basic award of £2100. The tribunal can make deductions from these amounts (a) where the employee's own conduct contributed to the dismissal, (b) where he has unreason-

ably refused reinstatement, and (c) where the employee also receives a redundancy payment or compensation under the Sex Discrimination or Race Relations Acts, which are set off against compensation for dismissal.

2. In addition to the basic award, the tribunal may make a *compensatory award*, assessed in a similar way to damages for breach of contract at common law. As at common law, the complainant must try reasonably to mitigate his loss, for example by seeking other work. The maximum compensatory award is, at present, £8000.

3. If an employee has been unfairly sacked or selected for redundancy because of trade union membership or activity, or because he is *not* a trade union member, the tribunal can order reinstatement or re-engagement as described above. If the ex-employee requested this order and the employer now disobeys it, the tribunal can make a *special award*. This is one week's pay multiplied by 156, with a minimum of £15 750 and no maximum. If the employer can show that it was not practicable to comply with the reinstatement or re-engagement order, the special award will be only one week's pay multiplied by 104, with a minimum of £10 500 and a maximum of £21 000. The special award can be further reduced (a) for complainants over 64 for men and 59 for women, (b) where the complainant's own conduct before dismissal made a reduction just and equitable, or (c) where the complainant unreasonably refused or prevented reinstatement or re-engagement.

    All of this can particularly apply if a 'closed shop' proves invalid because proper ballots have not been held. Employees dismissed for non-membership or for leaving the union in these circumstances may be entitled to a special award. Sometimes, moreover, the *union* (not the employer) may be ordered to pay it (see below).

4. In other cases, *not* concerned with trade unions, where a reinstatement or re-engagement order is disobeyed by the employer, the tribunal can make an *additional award* on top of the basic and compensatory awards. An additional award is between 13 and 26 weeks' pay unless the employer can show that compliance was impracticable. If failure to reinstate, etc., is due to race or sex discrimination, a *higher additional award* of 26–52 weeks' pay can be made, to a maximum of £7904.

Generally, the award is made against the employer who dismissed the worker. However, by the Employment Act 1980, an employer who dismissed someone for non-membership of a union, and did so because of industrial pressure by the trade union, can have the union joined as party to the proceedings. The tribunal can then order the union to pay the whole or part of any award which would otherwise have been payable by the employer. Since the 1982 Act, the employee too can ask that the union be brought into the proceedings and made liable.

Where there is a valid 'closed shop' agreement, a worker can also claim compensation from the union if he is unreasonably expelled or excluded from it.

Appeals from industrial tribunals lie to the Employment Appeal Tribunal and thence, on a point of law, to the Court of Appeal and House of Lords (Unit 4).

263

Exclusions from the Acts

1. Employees over retiring age on dismissal are not covered by the above provisions unless dismissed for an inadmissible reason. Note also the *Nothman* case (page 274).
2. Certain classes of employee are excluded: registered dock workers (who have their own scheme); share fishermen; police officers; and those ordinarily employed outside Great Britain. The Acts do govern Crown employees, except members of the armed forces.
3. Since the 1980 Act, unfair dismissal provisions do not apply on the expiration of a fixed-term contract for *one* year or more if, before the term expires, the employee has agreed in writing to exclude any claim in respect of such rights in relation to that contract. The exclusion may be in the contract itself or in a separate document.

   For this purpose, it was held in *BBC* v. *Ioannou* (1975) that a 'fixed-term' contract which gives either party a right to terminate it by notice before it expires is *not* sufficient, and an exclusion in such a contract is void. On the other hand, it is still a fixed-term contract in the sense that, if it is not renewed on expiry, the employee is dismissed.
4. Where employers, unions and employees in a firm or industry have agreed their own dismissal procedures, the Secretary of State may, if satisfied that the agreement is as beneficial as the Acts, designate the agreement as applying instead of the unfair dismissal provisions above.
5. Subject to the two previous points, any attempt to 'contract out' of the unfair dismissal provisions is void.

D. Wrongful dismissal

The common law action for damages for wrongful dismissal has not been replaced by the statutory concept of unfair dismissal. The latter has largely supplanted the former in practice, particularly because dismissal can be unfair even after proper notice, and proceedings before a tribunal are quicker and less formal than the ordinary courts. In some cases, however, it is only possible to proceed in the ordinary courts, for example if the worker has been employed for less than two years. Moreover, particularly in long fixed-term contracts, it can be more lucrative to succeed at common law, where there is no ceiling on the potential amount of compensation.

Dismissal with proper notice is never wrongful at common law but, if no adequate notice is given, this can be breach of contract by the employer unless he has the right to dismiss the worker summarily because of serious breach of contract by the latter.

If notice is not given, dismissal can apparently be wrongful without being unfair, in that it would be fair to dismiss the employee, but wrongful to do so without notice.

In *Treganowan* v. *Robert Knee & Co. Ltd* (1975), the complainant was dismissed without notice because she allegedly boasted about her sex life, thereby making the atmosphere at work difficult. She was held to have been fairly dismissed; but the tribunal said, *obiter*, that since about six weeks notice should have been given, the dismissal would have been wrongful at common law, because her conduct was not sufficient to justify instant dismissal. The tribunal, however, had no power to award damages for breach of contract, and felt that in this case the manner of the dismissal, as opposed to the reasons, did not render it unfair by statute.

If dismissal is wrongful, the employee may have the following remedies:

1. He can recover damages, which are normally based on the wages which would have been payable had proper notice been given. Other regular earnings may be included, such as bonuses, tips and commission, and there may be compensation for loss of pension rights. Where the employment is for a long fixed term, not terminable earlier by notice, damages may be based on the remuneration due if the employment had run its full term, subject only to the employee's duty to mitigate his loss. The sum can, therefore, be substantial.

   The first £25 000 of damages are based on the net salary, after deduction of income tax and social security contributions. Damages over £25 000 are based on gross salary which the employee would have received, but are then taxed in the hands of the employee.

2. In some circumstances, where a claim for damages is inappropriate because, for example, the plaintiff has worked under a contract which proved void, he can claim compensation on a *quantum meruit* basis, for so much as he deserves (Unit 15).

3. The personal nature of employment means that the remedies of injunction and specific performance will not normally be granted. Very exceptionally, the court may feel that damages would be inadequate, and make a declaratory judgment that the dismissal was wrongful; in this event, an injunction might be issued to delay dismissal until proper notice is given, or the proper procedure followed; see *Hill* v. *C. A. Parsons & Co. Ltd* (Unit 15).

The employer too has a right of action if the worker leaves without good reason or adequate notice. In practice, such actions are rare. The court will not compel a worker to continue his employment, but an injunction may be granted to restrain him from working elsewhere if the contract contains a valid restraint clause (Unit 17).

Apart from the difference between wrongful and unfair dismissal already mentioned, such as the need for qualifying employment under statute but not at common law, the relevance of proper notice, and the different remedies, there are other important distinctions. Only the ordinary courts have jurisdiction over wrongful dismissal, although the Lord Chancellor has power to give tribunals such jurisdiction in the future. Finally, the limitation period for breach of contract actions is normally six years, as contrasted with three months for unfair dismissal claims.

E. Dismissal for misconduct

In relation to both unfair and wrongful dismissal, the employer can justifiably dismiss an employee for sufficiently serious misconduct. Sometimes even summary dismissal is justified. The following are some examples.

Lack of competence, 'capability' or qualifications

In *Harmer* v. *Cornelius* (1858), a man who accepted a job as a scene painter proved quite incapable of painting scenes, and was lawfully dismissed without notice.

In *Mathieson* v. *Noble & Son Ltd* (1972), a travelling salesman was disqualified from driving. Although he had lost an essential qualification, his dismissal with notice was unfair because he had engaged a chauffeuse.

In *Burrows* v. *Ace Caravan Co. Ltd* (1972), Burrows was promoted but then dismissed with notice for alleged incompetence in his new post. Dismissal was held unfair, because he had received no adequate training or instruction in the new post.

Disobedience

The order must be lawful and be one which the employer was competent to give (Unit 23). Disobedience must be serious, and an isolated occurrence may not be enough.

In *Laws* v. *London Chronicle Ltd* (1959), the plaintiff was present at a meeting between her immediate superior and the managing director. The meeting was stormy, and her immediate superior walked out, telling her to follow. The managing director told her to stay. She chose to go, whereupon the managing director dismissed her summarily. The dismissal was held wrongful; an isolated instance of disobedience in these circumstances was not a repudiation of her obligations.

In *Pepper* v. *Webb* (1969), a gardener refused instructions to put in some plants, and observed, 'I couldn't care less about your bloody greenhouse and your sodding plants'. His employer was held justified in dismissing without notice.

Negligence

One careless act will normally be insufficient, but repeated negligence might justify summary dismissal, particularly if the worker has been warned. Much will depend upon the position held, the nature of the work and the damage caused, or likely to be caused, to property or to fellow workers.

Misconduct

This can include any serious breach of the employee's duties of good faith, such as making a fraudulent secret profit as in *Reading* v. *Attorney General*, or 'moonlighting' in circumstances which harm the main employer (Unit 23). Even honest but improper conduct can justify dismissal.

In *Sinclair* v. *Neighbour* (1967), the manager of a betting shop borrowed money from the till, replacing it with an IOU. He did not ask permission, and knew that such a request would be refused. The money was repaid the following day, but the employer found out what had happened and dismissed the manager. The dismissal was held justified.

Other misconduct can include immorality, persistent drunkenness, or a physical attack upon a colleague or superior; in general, any serious misbehaviour which is inconsistent with the position held and proper performance of the worker's duties.

Exceptionally, it can include behaviour in the worker's own time, if this is relevant to the position held.

In *Pearce* v. *Foster* (1886), a clerk holding a responsible position in a trading firm was discovered to be speculating heavily on the stock exchange in very risky transactions. Although this was in his own time and with his own money, his employers were held justified in dismissing him summarily.

In *Richardson* v. *City of Bradford Metropolitan Council* (1975), a senior meat inspector was convicted of theft from his rugby club. His employer, the Council, tried to find other work for him where honesty was not so vital but, unable to do so, dismissed him. This was held to be fair.

A conflict of interest

A conflict of interest can arise without misconduct on anyone's part.

In *Foot* v. *Eastern Counties Timber Co. Ltd* (1972), dismissal of a cashier who married her employer's business competitor was held to be fair.

Subsequent discovery of misconduct

A difficult situation occurs where an employee is dismissed for possibly inadequate reasons, but the employers subsequently discover more serious misconduct. Does this subsequent discovery retrospectively validate the dismissal? The common law differs from decisions on the statutory provisions.

In *Boston Deep Sea Fishing and Ice Co.* v. *Ansell* (1888), a director was dismissed from his employment contract for inadequate reasons, but it was later discovered that he had been pocketing large undisclosed commissions. It was held that this retrospectively justified dismissal.

In *Devis & Sons Ltd* v. *Atkins* (1977), Atkins was dismissed for alleged incompetence, with six weeks' notice and £6000 agreed compensation. It later transpired that Atkins, like Ansell, had been pocketing secret commissions. His employers promptly refused to pay the agreed compensation, and treated Atkins as summarily dismissed. The House of Lords held that Atkins's action for *unfair* dismissal succeeded because, by statute, only information known at the time of dismissal is relevant to determine whether it is fair. On the other hand, subsequently discovered misconduct is relevant in deciding what compensation should be awarded (see earlier).

Examination questions

1. (a) In what circumstances may an employee be dismissed without notice?
   (b) Kenneth took £5 from the petty cash in order to buy a birthday present for his girlfriend. He replaced the money the following day, but was discovered doing so and was summarily dismissed. Advise Kenneth.

   To what extent, if at all, would your advice differ if Kenneth had been dismissed because of a deficit in the petty cash and the deficit had arisen because of an over-payment which he had carelessly made?

2. Discuss whether or not summary dismissal is justified in the following circumstances:
   (a) Jane, a secretary, has been absent from work through illness on a number of occasions during the past two years. Her present illness has continued for six weeks.
   (b) Richard, an accounts clerk, is criticized by the office manager for careless work. An argument develops and Richard walks out of the office, slamming the door behind him.

3. (a) When may an employee claim compensation for unfair dismissal?
   (b) Explain whether or not the following dismissals are fair:
      (i) Albert is dismissed when his employer discovers that he does not have the professional qualification which he claimed to have when he applied for the post.
      (ii) Barry is dismissed for allegedly spending too much time on trade union activities.

4. (a) Termination of a contract of employment by notice is possible but certain obligations are imposed upon an employer who does so. What are these obligations?
   (b) Advise Eric, the employer, whether he is entitled to dismiss the following employees and, if not, the remedies which might be sought against him if nevertheless he does dismiss them:
      (i) Martin, who has been absent through illness for six months; and
      (ii) Norman, who is late for work on most days in the week.

Unit 27. Redundancy Payments and Other Rights

When an employee loses his job the effects for him (or her) can be serious, and the rights to notice and to compensation for unfair or wrongful dismissal already discussed recognize this. The Redundancy Payments Act 1965 gave further recognition to a worker's 'property' rights in his job, which are deemed to become more valuable with increasing age and length of service with the same employer. These provisions now form Part VI of the Employment Protection (Consolidation) Act 1978, which replaces the 1965 Act. This unit also describes financial protection for employees if the employer dies, is wound up, or becomes insolvent, and finally outlines the longer term social security provisions in the event of unemployment.

A. Redundancy payments

Qualifying period of continuous employment

An employee is not entitled to redundancy payment until he has been continuously employed with his employer for at least two years. The rules to determine what amounts to continuous employment are as set out in Unit 26.

Dismissal, lay-off, short time

The right to a redundancy payment arises only if the employee has suffered one of these fates, usually dismissal.

For the purposes of the Employment Protection (Consolidation) Act, Part VI, an employee is treated as dismissed if, but only if (section 83):

1. the contract under which he is employed is terminated by the employer, whether with or without notice; or
2. where he is employed under a fixed-term contract which expires without being renewed under the same contract; or
3. where the employee himself terminates the contract, with or without notice, in circumstances such that he is entitled to end it without notice because of his employer's misconduct or breach of the terms of the contract.

Under section 83(2)(c), therefore, an employee who leaves 'voluntarily' is still dismissed if the employer's misconduct has forced this on him; see *Marriott* v. *Oxford & District Co-operative Society Ltd* (Unit 22) and *Donovan* v. *Invicta Airways* Ltd (Unit 23). By section 85, moreover, when a worker has been given notice of dismissal, there are detailed provisions entitling him to serve a counter-notice and thereby voluntarily leave early without loss of redundancy payment.

Subject to this, no redundancy payment is made when the employee leaves voluntarily.

> In *Morton Sundour Fabrics Ltd* v. *Shaw* (1966), Shaw was warned that his job in the velvet department was *likely* to end at an unspecified time some months in the future. He, therefore, sought and found another job, and left his present employer. He was held not entitled to a redundancy payment, because he had left voluntarily. He never actually received notice from his employer, and, therefore, did not come within the provisions of section 85 above.

Similarly, there is no dismissal, and, therefore, no redundancy payment, if the contract is frustrated as in cases such as *Morgan* v. *Manser* and *Hart* v. *A. R. Marshall Ltd* (Unit 26).

An employee is not taken to be dismissed if his contract is renewed, or he is re-engaged under a new contract on the same terms as hitherto, in pursuance of an offer, written or not, made by his employer before the end of his existing employment, so long as the renewal or re-engagement takes effect either immediately or within four weeks of the end of his old job.

Alternatively, the employer may offer renewal or re-engagement on terms which differ, wholly or in part, from the old ones 'as to the capacity and place in which the employee is employed, and as to the other terms and conditions of his employment'. In this case, there must be a 'trial period' of at least four weeks under the new terms. If, during this trial period (a) the *employee* ends the employment for *whatever* reason, or (b) the employer ends it for a reason connected with or arising out of the change then, unless there is a further renewal or re-engagement, the worker is treated as dismissed as from the end of the original job.

The parties can, if they so wish, agree a trial period of longer than four weeks for the purpose of retraining the worker. Such an agreement must be in writing, before the employee starts work under the new employment; it must specify the end of the trial period, and the proposed terms of the worker's employment when the trial period ends. In either of the above cases, if the worker continues in his new employment after the trial period, he is regarded as not having been dismissed.

Since employers might attempt to avoid redundancy payments by using temporary lay-offs or short-time working, the Act provides for payment if either of these occurs. Lay-off occurs where a man, dependent upon being provided with work, is not so provided by his employer, and is consequently not entitled to remuneration. A claim may be based on short-time working where remuneration depends upon the hours worked, and work diminishes so that the remuneration for the week is less than half a week's pay. If the lay-off or short time lasts for at least 4 consecutive weeks in the last 8, or for any 6 of the last 13 weeks, the worker may give written 'notice of intention to claim' redundancy payment. The length of notice is either 4 or 6 weeks, depending upon which of the above periods of lay-off or short time the worker alleges. He must also give appropriate notice to terminate the employment. There are detailed provisions entitling the employer to serve a counter-notice if the work available is likely to increase in the immediate future.

Redundancy

The dismissal must have been due to redundancy and not, for example, to misconduct justifying instant dismissal. In a claim for redundancy payment before a tribunal, an employee who has been dismissed is presumed to have been dismissed for redundancy, so that the onus of proving misconduct or any other reason is on the employer.

By section 81(2) of the Act, redundancy occurs where the employee is dismissed because:

1. the employer has ceased or intends to cease to carry on the business for the purposes of which the employee was employed by him; or
2. the employer has ceased or intends to cease to carry on that business in the *place* where the employee was so employed; or
3. the work needed to be done by the employee has either diminished or ceased to be necessary to the business of the employer (either generally or at the place where the employee worked), or is expected to diminish or cease.

Even temporary closure of the business can be enough under paragraph 1 above. Provisions for temporary lay-off have been outlined already and, if the employee is absolutely dismissed, he is entitled to compensation even if he knows that the business will reopen soon.

> In *Gemmell* v. *Darngavil Brickworks Ltd* (1966), employees were dismissed while the works closed down for three months for repairs. Employees knew that their jobs would be available again when the works reopened. Nevertheless, they were held entitled to redundancy payments.

Where a *place* of business closes or moves (under 2 above), the main legal difficulty is to determine where, under his contract of employment, the worker has contracted to work. If, as in *UK Atomic Energy Authority* v. *Claydon* (1974), he has expressly agreed to work anywhere in the UK, he is not entitled either to redundancy payment or to compensation for unfair dismissal if he refuses to move. The 'place' where he is employed is the UK. The terms of the contract are not always so clear, however.

> In *O'Brien* v. *Associated Fire Alarms* (1969), an electrician who had lived and worked in Liverpool for many years was held impliedly to be bound to work only in the Liverpool area. He justifiably refused to move 120 miles to Barrow-in-Furness when the Liverpool branch closed, and was entitled to a redundancy payment (see also Unit 23).

> In *Stevenson* v. *Tees-side Bridge and Engineering Ltd* (1971), on the other hand, a steel erector stated when applying for his job that he would be prepared to work away from home. There was no express term to this effect in the nationally agreed terms upon which he was employed, but there was provision for travelling expenses and subsistence allowances. Moreover, the very nature of the construction industry meant that when work on one site was completed, work would move to another building site. For some time, Stevenson worked at a site near his home, where he could earn a lot of overtime pay. When this was completed, he refused to move to a more distant site where he would have to live away from home. He was held not entitled to a redundancy payment.

Where it alleged that the employee's own work has diminished (under 3 above), the main legal problem arises where the nature of his job has changed because of technical or other developments, and he cannot adapt. If he is dismissed, is it redundancy in that the work for which he was originally engaged has ceased; or is it incompetence in that he has failed to adapt to reasonable changes?

> In *North Riding Garages Ltd* v. *Butterwick* (1967), Butterwick had been employed by the garage company for 30 years, and had risen to become manager of the repair shop. In 1965, the business was taken over and new methods were introduced which placed more work on the manager. In particular, he now had to do costing work, which had never been demanded previously. Unable to adapt, Butterwick was dismissed, and claimed redundancy payment on the ground that the nature of the work had so changed that his former job no longer existed. His claim failed. The job was held to be basically the same; he was simply unable to meet its changing demands.

> In *Vaux and Associated Breweries Ltd* v. *Ward* (1969), the landlord and the brewery decided to give a younger and livelier 'image' to a public house. The name was changed, a discothèque was opened, and young barmaids of a 'bunny girl' type were engaged. A barmaid aged 57 was dismissed, and claimed redundancy payment. Her claim failed. It was held that the nature of the job was basically the same, but the landlord felt that she could not adapt to meet its changing requirements. Today Mrs Ward, like Mr Butterwick, might claim compensation for unfair dismissal, but this was only introduced after 1971.

There can be similar problems when the employer reorganizes his system of working. Are the new conditions still the old job, or are they so different as to be a new contract?

> In *Lesney Products & Co. Ltd* v. *Nolan* (1977), the firm had formerly worked for one long day shift. It changed to a two-shift system, which meant that the employees had different working hours and could earn less overtime. Employees who refused the new conditions were dismissed. It was held that they were not entitled to redundancy payments, because the old jobs still existed, albeit organized differently and paid less well.

Payment

Responsibility to make redundancy payments rests upon employers, but they are entitled to a partial rebate (at present 35 per cent) from the state 'Redundancy Fund', to which all employers must contribute according to the number of workers they employ. However, the Fund will give a rebate only in respect of the employer's *statutory* liability. If the employer has contracted to pay more than this, then he must pay all of the extra.

> In *Secretary of State for Employment* v. *Globe Elastic Thread Co. Ltd* (1979), *W* was persuaded to move to Globe Ltd in 1970 partly because Globe agreed that *W*'s earlier service for another employer, from 1948 to 1970, would still be counted for redundancy and similar purposes. The House of Lords (1) said that Globe's agreement to recognize the earlier service was almost certainly binding *on Globe*, but (2) held that even if it was, Globe could only claim a rebate from *the Fund* for its *statutory* liability, since 1970.

Ex-employees can claim directly from the Fund if, for example, the former employer is insolvent, but again the Fund will meet only the employer's statutory liability. If the insolvent employer had contracted to pay more, therefore, the ex-employees will probably lose the extra.

If the worker's statutory claim is contested by the employer, the claim must be pursued before an industrial tribunal, normally within six months of dismissal.

The amount of payment is calculated by reckoning backwards from the end of the employment. For whole years of service after the 41st birthday (until retiring age) in which the worker has been continuously employed by this employer, he is entitled to one-and-a-half weeks' pay per year; for years from the 22nd birthday to the 41st, one week's pay per year; and for years between the 18th and 22nd birthdays, half a week's pay per year. The maximum number of years to be taken into account for this purpose is 20, and all earnings over £152 per week are disregarded. The maximum sum payable, therefore, would be £4560. 'Week's pay' will usually be calculated according to the pay to which the worker would normally have been entitled during the last week before dismissal. The employer must give the worker a written statement showing how the amount of redundancy payment has been calculated, non-compliance being a criminal offence.

Redundancy payment does not affect a right to unemployment benefit, and is independent of any claim for *wrongful* dismissal. The Secretary of State does have power under the Act, however, to make regulations modifying the amount of redundancy payment where there are also damages for wrongful dismissal.

Redundancy and *unfair* dismissal are normally mutually exclusive, because dismissal for redundancy is not 'unfair' (Unit 26). Where an employee is selected for redundancy because of union membership activity, or non-membership, however, or in contravention of a customary arrangement or agreed procedure without good reason, the dismissal *can* be unfair. This can benefit the claimant because compensatory or special awards may, under Part V of the Act, be added to his payment.

Exclusion from redundancy payment

Certain categories of people are not entitled to redundancy payment:

1. *Those over retiring age*: normally men over 65, and women over 60.

    > In *Nothman* v. *London Borough of Barnet* (1979), however, the limit for a woman teacher was held to be 65, her *normal retiring age*. The limit of 60 applies only if no other age is fixed. Although Miss *N* was 62, a tribunal could, therefore, hear her unfair dismissal complaint (Unit 26).

2. *Persons rightfully dismissed for misconduct*, either without notice, or with notice where the employer had a right, which he did not exercise, to dismiss without notice.

3. *Those in excluded employments*: (a) registered dock workers; (b) share fishermen; (c) Crown employees; (d) an employee dismissed while abroad unless under his contract of employment he ordinarily worked *in* Great Britain.

4. '*Contracting out*'. An employee engaged for a *fixed term of two years or more* entered into after the 1965 Act, shall not be entitled to a redundancy payment in respect of the expiry of that term without its being renewed (whether by the employer or by an associated employer of his), if before the term expires he has agreed in writing to exclude any right to a redundancy payment in that event. The exclusion may be either in the employment contract itself, or in a separate agreement. This is not affected by the Employment Act 1980.

    Subject to this, any attempt to 'contract out' of redundancy entitlements is void. It should also be noted that if a 'fixed term' contract is terminable by notice by either party before the term expires, it is not a fixed term *for this purpose*, so that an extension in such a contract is void; see *BBC* v. *Ioannou* (Unit 26).

5. *Unreasonable refusal of new employment*. If an employee *accepts* renewal or re-engagement, even (subject to the 'trial period') on new terms, he is treated as not having been dismissed at all (see previously).

    Conversely, he is disqualified from redundancy payment if he unreasonably *refuses* either an offer of renewal or re-engagement on the same terms as hitherto, or an offer of different terms which are *suitable* alternative employment for him. The offer must have been made before the end of the old employment, and have been to take effect either immediately or within four weeks. It need not have been in writing.

    Similarly, an employee is disqualified if, having *accepted* different terms, apparently suitable, he then *unreasonably* leaves or gives notice during the trial period.

    What is suitable, and whether refusal is unreasonable, depends on the facts of the particular case. A job in a nearby factory might be suitable, but perhaps not in a distant town. A married man with family commitments might reasonably refuse to move home, but perhaps not a single man.

    > In *Taylor* v. *Kent County Council* (1969), a headmaster became redundant when his school was amalgamated with another. He was offered alternative employment in a mobile pool of teachers, serving to cover staff shortages, in another part of the county.

His headmaster's salary would be unaffected, but he would have to move home. The inconvenience and loss of status were held to justify his refusal. He received a redundancy payment.

6. *An agreement between employers and trade unions* as to redundancy payments for certain workers may, on application by *all* parties, be approved by the Secretary of State in substitution for the statutory provisions.

B. Procedure for handling redundancies

Because of the economic and social effects of redundancies, particularly on a large scale, new legal duties were placed on employers by the Employment Protection Act 1975, sections 99–107, and these provisions still apply.

Duty of employer to consult trade unions

In relation to *all* proposed redundancies, the employer must consult any independent trade union recognized by him in relation to the employees concerned. Consultation must be 'at the earliest opportunity', and must take place whether or not those to be dismissed are actually members of the union concerned.

Where 100 or more dismissals at one establishment are proposed within a period of 90 days, consultation must begin at least 90 days before the first dismissal takes effect. Where 10 or more dismissals at one establishment are proposed within a period of 30 days, consultation must begin at least 30 days before the first takes effect.

In consultation, the employer must disclose the following details in writing to the union representatives:

1. the reasons for his proposals;
2. the number and description of proposed redundant employees;
3. the total number of employees of that type at the establishment;
4. the proposed method of selection for redundancy;
5. proposed ways of carrying out the dismissals, with regard to any agreed procedure, including the period over which dismissals are to be spread.

The employer must consider any representations made by the union, reply to them and, if he rejects any representation, say why.

If circumstances render compliance with all of the above impracticable (e.g., because redundancy resulted from unexpected loss of a large order), then it is sufficient for the employer to do all that is reasonably practicable in the circumstances, so long as he does consult at the earliest opportunity.

If an employer fails to satisfy the above requirements, then a *trade union* (not an individual worker) may complain to an industrial tribunal, normally within three months of the date set for the dismissals. If the complaint is held to be well founded, the tribunal must make a declaration to this effect. It *may* also make a *protective award* to the employees concerned, under which the employer must continue to pay normal wages to the employees for such 'protected period' as the tribunal specifies.

The normal maximum protected period is 28 days, but up to 90 days' payment can be awarded if 100 or more dismissals are proposed within any 90 days, and up to 30 days' payment if 10 or more dismissals are proposed within any 30 days. Subject to these maxima, the length of any protected period is at the tribunal's discretion.

If an employer fails to comply with a protective award, the worker personally may complain to the tribunal, which will award payment if the complaint is well founded. The protective award is set off against any damages for wrongful dismissal, and vice versa, but does not affect the amount of any redundancy payment. (Note that a worker is only entitled to a protective award if dismissal is for *redundancy* and not, for example, because of misconduct or because he unreasonably refuses re-engagement.)

Duty of employer to notify the Secretary of State

In addition to his duty to consult appropriate trade unions, an employer proposing 100 or more redundancies at one establishment within any 90 days must notify the Secretary of State for Employment at least 90 days before the first dismissal takes effect. If 10 or more redundancies are proposed within any 30 days, 30 days' notification is required. The notification must identify any unions concerned, and contain such further particulars as the Secretary of State may direct.

If proper notice is not given, the employer's rebate from the Redundancy Fund may be reduced by up to one-tenth, or the employer may be prosecuted and subject to a maximum fine of £2000.

C. Death, winding up, etc., and insolvency

Of the employer

Death of an individual employer will, because of the personal nature of employment, almost invariably end the contract. This can have the following effects.

1. *Wages.* The employer's death does not affect accrued rights, and employees are entitled to arrears of wages up to the date of death. If the employer dies insolvent, all employees are preferred creditors for up to four months' wages or £800, whichever is less. An employee has no right to wages after the employer's death unless, as is usual, the personal representatives expressly or impliedly employ him under a new contract.
2. *Redundancy payment.* If the employer's death ends the employment, an employee is entitled to a redundancy payment unless the personal representatives re-employ him, or offer to do so, within eight weeks of the employer's death.

Dissolution of a partnership may similarly end the contracts of employees, but only if the identity of the partners is clearly material.

In *Brace* v. *Calder* (1895), the plaintiff was employed for a fixed term by a partnership of solicitors, which was dissolved when two partners died. The business was carried on by the remaining partners, but the plaintiff, whose term had not expired, claimed that his employment had ended and demanded damages for breach of contract. He was held entitled to damages but, since the remaining partners had offered to re-engage him on the same terms, the damages were nominal because he had not taken the opportunity to mitigate his loss.

Winding up of a company will end the employees' contracts if the winding up is compulsory, for example because of insolvency. A voluntary winding up (for example on reconstruction or amalgamation) will end employments only if the business is being terminated.

Bankruptcy or insolvency of the employer does not necessarily terminate the contracts of employees; only if the solvency of the employer was relevant. On the other hand, insolvency will often bring the employer's business to an end, which is of course relevant. Employees are preferred creditors for arrears of wages as described above, but this may be little comfort if the employer has no money at all. By the Employment Protection (Consolidation) Act 1978, section 104, therefore, an employee may claim in writing up to eight weeks' arrears of wages from the Redundancy Fund (see earlier), to a maximum of £152 per week. He can similarly claim up to six weeks' arrears of holiday pay accrued during the last 12 months, amounts due to him if the employer has not given due notice, any basic award for unfair dismissal, and entitlements such as guarantee payments or protective awards.

If the employee becomes redundant, we have seen that he can recover any redundancy payments from the Fund, in so far as the employer cannot pay, to a possible maximum of £4560.

Of the employee

Death of the employee obviously ends the employment. His estate is entitled to arrears of wages to the date of death. Insolvency of an employee will not automatically end the employment; it may or may not justify dismissal, depending upon the nature of his job.

D. Social security rights

Unemployment benefit

The national insurance scheme was introduced in broadly its present form in 1946. It is now governed by the Social Security Acts 1975 to 1980, and provides a wide range of benefits for those in need, in return for weekly contributions from employers and workers. A worker whose employment is terminated may, therefore, be entitled to weekly unemployment benefit payments. In order to qualify, he must have satisfied certain contribution conditions, i.e., paid specified amounts in contributions. The benefit includes increases for dependants. Unemployment benefit itself can last for up to one year.

A person who is not entitled to unemployment benefit, or whose benefit has expired, or whose benefit is not sufficient for his requirements, may be given supplementary benefits. These are partly discretionary payments made, today, under the Supplementary Benefits Act 1976 as amended. This is designed to ensure that no one is left entirely without means.

On the grounds that the national insurance scheme should not be used to finance trade disputes, unemployment benefit will not be paid to a person who has lost employment because of a stoppage of work due to a trade dispute at his place of work. (There is a similar disqualification from supplementary benefits for the claimant and, to some extent, his family.) This disqualification does not apply, however, if the claimant can show that he was not participating or directly interested in the dispute which caused the stoppage. If a worker loses his job because of a trade dispute and bona fide obtains regular employment elsewhere, his right to unemployment benefit is revived should he subsequently be unemployed during the trade dispute.

There is also a discretionary power for insurance officers to disqualify a worker from benefit for a period not exceeding six weeks for misconduct or lack of cooperation. This applies where he has been dismissed for misconduct or has left his job voluntarily without good cause, or has refused to avail himself of a reasonable opportunity for suitable employment by refusing to apply for or to take another post, or to receive training. Employment is not suitable if it is on less favourable terms or at a lower rate of pay, or if the vacancy has arisen because of a trade dispute.

Pension rights

If a worker's employment ends when he reaches pensionable age, he may have certain pension rights. If he has satisfied the prescribed contribution conditions, a state retirement pension is payable under the social security scheme. In addition, he may qualify for a further pension arising from the terms of his employment. The scheme generally is governed by the Social Security Pensions Act 1975, as amended.

Examination questions

1. (a) When may an employee claim a redundancy payment?
   (b) John had been employed by Electrics Ltd for 20 years on security work at a factory making small electrical components. The factory was then bought by Panther Ltd, a motor manufacturer, for the purpose of producing electrical fittings for its cars. John's employment was continued by Panther Ltd for a period of 10 weeks. He was then told that his services were no longer required and he was given four weeks' notice. John found another job immediately, gave his employer one week's notice and left.
   Advise John of any rights he may have against Panther Ltd.
2. (a) Compare and contrast compensation for unfair dismissal and redundancy payment.
   (b) John is the chief accountant of an engineering company. His company is taken over by another company and John is offered the post of deputy accountant

with the new organization at a lower salary. He writes a letter of protest to the managing director but takes up the new post and works for three weeks while looking for another appointment. Upon finding this, he leaves. Discuss the legal position.

3. Expanso Ltd decides to close down its Barchester factory and gives notice to the following persons that their services will no longer be required:
   (a) Albert, a foreman, who has been employed for 20 years and who has turned down the firm's offer of a similar post in another factory 100 miles away;
   (b) Bertha, a typist, who has been employed for 10 years for 15 hours each week;
   (c) Colin, a labourer, who has been employed for 18 months;
   (d) David, a local taxi-driver, who has been engaged whenever the firm has required transport during the past five years.
   Explain, with reasons, whether or not a claim for a redundancy payment may be made in each of the above circumstances.

4. On his 17th birthday, 1 January 1968, Eric was engaged by John as a trainee accountant. In April 1970, John died and Simon, his son, took over the business.
   In July 1971, Eric and other employees went on strike and they were told by Simon that they would be dismissed unless they returned to work immediately. They did not do so, and they were dismissed, but four days later the dispute was settled and they were re-engaged.
   Simon reorganized the business in September 1972, and told Eric that, in consequence of the reorganization, his services in his present capacity were no longer required. Simon offered Eric an alternative post as a storekeeper.
   Discuss Eric's right to claim a redundancy payment.

5. Albert is employed by a drug firm as the manager of a department in which new drugs are tested on animals. He refuses to administer a particular drug on the grounds that it would cause unnecessary suffering to the animals, whereupon the firm closes down the department and dismisses Albert without notice. Discuss Albert's right to claim:
   (a) compensation for unfair dismissal;
   (b) redundancy payment; and
   (c) unemployment benefit.

6. After five years' employment as chief cost accountant to a medium-sized engineering company, you have recently been appointed to the board of directors. Consultations are now taking place to appoint your successor. Draft a report for the other members of the board outlining the matters which should be included in the contract of employment of the person appointed.

Appendix A. Specimen Questions

The following questions were published by the Institute of Cost and Management Accountants as a guide to students. They are reproduced here by kind permission of the Institute to provide additional exercises.

1. (a) Which court or tribunal would hear the following cases:
     (i) a prosecution for breach of the Factories Act;
     (ii) a claim for breach of a contract to supply goods to the value of £5000;
     (iii) an action for unfair dismissal;
     (iv) an action to re-possess goods following the breach of a hire-purchase agreement?

   State in each instance the court to which an appeal might lie.

   (b) In what circumstances might a commercial dispute be more appropriately settled by arbitration rather than a court action?

2. (a) To what extent may an action for negligence be based upon:
     (i) a careless statement, and
     (ii) financial or economic loss?

   (b) Sharp, who is in practice as an accountant, regularly prepares tax returns for Rich for which he receives an annual fee. On one occasion Rich telephones Sharp and asks his advice on the investment of some money which he has just received from the maturing of a life assurance policy. Sharp is busy at the time and, without giving the matter much thought, suggests Lunar Development Ltd. The financial operations of this company had in fact been criticized in a recent article in Sharp's professional journal. Rich invests in the company without seeking further advice. The company shortly afterwards goes into liquidation and the money is lost. Advise Sharp as to his possible liability.

3. Clutch, who is employed as a lorry driver by Speedy Transport Ltd complains to his employer about the poor condition of the brakes on his lorry. He is told that the brakes will be repaired the following day, and is persuaded to make an urgent delivery. He is told to drive slowly and carefully and is also forbidden to give anyone a lift in the lorry. During the course of his journey Clutch gives a lift to Hiker. While driving far too fast, having regard to the state of the brakes, Clutch is involved in an accident in which Walker, a pedestrian, is seriously injured. Clutch and Hiker also receive injuries. Advise Speedy Transport Ltd as to their possible liability towards Walker, Clutch and Hiker.

4. *T* has been employed as head of a research department for the past five years on a fixed contract for one year, which has been renewed annually. He has been repeatedly warned that his department is pursuing lines of enquiry of no benefit to the company and has been told to discontinue them, but he has persistently refused to change the department's policies. Finally, the company closes down the department and does not renew *T*'s contract. Discuss *T*'s right to claim:
   (a) unemployment benefit;
   (b) redundancy payment; and
   (c) compensation for unfair dismissal.

5. (a) Explain the effect of mistake upon the validity of a contract.
   (b) Garish Garages are approached by Harry who offers to buy a car from them on hire-purchase terms. Harry falsely states that he is Blackstone, a solicitor. The agreement is concluded and Harry is allowed to drive away the car in return for a cheque for the deposit. Garish Garages now find that the cheque is worthless and that Harry has disappeared after selling the car to Tom. Advise Garish Garages.

6. Factory Suppliers Ltd enter into a contract to build a factory for £100 000, payable in instalments as the work progresses. They also agree to import and install machinery in the building for £50 000, of which £10 000 is paid immediately and the balance is due upon completion. The building is begun and the first progress payment of £5000 is made. Factory Suppliers Ltd then discover that as a consequence of a serious costing mistake, they can only complete the factory building at a considerable loss. At about the same time the import of the foreign machinery is forbidden by the Government. Advise Factory Suppliers Ltd, who no longer wish to proceed with the work.

7. The heating plant at your employer's factory is operated by smokeless fuel. One consignment of fuel contained explosive which seriously damaged the plant and caused the factory to be closed for three weeks. In addition to loss of normal production, a particularly profitable contract was lost. Both the supplier and the manufacturer of the fuel disclaim responsibility, each blaming the other. Advise your employer.

8. (a) Under what circumstances may an agent incur personal liability to third parties with whom he contracts on behalf of his principal?

281

(b) *A*, the purchasing officer of an electrical goods manufacturer, is authorized to buy materials for the company at prices which must not exceed those laid down by the directors. *A* agrees to buy copper wire from *X* at a price which is higher than the prescribed maximum price. *A* also enters into a second agreement to buy switches from *Y* in return for which *Y* promises to pay a commission to *A* which *A* is not authorized to accept. The details of these two transactions are now known to the company. What action may the company take?

9. Your company will shortly open a multi-storey car park. It is concerned about the possible liability which may arise from theft or damage while cars are on its premises. Draft a report explaining the nature and extent of this liability and how, if at all, it may be avoided.

10. (a) An employer is vicariously liable for the negligent acts of his employees but not for those of an independent contractor. Discuss.

(b) Road Contractors Ltd engages a number of drivers to move earth and rubble during the construction of a motorway. Each driver provides his own lorry and payment is made on a piece-work basis subject to guaranteed minimum earnings. During prescribed hours of work the drivers are subject to control by the company's supervisors. One driver overloads his lorry, contrary to instructions given by a supervisor, and this is the cause of an accident in which a third party is injured. Advise Road Contractors Ltd as to its possible liability.

Appendix B. Further Reading

The following books are suggested for further reading and reference. Care should be taken to use the latest edition.

English Legal System
Learning the Law, by Glanville Williams (Sweet and Maxwell)
The English Legal System, by R. J. Walker and M. G. Walker (Butterworths)
The Machinery of Justice in England, by R. M. Jackson (Cambridge University Press)

European Community Law
Introduction to the Law and Institutions of the European Communities, by D. Lasok and J. W. Bridge (Butterworths)

Contract
Contract, by F. R. Davies (Sweet and Maxwell)
Law of Contract, by G. C. Cheshire and C. H. S. Fifoot (Butterworths)
A Casebook on Contract, by J. C. Smith and J. A. C. Thomas (Sweet and Maxwell)

Tort
Tort, by C. D. Baker (Sweet and Maxwell)
Cases and Statutes on Tort, by P. L. Bradbury (Sweet and Maxwell)
Tort, by Sir P. H. Winfield and J. A. Jolowicz (Sweet and Maxwell)

Sale of Goods
The Sale of Goods, by P. S. Atiyah (Pitman)

Agency
The Law of Agency, by G. H. L. Fridman (Butterworths)

Consumer Credit
Commercial and Consumer Credit: An Introduction, by A. Diamond (Butterworths)

Industrial Law
Law of Employment, by N. Selwyn (Butterworths)
Law of Health and Safety at Work, by N. Selwyn (Butterworths)

Index